Lewis Naphtali Dembitz

Jewish Services in Synagogue and Home

r

Lewis Naphtali Dembitz

Jewish Services in Synagogue and Home

ISBN/EAN: 9783743310438

Manufactured in Europe, USA, Canada, Australia, Japa

Cover: Foto ©Thomas Meinert / pixelio.de

Manufactured and distributed by brebook publishing software
(www.brebook.com)

Lewis Naphtali Dembitz

Jewish Services in Synagogue and Home

JEWISH SERVICES

IN SYNAGOGUE AND HOME

By

LEWIS N. DEMBITZ

ISRAEL'S MISSION IS PEACE

Philadelphia:

The Jewish Publication Society of America

1898

PREFACE

Five years ago I entered upon the work of drawing up an analytic sketch of the Jewish Services, but was prevented by work more in the line of my profession from finishing the task or even studying up the material in the fullness demanded by honest authorship. Some years later the Chairman of the Publication Committee of the Jewish Publication Society, hearing of my labors in that line, opened a correspondence with me about getting up a book on the subject, to be published by that body. At a meeting of the committee in charge the wish was expressed that the sketch should be historical as well as analytic, and I assented to this proposal, which greatly increased my labor; for, in our days, history means, above all things, going back to original sources; and to one residing in a Western city, with no great libraries at hand, with but few friends near him with whom to advise; to one not a professional but an amateur only in Rabbinic lore, and who has to attend his business office in business hours, it is a weariness to the flesh to hunt up and verify authorities in the oldest and the original sources on such a wide subject as the Jewish Services in Synagogue and Home.

Hence, like a careful bookkeeper, I put an E. O. E. at the head as well as at the bottom of my statement:

ERRORS AND OMISSIONS EXCEPTED

I have availed myself freely of the historical researches made by others, from Abudraham's work, written about 1340, to pamphlets bearing the date in 1897. Much of the original material was not otherwise accessible to me, and much more time would have been wasted in finding what is hidden away in the Talmud and Midrash, often in the most unexpected places. Wherever the usage of authors demanded it, credit has been given to the scholars and investigators of whose work I have availed myself.

The volume has been much swelled by the necessity of laying before my readers the chief parts of our liturgy and samples of the later and less essential parts in a faithful English translation, as the greater number of those whom this book will reach are not acquainted with the old Prayer Book, that peculiar treasure of Israel, nor even possessed of a copy, otherwise I might, like German authors on the subject, have referred to parts of the prayers by name without embodying them in the text. Longer passages from the Bible, such as whole Psalms, are not copied, but simply cited.

Citations from or references to the Bible are marked in the text, as all readers have a copy within easy reach. The chapter and verse number follow the Hebrew text; in Psalms with a long title the verse number is higher by one than in the English common version. Other citations are made in the notes, to which also much of the minor historical detail is relegated. The name of a Talmudic treatise with chapter and section means the Mishna; the Babylonian Talmud is cited by the letters T. B. before the treatise, and the folio, with *a* or *b* for the page; the Jerusalem Talmud in the ordinary way, by the section or Halacha of the Mishna on which it comments. The citation of "Hilchoth" indicates the Code of Maimonides.

With these few preliminaries I submit my work to the kind reader, unlearned or learned.

LEWIS N. DEMBITZ.

Louisville, August 1st, 1897.

TABLE OF CONTENTS

BOOK I

GENERAL AND HISTORICAL INTRODUCTION

BOOK II

THE DEVOTIONS OF THE SYNAGOGUE

BOOK III

THE DESK AND THE PULPIT

BOOK IV

INCIDENTS AND CEREMONIES

BOOK V

THE JEWISH HOME

BOOK I

General and Historical Introduction

BOOK I

GENERAL AND HISTORICAL INTRODUCTION

CHAPTER I

DIVISIONS OF THE JEWISH BODY

THE word "Services" has been chosen as a part of the title of this work rather than "Ritual," which is too comprehensive, or "Liturgy," which is too narrow. The work is to treat of everything that is spoken or read in the Synagogue or in the Jewish Home by way of religious duty, and incidentally of what is done to suit the action to the word.

We treat only of the services according to the old rituals, unaffected by those reforms, beginning at Hamburg in 1819, based on the rejection of a part of the beliefs on which the old order of services was founded. Although the number of Jews and Jewesses who no longer share these beliefs is quite considerable, the number of Synagogues that have adopted a reformed service is, at the time of this writing, quite small except in the United States and in Germany.

But in many congregations of Europe and America the services have been modernized without the abrogation of anything that had been deemed obligatory in the order of worship. Music suited to Western tastes has taken the place of a drawling chant or of wild license and inharmonious noise, and sermons in correct speech have become an integral part of the service, in place of long and disjointed talks in an uncouth jargon, filled either with bold misinter-

(11)

pretation of Scripture or with dry, legal hair-splitting, which
were formerly heard in the Synagogue at odd times. Moreover, many of the "poetries," composed in the middle
ages to fill up time on Festivals and favored Sabbaths in
the absence of a preacher, have been dropped by the "pro-
gressives," as indeed they had always been discountenanced
by many otherwise strict and old-fashioned Jews. As the
Jews are naturally gifted with a good ear, and many
also with a good voice for music, the "progressive" or
choir Synagogues have spread rapidly since Samuel Sulzer
introduced the beginnings of his "Song of Zion" at the
great Synagogue of Vienna in 1829. Even in Russian
Poland and Russia, at least in the great cities, the prejudice
against the innovation has been overcome, and many congregations lack the choir or the musically-trained leader
only by reason of their poverty.

· But there is a division much older than any between
orthodoxy, progress, and reform; it is that between the
Sefardim, or Jews of the Spanish and Portuguese ritual, and
the Ashkenazim, or German and Polish Jews. The Hebrew
names for the divisions are based on a notion which iden-
tifies Sepharad, mentioned in the prophecy of Obadiah, with
Spain, and another which makes Ashkenaz, a grandson of
Noah, the ancestor of the Teutonic race.[1] The Sefardim,
embracing the Jews dwelling in Spain and Portugal, in
Provence, Italy, North Africa, and Turkey, were, in 1492,
at the time of the expulsion from Spain, the more important
branch in wealth, in learning and refinement, probably also
in numbers: but they have dropped into the background
since the culture of the times has reached the Jews of Germany and adjoining countries, and since those in the
east of Europe have increased to such vast multitudes. At
present the Ashkenazim outnumber the Sefardim by fully
twelve to one, but the customs of the latter have by no
means lost their historic importance.

The services of the Synagogue are carried on in Hebrew.

The Sefardim and Ashkenazim differ mainly in their ways of reading this language. The former have pretty nearly kept up the classic pronunciation of Judea, the same by which Hebrew names of persons and places were transliterated into Greek, as we find them in the Septuagint (or Greek Old Testament) and in the New Testament, as far as Hebrew sounds could be represented by Greek letters. Hebrew, read in the Sefardic fashion, is "the Jews' language" referred to in Isaiah 36: 11 and Nehemiah 13: 24. The Ashkenazim have, on the other hand, brought with them the pronunciation of Galilee,[2] from which district a great colony is said to have been deported to the lower Rhine in the days of Hadrian. Thence their descendants overflowed the north of Europe, especially Bohemia, Hungary, Poland. Witness the German speech, or at least the German jargon which the Jews of these countries have employed among themselves for hundreds of years in the midst of a Slavonic population. Lately millions of them have overflowed further east, into Russia, Roumania, and Turkey.

But before we can speak of these differences we must first fix the sounds which the English letters are to designate. The vowels, *a, e, i, o, u,* have their "Roman" values, the same as in German and Italian; *j* that of consonant *y; ch* has the Scotch or German sound; *s* is always sharp. We might mark *h* with some diacritical mark when it represents in Hebrew the stronger breath *Heth,* and employ an inverted apostrophe for that peculiar guttural, the Hebrew 'Ayin; but to do so regularly would be needless trouble for the printer and the reader. *Tz* will be written for the Hebrew Tzaddi.

I. The chief differences in reading are these:

The vowel called Kametz is to the Sefardim generally long *a,* rarely short *o;* to the Germans, always *o.* Hence, the latter read the name of the first man *Odom.* There is a short *a,* which is pronounced alike by both branches.

The vowel Tzere is to the Sefardim and to many Germans and Poles long *e*, but in eastern Germany and with the Ashkenazim of England it sounds like the diphthongal English *i* (the short *e* all pronounce alike).

The vowel Holem is to the Sefardim long *o*, to the Germans and Poles *ou* or some corruption thereof. Thus a Cohen is in a London Synagogue a *Cowhine*.

The vowel Shurek, pronounced by the Sefardim *u*, is by most Polish and Hungarian Jews sounded like the French *u* or German *ue*. This peculiarity may indicate an overland immigration into these countries independent of the German element, for to the Germans proper it is *u*.

The letter Beth is to the Sefardim always *b*. But when "weak," that is, when it follows a vowel and is not doubled, it is to the Germans and Poles a *v*.

The letter Tav is to the Sefardim always *t*, but when "weak" it is to the Germans and Poles a sharp *s;* the West Africans then sound it *ts*, the English Bible turns it into *th*. Hence, Rut and Rus are the Sefardic and German for Ruth.

The Sefardim put a short vowel between the two consonants which would otherwise introduce the same syllable (known in grammar as the *Sheva mobile*). In the English Bible this vowel is generally marked by an *e*, in a few well-known names by *a* or *o;* the Germans and Poles read the two consonants closely together. The last three points are illustrated by the word *Ketubim* (meaning the books of the Bible after the Law and the Prophets), which in the German pronunciation becomes *Xuvim*.

The letter 'Ayin denotes a guttural peculiar to the Semitic tongues, produced by breathing while the back of the mouth is compressed. The Sefardim in Mohammedan countries give to this letter the true old sound; those in Holland, England, and the United States have turned it into *ng*, which is wholly wrong; the Germans and Poles drop it altogether, and thus fail to distinguish between 'Ayin and

Alef. Moreover, the Sefardim observe the rules of the word-accent, which in most words ought to fall on the last syllable; the Germans and Poles do not observe them, generally letting the accent rest on the last syllable but one.

II. Next comes the difference in intoning prayers and Bible lessons. The Sefardim have pretty much maintained the old Oriental chants, which move in a very narrow compass, while the Germans and Poles have allowed a strong European element to enter their religious music. Their tunes and chants are lively and run through a considerable compass.

III. There is lastly a considerable divergence between the German and the Portuguese service books. The more important and old established devotions are the same, or differ only in a few words (nearly always so, in that the form used by the Sefardim is fuller of synonyms and more diffuse), but the later additions have not always been accepted by both branches. The German service book came originally from Tiberias in Galilee, that of the Sefardim (the "Ritual" of R. Amram) from the schools of Babylonia early in the ninth century. In later times the two great branches often borrowed new compositions or the use of Psalms and other Biblical passages from each other.[3]

The old standards fully recognize the right of congregations in different lands to vary in their customs in all unessential details, and make it the duty of the individual to conform to the customs of his own community.[4] The Mishna, after the Law of Moses our oldest Code, often uses the phrase, "Everything according to the custom (*Minhag*) of the country," and we speak now of the "Portuguese Minhag" and the "German Minhag." The latter is divided into the German proper (Western Germany) and the Polish Minhag, that of Eastern Germany and the countries east and southeast of it. The many migrations of Israel have brought together in new abodes numbers of Jewish families, who had for generations respectively used one or the other *Minhag* in their several homes. Old associations being stronger than mere nearness in space, several communities would grow up, those of the same custom herding together, and each of these communities would, in the same city, set up a Synagogue for worship according to its own *Minhag*. Thus there are Spanish or Portuguese Synagogues in London, Paris, Hamburg, and Vienna, although in each of these cities the bulk of the Jewish population adheres to the German or Polish ritual. We find a like condition as early as the twelfth century at Cairo, where a Palestinian and a Babylonian congregation worshipped within the walls of one city, the former reading the Law in a cycle of three years, the latter in one year.[5]

In this book the sounds of Hebrew words and names occurring in the text will, after the usage of all modern writers, follow the Sefardic mode of reading, and be represented by English letters as indicated above; but wherever the name of a person or place occurs in the English Bible the spelling there used will be followed. In fact, this cannot differ much from the proposed system, being also based on the Sefardic way of reading and on the use of the English letters indicated above, except that simple *z* is used for *tz* (Zion ought to be Tzion), and in all best-known names, such as Moses (Mosheh), Samuel (Shemuel), Solomon (Shelomo), which had become part of the language before the Reformation, the English Bible follows the Latin version, the Vulgate. But while we go with the Sefardim in pronunciation, we shall, in most cases, present the forms of prayer of the "Germans," as the Ashkenazic division of the race is vastly in the majority, and as, moreover, these forms are generally more concise.[6]

But while the Sefardim are painfully prolix in many of the older prayers, they have kept their services almost free from the "poetries," which began to overwhelm the liturgy of the Synagogue late in the ninth century, soon after the standards for the two branches of Jewry had been established. Of these compositions the German branch has adopted many that have no devotional value, and some, moreover, almost or quite unintelligible even to the best Hebrew scholars. In giving very few specimens of this literature, this work will, at least in a negative way, side with the Sefardim and with the progressive party among the Germans.

The Jews of Yemen, few in number, poor, without worldly power or much learning, are nevertheless of interest because some customs survive among them that have died out everywhere else, and because, in the pronunciation of Hebrew, they stand midway between Sefardim and Germans or Poles. Like the former they sound the *Sheva mobile*, i. e., they do not begin a syllable with two consonants, and they do not modify the aspirates of Beth and Tav. They pronounce the vowels nearly like the Germans, and they use in their manuscripts generally the "supralinear" vowelling, which is suited to their pronunciation. In their ritual, which, through the influence of Maimonides in the twelfth or thirteenth century, was assimilated to that of the Sefardim, there are yet some traces of the German ritual which came to them from Palestine.[7] It lies beyond our purpose to analyze the services of the Karaite sect in the Crimea, who profess to have cut loose entirely from the Rabbinical traditions, or of the one small congregation of Samaritans who are worshipping in their little Synagogue at Nabloos in central Palestine, and who still sacrifice their Passover lambs every year.

But there is a sect numbered by hundreds of thousands, spread through large parts of Poland, Russia, Northern Hungary, and Roumania, who should not be passed over: the *Hasidim*, or "Pious," the followers of Israel Ba'al Shem Tob (possessor of the good name, i. e., wonder-worker by the use of divine names). This sect was founded in the first half of the eighteenth century, and has grown considerably

2

in the second half of the nineteenth in measure as it moderated its divergences from the general body. The *Hasidim* do not deny the binding force of the laws and customs of ordinary Jews, but they ascribe a higher value to the mystic writings, the Cabbala, than to the Talmud, and their spiritual guides are chosen not for their learning, but for their supposed miraculous gifts. They pronounce Hebrew like the other Jews of the countries which they inhabit, but their Prayer Book is borrowed in the main from the Sefardic ritual.[8]

CHAPTER II

As we shall in these pages seek to assign every part and every feature of the Jewish worship of God, by spoken words in the Synagogue and at the home, to the time of its origin, we must first sketch and define the periods through which the Jewish community has passed since the first beginnings of the order of services which has come down to our days. These periods fall naturally into two divisions— the older, when the life of our religion centered within the Holy Land, at Jerusalem, at Jamnia, and lastly in Galilee, down to the compilation of the Mishna in or about the year 220 of the present era; and the later, in which the leadership of Israel, after remaining for a few hundred years with the schools of Babylonia, fell into abeyance altogether, and the nation had no longer a religious any more than a political center.

In treating of the Palestinian times we need not go back of the Babylonian exile. The destruction of Solomon's Temple is usually assigned to the year 588 before the common era. In the year 538 Cyrus became King of Babylon, and in the first year of his reign as such he published his famous decree allowing the Jews to return to Jerusalem. The first colony went out under Zerubbabel of the House of David, and built an altar on the sacred spot. In the account which the Book of Ezra has left us of this great event, we find the one line of our present Prayer Book of which the continuous use may be traced back to the days of the old Commonwealth. It was sung by men who had seen the first Temple, as we know also on the independent testimony of Jeremiah: "Give thanks to the Lord for He is good; for His mercy endureth forever."[1]

Much indeed of the Scriptures written before the exile is read in our Synagogues either as a lesson or by way of devotion. The Mosaic Code even commands the recital of some set forms of words, among them the Priestly Blessing; and Moses in his farewell address demands that the whole book should be read to the assembled men, women, and children once in seven years. Conceding, as orthodox believers maintain, that these precepts are as old as the day of Moses, we know from other parts of the Bible, that for hundreds of years the Mosaic Law was forgotten, and not a copy of it was in common use.

The exiles in Babylon had no altar nor sacrifice, hence their strong religious feeling took form in song and praise, and in listening to the words of inspired teachers. The "Sons of Asaph," who had acted as the choir in Solomon's Temple—some of them as the poets and composers for the choir—kept up their identity while on the banks of the Euphrates, and sang before the new altar when they came back to their old home.

There were delays in the building of the Temple; it was not finished until the sixth year of King Darius. Little or nothing is known of the religious life of the colony between the Festivals in that year and the coming of Ezra, the Scribe, and of Nehemiah, the governor, in the reign of Artaxerxes Longimanus, nearly sixty years later. Here we come to a great epoch in the life of Israel—the assembly of the people on the first day of the seventh month, when Ezra read the Law of Moses to them between sunrise and high noon.[2]

And herewith begins the first historic period in which the mode of worshipping God otherwise than by sacrifice was developed in Israel; it is the age of the men of the Great Synod. As to all details, this period, say from the year 458 to the year 201 (the date assigned for the death of Simeon the Just), is a blank. The Book of Chronicles, written during this time, records the names of some of the High Priests; Josephus tells a few incidents of Alexander's entry into Jerusalem, and how Palestine became an apple of discord between the Ptolemies in Egypt and the successors of Seleucus, the "Kings of Asia;" but of the inner history of the people, in law, religion, or customs, we know nothing but the results. Whether the Great Synod was a council or only a collective name for many teachers and lawgivers, and how many men were counted as members of the Synod, is unknown. The only names handed down to posterity are those of Ezra, the founder, and of Simeon the Just, who was the last among them.[3]

The men of the Great Synod gathered the national writings; they decided what books should and what books should not be considered as sacred. We are informed in the Talmud that they put several of these books, namely Ezekiel, the twelve smaller Prophets, Daniel, and Esther, into shape.[4] Although the Book of Daniel, many of the Psalms, and probably the Book of Ecclesiastes were written in later times, it is clear that with the end of the days of the Great Synod the idea of a collection of sacred books —Law, History, Prophets, Songs, and Reflections—had taken firm root in the Jewish mind.

But the feeling of the necessity for an "oral law," carried down by honored teachers from generation to generation, had also grown up. We find a fully developed germ of the "Oral Law" in the second chapter of Haggai, where the prophet asks the priest questions in the Law. Where the Pentateuch laid down a command in a few words, in broad outlines, the tradition of the fathers would fill in the details. As to the worship of God by prayer, praise, or study, the Mosaic law is almost silent. In this field tradition, taking its root mainly in regulations by men in authority, was most needed. At the end of the period an outline of a daily service seems to have been known and in common use by the more faithful among the people, as will be shown hereafter.

Three maxims of the Great Synod are reported: "Be slow in judgment" (showing that the men composing it were judges as well as teachers); "set up many disciples" (evidently in interpretation and in traditional law), and "make a fence around the law" (showing that they assumed a law-making power even beyond interpretation). One saying is ascribed to Simeon the Just: "The world stands on three things, on the (study of the) Law, on the Service, and on Charity."[5] The very opening of the Mishna proves that the Great Synod did not regulate worship by spoken words until it had first settled priestly usages.[6]

The next period after that of the Great Synod may be reckoned to the death of Antigonus, the last of the Hasmoneans, in his futile struggle against the Roman power, about 35 years before the Common Era. It comprises a few years of quiet and prosperity before Antiochus sought to force his pagan worship upon the Jews;[7] also the war of twenty-five years which ended with the full independence of the country under Simeon, the brother of the heroic Judas Maccabeus; the reigns of the Hasmonean princes, the invasion of the Romans under Pompey, and the fitful struggles that followed till the Hasmonean race, in the male line, was extinguished. We find in this period of one hundred and sixty-six years the names of a few great teachers, not more than two in any one generation, whose opinions are recorded in the Mishna as authority in the Law; the oldest of the line of teachers known as Tannaïm.[8] The Bible took its final shape during this age, except that even at its close there was still a dispute about the right of the Books of Ecclesiastes and Canticles to a place in the Canon.[9]

The first of the bearers of the tradition in this period is "Antigonus, of Socho," of whose views little or nothing is known but his motto: "Be not like servants who serve the master in order to get their rations, but like servants who serve the master without regard to their rations; yet should the fear of Heaven be before your eyes." Talmudic story, doubted by some modern writers, gives him two disciples, Zadok and Boëthos, who construed his motto into a denial of rewards in a future life. The latter turned to Epicurean philosophy, the former became the founder of the sect of Sadducees (*Tsedukiyim*), who denied the resurrection, insisted on a literal construction of the Pentateuch, and rejected all traditional interpretation. They carried out "eye for eye, tooth for tooth," by taking the eye or tooth of the offender, while to the followers of tradition this precept meant no more than an award of money damages for the loss of the member or organ.

The latter, the men of the tradition, by their refinements in criminal procedure almost abolished the death penalty, and showed how its infliction by stoning or burning could be rendered nearly painless.[10] The Sadducees were numerous only among the wealthy and powerful classes; the learned men, whom the mass of the people obeyed, were in somewhat later times called Pharisees (*Perushim* or *Perishin*, i. e., the Separated), while among themselves they took the name of Companions (*Haberim*). But both of these names were coined to distinguish them, not so much from the Sadducees, as from the unlearned and indifferent mass, the "people of the land" (*Am ha-aretz*).

As all subsequent religious life and learning were drawn from Pharisaic sources, the leading tendencies of their school must be briefly stated. They believed in an aristocracy of learning, that is, of course, learning in the Law. Hence the rule in the Mishna, that though the High Priest must be of the noblest blood and purest descent, yet if he be "of the people of the land," i. e., unlearned, he is of less account than a bastard who is a "disciple of the wise" (a man of Rabbinic learning).[11] In their ideal polity the Sanhedrin, made up of learned judges, was the supreme ruling body; the King or High Priest must act only under its advice.[12] Though they scrupulously gave tithe of their produce to the priests, yet they thought that every man should be priest in his own house, and every dining-table his altar; hence their rule to wash the hands before each meal and to put salt upon the morsel first eaten.[13] The written law hardly knows of any other mode of worship but that of the altar, and though this was accompanied by beautiful hymns and prayers composed for that very purpose, it could not satisfy the hearts of the vast majority of Israel, who seldom or never entered the court-yards. The Sadducees, tying themselves to the letter of the Mosaic Code, could hardly busy themselves with composing prayers for the Synagogue, as, in the language of the Sages, the obligation to pray at all "floats in the air," i. e., has little or no support in the Scriptures. But for the greater freedom with which the Pharisees handled the Law, the religion of Israel must have come to an end with the permanent destruction of the Temple. They had the courage to add to the two hundred and forty-eight positive commands found in the Pentateuch their own further commands, to read Bible lessons in the Synagogue at stated times, to sing Psalms of praise on the Festivals and on the Feast of the Maccabees, to say prayers three times a day, to bless God not only after, but also before meals; indeed, they went so far as to draw up benedictions according to which God has "commanded us to read the scroll" (the Book of Esther), or "to read the Praise" (Psalms 113-118).[14]

The Sadducees of earlier days must not be confounded with the unpatriotic or Hellenizing Jews who sided with Antiochus, and were by the *Hasidim* (the pious), or Patriots, denounced in the later Psalms and in early parts of the Prayer Book under the name of the Wicked, or Deserters of the Covenant. In fact, the Sadducees became important and powerful only in the reign of the Hasmonean

Priest-Kings, John Hyrcanus and Alexander Jannæus, who were driven into their arms by the sharp opposition of the great popular party, led, during the reign of the latter, by Simeon ben Shetah, his brother-in-law, and Vice-President of the Sanhedrin. The "Sages" were cruelly persecuted, and though, after the King's death, his widow and successor, Queen Salome, restored the Pharisees to power, the feeling between the two sects remained very bitter, and the Sadducees drifted away so far from patriotism that in Roman times they were generally preferred by the foreign oppressor for the positions of High Priests and Judges.

We come now to the second period of the Tannaïm and the last period of the Temple service. Antipater for a few years and after him his son, Herod, Idumeans by descent, but Jews by religious profession, were kings by the support of the Roman arms and in spite of the protest of all patriots, who looked upon them not as kings of Israel, within the meaning of the Scripture, but as tools of a hated conqueror. There was no hope of getting rid of the foreign yoke by the unaided bravery of the nation, not even by such bravery as the highest religious fervor could inspire, such as gave to the Hasmoneans victory over the Syrian armies. Nothing would suffice but a deliverance by signs and wonders, like God's battling in behalf of His people when He brought them out from under the burdens of Egypt. Herod sought in vain to offset his cruelties against the people and their learned leaders by an ostentatious observance of the ceremonial law and by building a Temple greater and fairer than that of Solomon; still he was to the patriots nothing more than an enemy whom God had permitted to rule over them, to punish them for their sins. And times got worse and worse; the Jewish courts, under the advice of the Sanhedrin, refused to try capital cases; the land was overrun with robbers and guerrillas in the guise of patriots;[15] and thus things went on for many years, except during the short interval when Agrippa, Herod's

grandson, by the favor of the Emperor Claudius reigned
as King of the Jews, acknowledged and beloved as such by
the Sages.[16] It was natural that in these times the mind of the
people should turn to the Messianic prophecies in Isaiah,
in Micah, in Zechariah, should connect them with the predictions of God's conciliation with Israel in Deuteronomy
and with the promises of universal peace and well-being and
true belief which are scattered through the Prophets and
Psalms.[17]   Hence in this age the hope for the speedy coming of a Messiah (*Mashiah*, i. e., Anointed), a King of
Israel from the seed of David, took strong hold of the
people. The critical remark of a scholar that the Israelites
"have already consumed their Messiah," meaning that in
King Hezekiah the most striking prophecies had been
fulfilled, could not change the popular faith.[18] Only in this
age, during the first fervor of Messianic hopes, and while
claimants to the Messiah's office fought bravely against
the Romans,[19] could Christianity arise; a religious belief
in which the personality of a man, claiming to be the promised Messiah, fills the chief place.

As the hope of a coming Redeemer and the wish for his
speedily coming and ushering in the Kingdom of Heaven
on earth had a marked influence on the Prayer Book, we
must for that reason alone distinguish the last one hundred
and five years of the Temple from the preceding ages. But
there is another change; the Jews are no longer a Commonwealth; they are only a Church; not only in their own eyes,
but in those of the heathen. Their minds are turned from
politics to the study and practice of their religious law more
than ever before. The schools of Hillel and Shammai
gather many hundreds of pupils, who in their turn become
teachers for another generation. The Patriarchate, stripped
of its political power, becomes hereditary, with few breaks,
with the descendants of Hillel, who for four centuries
remained faithful to the cause. While only a few sayings
of the older Sages are recorded, the disputes between the

schools of Hillel and Shammaï cover hundreds of points, sometimes weighty, as in the matter of divorce, oftener on unimportant ceremonial questions.[20] For those who lived at a distance from Palestine, took no part in the services of the Temple, and were not bound by the laws of tithing and tribute and first-fruits, etc., applicable to the Holy Land alone, orthodox Judaism took pretty much the shape then which it had within living memory and which it still has in the East.

A grandson of Hillel was Rabban Gamaliel, so well known to the Gentile world as the teacher of Paul of Tarsus, and it seems that he was the last President of the Sanhedrin while it sat at Jerusalem.

Among the other great names of this century are Jonathan ben Uzziel, the expounder and translator of the prophetic books; Rabbi Ishmael, one of the latest of the High Priests; and Rabban Johanan ben Zaccai, who survived the tragic end of Jerusalem, and became the founder of the new Judaism.

In the period just considered a sharp difference was developed between the "Haberim," or companions, or "disciples of the wise," in short, the Pharisees, and the common people (*Am ha-arctz*). Of this the Synoptic Gospels bear abundant witness. The dislike was mutual. Rabbi Akiba, who died as a very old man and as the most esteemed Rabbi of his age in the next following period, had in his younger days been one of the "people of the land," and he acknowledges that while he was such he felt, at the sight of a "disciple of the wise," the desire to "tear him to pieces like a fish."[21] Many differences between the "companions" and the "people" are found both in the Gospels and in the Talmud. The most striking is the unbending custom of the former to wash their hands before partaking of bread; another, their distrust of the latter as to regularly tithing their corn, oil, and wine; for both of which reasons the former were unwilling to eat "with publicans and sinners."[22]   The great practical difference was that between learning and ignorance.   As the religious law embraced not only ceremony and dogma but the moral duties of man to man and the mutual rights of men and of women in all questions of contract, of tort, of inheritance, of marriage and divorce, and of criminal procedure, and as in those days there were very few branches of knowledge outside of law and religion to which studious minds could turn, it came naturally that the Pharisees, notwithstanding their aversion to Greek philosophy and heathen influences, were much more enlightened than the "people of the land."   The latter wanted an emotional religion in which good and evil spirits, especially the latter, played a prominent part.   They were fond of miracle workers, while the learned Rabbis, from the days of Joshua ben Sira (Jesus Sirach) down, looked upon medicine as a science.[23]   The "people" were in constant fear of hell and its torments, while the learned of the age referred to Ge-Hinnom seldom and then only by the use of popular sayings.   Enlightenment remained in the lead as long as Jewish life centered in the Holy Land.

After the destruction of the Temple, Rabban Johanan ben Zaccaï obtained leave from Vespasianus to establish a school of the Law at Jamnia,[24] and there laid the foundation of the present Synagogue, which has no need for altar or offerings.   But the people continued to long for the old service; they had been told that the blood of sacrifice was indispensable to the atonement of sin; there could be no sacrifice but on the Holy Mountain, and access to that was denied by the stern Roman.   For all national holidays, all great rejoicings, Jerusalem had been the scene.   "Who has not seen the gladness of the water-drawing house, has never seen gladness in all his days," was the sad plaint of the survivors to the younger generation.   We thus find a new element naturally introduced into the order of prayers: Build thy Temple again, which has been destroyed through our own sins, and restore its service!   The desire for a speedy

coming of the Messiah became stronger, and was intertwined with the hopes for the recovery of Jerusalem and
the rebuilding of the Temple.

Fifty years after its destruction by Titus, the Jews in
northern Palestine had so increased in numbers and prosperity that they felt strong enough to essay a new rebellion
against the Roman Colossus. Its military leader, Simeon
bar Cochba (son of the star), announced himself as the
promised Messiah, and it found spiritual support from R.
Akiba, the most learned and pious Sage of his time, who
accepted Bar Cochba's claims only when, after a learned
and labored research, he had come to the conclusion that
there could be a restoration without the previous re-appear-
ance of the lost tribes.[25] The rebellion or series of rebellions was not finally put down for twelve or thirteen years.
The forces under Bar Cochba finally stood a siege in the
mountain fortress of Bethar; they were, of course, overcome; five hundred thousand men, women, and children
lost their lives; R. Akiba and many of his colleagues died as
martyrs; thousands of the survivors were deported to the
shores of the Rhine; Northern Palestine for twenty years
became a waste, as the South Country had been before.
Yet the cruel lesson left the hopes for the coming Messiah
as deep-seated as before.[26] The school and Sanhedrin at
Jamnia were now broken up; it took many years before the
torn threads were gathered up and a new school and new
Sanhedrin were established at Usha, further north. Under
Simeon ben Gamaliel, of the old line of Patriarchs, the
school soon attained high standing, and drew to itself great
numbers of eager learners. The Sanhedrin again fixed the
New Moon and Feasts for the Jews of the dispersion; this
being the badge of supreme authority. It attained its highest splendor with Rabbi Judah the Saint, a man noted for
his great learning, the purity of his life, for his wealth, and
for the favor in which he was held by the Romans.[27] Two
generations before him R. Meïr had made an attempt to

codify the tradition, or Mishna (perhaps R. Akiba before him); this was probably only by word of mouth, or in a privately-kept manuscript, in short aphorisms which the disciples might learn by heart; for it was still deemed dangerous to write down the oral law and thus put it on a level with the Mosaic Code.[28] With these older works before him, Rabbi Judah undertook to collect the substance of all the Pharisaic learning down to his own time.

The product is the Mishna, with its sixty-three treatises, which, in turn, are subdivided into chapters and sections, all arranged in six "orders."[29] This became henceforth the basis of all discussion, and thus a broad line was drawn between the old Sages, whose opinions were here recorded, and their successors in later ages. But much of the old lore remained outside of the compilation, and is known as Baraïtha (the outside). This has been preserved either in certain commentaries on the second, third, fourth, and fifth books of Moses and in additions to the Mishna, written by Rabbi Judah's disciples,[30] or by quotations in the Gemara, of which hereafter.

The Mishna treats in full detail of King and of High Priest, of capital crimes and punishments, of the Temple and of sacrifice,[31] not for historic information, but for the day when Israel, free from foreign yoke, will again live under its own King and High Priest and its own laws, and bring grateful offerings on Mount Zion. One passage sets forth the signs which will indicate the speedy coming of the Messiah; but this is generally thought to be a later addition to the Mishna as first compiled.

In the disapproval of superstitions the later Tannaim are even more decided than their predecessors; probably by way of reaction against the miracles and exorcising of the Jewish Christians. R. Akiba reckons among those "who have no share in the world to come," him "who whispers over a sore," that is, who pretends to cure it by incantation or by casting out devils.[32] The same sober and enlightened tone is not always found in the Baraïtha as in the Mishna; perhaps because superstitious sayings were rejected by the great compiler of that Code; more probably because those who in the Gemara claimed to quote ancient sayings from hearsay after hearsay, projected their own superstitions into an earlier and more enlightened age.[33]

The moral standard of the Mishna for the daily intercourse between man and man is very high. After the legal requisites to make a binding contract of sale are minutely set forth, the vengeance of God is invoked upon him. who takes advantage of these rules to break his plighted word. To hurt a man's feelings by reminding him of his weaknesses is deemed as wrong as to cheat him in trade; to "blanch a man's face in public" is one of the unpardonable sins. One of the old heroes refuses the Patriarchate because to gain it he would have to yield to the majority his opinions on a few trifling points of ceremonial law; he answers, "I would rather be thought a fool all my life than be wicked for even one hour."[34]

The language of the Mishna is Hebrew of the Galilean dialect in its decay, with some Aramaic and some Babylonian forms, and mixed with many Aramaic and Greek and a few Babylonian and Latin words, but it is still Hebrew.[35]

Some noted Rabbis of this period will be spoken of hereafter as identified with some one or other tendency or institution.

During all these ages in which "the law went forth," if not from Jerusalem, at least from Palestine, many Jews, and towards the last a majority of them, lived outside of the sacred borders. In Babylonia and Mesopotamia descendants of those whom Nebuchadnezzar had carried there lived, multiplied, and prospered; Hillel himself was born there, but became a leader of thought only after coming to Jerusalem. We also hear in the Mishna often about the Jews settled in Syria, right north of the border, and in Cappadocia. All these adhered closely to the teaching of the Pharisaic Rabbis. Then there were vast numbers at Alexandria and in other cities of Lower Egypt, who carried on their worship and studies mainly by the aid of Greek translations, and who were, in a measure, allowed to go their own way. Among them Philo, a contemporary of Paul of Tarsus, is most noted. Among books which have come down to our time, his works are the first to exhibit Hebrew faith blended with Pythagorean and Platonic and perhaps with Hindoo speculations. Of this hereafter. There were also Greek-speaking Jews in great numbers in Cyrenaica, the present Tripoli, thoroughly in sympathy with their brethren at the old home. Many of them fought under Bar Cochba in the last war for Israel's independence. There were Synagogues in Rome even in the days of Cæsar, *and they have been there ever since.* Horace and other Latin writers speak of the wide spread of Jewish beliefs and of Sabbath observance.[36] The New Testament bears witness to the diffusion of Jews through Greece and its colonies; Josephus, to the conversion of the King and many of the citizens of Adiabene, or "Little Media."[37] But, with the exception of the Alexandrians, all took their law as it came to them from Jerusalem, Jamnia, and the seats of the Patriarchs at Usha and Beth Shearim in Galilee.

Besides the divisions of the Jewish body named above, there were, according to the Mishna, both before and after the destruction of the Temple, sectaries, hated and considered as dangerous, known as *Minim.*[38] What the origin and what the tenets or distinguishing marks of these sectaries were, whether in fact one or several bodies of dissenters were thus designated, is uncertain. It is possible that Jewish Christians are generally meant, but some passages forbid this assumption.[39]

CHAPTER III

HISTORIC BACKGROUND—CENTER NO LONGER IN PALESTINE

In about 220 the Patriarchate was moved to Tiberias on the Syrian border, where it remained till it disappeared two hundred years later. But no great men arose like Johanan ben Zaccaï or R. Akiba or Rabban Gamaliel. Tiberias could not rule the dispersion; the leadership of Israel fled to schools planted on the Euphrates among the descendants of those whom Nebuchadnezzar had carried from Judea. Of the later teachers at Tiberias only three need be named, . R. Hiya, the foremost pupil of Judah the Saint; R. Simlaï, who counted the 613 (365 positive and 248 negative) precepts of the Tora, and showed how Prophets and Psalmists had reduced them to their kernel in eleven principles or even one, and, lastly, the Patriarch, Hillel the Younger, who, yielding to the growing enmity of the Christian emperors in about 360, gave up the old badge of Palestine's supremacy, the proclamation of New Moons and New Years, and adopted the Athenian calendar, modified for Jewish purposes, as will be shown in another chapter. To these might be added Resh Lakish and Joshua ben Levi, masters of legend in their own time and its heroes in following generations.[1]

The discussions of the Sages of Tiberias upon the Mishna have been collected into the so-called Jerusalem Talmud, but by reason of the low esteem in which they were held by the Jews of other countries, great parts thereof have been lost, and other parts preserved only in single, often quite imperfect and incorrect copies. The treatises on civil law

3   (33)

are treated least fully, and in these discussions, as far as they have reached us, very few new forms of prayer are found; but they contain much important information not found elsewhere on the growth of the liturgy.

About the life of the Jews in Babylonia down to the revival of the Persian Kingdom by Ardeshir, son of Sassan, in the year 227, nothing is known. But at this time, when by the decay of Palestine the men of the East came to the foreground, history dawns upon them. We find the institution of a hereditary Chief of the Exile (*Resh Geluiha*), to whom the former Parthian, and now the Neo-Persian, Kings allowed very large governing powers over the Jewish population, which appears to have lived in compact settlements and to have consisted mainly of industrious, well-to-do. contented farmers. It was afterwards contended that these Chiefs had had a continued succession from the days of Zerubbabel, and were through him descended from King David; but this is hardly more than a myth. The Chief of the Exile, often himself a man of Rabbinical learning, appointed the chiefs of the colleges, which took rise about the year last mentioned.[2]

The subject to be taught in these schools was the whole mass of traditions and a world of thought and of method which had grown up in the course of at least four hundred years. Naturally, therefore, the first two teachers of the East had studied in the West; they were Abba Areka, afterwards known as "Rab," and Samuel, a man possessed of all the learning of his time, including medicine and astronomy. The former became head of the school at Sura, the latter at Nehardea, and as such they formed the first of the Babylonian "couples," whose opinions the Talmud habitually gives side by side. These two men, especially the former, did much towards bringing the order of prayers into the fixed form which it has at the present day. Both died before the middle of the third century.[3]

The discussions of the Eastern schools or colleges (*Methi-*

batha) are very full on the laws of Mine and Thine, on the observance of Sabbath and Festivals, and on the service of the Synagogue, but leave untouched parts of the Mishna dealing with tithes and other burdens on the farm (as these applied to the Holy Land only) and those which deal with Levitical cleanness. The teachers who appear either at Tiberias or in the East, and whose discussions are based on the Mishna, are known by the general designation of Emoraïm, as distinguished from the Tannaïm that preceded them; and their discussions are known as "Gemara," that is, completion. The Jerusalem Talmud seems to have been completed in the second half of the fourth century; the Babylonian Talmud (which records many of the best sayings of the later Palestinian teachers) was not closed till about the year 480, and in its present form contains a few somewhat later additions. The sudden outbreak of a persecuting spirit in the Persian government, which dispersed teachers and scholars, may have been a determining cause for reducing into a written collection, and thus preserving for the Jews elsewhere and for later generations, the best results of what had been said and done in the schools, now of Sura (or Mahasia) and Pumbeditha (which succeeded Nehardea), during the lapse of almost three hundred years. In this collection, known as the Babylonian Talmud, is preserved, forming its most valuable part, much of the Baraïtha, that is, the sayings of the olden ante-Mishna times, which are quoted therein from recollection and tradition, often to exhibit their conflict with the official body of the Mishna; and though not so reliable as the latter, yet needed as material for the history of Jewish institutions, such as the services of the Synagogue. The best sayings of the Palestinian teachers (such as those named in the beginning of this chapter) are also found in the Babylonian Talmud. The chain of tradition is carried down to five sets of disciples, who became in turn the leading teachers of their day, as Rab and Samuel had been in their day; the

fifth and last of these, R. Ashe and Rabina, are called the
"end of authority," and they made the first attempt to write
down the Babylonian Talmud.[4]

After Rab and Samuel all touch of the Eastern schools
with Hellenic learning was lost. Thus, where the Mishna
declares that an "Epikuros" has no share in the future
world, the Babylonian doctors, commenting thereon, have
no idea that this is the name of a Greek philosopher; nor
do they know the bearings of his system, and they try to
derive the word from a Hebrew or Aramaic root. They
often disclaim all knowledge of geography or of astronomy,[5]
though Samuel still claimed that the paths of the starry sky
were as familiar to him as the streets of Nehardea,[6] and the
opinions of the Talmud on all branches of science, on language, and on history are in most cases crude and unschol-
arly. But in the face of much ignorance and of not a little
superstitious ghost-lore, the freedom with which opinion
was expressed in discussion would do honor to later and
more enlightened ages. Thus, in a discussion about the expected coming of the Messiah, we find one Rabbi (Giddol),
whose authority is often quoted as good law, making sport
(as it seems to the writer) of all Messianic hopes, while
another (Hillel), like our higher critics, says: Israel has
already "eaten" its Messiah in King Hezekiah. For this
view he is not excommunicated, but only confronted with
the words of a prophet who lived after that King: "Rejoice
greatly, O daughter of Zion, etc.: behold, thy King cometh"
(Zech. 9: 9).[7] The high moral standard set by the Sages of
the Mishna is fully maintained; the law of Mine and Thine
is worked out in a righteous spirit and with wonderful
acuteness; woman is cherished and honored. Abhorrence is
expressed for him who divorces a wife that is the mother of
his children. Raba, chief of the school at Mahusa, tells his
towns-people: "Do honor to your wives; only thus can you
prosper." And whatever wild fancies the Babylonians may
have entertained about angels and devils, hell and paradise,

they never gave expression to them in the benedictions and devotions which they drew up and recommended to their people.[8]

The Talmud often speaks of the old divisions between Pharisee and Sadducee, between "companions" and "people of the land;" but, when we scan it attentively, we see that this is altogether "ancient history." There was no organized body of Sadducees on the Euphrates; if men in power at times acted on Sadducean principles, it was from ignorance or inborn cruelty.[9] The laws of Levitical purity and of tithes, by the careful observance of which the "companions" had mainly distinguished themselves from the "people," had fallen into disuse, or never were applicable "outside of the land." Occasionally we hear of the mass of Babylonian Jews becoming weary of Rabbinical hair-splitting;[10] but, upon the whole, they followed the leadership of the learned, and attended in great crowds the half-yearly meetings in the month before the Passover and in that before the autumnal feasts, to listen to the popular teachings of the Heads of Assembly (*Reshe Calla*).[11] Nor were they disturbed by the Christian heresy; it is said, "There are no Minim at Nehardea."[12]

Both the Talmuds are written in Aramaic dialects; the Palestinian in one nearly allied to that of the Christians of Antioch and Edessa; the Babylonian in one which seems to be the natural outgrowth of the Biblical Aramaic, found in the books of Ezra and Daniel.[13] It is necessarily much mixed with Hebrew, the former also greatly with Greek and Latin, the latter slightly with Persian. The quotations of Mishna and Baraitha and Scripture maintain, of course, their original garb.

So much had to be said about the Talmud, because it, and particularly the part elaborated on the banks of the Euphrates, was for almost fourteen hundred years the chief mental food of the Jewish nation.

Wholly independent of the Babylonian schools, and long

after the authoritative teaching of the Oral Law had ceased at Tiberias and Cæsarea, a band of men in Northern Galilee, whose names and exact era have been utterly lost and forgotten, performed a great service not for their race only, but for men of all races and creeds who seek to understand the Hebrew Scriptures. They contrived a system of vowel signs and other diacritic marks (such as the Dagesh for doubling consonants or for taking away the aspiration from some of them), and they applied these signs and marks with great consistency to the text of the twenty-four books. Their system, as the names of some of the vowels show, was borrowed from that of the Syrians, which in turn was due in part to Greek influences. For a language no longer spoken, in which the change of vowels is so frequent and means so much, this help to the learner had become almost indispensable. It seems that the system took shape in about the year 600.[14] During the sixth and seventh centuries the Babylonian schools did but little to affect the current of Jewish life. However, in this time efforts were made in the *Tosifta* (Addition) to collect and to write down at the end of each treatise of the Mishna such of the old traditions on the Law as were not elsewhere to be readily found. The Treatise of Scribes (*Soferim*) as to the preparation of scrolls of the Law and of phylacteries and about their use in the services, and the Treatise on Joys (*Semahoth*), so called by euphemy, which treats of the rules of Mourning, were also elaborated in this period, or not much later.[15] The men in authority were known as *Seburaïm*, "opinion givers."

In the eighth century, under the powerful and benign government of the Khalifs of Bagdad, the schools at Sura (or Mahasia) and Pumbeditha again rose in importance. The head of the former took the title of *Gaon* (excellency), in imitation of that of Illustrissimus, which the Patriarchs at Tiberias had enjoyed under Diocletian and his successors. The Gaon was a sort of Grand Rabbi for all the Jews of the world by means of "Questions and Responses" (*Sheelthoth u-Theshuboth*), of which volumes are still extant. Questions were directed to him from distant lands, which he answered, and these answers generally were regarded as law. Natronaï and Amram were particularly active in the ninth century; the latter, by way of a response, sent out to Spain the sketch of a liturgy which goes by his name. Saadia, in the tenth century, is better known through other literary work than through what he wrote or said *ex cathedra*. Sherira, who died at the end of the tenth century, is mainly known as an historian, the predecessor and in part the authority of Jost and Graetz. With R. Haï, who died in 1040, the line of the *Geonim* came to an end.

And now a Grand Rabbi on the Euphrates was no longer needed. In the ninth century the Jews of Europe and Africa show signs of literary activity. The earliest name is that of an Italian, Moses ben Kalonymos, who carried Rabbinic learning to Germany, where it flourished among his descendants for four centuries. Eleazar, surnamed Kalir, was about the first author of poetry for the service; some derive his surname from Cagliari, some place his birthplace in Africa. Saadia, of Fayum, in Egypt, reached such fame as a philosopher, poet, and commentator that he was called thence to the post of Gaon, or Excellency, at Mahasia. R. Isaac Alfassi (i. e., of Fez) in the eleventh century worked out a Code of Talmudic law, which is still studied, as the pioneer in its line. In the eleventh century the "golden Spanish Age" began and ran its course to the end of the thirteenth. Its brightest stars are Solomon Ibn Gebirol as poet, both sacred and secular; Jehuda Hallevi, who alone wrote poetry in the truest sense in Hebrew after its extinction as a living tongue, and who, in his Cuzari, has left a monument to his own scholarship and clear head, and an immortal defence of his religion; the brothers Ibn Ezra, sacred poets; the keen-witted philosopher, Abraham Ibn Ezra, the first who taught men to read the Bible according

to its context and natural sense, and not as a quotation
book; the grammarian, David Kimhi, and after these Moses,
the son of Maimun, scholar, physician, Talmudist, creed-
maker; the man who identified the God of the Bible with
the God of philosophy; the author not only of the rationalizing "Teacher of the Perplexed" (*More Nebuchim*), but of
a commentary on the Mishna and of that Code of Talmudic
Law (including much of the service book) which for nearly
three centuries was acknowledged as authority in all the
countries along the Mediterranean; for when Maimonides
left Spain for Egypt and took service at Cairo with Sultan
Saladin, his overmastering fame imposed on the Orient
the customs and ritual of Spain. All these and others who
wrote on ethics and metaphysics from the Jewish standpoint were born and raised under Moslem surroundings,
and many of their works were written in Arabic. But the
fall of the Kingdom of Cordova, in 1212, did not cut off the
line of great men in Israel. Even in the Kingdom of Ara-
gon, which had been Christian for centuries, a man arose
almost equal in genius and importance to the *coryphei* of
Arabic Spain, R. Moses ben Nahman (Nachmanides), of
Gerona. Though a thinker and deeply versed in the secular
learning of his age, he was, by the warmth of his temperament, led to favor the Mystics in some of their vagaries.
But the Commentary on the Pentateuch, supplementing
those of Rashi and Ibn Ezra, which he wrote in Palestine as
an exile from home, in his last days, proved his well-bal-
anced mind and clear understanding; it was not improved
on till the new weapons of modern science were brought to
bear on the exegesis of Holy Writ. The Jewish scholars
of the thirteenth century did a great service to their brethren
in northern Europe as well as to their own countrymen by
translating from Arabic into Hebrew the works of Jehuda
Hallevi, Maimonides, and their fellow-workers.

A Spanish Jew of much less ability or fame cannot be
passed by here; it is David, son (or grandson) of Abu-

Dirhem, generally known as Abudraham, of Sevilla, who, about the year 1340, wrote a critical analysis of and commentary on the services of the Synagogue as they were then carried on in Spain. His book has been to the writer one of the richest sources for the historic features of this work.

In France (of which the Jews of Angevin England were an outlying post) and in Germany, there was none of the broad culture reaching back through Arabic channels to the philosophers and mathematicians of Athens and Alexandria. But, as far as the old traditions, common sense, and hard work sufficed, great results were achieved. Rabbi Solomon ben Isaac, better known by his initials as Rashi, who was born in northwestern France and died at Worms in 1105, performed alone the stupendous task of commenting by running notes on the Pentateuch and other parts of the Bible and very nearly on the whole of the Babylonian Talmud. The great Spanish commentators on the Pentateuch, Ibn Ezra and Nachmanides, had his commentary of the Pentateuch before them, and added their own notes where his seemed to them either insufficient or erroneous. His comment on the Talmud was accompanied, in the twelfth century, by "Additions" (*Tosefoth*), the work of his immediate or mediate disciples, foremost among them his grandson, Rabbenu Jacob the Perfect (*Tam*). The last in time of the "Tosafists" was R. Meïr of Rothenburg, who died in prison, in 1293, the victim of oppression.

In northern Europe there was then much less tolerance of opinion than among the Sefardim. Some of the Rabbis along the Rhine hedged the Prayer Book about with a sacredness hardly less than that due to Scripture. Foremost among them was R. Jehuda, the Pious, who denounced all changes from the "type" as wicked and blasphemous.[16]

In the year 1208 (4968 A. M.) Rabbi Simha, of Vitry in France, who calls himself a disciple of Rashi, but was so only in an indirect way, published his Mahzor, or Cycle, for the year. It has reached our days in several manuscript copies; it was brought out in print by the Mekitze Nirdamim Society in 1892.

During the later middle ages Spain and Germany remained in touch. While Rashi formed the starting point for the Spanish commentators of the Pentateuch, the Arabic works of the great Spanish writers, in Hebrew translations, were studied in the North, and though the rationalizing of Maimonides in his "Teacher of the Perplexed" and in the opening chapters of his Code met with violent opposition in France and Germany, his creed of thirteen articles was approved, and, when set to measure, sung in all the Synagogues on both sides of the Rhine. The successors of Rashi down to Meir of Rothenburg were quoted and admired in Spain, and a disciple of R. Meir, R. Asher, known as Rosh, fleeing from oppression at home, became Rabbi at Toledo, where he died in the early part of the fourteenth century.[17]

The next important events in the religious history of the Jews to be considered are the compilation of a new Code by R. Joseph Karo, a Palestinian of Spanish origin, in the middle of the sixteenth century, in accordance with the Sefardic custom, and its annotation by R. Moses Isserles (R'mo) of Cracow, said to have been a friend and assistant of Kepler, early in the seventeenth century; the modifications being made to adapt the book to the usages of the German and Polish Jews. This code, especially in the form put upon it by the young scholar of Cracow, shows an iron rigor worthy of the mathematician. Its leading rule is this: Whatever restriction or irksome duty the Jews or any large section among them have laid upon themselves, is and remains the law for all and for all time.

Karo's Code is known as the "Set Table" (Shulhan Aruch). Of its four parts, one, the "Path of Life" (Orah Hayim), treats of the services and of the Sabbath and Feasts; one deals with the dietary laws; one, with husband and wife; the last, with property rights. Unlike Maimonides' Code it does not start on a dogmatic basis nor deal with things long since out of date. Property rights are treated because, in those times, Jews everywhere enjoyed a kind of autonomy in their disputes. Joseph Karo's work was soon acknowledged as the standard in all Sefardic communities, and, as annotated at Cracow, by all the German Jews. It regulates carefully every act of life from the cradle to the grave; its rules are well arranged, and each of them is easily found. By the common herd in Germany and Poland, young Moses of Cracow was long held in higher esteem than old Moses himself and all the Sages of the Mishna.

Thus, much that had been liquid became fixed. However, additions were still made to the liturgy, some by the sinister efforts of the Cabbalists, some through the wondrous effects of one short poem, some through the desire of orphans to procure "merit" for their dead parents.

The establishment of wealthy colonies by the fugitives from Spain and Portugal in Amsterdam, London, and Hamburg, during the seventeenth century, brought about some mutual borrowing between the Jews of the German and those of the Sefardic Minhag. It was always easy to add, but until within living memory almost impossible to drop, anything once introduced into the service book.

The persecutions to which the Jews were subjected at different times and in different countries for eighteen hundred years have had very little effect in modifying the services or in producing new prayers or plaints except in the fast day services. Their effect was simply to intensify Israel's faith and render it less receptive of foreign beliefs and modes of thought. Hence it is not necessary to speak of them in this place.

In the next chapters the history of two kindred lines of religious thought and literature, having a strong bearing on our services, will be touched upon separately.

CHAPTER IV

MIDRASH AND AGGADTA

THE Talmud, taken in its widest sense, deals not with rules of conduct (Halacha) only, but with matters of belief as well. It tells many stories, both about Biblical personages, filling out the loose outlines of the text, and about the wise and great men (and a few women also) of whose thoughts and discussion the Talmud is made up; other stories too: bold metaphors about things divine; not a little about angels and evil spirits; homilies on detached verses of Holy Writ; guesses (sometimes containing a grain of history) about the origin of Biblical books; views of nature, of medicine (always rather crude), and what not. These things are not discussed between contending schools or between the greater and lesser number; they are simply accredited to the one man who says thus and so. Beside the Talmud and the old Commentaries already spoken of, which in some sense are a part of the Talmud, there is a literature of works, known as "Midrash,"[1] reaching down to a very late age, not dealing with matters of conduct, but only with the other subjects of religious and national life comprised under the Hebrew word Haggada, i. e., Tale, or its Aramaic transformation, Aggadta.[2] Midrash means literally a searching, and denotes an interpretation of Scripture other than the obvious one. When the search is not to lead to rules of conduct, but only to an impressive saying, a sense is arrived at neither obvious nor seriously meant for the true one; in fact, two or three different meanings are often suggested for the same verse. In short, the Midrash is hardly more than a collection of heads for sermons.[3] This whole branch of literature belongs much more to Palestine than to Babylon; the teachers quoted in the Midrash are mainly Palestinians; on disputed points it agrees more with the Jerusalem Talmud than with the Babylonian, and the language is richly interspersed with Greek words, the distinguishing mark of the "West."

Our old Sages would not, or could not, vote on points for belief. Thus, when they wanted to decide which books should be received into the Canon, they first made a rule that whoever touches a sacred book must afterwards wash his hands; then they voted whether you must wash your hands after touching Canticles or Ecclesiastes.[4] But on a few great questions, such as the belief in a future life, or the hope for a coming redeemer, a decision was practically made by embodying such belief and hope in the form of prayer and then ordaining, as a matter of conduct, that every Israelite should recite this prayer thrice a day. Fortunately the portions of the service which law-observing Jews of any learning consider as obligatory were framed when good sense and enlightenment still ruled; that is, either before or very soon after the compilation of the Mishna. The formulas of those early days were extended, and somewhat "enriched," between the first half of the third century and the close of the eighth. But beyond a multiplication of words of like sense, in a manner repugnant to Western taste, hardly any fault can be found with these extensions; there is very little allusion to "Aggadta," and none that is offensive to reverential feelings,[5] and this for a good reason—there was still a central authority in the schools of Tiberias and of Nehardea, Sura, and Pumbeditha. As Midrash and Aggadta represented at most the opinions of single men, often only their suggestions or the play of their wit, the Patriarchs or Geonim at the heads of these schools would not lightly, by embodying this material in the order of prayers, force it upon the consciences of the people.

A strong instance of a Midrash which has borne fruit

in an important part of the services is that which turns
the Day of Memorial, or New Year's Day, into the Day
of Judgment. Psalm 81: 4, 5 reads according to the Jewish rendering: "Blow ye the cornet (Shofar) in the new
moon: at the darkening, the day of our feast; for it is
a statute for Israel, a *judgment* with the God of Jacob."
The plain meaning of "judgment" here is a synonym for
statute; the Hebrew word (Mishpat) is very often used in
this sense. But the "search" of Scripture leads elsewhere.
The only Feast which falls on a new moon, or darkening, is
that on the first day of the seventh month, when the Law
bids us blow the cornet. This is a "statute for Israel," but it
is a Day of Judgment not for Israel alone, but for all nations;
the day of "judgment with the God of Jacob," the one day
in the year on which he judges all the world.[6] It is not at
all improbable though, that the belief in this yearly judgment
day had grown up independently before the research into
this Psalm verse yielded a ground for such a belief. But
there is hardly any other Midrash, any other view or
thought not plainly or apparently Scriptural, which can be
found in the old liturgies as they were received in Europe
and Africa early in the ninth century.[7]

Again: The eighth or concluding day of the Feast of
Tabernacles became at an early day a symbol for the time
when the Messiah should deliver Israel. The wars of Gog,
of the land of Magog, predicted by Ezekiel, were expected
to occur shortly before the Messiah's triumphant entry into
his Kingdom.[8] Hence a chapter from the prophecy on
Gog, prince of Rosh, is read as a lesson on the Sabbath
preceding that festive day. The choice of the lesson rests
on a Midrash, but the lesson might have been chosen on
other grounds, and few inquire why Gog-Magog is read on
that day.

But when we come to the so-called "poetries" which were
added from time to time to the old liturgy, then Midrash
and Aggadta enter largely. Sometimes the old materials

are simply thrown into better Hebrew and poetical form, and have thus become better known to the Jewish public through the service book for the Festivals than they ever could become through the heavy volumes of the Talmud or Midrash, from which the poet culled them. Such is the story of the Ten Martyrs, ten highly-learned and pious Rabbis, murdered cruelly by the order of Roman emperors; true in the main, but full of legendary embellishments.[9] There is a story about Abraham, extensively known even among Christians and Moslems, how, in his youth, he was by Nimrod's commands thrown into a fiery furnace for his refusal to serve idols. It comes from a "search" into the words "Ur of the Chaldeans," from which the patriarch was brought. Ur in Hebrew means a bright fire; but in Babylonian, Ur means "city," and is the name of a city. The story is briefly told in Festival hymns among the trials of the Patriarch.[10]

There is another class of Midrashim in which the Israelite as the child of God takes some liberties in speaking of his Heavenly Father. We quote an example. A Rabbi says: Whence do we know that God puts on phylacteries? It is said (Isa. 62: 8): The Lord has sworn by his right hand, by his strong arm. The strong arm means the phylacteries; for it is said (Ps. 29: 11): The Lord gives strength to his people! And how do I know that the phylacteries are a strength to Israel? Because it is written (Deut. 28: 10): All the nations of the earth shall see that God's name is pronounced upon thee, and shall be afeard of thee. To the question which is naturally asked, what is written in these phylacteries? the answer is: Where is like thy people Israel one people on the earth (1 Chr. 17: 2)? In other words, as Israel in the words inscribed professes the One God, so their Heavenly Father makes a corresponding profession of one people.[11] The notion of God putting on phylacteries being once started, there was a ready explanation of the words with which Exodus 33 closes: Thou shalt see my back parts, but my face cannot be seen. This

means naturally then that God showed Moses only the
knot in the rear by which the phylacteries are tied round
the head.[12] These passages are alluded to in the words of
the "Song of Glory:" "He showed the knot of the Tephil-
lin to the meekest of men."[13]

Sometimes a Midrash has been thought out after the
introduction of words or ceremonies in the service, osten-
sibly to find grounds for them, but really to awaken pious
feelings or memories when these words are spoken or the
ceremony is performed. Thus the Sages at Tiberias give five
several reasons for the custom of drinking four cups of wine
at the Passover night service. The first of them derives the
number four from the fourfold promise God made through
Moses to Israel (Ex. 6): I will bring you forth, I will
deliver you, I will redeem you, I will take you for a people.
The other reasons are rather far-fetched. This alone is
widely known. A well-posted father tells it to his children
at the Passover supper, and it thus becomes part of the
exercises.[14]

In fact, much of the matter read on that night is Midrash, i. e., free interpretation, or Haggada, written expressly
for the occasion. Perhaps the service of that night is
called the Haggada of the Passover, not in the sense of the
story, but in that of homiletics for the Passover night.[15]

But Midrash and Aggadta have entered the Jewish
services mainly by becoming the groundwork of the
sermon, and it is so yet wherever the preacher can find an
appreciative public. The old-fashioned "Darshan," or
"Maggid,"[16] in his "Drosho" could string out the legends
and wonderful interpretations found in the old repositories,
with his own additions, for hours at a stretch without fatigu-
ing his hearers. As Aggadta is the opinion of only one man,
which none need believe unless it strikes him as plausible,
the preacher may develop his material according to his own
taste, with only this limit set to his free movement, that
he must not land at some conclusion at war with the
Halacha, or laws of conduct, or with the fundamental

beliefs of Israel, or, as it would be put in short, he must not go off into "Epicurism."[17]

The reader who has no Jewish books at hand can find the most typical example of the Midrashic style (without the above limitations) by reading in the New Testament the Epistle to the Hebrews. The writer of this Epistle not only misconstrues every verse, but also misreads several words of the Scriptural text. Even this he has in common with good Jewish masters of Midrash, who often, in order to point a moral or adorn a tale, tell their hearers or readers: Do not read thus (the true reading), but thus (a slightly changed reading with a fanciful sense). Of the narrative Aggadta, a very striking example is found in the fourth chapter of the Gospel of Matthew, where Jesus of Nazareth and Satan are represented as pelting each other with quotations from Holy Writ, the victory of course remaining with the former.

Among the ignorant some mischief has been done by Midrash and Aggadta. They do not understand its extent and true nature; they do not know its undisguised contradictions nor the principle taught by even the deeply orthodox, that Aggadta is binding on no one's conscience;[18] hence the unlearned, and particularly Jewish women, have often taken the most striking and most easily remembered legends, which are apt to be also the most grotesque, as true coin, thus throwing discredit on our literature, if not scandal on our religion. It must, however, be said in defence of the Talmud, that while many of the Emoraïm speak of God in bold metaphors without rebuke from their companions, there is an undercurrent of protest against all anthropomorphic thought, which breaks out frequently in an observation on some Bible verse like these: "If it was not so written we should not dare to say it," or "The Tora spoke in human language," or "The Tora said so only to break it to the ear," and very often by a word meaning, "were it possible," coined on purpose to indicate that anything human predicated of the Almighty is not to be literally understood.[19]

4

CHAPTER V

SECRET LORE, OR CABBALA

POSSIBLY in very early and certainly in very late times the secret lore, known as Cabbala, had its influence on the service book, and some of its features must be here stated, and its history briefly sketched. While in their outward form the writings of the mystics often resemble the ordinary Midrash, they differ greatly in this: they are always painfully serious. The believing reader feels that these books should be approached in awe and by none but the worthy.

The speculations of the Cabbala, like those of the Gnosis, of Neo-Platonism, and of Christian dogma, flow from one source—the dissatisfaction of brooding minds with the stern simplicity of the One God idea. The First Cause[1] is infinite in space and time; one and undistinguished by parts or qualities; how can we conceive the transitions from the undivided and Infinite One to the manifold, the complex, and the small, in the phenomenal world? How can we grasp the thought of that moment in past eternity when, in the words of the Lord to Job, he "cast the corner-stone of the earth."[2] Even in our days of evolution it is as hard as ever to think of the moment when the slow changes began with which it deals, and still harder to conceive that they have gone on from evermore.

Hence men contrived something to interpose between the First Cause and the phenomenal world, an emanation or successive emanations, or the Demiurgos, or Mechanician, of Plato, Wisdom personified, the Word, or Logos, of the Gospel of John, the First Effect[3] of later Cabbalists. The *Shechina*, that is, the residence or presence of God on earth, was also turned by the mystics into a phase or person of the Deity, somewhat like the Holy Ghost of the Christians.[4] Beneath the lower aspects of the Deity, created beings of vastly greater than human power were conceived—the angels or messengers of God's will. In the Bible the distinction between God's action and that of his messenger is not always clear; the "Angel of the Presence" is introduced by the Prophets when the action is God's own; and so with the Metatron[5] of the Talmud. In the older books of the Bible the angels who appear have neither name nor individuality; each of them comes on his one errand, does it and disappears.[6] Neither Isaiah with his six-winged Seraphim, shouting Holy, Holy, Holy, nor Ezekiel, with his Beasts and Wheels, intended to teach the comparative rank of the celestials; and the angel who encourages Zerubbabel and the High Priest in Zechariah's dream is but a passing phantom. In the late Book of Daniel, however, the Persian influence tells; his angels bear names, and are strictly personal. He speaks also of a heavenly "prince" of Persia and a like "prince" of the Greeks, national types, genii, and champions of earthly Kingdoms in the realms above; an idea fully developed in the later Cabbala, in which the "Prince of Edom," i. e., of Christendom, plays a great part.[7]

Later on a heavenly hierarchy was built up: Cherubim, Seraphim, Hayoth, and Ofannim (the beasts and wheels of Ezekiel), and six other classes, which it is needless to name. Many individual names were invented, some of which became common property, while some were known only to the initiated. The study of the opening chapters of Ezekiel the "Work of the Chariot," or "Mercaba," became a special branch of learning; the full acquisition whereof was expected to confer on the possessor powers beyond those of ordinary men. The teachers of the Mishna thought that only the wisest could be trusted with such dangerous knowledge.[8] It is reported that only four entered this "Paradise," and that R. Akiba alone among the four "entered in peace and came out in peace."[9] A majority, which unfortunately was afterwards overruled, held that the first chapter of Ezekiel should never be read as the lesson for the day.[10]

Men who looked on every word and letter of Scripture as inspired held, of course, that whichever of God's names is employed therein is always chosen to denote the aspect or attribute at work in the passage or connection. The Talmud shows that it was publicly agreed on and taught, that Elohim implies the quality of Justice, and the Tetragrammaton, the Attribute of Mercy.[11] But the Mystics went much further; they set up their ten Sephiroth—ten Categories at first, afterwards ten Attributes of God, the nature of which is understood only by them; the seven lower[12] and the three higher, Wisdom, Reason, and Knowledge, or the Crown.[13] Thus, with the Cabbalists, God's name coupled with that of Abraham, of Isaac, or of Jacob, would indicate the first, second, or third lower Sephira; the Tetragrammaton itself, according to position, might imply the effects of this or that of the ten, or perhaps of all of them together.

The Sephiroth were combined into the figure of a man, the Adam Kadmon, or heavenly archetype of the terrestial man; a notion which became in the early middle ages known to the Gentile world.[14] The mystics found divine names and groups of Sephiroth in passages from Holy Writ and from the oldest prayers, where the uninitiated would not even suspect them. The "names" thus picked out and built up like anagrams were thought to work wonders when recited with proper devotion or when transcribed.

The oldest text-book of the Cabbala, the "Book of Formation" (Jetzira), is ascribed to R. Akiba (though the most ardent claim Abraham himself as the author), and it seems, after weighing the discordant opinions of modern writers, that the book was written either by R. Akiba or at least in his time.[15] The book has come down to our times in recensions of varying length, but the longest contains less than four thousand words. It sets forth the "thirty-two paths of wisdom," along which God has shaped and governs the world; that is, the ten Sephiroth and the twenty-two letters of the Hebrew alphabet. The Sephiroth of this book are neither the Spheres of Ptolemy and of Dante, nor the first ten numbers; nor are they divided into seven lower and three higher; nor do they bear the names afterwards bestowed on them; they are simply six directions in space, two in time, and the two extremes of good and evil.[16] No important secrets can be obtained from the little volume.

The love for numbers, on which to base the nature of all things, came down from Pythagoras, who probably had himself acquired it on Semitic ground, to the Cabbalists of the middle ages. Beside the Sephiroth and beside the letters, grouped in three and seven and twelve in this first textbook, we find later on the four worlds: that of Creation (Beria), that of Deed ('Asiya), that of Formation (Jetzira), and that of Uplifting (Atziluth), a distinction which captivated the philosophic mind of Leibnitz, when, as a young man, he entered into the circle of the Rosicrucians at Nuremberg. The five stages of .the human soul, derived from its five Hebrew names found in Scripture, also were deeply studied; the distinctions were deemed important truths; in our times they have given rise to the seven souls of esoteric Buddhism.[17] The forty-nine days between Passover and Pentecost played a great part in the younger mysticism; and seventy-two "names" were built up from three verses in Exodus 14, which happen, each of them, to be made up of seventy-two letters.[18]

While these tendencies were at work, new books, bolder and bulkier than those preceding them, would come out from time to time, either as commentaries on the "Book of Formation," or as separate treatises under the assumed name of some of the early Sages of the Mishna.

Such were the two books which first appeared late in the

tenth century under the name *Hechaloth* (Temples), purporting to be the work of R. Ishmael, a Sage of the second century, from which Cabbalistic notions spread among the learned of the time, not only in the shape of new prayers, but also in the way of new meanings to old parts of the liturgy.[19] The great teachers of the Arabic period in Spain, Jehuda Hallevi, Maimonides, and Ibn Ezra, all of whom flourished in the twelfth century, held aloof from the Cabbala. The latter was, like the teachers of the secret lore, fond of Pythagorean dalliance with numbers, but he struck out on independent lines. However, in the next century, Nachmanides, of Gerona, in Christian Spain, the most beautiful character among Jewish scholars since the days of Hillel, imbibed a leaning to mysticism from his early teachers, which he shows in his writings, though he never became a declared adept.

In the same century and in Spain, two new publications appeared, more bulky than any of the former, in which the Cabbala is set forth as a system. The first of these is the *Bahir* (the Bright) ascribed to Nehonia ben Hakkana, one of the oldest Sages of Mishna times, of the contents of which nothing is now read except a short prayer; for after about forty years it was supplanted by a much more ambitious work, the *Zohar* (Radiance), which, even in small print, makes three stout octavo volumes. The Zohar has ever since been the leading text-book of the Cabbala. It was undoubtedly written by R. Moses de Leon, a Jewish scholar of the thirteenth century; all from his own head except as far as he used well-known materials; but he gave out that the book had been discovered in Palestine, and R. Simeon ben Johai, of the days of the Antonines, figured as the author. The Zohar takes the shape of a running commentary on the five books of Moses, in discourses by R. Simeon and his son, purporting to have been delivered while he was, according to a Talmudic story, for twelve years a fugitive from Roman persecution, hiding in a cave, where he was fed and attended by his disciples. It is written in the Aramaic of Northern Palestine. The forgery, however, is apparent enough. In the first place, the scant vocabulary betrays an author who has never spoken Aramaic as his mother tongue; secondly, conditions much later than the times of the Antonines are often referred to. Thus the inhabited earth is divided out between Edom and Ishmael, i. e., between Christianity and Islam; the Messianic time is predicted in numbers of the Era of Creation, which was unknown and not even thought of in the days of R. Simeon and for many centuries after him. But positive proof of the fraud perpetrated by R. Moses de Leon has been unearthed and published in recent years.[20]

The Zohar, grown on Spanish soil, shows a strong impress of Christian dogma. Its Messiah is superhuman, and there is a sort of Trinity, though it differs greatly from that of the Christians.[21] For more than two centuries it was but little read; the Aramaic tongue, once popular, was now much less known than Hebrew. Moreover, simple-minded Jews were unwilling to read it, deeming themselves unworthy to delve in the most sacred mysteries. But in the middle of the sixteenth century Isaac Luria, surnamed from his birthplace Il Calabrese, studied it, found in it the consummation of all divine truth, and made its contents known to the Jews of three continents. The art of printing came to his aid. The Zohar was translated into Latin, and captivated many Christian minds. The fearful calamities which afflicted Israel in the sixteenth and seventeenth centuries prepared them to read and to believe anything which would transplant them from their sad surroundings into heavenly spheres and amidst choirs of angels. Books in the spirit of the Zohar followed to supplement its work.[22] Passages from it (among them a truly sublime prayer) passed into the service books.[23] The false Messiah, Shabbathai Tzebi, who appeared at Smyrna in 1666, found in the mystic tendency of the Jews of the time a great help for his unholy ambition, and so did his successors, Hayim Vidal and Jacob Frank, in the next century. But the wholesale apostasies caused by these men led to a strong reaction against the Zohar and Cabbalism, the story of which is well told in the last volume of Graetz's History of the Jews. But there is a considerable sect in Eastern Europe, that of the Hasidim, founded by Israel Ba'al Shem Tob, and counting its adherents by hundreds of thousands, to whom the Zohar is still as sacred as the Bible itself.[24] Outside of that sect, the un-Jewish dogmas of the Zohar and its arbitrary assertions of knowledge about things unknowable are now becoming better understood even in the most orthodox circles;[25] yet it seems almost impossible to erase from the service books all the follies and blasphemies which have crept into them from this source, mainly in the eighteenth century.[26]

The very name of Cabbala, i. e., tradition, given by its adherents to the secret lore, is a usurpation. In the Mishna this word is usually applied to the sayings of the Prophets, on the ground that the tradition passed from Moses and Joshua to the Prophets.[27]

The Midrash, or Aggadta, often seems to flow imperceptibly into Cabbala; but there is always this distinction, that the former is open to the public, while the books of the latter, even when printed, profess to belong to the initiated alone.

CHAPTER VI

THE elements of the Jewish Calendar are the day, the month, and the year. The day begins in the evening at the moment when, on a clear night, three stars are first visible, which is supposed to be about twenty-five minutes after sunset. Hence the Sabbath begins on Friday evening, earlier in winter than at the equinoxes; earlier at these than in midsummer; also earlier in the winter, and later in the summer, in the high North than in sub-tropical countries.

The Bible says, "from eventide to eventide ye shall observe your Sabbath," and as the law and usage grew up before the time of clocks, they naturally conformed to the actual night-fall of the place and season.

The month on which the Jewish Calendar is based is that which begins with the new moon. In astronomy this means the moment at which the center of the sun's disk and that of the moon's disk are in the same longitude; but in the Rabbinic traditions it meant the time when the moon had so far overtaken the sun in longitude that its sickle with the convex edge turned to the right could be seen. Upon the evidence of witnesses who had observed it, the Sanhedrin or the Patriarch would, as long as these authorities were recognized, proclaim the new moon.[1]

When the Patriarchate at Tiberias felt its power waning, it adopted the rule of the Calendar which Meton had introduced at Athens in the days of Pericles, by which a constant period of time, the average of many lunar months, was made the measure of each month. The length of this period was known with a great degree of correctness. It

(57)

must have been calculated from two solar eclipses several hundred years apart, which could be easily done, considering the early times in which Egyptians and Babylonians had observed such events. The length of this month was taken at 29 days, 12 hours, and 793 "parts," there being 1080 parts to the hour; or 29 days, 12 hours, 44 minutes, $3\frac{1}{3}$ seconds. This is correct within less than a second. The moment at which the month begins is known as its *Molad*, or birth, and this is noted in every Jewish calendar for each month.[2]

As twelve of such months make only 354 days, 8 hours. 48 minutes, 40 seconds, the Festivals set for days in named months would soon drift back into the wrong seasons of the year. As a sheaf of barley was to be offered during the Passover, it must have been within the province of King, or Senate, or High Priest to add a month to the twelve when necessary to bring the Feast to its proper season. The Sanhedrin, when constituted, deemed the right to proclaim the new moon and to make a "pregnant" year, that is, to add a thirteenth month, as the highest mark of their sovereignty in Israel.

Before the Babylonian exile, the twelve months had Hebrew names, of which only four have been preserved: that of the first month, including the Passover, Abib (corn-ear); the second Ziv (splendor); the seventh Ethanim (constant streams); the eighth Bul (of uncertain meaning). Generally the Bible speaks of the months by number, the first, the third, the seventh month. After the exile we find the Babylonian names of the months, which are still used in every Jewish Calendar, i. e., Nisan, Iyar, Sivan, Tammuz, Ab, Elul, Tishri, Marheshvan, Kislev, Tebeth, Shebat, Adar. If these are insufficient, an Adar Sheni (second Adar) is added.

It was long an open secret that the Sanhedrin would add or not add a thirteenth month by the rule that the Passover must always be celebrated on the first full moon after the vernal equinox; hence the canon of the Council of Nice fixing Easter on the Sunday following this first full moon. But as disputes might easily arise as to the true time of the equinox, Hillel the Younger, the Patriarch, thought it better to adopt a rule based on a simple count rather than one resting on astronomical observation. The Metonic cycle, or Athenian calendar, is made up of nineteen years. that is, twelve of twelve months each, and seven of thirteen months each. In the form in which the Jews adopted this cycle, the following years have thirteen months each: 3. 6, 8, 11, 14, 17, 19. These 19 years have 235 months, or 6939 days, 16 hours, 33 minutes, $3\frac{1}{3}$ seconds, and this period is more nearly correct than 6939 days, 18 hours, the length of 19 years by the Julian calendar, but it exceeds by over two hours the length of 19 tropical years as it has since been ascertained.[3]

The Bible always counts the Passover month as the first, and what we call nowadays the New Year is known in Leviticus and again in Nehemiah as the first of the seventh month. The Era of Seleucus, which was in use among the Jews for many centuries, was counted from a new moon near the fall equinox in the year 311 before the Christian era, and has undoubtedly had its effect upon the Jewish year; but Nachmanides, in his Commentary on Leviticus, argues strongly for the position that the Mosaic Law contemplates two beginnings of the year; one in our Tishri, as well as that which Exodus 12 fixes on the first day of the Passover month. For in the Sabbatic year there was to be neither sowing nor harvest, and as the grains of Palestine are all winter crops, seed and harvest fall into one year only if it begins in the fall.[4]

In practice the month can contain only whole days, and so the twelve hours and a fraction above 29 days are disposed of by making the months alternate between 30 and 29 days. Nisan, Sivan, Ab, Tishri, Kislev, and Shebat have each 30 days, the other six months, each 29 days. When

Adar is doubled, the first Adar has 30 days, the second 29. This does not fully absorb the 44 minutes $3\frac{1}{3}$ seconds above the twelve hours. For this purpose Marheshvan is as often as necessary lengthened to 30 days. But for ritual purposes the year is occasionally shortened by having only 29 days in both Marheshvan and Kislev. Here of course considerations enter that were unknown to the Athenians, from whom the calendar was borrowed.

It is a rule that the Day of Atonement (Tishri 10th) may not come on a Friday or a Sunday on account of the great inconvenience of preparing food on Sabbath for the fast day or *vice versa*. Another rule forbids putting on a Sabbath the old national holiday, the seventh of the Feast of Huts (Tishri 21st); hence the first of Tishri, the Day of Memorial, or modern New Year, cannot come on a Sunday, Wednesday, or Friday.

Then there is the older rule that the *Molad* of Tishri must occur before midday, otherwise there would not have been time for the sacrificial service, and the next day is the New Year.

Thus, if by calculation this *Molad* should strike Saturday afternoon, the first of Tishri must be put off to Sunday, and this being disallowed, further on to Monday; the adjustment for this purpose is made at the end of the months of Marheshvan and Kislev in the preceding year. There are some niceties in the calculation which it is needless here to pursue.[5]

The first of every Jewish month is celebrated as a half holiday, the Rosh Hodesh, or New Moon, of the Bible. When the preceding month has thirty days, its last day is celebrated in like manner. Thus Iyar has "two days of Rosh Hodesh;" namely, the 30th of Nisan and the 1st of Iyar, while Nisan itself has only one, its own first day.[6]

The Biblical yearly days of holiness and rest are enumerated in Leviticus 23 and again in Numbers 28 and 29, thus: Passover on the 15th and 21st of the first month (Nisan);

the Day of Memorial on the first of the seventh month (Tishri); the Day of Atonement on the tenth, the first day of Huts on the fifteenth, the "Eighth a rest" on the 22d of Tishri. Pentecost is to be celebrated fifty days after a "Sabbath" in or near the Passover. Taken literally, as the Samaritans did, Pentecost would always fall on a Sunday. The Pharisees for good reasons construed the word "Sabbath" to mean the first day of the Passover, which always brings the Pentecost on the 6th of Sivan, the third month; and they construed the nineteenth chapter of Exodus so as to locate the Revelation on Mount Sinai on that day. Hence Pentecost, which in the words of Scripture is only a harvest feast for the first-fruits of wheat, attained a higher meaning; it became, in the words of our Prayer Book, "the day of the gift of our Law."[7]

New Year is celebrated for two days even in Palestine, on the ground that, if the new moon were still proclaimed, it might be announced so late as to require the next day for the completion of the service. The Day of Atonement being a fast cannot be doubled.

The five other holidays are doubled outside of Palestine on the following historical grounds, which would *a fortiori* apply to the New Year too. While the Sanhedrin at Jerusalem or, in later days, the Patriarch at Tiberias announced the new moons, the news was flashed from mountain top to mountain top throughout Palestine but not to other countries; those in Babylonia would not receive the news even in two or three weeks. Hence, not feeling sure whether the preceding months should not have thirty days, they kept two days of each Feast; and this usage became so deeply ingrained that when, about the year 361, the fixed calendar was introduced, nobody felt himself authorized to abolish these double holidays.[8] The reason for them has wholly ceased since Palestine is connected by electric wires with all parts of the world. For if there were a Sanhedrin or Patriarch now to proclaim the new moon, the Jews of Chicago or Melbourne would know its true date within the next twelve hours.

Besides the Festivals and New Moons mentioned in the Law, we find in other parts of the Bible a reference to certain other days. *First*, Purim, or the Feast of Esther, on the 14th of Adar, in lengthened years on the same day of the second Adar. *Second*, the four Fasts for commemorating sad events in the downfall of the first Jewish Commonwealth, that is, the 10th of Tebeth, when Nebuchadnezzar began the siege of Jerusalem; a day in Tammuz, when he entered the city through a breach, which has been fixed on the 17th of that month, i. e., on the same day on which Titus entered at the downfall of the last Commonwealth; the day in Ab when Nebuchadnezzar destroyed the first Temple, now fixed on the 9th of Ab, when the Romans burnt the last Temple; and the third of Tishri, when Gedaliah, the prince of the House of David, whom Nebuchadnezzar left as governor of the remnant of Jews in Judea, was murdered, and the last trace of the first Commonwealth was wiped out.

Lastly the calendar gives us the eight days of the Feast of Maccabees, or Hanucca, beginning on the 25th of Kislev.

It remains for us to speak of the Jewish era. In the Books of Maccabees we find all dates fixed by the Era of Seleucus. This was still used for historic dates by the leading Rabbis in Babylonia late in the tenth century. For dating documents the Mishna requires the year of the reign, meaning that of the Roman Emperor, and for Eastern countries that of the Kings of Parthia; but it became afterwards the custom to date all documents by the Era of Seleucus, which thus became known as the "year of deeds." But when Jehuda Hallevi wrote his Cuzari about the year 1140, he speaks of the Year of the World (then 4900) as something in common use among the Jews, and claims that they reckoned already by it in the year 4500, in which he lays the story which is made the vehicle of his teaching. It is clear, therefore, that this mode of counting years could not have been a new thing with Jehuda Hallevi's contemporaries.⁰ At what particular time it was first suggested or introduced, and when it displaced the other Era (which survived in Arabia long after Jehuda Hallevi's days) cannot be ascertained. It is said that the Year of the World is found earliest on epitaphs in Italy. The Jews of Yemen reckon by the "year of deeds" to this day.[10]

CHAPTER VII

THE first Jewish Commonwealth, which came to its sad end when Nebuchadnezzar destroyed Jerusalem, seems to have known no such institution as the Synagogue, though there must have been even in it some public worship of song and prayer, both in the Temple and outside of it. The beginning of the Synagogue as a place, not only for worship, but also for instruction and edification, is shown in the eighth chapter of Nehemiah, when Ezra read the Law of Moses to the assembled people, men, women, and children old enough to understand; he and the other chiefs of the community standing upon a wooden turret, and the hearers surrounding them upon all sides. That wooden turret survives in our times in the platform with the reading desk upon it. The late Hebrew word for the platform is *Bima*, derived from the Greek *Bema*, the tribune from which speakers address the public. It is in Germany and Austria generally known by the Arabic name *Almembar* (pulpit), corrupted into *Alemmer*. This platform should stand in the middle of the Synagogue, after the pattern of Ezra's turret; but in all more or less modernized German Synagogues it has been pushed forward to the "Ark."[1]

The Talmudic tradition traces the Synagogue as a place for reading the Law at stated times (say every Sabbath, Monday, and Thursday) back to Ezra in an unbroken line. But this is hardly possible. The Book of Chronicles, written long after Ezra, which carries some of the genealogies down for over a hundred years after him, nowhere alludes either to the place or to the weekly readings.

(64)

Some of the later Psalms, especially Ps. 119, may possibly allude to frequent readings from the Law, but hardly to any consecrated places other than the Temple and its court-yard, which in a sense might be called a Synagogue.[2]

The Greek name of the Jewish house of worship means simply a meeting; it is but a translation of the Hebrew *Beth ha-Keneseth*, the House of Meeting. Not only is the word foreign to the latest Biblical books, but also to the older works among the Apocrypha, such as Ecclesiasticus and Maccabees. But in these latter books (e. g., 1 Macc. 12: 11) we find the Greek word *Proseuche* (house of prayer) as a place of devotion other than the Temple. It seems probable that the new word *Synagogue*, with its wider meaning, came into use when other exercises were added to prayer. At any rate, in the Gospels we find this new word in full and exclusive use for all houses of worship outside of the Temple, and these are already so numerous, being found in all the villages, that the institution cannot have been recent at that time. In the Synagogues of Galilee, as the Gospels relate, lessons were read from the Prophets, and persons of learning and piety were expected to preach on the lesson; it is very evident that there was also prayer and readings from the Law; in short, all the elements from which the exercises of the modern Synagogue are made up.

The "Ark," called in the Mishna *Teba*, i. e., box, chest, but in modern Hebrew *Aron*, like the Ark of the Covenant, whose place it has taken, is a press or wall closet in which the Scrolls of the Pentateuch are kept stand-ing upright. It is placed slightly above the floor of the nave, and is reached by steps. The Ark is set in or against that wall of the Synagogue towards which the worshippers turn, at least in that part of their devotions known more especially as the Prayer. The leader, who reads the liturgy aloud, stands in the same direction as the people. He does not address them, but is their messenger, or representative. The wall in or against which the Ark stands is in the

5

direction of Jerusalem, according to the request of King Solomon, that the people of Israel may pray "towards this place," the Temple which he built. Hence in Europe and America the Ark stands towards the East, but no attempt is ever made to strike the exact point of the compass, as the Moslems do when turning towards Mecca.[3]

Before the Ark is a heavy curtain, which is named after the curtain which, in the Tent of Meeting and in the Temple, screened the Holy of Holies.

The *Sefer Tora* (Book of the Law) is a parchment scroll in which the whole Pentateuch is written by hand upon calfskin or sheepskin, with an ink made of lamp-black, in the Hebrew text and in the so-called square or Assyrian character,[4] without vowel points, accents, or verse divisions; but the paragraphs are marked according to the *Masora*, or tradition of the text, some by starting on a new line, some by leaving a shorter or longer blank in the same line. The scroll is mounted on wooden rollers, is first wrapped in a white band, and then encased in a silk or velvet robe. A silver hand for pointing is hung by a cord or chain; often silver ornaments are placed on the heads of the rollers. Every Synagogue of any pretensions has three or more scrolls of its own.

According to the best approved usage the leader in prayer does not stand on the platform from which the Law is read, but in a low place near by the Ark, according to Ps. 130: 1: "From the depths have I cried unto thee." In olden times the leader "went down before the Ark" only when the Prayer in the narrower sense (see Book II, ch. 1) was reached.[5]

The Lessons from Law and Prophets are read from the platform, the scroll or book of Prophets being laid on the desk (*Shulhan*, i. e., table). The preacher usually stands on the steps before the Ark with his back towards it and his face towards the people.

The main floor is occupied by men and boys only; a

raised gallery or, in small Synagogues of insufficient height, a side room is set aside for the women.[6]

Pretty much every Synagogue has an anteroom; one of its uses is that those who mourn for a parent or other close kindred may tarry in it on the first Friday evening after the funeral to await the announcement of the Sabbath, when they are formally ushered in by the leader and presiding officer with words of comfort. This anteroom or some other small apartment in the building is in the larger Synagogues used for work-day services.

The so-called Temples of our times are simply Synagogues. The word Temple for a Church or Synagogue is a misnomer, or at least a fancy name; it means really a place of sacrificial worship.

Synagogues, unlike Mosques or Catholic churches, were always furnished with benches and chairs.[7]

Near a Synagogue a *Beth Hammidrash*, or House of Study, is often found, a room filled with theological books, the Bible and its commentaries, the Mishna, the Talmud, the Midrash, the Codes, and whatever else may be deemed of interest. Some of these rooms are nothing but reference libraries, that is, study is carried on privately, every man poring over any book that suits him; but in most of them the Rabbi holds forth at stated times, at least for an hour or so about sunset, reading and expounding consecutive parts of Bible, Mishna, or Talmud.[8]

When ten or more are together in such a room, and the time for services comes around, they hold them in the *Beth Hammidrash*, as they would in a Synagogue, and this was done already in the days of the Talmud. It may be remarked here that this number of men and boys (over thirteen years of age) is indispensable for public services with their responses and for the readings of the Law and Prophets from the desk.

This number ten according to the Mishna is the minimum of the "congregation," not only for liturgic, but also for political purposes, and this rule is probably as old as the institution of the Synagogue.[9]

It is the better opinion that if nine fully qualified persons are present, a boy under thirteen, but old enough to have some religious ideas, will do for the tenth.[10]

The highest functionary of a Jewish congregation is the Rabbi, literally "my Master," originally, in the days of Jewish independence, a Judge in civil and criminal matters, as well as an adviser in religious questions.

Among the Sefardim this official is generally known as *Hacham*, the learned.

Where Jews live together in sufficient numbers to maintain a Rabbi or a Rabbinical Court (*Beth Din*) of three Judges (*Dayanim*), they form a Congregation, and this may worship at one or at a hundred Synagogues, big and little. Where the community is too small to maintain a Rabbi, it is known as a *Jishub* (settlement), and is generally dependent upon the Rabbi in the nearest town. The establishment of several congregations in the same city has in late years often happened through disagreement between the more orthodox and more progressive or reforming elements, and in the eighteenth century already through the schism of the *Hasidim*, and even before that time, as above seen, when Jews of the Sefardic and of the German ritual settled at the same place in sufficient numbers of each.

The title of Rabbi certifies the recipient's learning in the traditional law. It is conferred by one or more Rabbis in continuous succession by means of a *Hattarath Horaa*, a license to teach or rather to decide. In olden times, but in Palestine only, the succession of Rabbis was perpetuated by the laying on of hands, and this ceremony was thought to confer privileges which neither learning by itself nor a written certificate thereof could impart.[11]

With the services of the Synagogue the Rabbi as such has nothing to do. Not being chosen for his good voice, he is not expected to read either the prayers or lessons;

he is indeed, by his learning, fitted to preach in the Synagogue, but anybody else who has sufficient acquaintance with Bible and Talmud and eloquence enough to interest an audience may preach without holding the "license to teach."

The English Bible uses the word "priest," a corruption of the Greek *presbyteros*, literally, an elder, to translate the Hebrew *Cohen*, a sacrificer, the *Hiereus* of the Septuagint and Greek Testament. There are *Cohanim* at the present day, great numbers of them, who claim descent from those who acted as such in the days of the Temple; and there are Levites claiming descent from the Levites of those days. At present the Cohen is not a functionary; his presence is not required, except to impart the priestly blessing (Numbers 6: 22-27), which in modern times is only done on the Festivals, and a certain precedence is given to the Cohen, and after him to the Levite.

The word *Minian* (number) designates the presence of ten or more male Israelites when met for public service. One of them, as "messenger of the assembly" (*Sheliah Tzibbur*), reads or chants the prayers. The needful qualifications are correct Hebrew reading, understanding the contents of the Prayer Book, and a good moral and religious standing.[12] No man who is under excommunication can act as leader, or be counted of the ten.[13]

Where a permanent congregation erects a Synagogue it nearly always employs a man to read the services on Sabbaths and Holidays. Such a man is in modern phrase called the *Hazan*, a word meaning literally "overseer" (whence the Christian *episkopos*), which formerly, before the vowel points and accents were placed under the text of Scripture, denoted an official who held the traditions as to the true pronunciation, and saw to it that the lessons were correctly read.[14]

In German a regular Hazan is called *Vorsänger* or *Vorbeter*, i. e., leader in song or leader in prayer; also Cantor, the corresponding Christian title. The professional Hazan is chosen with a view to a good voice, musical training, and thorough acquaintance with chants and accustomed tunes; his shortcomings in morals and religion being too often overlooked. In progressive Synagogues he has to be a thoroughly trained vocalist, for he is the tenor solo of a series of oratorios.

The Hazan, or oftener in the great Synagogues another man with other qualifications, reads the lesson from the Pentateuch; he is known as *Ba'al Kore* (master reader). This title is modern; formerly to know this lesson was the main duty of the Hazan, or overseer; for the members in turn were expected to read parts of the lesson, while the Hazan prompted them. The *Ba'al Kore* should know all the niceties of Hebrew grammar, and be able to read with the proper feeling and expression; his voice should be loud and clear, so he may be readily followed and understood. But the chant prescribed for him is simple, and requires for its rendering very little vocal skill.

In olden times, when everything was written without vowel points and accents, the reading of the prophetic lesson was the most difficult function, the style being more rugged than the prose of the Tora and less familiar than the prayers. Hence, when any one was found with the skill and learning to read the prophetic lessons well, he would generally (if over thirteen years of age) be invited to read the prayers too; and it seems that occasionally, as early as Talmudic times, he would be paid for the exercise of his skill.[15] Nowadays to read this lesson is rather an honor to pay for than a task to draw wages for, except in such congregations in which few can read correctly, even from our printed volumes with their vowels and accents. There are still Synagogues in Poland and elsewhere in which parchment copies of the Prophets are kept with the bare letters, like the Scrolls of the Law, and a permanent official has to read the lessons.

Every Synagogue has a lay member for its business head, who presides at the services to preserve order and to give directions. He is known as *Parnas* (provider, a word probably derived from the Greek *pronoos*). The next in command, or Vice-President, bears the title of *Gabbai* (literally, collector). Whoever performs the duty of presiding officer at the desk upon the platform is for the time being the *Segan* (assistant), a title borne in the Temple by one of the foremost priests. The usage demands that lay officers of the congregation should stand by the reader during the lessons by way of respect for the Law.[16]

The Parnas commands the services of a paid official, the *Shammash*, the same as the *diaconos* of the Acts; he is sexton, beadle, and usher, and goes all the errands to be run in the progress of the services.

BOOK II

The Devotions of the Synagogue

BOOK II

CHAPTER I

OUTLINE OF THE LITURGY

It may seem strange to our young men and women, but it is true, that the devotions of the Synagogue differ but slightly from those which the law-observing Israelite recites at his home when he does not attend public worship; the difference lying mainly in the responsive passages in the latter, which are not fitted for private worship. It may astonish them still more to hear that the services for the Sabbath and Holidays are built up on the same plan as those for work-days, and that the orthodox Jew considers it just as wrong to miss his prayer on Monday night or Tuesday morning as on Friday night and Sabbath morning.[1]

The most important parts of our liturgy are two, the reading of the *Shema* (Hear, O Israel) and the Prayer proper, or *Tefilla*, called by the Portuguese Jews and those of England generally *Amida*, the "standing," a convenient name. We shall hereafter denote it either as Prayer, written with a capital, or as "Amida."[2]

The "Shema" is to be recited, preferably to be read, twice a day, in obedience to the command in Deuteronomy 6: 7: "Thou shalt impress them upon thy children, and shalt talk of them, when thou sittest in thy house, and when thou walkest by the way, and when thou liest down,

(75)

and when thou risest." A like command is found in Deut.
11, and each is applied to the paragraph of which it forms
part. Another command is found in Deut. 16: 3: "That
thou mayest remember the day when thou camest forth
out of the land of Egypt all the days of thy life," which from
early times was understood to require a mention of the
great event on every day and in every night. Not everybody took these commands so literally, for it is said of the
saintly R. Judah that his reading was confined to the first
verse, "Hear, O Israel, etc." He evidently trusted that
in his studies and discourses he would speak sufficiently
on the subjects embraced, and that recital in the very words
of the Bible was not necessary.[3]

The words, "when thou liest down and when thou risest,"
were, as far back as tradition reaches, construed to be
addressed, not to the individual, but to the nation. Hence
each Israelite may "read" his Shema for the night at any
part of the time during which men usually go to bed, and
for the morning during the whole time at which people
of any class rise; and thus alone public services could be
held, of which the reading of the two passages in the sixth
and eleventh of Deuteronomy and the mention of the deliverance from Egypt are the most weighty parts. The limits
drawn by the old standards are pretty wide for the reading
at night, from early starlight till midnight, for the morning
service, from the light of dawn till nine o'clock in the forenoon.[4] These limits were pushed out even further with
the view of bringing worshippers together in the House
of God; that is, the night service, except that which follows
a Sabbath or Festival, may be read at the Synagogue before
starlight, in order to make it follow an afternoon service at
the same place; and even should the morning Shema
be reached after nine o'clock, the service goes on nevertheless, including the "benedictions" preceding and following the Shema.[5]

The other main element, the Prayer, or *Amida*, is known

among the Jews of the German and Polish Minhag as the *Shemone Esre*, or Eighteen, a name, as will be shown, not quite appropriate.[6] This Prayer contains, not only petitions for Divine grace and help, but praise and thanks as well. It is intended to satisfy the cravings of a pious heart for communion with God and at the same time the command of the Law that we should serve God, and its assumption that we will serve him with all our heart and with all our soul.[7] But the Pentateuch nowhere intimates how many times the Israelite should pray, or what he should have to say. The forms now in use took their rise under the men of the Great Synod. One reason assigned for their work is the decay of the Hebrew language, the inability of the people and perhaps even of priests and preachers to pour out from their hearts well-worded devotions in that tongue, and the resulting need for set forms of prayers, in which all could unite, which all would soon know by heart, and then repeat even in private.[8]

In Psalm 55, written probably after the institution of the regular Prayer, the righteous man declares, "evening, morning, and at noon-day will I complain, and moan, and he shall hear my voice;" and this praying thrice a day is found also in Daniel as a custom which the Israelite cannot forego without incurring the guilt of impiety.[9]

Of the three daily Prayers, two are joined to the reading of the Shema, following upon it both in the night (or evening) and in the morning service; the third is recited in the afternoon, and is known as *Minha*, literally, a gift, thence the meal-offering, the name being suggested by the passage in 1 Kings 18: 29, where Elijah prays in the afternoon at the time of the "evening oblation." The Prayer in the morning and that for the afternoon, or Minha, are deemed more obligatory than that in the night service, for the two former correspond in point of time to the daily sacrifice in the Temple, and by reciting them the worshipper complies in spirit with the words of the Prophet Hosea (14: 3): "We shall render as bullocks (the offering of) our lips." The Prayer in the evening is not demanded as a duty, and though law-observing Jews will not miss it any more lightly than the two others, there is yet the broad practical distinction, that in public service the morning and afternoon Prayers are repeated by the leader, or Cantor, while the evening Prayer is not repeated.[10]

The accounts in Daniel and in Psalm 55 present one man in solitude uttering his Prayer, but the Mishna shows that some of its benedictions were publicly recited in the Temple, and it often refers to a leader reciting it before an audience. It seems that any one could say his Prayer privately, but when a sufficient number met, one would lead and the others listen. But there is the custom, fully established in the times of the Palestinian Talmud, that in the Synagogue everybody says his Prayer silently, and that the leader repeats it aloud. The reason given is that he must thus relieve those unable to recite the Prayer of their duty; but this does not fully explain why the others should first speak it in low tones, unless to the end that each may add his own heart-felt supplications.[11]

When time presses, e. g., when night-fall is too near for finishing the afternoon service, the leader begins the Prayer aloud with the rest and recites three benedictions, then all proceed silently. Some congregations, otherwise carefully observant of the old forms, act thus regularly with the "Additional Prayer," as to which many of the old Sages held, that it is fitted only for public worship ("town company" they call it), and this view would justify such a shortening.

As to this service it should be remarked that, as the Prayer takes the place of the communal sacrifice, on those days for which the law prescribes additional offerings, there is another Prayer "added" (*Musaf*) after the morning Prayer and before that for the afternoon; in most places right after the former, without any intermission beside the "lessons" for the day.[12] But in many Synagogues of Austria and Hungary, and in Western Asia also, the true morning service for the Sabbath is held at a very early hour, at six or seven; the worshipper then goes home, takes breakfast, and comes back at ten o'clock for the "lessons," for the sermon, and for Musaf. This is correct, for it is a leading Jewish principle that whatever duty can be performed at break of day should be performed before the morning meal and before any business or pleasure is entered on; and this principle applies most strongly to the Reading of the *Shema* "when thou risest."[13]

Thus there are three Prayers on work-days; that for the afternoon can be joined with the Reading of the Shema and Prayer for the following night into one continuous service; there are four for Sabbaths, New Moons, and Festivals, generally making three distinct services, and there is a fifth Prayer on the Day of Atonement known as *Neïla*, the "door-closing," which is begun shortly before sunset.[14]

The morning service has been much lengthened beyond the two essential elements above named. It begins (leaving out one or two poems) with benedictions and prayers which express a devout man's feelings when he has risen from bed, and has cleansed and dressed himself, and which were really intended for the home;[15] then come passages from Pentateuch, Mishna, and Baraïtha as a minimum of study; then the "hymns," Psalms, and other Bible poetry with befitting benedictions; the two essential elements named come next; then on New Moons, on the three Festivals, and on Hanucca the "Psalms of Praise;" then the lesson or lessons. There are other accretions towards the end of the morning or of the "additional" service, but few in the afternoon and evening. One of these is the recital, thrice a day, of Psalm 145, on which the Talmud lays great stress, first as one of the morning hymns, again after the morning Prayer, and again in the afternoon, when it and the *Amida* make up, in the main, the *Minha* service.[16]

The question as to the order of the evening service, whether the Prayer is to precede or follow the Shema, was still in dispute in the third century; some insisted that the latter should be last and thus nearest to bed-time. The prevailing usage was probably always the same as it is now, so as to give to the morning and evening services a similar structure.[17]

We do not speak here of the responses, as their place and nature cannot be understood before the material which the home has in common with the Synagogue is fully explained. We may here speak of the persistence of new elements when once introduced into the service on any ground. Abudraham, writing in Spain early in the fourteenth century, says of the abstract of the Prayer which the leader chants in the Friday night service after the congregation have silently read the full text: It was introduced in Babylonia, when most houses of worship were in the fields, lest those coming late would have to walk home alone, for while the leader chants it, they can catch up and then go home, free from danger, in company. With us, who live and worship in towns, there is no danger in walking alone, but the custom of our fathers remains with us. And about the *Kiddush* (Sanctification) made on Friday night over the wine cup in the Synagogue he says: It is really improper, for the Sabbath must (quoting the Talmudic saying) be consecrated only at the supper table, and he quotes R. Haï, the last Gaon, that is, the last man who spoke with authority to all Israel, in reproof of the custom, which arose at a time when a room was usually attached to the Synagogue for lodging and feeding travellers on the Sabbath, so that they might hear the Sanctification over the cup of wine. He says the reason has ceased; we no longer lodge travellers in the Synagogue building; "yet, as our predecessors have set up the rule, though for a reason which no longer exists, the rule remains unshaken."[18]

As matters thus stand, with all the old and new elements,

the work-day service, except on Mondays and Thursdays, including responses and the repetition of the Prayer by the leader, is gone through with without undue hurry in about forty-five minutes; on New Moons, including Musaf, in about an hour. The afternoon service on work-days takes at most ten minutes, the evening service fifteen minutes or less.

On Sabbaths and Festivals, even without preaching, more time is required, first, on account of the longer "lessons" and additional Psalms in the liturgy; secondly, because the leader, with or without a choir, will give free rein to his musical tastes, seeing that his hearers are not supposed to have any other business on hand than to enjoy the glad and solemn service.

In a very few parts the liturgy has in late centuries been shortened by the omission of redundant matter. We shall be so much occupied with an analysis of the Prayer Books of the present day and the history of their gradual growth that we will be unable to give much time and space to an account of such parts of the liturgy as have been discarded in the orthodox rituals of our time.

One class of services has fallen into disuse since Talmudic days, or is now attended only by those of avowedly ascetic habits. These are the Watches, or Posts (*Ma'amadoth*, literally, "stands"), growing out of the public fasts which, during the days of the Temple and for some centuries thereafter, were called by the spiritual chiefs in the time of distressing drought, yet distinct from them. The liturgy for those fasts, which are now quite obsolete, is minutely set forth in the Mishna. The *Ma'amadoth* are given pretty fully in the oldest "Arrangements" and in some modern prayer books, but they are not deemed at present, even among the most orthodox, of universal *obligation*, and therefore lie out of the province of this volume.[19]

6

CHAPTER II

SOURCE AND STYLE

A GREAT part of the services is made up of entire Psalms or other long passages of Scripture, such as the Red Sea Song (Ex. 15); another considerable part, of single verses, culled from different books and chapters; thus, the verses sung in German congregations at the return of the Scroll to the Ark are taken from Numbers, from the Psalms, from Proverbs, and from Lamentations. Sometimes a verse will be found intertwined in a non-Biblical composition as if it were a part thereof, or changed only by turning the first person singular into the first person plural, in which, as a rule, all the prayers are composed; as Jeremiah's verse, "Heal me, O Lord, and I shall be healed, save me and I shall be saved, for thou art my glory," becomes, in one of the Eighteen, "Heal us, O Lord," or by turning promise into request, as Isaiah's prophecy, "I will restore thy judges as of old, and thy counsellors as at the beginning," becomes "Restore our judges." Oftener a verse is quoted with an introductory, "it is said," or "it is written," as a foundation of our hopes, or as a reason for what we say or do; thus, in the after-dinner grace, "For all this may Thy name be blessed, etc., as it is written (Deut. 8: 10), Thou shalt eat and be full, and shalt bless the Lord, thy God, for the good land which he hath given thee."

But, leaving aside whole chapters or whole verses, a set purpose can be seen in the earlier compositions to keep close to the spirit and to the very words of Scripture. Thus, where a benediction begins, "Thou hast loved thy people, the house of Israel, with everlasting love," it is an echo of Jeremiah's words (31: 3): "I have loved thee with an everlasting love;" and when, a few lines further on, we declare that "we meditate on them (the words of the Law) by day and by night," it is only because it is written that the righteous man "meditates by day and by night" (Ps. 1: 2; cmp. Josh. 1: 6). We shall, wherever it is of interest, point out the Scriptural materials from which the prayers are compounded like mosaic work; it would be a waste of space to go through the whole service book, tracing each phrase to its original. It was done by Abudraham in the fourteenth century so fully and patiently that he frankly says of every expression which he cannot trace, "this is the language of the Sages."

The devotions that are not taken bodily from Scripture are almost always drawn up in the first person plural, the "we" standing for all Israel,[1] and the people are always called by that name, never Jews. Jerusalem or Zion is mentioned only as a place, not as the embodiment of the nation. It will be seen that in some passages we are taught to pray for the welfare of mankind, especially that all may be brought to the knowledge of the One God, and we are made to acknowledge God's kindness to all flesh.

The names given to the Supreme Being in the older prayers are the same that are used in the Bible; no wonder, as these compositions are as old as many of the Psalms, or older. But later on we meet with the paraphrase, "The Holy One blessed be He," which the Rabbinic schools employed in order not to pronounce a real Name too lightly or too often, and occasionally with a very distant circumlocution for God, "the Place" (*ham-Makom*), as to the origin of which Hebrew scholars are very much in the dark.[2] We also meet in our liturgy, "our Father who (art) in heaven;" oftener, "our Father and King," and in one composition we praise and pray to "the Merciful" by a half Aramaic name (*ha-Rahaman*), which has been borrowed by Mohammed, and plays a great part in the chapter headings of the Koran.[3] We also find "the King of kings," an appellation suggested by Daniel.

The "four-lettered" Name was not sounded by the Jews as written (Yod He Vav He), but was read Adonai (in Galilee *Adounoy*) i. e., the Lord, even before the Maccabean wars. (Where it is preceded by the name Adonai the unspeakable Name is read *Elohim*, and our version says, "the Lord God.") The Greek version, made in part in the third century before the Christian era, turns the Name regularly into *ho Kyrios*, the Vulgate says *Dominus*, the Syriac version *Morio*, all according to the pronunciation, not according to the spelling. But in the Temple, till its destruction by Titus, the High Priest in the three confessions of sin on the Day of Atonement pronounced the Name as written. The common priests did the same in blessing the people in the words of Numbers 6: 24-26, at least in the Temple, for they were bidden to do so: "They shall place my name on the children of Israel and I shall bless them." But outside of the Temple, in the Synagogues even of the Holy Land, they ceased doing so long before the fall of Jerusalem, being persuaded of their unworthiness to utter the great Name except under the most solemn command.

At any rate, before the redaction of the Mishna it was deemed impious even to *think* of the sound of the four letters, probably because adepts in the secret lore claimed that by correctly sounding and properly thinking the Name they could work miracles, not always of mercy, and thus it was thought best that the true vowelling of the Name should be forgotten.[4] The vowels put under and over the letters in our Hebrew Bibles are those of Adonai or, in the exceptional case, of Elohim.

The Name as written is now never heard in a Jewish Synagogue, except in the sermon of a very modern preacher.

The Hebrew of the older compositions differs but little from that of the Bible; some of the later ones fall more or less into the jargon of the Mishna, while in others a pure

Biblical Hebrew, with its older grammatical forms, is introduced, not as a living, but as a learned tongue. The few
Aramaic or half-Aramaic pieces will be noticed separately.

We must here explain the Benediction (Beracha), which
is the unit of the older non-Biblical parts of the service. The
word may mean a blessing bestowed on man by God, or
asked from him, but in the law of the liturgy it denotes a
devout passage which opens, or the closing sentence of
which opens: Blessed (be) Thou, O Lord. The formula
grew up in the Temple (see 1 Chron. 29: 10), "Wherefore
David blessed the Lord before the whole Congregation,
and David said: Blessed be Thou, O Lord, God of Israel,
our Father, from everlasting to everlasting." According to
the Mishna, at the service in the Temple Court, all benedictions before any special thanks or praise proceeded, "God
of Israel, from everlasting," till the words "unto everlasting" were added to confute heretics who said there is only
one world ('Olam, everlasting, came later on to mean also
world).[5] .

Outside of the Temple the words, "Blessed (be) Thou, O
Lord," alone characterized the benediction. When they
stood at the beginning of a piece, the further words, "Our
God, King of the world," were added, except in the oldest
and most important benediction, the first of the Prayer, in
which "King of the world" is not found, probably because
at the time of its composition these words had not yet come
into vogue. When a number of benedictions are strung
together, as in the Prayer, the first alone has the characteristic words at the beginning and again in a short concluding sentence, while the following have them only in
such sentence at the end. Thus the first benediction of
the Prayer opens: "Blessed be Thou, O Lord, our God,
and God of our fathers," and closes, "Blessed be Thou,
O Lord, shield of Abraham." But the second benediction opens, "Thou art mighty," and gains its character

only from the closing words, "Blessed be Thou, O Lord, who reviveth the dead."[6]

There are many short benedictions for things enjoyed or by way of thanks for the merit of doing a religious act which have the characteristic words only at the beginning, e. g., that before eating bread: "Blessed be Thou, O Lord, our God, King of the world, who bringest bread forth from the earth."[7]

Such sanctity is ascribed to the "benediction" in this sense, that it is deemed a profanation of God's name to pronounce one that for any reason is not obligatory. Excepting the grace after meals, which is of Scriptural obligation, if you are in doubt whether you have already recited one of the prescribed benedictions, do not say it again, for the obligation is only Rabbinical, and it is worse to say a benediction twice than not at all.[8]

The Rabbis who, in the Babylonian Talmud, lay down such a principle, disable not only their successors but themselves from drawing up any new benedictions, though they may lengthen the old ones by the insertion of new matter. In fact, the two or three benedictions which cannot be traced back to the days of the Mishna or to the next hundred years following its completion have never received the full and undivided assent of all sections of the Jewish people.

In putting most of the benedictions into English there is a peculiar difficulty. They start with the second person, "Blessed be thou," and almost invariably pass into the third. For instance, "Blessed be thou, etc., who by *his* word darkeneth the evenings." The verb, it is true, is in the original a participle, as if we said, "the darkener of the evenings," but the pronoun *his* is there explicitly. This apology must be given beforehand for our shortcomings in this respect. To turn all the pronouns and forms of the third into those of the second person is hardly feasible; the writer has tried it as far as he could, but in a few benedictions he has let the third person stand as in the original.

From the tone in which the Talmud speaks of the services, it appears that the outline was fixed long before the filling up of the several benedictions. The leader had much discretion when he prayed aloud for the congregation. The individual worshipper was expected, at least in the Prayer, to insert his own petitions according to his wants.[9] And besides this testimony of the dead, we have the living evidence before us that the general contents of the benedictions and the closing words of each are the same in the Sefardic and in the German Ritual, but the words of request which precede the close, or "sealing," nearly always differ more or less. It follows that the contents of a benediction will generally throw but little light on the true time when it was first introduced. Thus, a benediction in which the speedy advent of the Messiah is prayed for may have been used before a coming Messiah was thought of, for it closes, "Blessed be, etc., who causes salvation to grow," a sentiment to which no one could ever object.

Another formula, not nearly so important or sacred or old as the benediction, should be mentioned, the petition opening with the words, "Be it thy will (literally, the will be before thee), our (or 'my') God and God of our ('my') fathers, that, etc." It is not found in the oldest and most obligatory devotions. The modern Cabbalists use it very freely.[10] A petition beginning, "Be it thy will," is sometimes made part of a benediction, though never in the oldest and simplest form of the older benedictions.

The Mishna and Talmud refer to many benedictions and other devotions by the first two or three words, thus indicating that the compositions were already in common use, and would be recognized by such short reference.[11] The short benedictions before enjoyment or before the performance of some duty are always given in full, yet many of these must have been in common use long before, and mention

is made only to clear up some fine point in the wording or
some casuistry about the occasion on which the benediction should be spoken. Some of the longer prayers given
in full and recommended by this or that Rabbi must also
have been in vogue in much earlier times, as will be pointed
out hereafter by comparison with the so-called Lord's
Prayer.[12]

CHAPTER III

THE first treatise of the Mishna begins with the reading of the Shema, as if it were the most solemn and most important act in the life of the Israelite. The precept implied in the first two verses of the first section is recognized in one of the Gospels (Mark 12: 29-30) as one of the two weightiest commands of the Law. It is the desire of every good Israelite to die with the words declaring God's unity upon his lips. The Moslem has learned from the Jew to say with his last breath: I witness that there is no God but the God (Allah).

From immemorial times the reading of the Shema has been preceded and followed by benedictions.[1] In the evening and in the morning two benedictions precede the reading. The first of these refers to the time of the day, and gives the name to the whole morning or evening service; the second in each service thanks God for his love in teaching us the Law, and prays for the continuance of this love. It is known as *Ahaba* (Love). The benediction which follows the reading leans upon the deliverance from Egypt, told in the last verse thereof, and is known as *Geulla* (Redemption); in the evening service another benediction follows, in which God is besought for his protection during the night. Here follow the evening benedictions:

I. Blessed be thou, O Lord our God, King of the world, who by his word darkeneth the evenings, who in wisdom openeth the gates, and with reason changes the times, and causeth the seasons to alternate, and who orders the stars in their watches in the expanse according to his will. He createth day and night, he

rolleth light away before darkness, and darkness before light;
he who moveth the day, and bringeth on the night, and who
divideth between day and night; the Lord of Hosts is his name
[The Germans add: The living and steadfast God, may he always
reign over us for evermore]; blessed be thou, O Lord; he who
darkeneth the evenings.

Here the Germans are guilty of a needless interpolation,
foreign to the matter in hand. The word rendered "steadfast" is rather late Hebrew; it is found in Ecclesiastes in the
phrase, the earth "standeth" forever, but is not applied to
God either in the Bible or anywhere else in the older liturgic
pieces.[2]

In the next piece the Sefardic Minhag differs from the
German only by the insertion, in the form given below, of
single unnecessary words:

II. Thou hast loved thy people, the house of Israel, with everlasting love, thou hast taught us Law and commandments, ordinances and rights. Therefore, O Lord our God, when we lie down
and when we rise, we shall talk of thy ordinances, and rejoice in
the words of thy Law, and in thy commandments for evermore.
For they are our life and the length of our days, and we will
meditate on them (or breathe in them) by day and by night. And
do not withhold thy love from us forever. Blessed be thou, O
Lord, who loveth his people Israel.

FIRST SECTION

Hear, O Israel, the Lord thy God, the Lord is One. (Blessed
be the name of his glorious Kingdom forever and aye.) And thou
shalt love the Lord thy God with all thy heart and all thy soul and
all thy might. (Here follow four more verses, Deut. 6: 6-9.)

Rashi gives a most natural meaning to the first verse.
Let us understand that the Lord who now is worshipped
by Israel will hereafter be alone worshipped by all mankind,
and will thus be the only God in recognition as he is already
in truth. The un-Scriptural line which follows the first verse

took rise in the second Temple; it was deemed the proper reaction to the spiritual shock of hearing the otherwise unspeakable Name pronounced,[3] and was thence transferred as a sort of rest after the solemn announcement of the highest truth.

The second section treats of reward and punishment, not of the individual saint or sinner, but of Israel as a whole; it is in Deut. 11: 13-21.

The third section consists of the last five verses of Numbers 15. It treats of the fringes on the corners of the garments, and ends thus:

> In order that ye may remember and do my commandments, and that ye be holy to your God, I am the Lord your God, who have brought you out of the land of Egypt to be your God; I am the Lord your God.

It seems, from Jeremiah 23: 7, that mention of the Exodus had been made in public worship even during the first Temple, perhaps in the evening as well as in the morning. But the "fringes" belong to the day; the verses treating of them were read at night only for the sake of uniformity, and their recital in the evening service was at one time in dispute.[4]

In public worship the last two Hebrew words (The Lord) (your God) are joined to the first word "True" in the following benediction.[5]

The *Geulla* for the evening service is marked by the word "faithful," suggested by the words of Psalm 92, "and thy faithfulness in the nights." It reads:

> III. True and faithful is all this, and standeth firmly for us: that he, the Lord, is our God, and no one else; who ransoms us from the hand of kings, our King who delivers us from the hand of all the fear-inspiring; the God who avengeth us upon our adversaries, and requiteth on all our enemies their deserts [Germans insert: Who doeth great things past finding out; yea, marvellous things without number (Job 9: 10)]. Who holdeth our soul in life, and

suffers not our feet to be moved (Ps. 66: 9); he who leadeth us
over the high places of the earth, and who lifteth our horn above all
those that hate us; who worked for us miracles and vengeance,
signs and wonders in the land of the sons of Ham; he who smote
in his wrath all the first-born of Egypt, and brought his people
Israel from the midst thereof to everlasting freedom; he who made
his children to pass between the parts of the Red Sea, and sank
their pursuers and enemies in the deep; then his sons saw his
might, they gave praise and thanks to his name, and willingly
received his dominion; Moses and the children of Israel broke out
into song before him, with great rejoicing, and thus they all said:
(Ex. 15: 11). Who is like unto thee, O Lord, among the Gods?
Who is like thee, glorious in holiness, fearful in praises, doing
wonders.

Thy children saw thy Kingship, even the sea parting before
Moses; they struck up: "This is my God," and cried:
(Ex. 15: 18). The Lord shall reign forever and ever!
It is said (Jer. 31: 11): For the Lord hath ransomed Jacob, and
redeemed him from the hand of one stronger than he.
Blessed be thou, O Lord, who hath redeemed Israel.

The two verses from Exodus are joined in by all present:
they are sung by the choir when there is one.

We find a short form of the *Geulla* in the Talmud, for
either the evening or the morning: "We thank thee, O Lord
our God, for that thou hast brought us forth from the land
of Egypt, and ransomed us from the house of bondage, and
hast done for us wonders and mighty deeds upon the sea;
and there we sang to thee." The words, "true and faithful,"
are supposed to precede this form, and that which was sung
must follow it; that is, the verses from the Red Sea Song
given above. But this was evidently not the established
form of the benediction, only what the men of the Law
declared to be the minimum of its contents. It is
too dry and bare for the Jewish taste in liturgical matters.
In the benediction as now known there is no trace of either
rhyme or acrostic and only three or four un-Biblical
words;[6] hence it is quite probable that it was from its first
constitution not much shorter than at present. Another

opinion in the Talmud demands a reference to the smiting
of the first-born, which is made both in the evening and in
the morning benediction. Another calls for the words, "the
rock of Israel and its redeemer;" and these words are used
by way of conclusion in the German Minhag whenever on
Festivals "poetries" are inserted.[7]

The next benediction is peculiar to the evening:

Let us, O Lord our God, lie down unto peace; let us rise, our
King, unto life; spread over us the tabernacle of thy peace, and
build us up with good counsel of thy own; be thou a shield about
us, and remove from us the enemy and pestilence, the sword and
famine and grief, and remove the adversary from before us, and
from behind us, and hide us in the shadow of thy wings; for thou
art the God who guardeth and delivereth us, for thou art a gracious
and merciful God and King; guard thou our going out and coming
in for life and peace from henceforth and for evermore.

Blessed be thou, O Lord, who guardeth his people Israel forever.

"The adversary" is the English for "Satan." It is not
clear, however, that a personal devil is here meant any
more than in the story of Balaam, where the angel tells
him, "Behold, I came as an adversary (Satan) to thee." The
adversary before us is the man, the spirit, or the evil impulse
who or which seduces us to do wrong; the adversary behind
us is the human or superhuman being who accuses us of
wrong done.

On the Sabbath and on Festivals, in the German Ritual,
only the "Blessed be thou" at the end is taken off, and the
following substituted:

"And spread over us the tabernacle of thy peace: Blessed be
thou, O Lord, who spreadeth the tabernacle of peace over us, and
over all his people Israel, and over Jerusalem."

The Sefardim go further back in this change from work-
days to holy days; on the latter, they say, we should not ask
God to guard us—the Sabbath or Festival is in itself a pledge
of his watchful care—nor think of sword or pestilence;

hence they stop with "be thou a shield about us" in the work-day form, and there add on the Sabbath and Festivals, "And spread," etc., as above.[8]

Here, in Talmudic times, the Prayer would have followed at once, but a third benediction has grown up which has never been fully recognized by all; of this hereafter.

CHAPTER IV

THE doubts about the third paragraph of the Shema do not touch the morning service, nor was there ever an attempt to add another benediction to those established in the first age, for the old Sages insisted strongly on joining "Redemption to Prayer," with nothing to intervene.

But while the number of parts, three paragraphs and three benedictions, was always undisputed, the volume of the latter has been very much swelled from their small beginnings.

It is generally believed that the first benediction in the morning was made up originally of forty-five Hebrew words, equivalent to over eighty English words. Below, all the rest is enclosed in brackets, each accretion separately, while the original parts are marked by the number of words.[1]

I. (1-6). Blessed be thou, O Lord our God, King of the world. (7-15) who hast formed light and created darkness, who makest peace and createst all; (16-26) who dost in mercy light up the earth and those who dwell thereon, and renewest on each day unceasingly the work of creation. [Ps. 104: 24. How manifold are thy works, O Lord; in wisdom thou hast made them all; the earth is full of thy riches.] [The King, who alone is exalted from evermore, who is praised and glorified from the days of eternity! Everlasting God, in thy abundant kindness be merciful to us, Lord of our strength, rock of our refuge; shield of our salvation; fortress around us!* God, the blessed, great in knowledge, has set up and made the beams of the sun; the Good One has created glory for his name; he has placed lights around his power; the heads of his hosts are holy, exalting the Almighty, always** telling God's glory and holiness.] (27-40.) Be thou blessed, O Lord our God, for the

(95)

excellent work of thy hands and for the luminaries of light, which thou hast made, they should glorify thee.   Selah.

[Be thou blessed our Rock, our King, our Redeemer, who hast created holy beings; may thy name be ever praised, our King, who hast shaped attendants, and all of whose attendants stand in the heights of the world, and proclaim in awe together aloud the words of the living God and everlasting King.   All of them are (*a*) beloved, all of them are (*b*) pure, all of them are (*c*) mighty; all of them (*o*) do in awe and fear the will of their Master; and all of them (*p*) open their mouths in holiness and purity, with song and music, and they bless and praise, they glorify and revere, they hallow and honor with homage

The name of the God, the great, mighty, and fearful King, holy is he.

And all of them (19) receive from each other the yoke of the heavenly Kingdom, and give leave to each other to sanctify their Maker with calmness of spirit; with pure and pleasant speech, all as one sound the Thrice-Holy, and say in fear:

Holy, holy, holy is the Lord of Hosts, full is the whole earth of his glory.

But the wheels and holy beasts arise with a great rush to meet the Seraphim; over against them they praise and proclaim:

Blessed is the glory of the Lord from its place].

[They put forth sweet songs to the blessed God; they discourse music and sound praises to the King, the living steadfast God; to him who alone worketh *mighty deeds, who maketh* new things, the Master of *battles, who soweth *righteousness, who causes *salvation to spring forth, who worketh *healing, who is fearful in *praises, the Lord of *wonders, who reneweth in his goodness always and on each day the work of the beginning.]

[As it is said (Ps. 136: 7):   *Thank him who made the great lights, for his mercy endureth forever.*]   [Let a new light shine over Zion, and may we all soon deserve its radiance.]   (41-45.) Blessed be thou, O Lord, Maker of the luminaries.

The first sentence (7-15) is taken from Isaiah 45: 7:   (I) form light and create darkness; (I) make peace and create evil; but toned down in the last word: it is a protest against the dualism of Persia, with its Ormuzd and Ahriman, the gods of light and of darkness.   The third sentence in the old form and the close of the benediction, by asserting that the

Lord made "the luminaries of light" (emp. Gen. 1:16), stand out as a protest against Greeks, Canaanites, and Babylonians, who worshipped the sun and moon and the stars. Nay, the Israelites of the second Temple who learned to recite this benediction felt a proud distinction over their forefathers of the first Commonwealth, many of whom at sunrise turned to the rising luminary in worship.[2] The middle part of the old formula is a protest against the teachings of Epicurus.[3]

The Hebrew word therein for Creation is *Be-Reshith,* "In the beginning," which, from the first two words of Genesis, has in the later language grown into a single word answering to Creation in English. The meaning of the sentence is that God does not leave the world to blind forces, but by watching over it he renews the work of Creation.

Of the later insertions the oldest were most probably the two Psalm verses, one near the beginning, the other near the end.

Next is the account of the heavenly bodies, who are endowed with life, and identified with attendants at God's throne, who sing the Thrice-Holy, and who bless his glory. These responses will be met with hereafter in the repetition of the Prayer in public; they may have been put here to give them a place in private devotion.

That this accretion is pretty old, dating at least to the year 300, appears from a reference in the Jerusalem Talmud to a leader in the services who became confused at the mention of the Ofannim (Wheels).[4] The words "beloved, pure, mighty, do, open," are marked with the letters a, b, c, o, p, to indicate the letters of the Hebrew alphabet with which they begin. There may once have been a composition running thus through all the letters, which was recited only on occasions, and was afterwards shortened for every-day use.

The other pieces, "The King who alone," near the beginning, and "They put forth," near the end, are written in a more labored style, and betray a later date. There are five rhyming clauses in the sentence "Everlasting God;" easy enough, as the rhyme is made by the suffix for "us" or "our." The next sentence (* — * *) is made up of twenty-two words with initials in the order of the alphabet at some sacrifice of grammar. In the new piece near the end there are eight words,* all ending in *oth*, the mark of the feminine plural. Then follow the simple words, "who reneweth," which are borrowed from the old formula, in order that the benediction at its end might be brought back to its *motif*.

The idea of imparting life and personality to the heavenly bodies is not drawn from the Aggadta but from Biblical sources, such as Psalms 104 and 148.

The last sentence before the sealing, "Let a new light," is not found in the Sefardic ritual nor in the Mahzor Vitry, the oldest standard for the Germans. It has been opposed by the greatest authorities, such as R. Saadia, as being out of place, for this benediction deals with the natural light of day, such as it now shines for all alike; not with light in any figurative sense which is to shine in the future.

Altogether the two rituals agree pretty closely on the whole of this benediction.

For the Sabbath it has been much extended. Before (16-26) of the oldest form is inserted:

All should give thanks to thee, all should praise thee; all should say: none is holy like the Lord. All should exalt thee, Maker of all; God who opens each day the doors of the eastern gates, and hews out windows in the skies; who bringeth the sun from its place, the moon from its wonted seat, and illumines all the world and its inhabitants, whom he has made through the quality of mercy.

(After 16-26 of the old form, and the work-day insertion
to "fortress around us," proceed:)

None is of a kind with thee; there is none beside thee; there is
none but thee; none is like thee. None of a kind with thee, O
Lord our God, in this world; none beside thee in the next world;
nothing outside of thee, our Redeemer, in the days of the Messiah;
none compareth to thee, our Saviour, at the resurrection of the
dead.[5]

> Almighty Master of all creatures,
> Blessed and praised by each breathing mouth;
> Grace and greatness fill his world,
> Deepest wisdom encircles his seat.
> He is enthroned above the heavenly forces,
> Worshipped in reverence upon the chariot.
> Zeal for the right stands at his throne;
> Highest mercy pervades his presence;
> True and good are his luminous spheres:
> In wisdom, reason, knowledge he shaped them,
> Kingly might he placed in them,
> Letting them rule o'er the living world.
> Massive with light, pouring forth radiance,
> Nowhere and never their brightness endeth.
> Setting with joy they rise with gladness,
> Obedient e'er to their owner's will.
> Praise and honor they yield to his name;
> Cheers and songs to the fame of his empire.
> Quick to his call the sun shone forth;
> Round, like it, he built the disk of the moon.
> Shouts of praise rise from all the host on high;
> Thronging seraphs and angels sing glory and greatness.[6]

The above twenty-two verses represent as many Hebrew
lines, the first two of five words each, the last two of six,
all the rest of four each, and ordered by the letters of the
alphabet; the same arrangement has been followed in the
version, substituting the nearest equivalents for the Hebrew
letters. The original runs much more smoothly than this
version, for Hebrew acrostics of even short lines are easily

made by reason of many synonyms and of the great freedom in the order of words.

Connecting with the last clause above, the benediction for
the Sabbath proceeds thus:

> To the God who rested from all his works, and on the seventh
> day sat exalted on the throne of his glory; who wrapped the day of
> rest in beauty, and who called the Sabbath delight. This is the
> excellence of the seventh day, that thereon God rested from all his
> work. Nay the seventh day itself says praises and speaks: "A
> Psalm, the song for the Sabbath day. It is good to give thanks to
> the Lord." Therefore, let all creatures glorify and bless God, and
> give praise, honor, and greatness to the divine King, the Maker of
> all, who gives a holy rest as a heritage to his people Israel on his
> Holy Sabbath. May thy name, O Lord our God be hallowed,
> and thy memorial, O our King, be glorified, in the heavens above
> and on the earth beneath. Be thou blessed, our Saviour, for the
> excellence of the work of thy hands and for the luminaries of light
> which thou hast made, they should glorify thee. Selah.

After this the Sabbath form is like that for week-days.
On Festivals falling on week-days there is no change,
unless "poetries" of later ages are inserted.

The insertion for the Sabbath is written in a language
and style as late as or later than the latest insertions in the
common form.

In the paragraph last given, the seventh day is personified
and named as the author of Psalm 92 from its title,
as Asaph is of Psalm 83, or David of Psalm 23. This
notion is found in the Midrash on the Psalms, written
towards the end of the ninth century. But the piece in the
Prayer Book seems older than the Midrash. It seems that
this imagery, turning the Sabbath into a Psalm writer, was
first conceived by him who composed this part of the morning service.[7]

In the second benediction known as "Love" (*Ahaba*),
thanks are rendered for the Law and for Israel's mission.

It stands in the German ritual, putting in brackets those parts which, in the opinion of scholars, are of later origin, as follows:

II. Thou hast loved us, O Lord our God, with abundant love, thou hast foreborne with us in great and overflowing pity. Our Father! our King! for the sake of our fathers, who trusted in thee, and whom thou taughtest the laws of life, teach us also graciously. [Our Father, the merciful Father, who showeth mercy, show it to us, and put it into our hearts to understand, even wisely, to hear, to learn, and to teach, to keep, to do, and to fulfill all the words of the study of thy law lovingly.] Illumine our eyes in thy law, let our heart cleave to thy commandments, and unite our hearts to love and to fear thy name, so that we may never come to shame. [For we trust in thy great and fearful holy name, we rejoice and are glad in thy salvation; and bring us unto peace from the four corners of the earth, and lead us walking erect unto our land.] For thou art the God who worketh salvation, and thou hast chosen us from every people and tongue, and hast brought us near to thy great name [Selah] in truth; to give thanks to thee and lovingly to proclaim thee One. Blessed be thou, O Lord, who hath chosen his people Israel in love.

The Sefardic Minhag adds over forty words, a few here, a few there, both in the older and in the later parts of the benediction. The Mahzor Vitry contains the same padding.

The bracketed parts betray their late origin, because the benediction, to judge from its counterpart in the evening, is a place rather for thanks than for supplication; the second of these parts also, because to pray for the gathering of the dispersion is out of place in the context, and those who drew up the old formulas were great sticklers for the "unities." The four corners of the earth were probably suggested by the fact that the worshipper took into one hand the four fringes at the corner of his shawl, as he is soon to read the section from Numbers concerning them.[8]

The three Scripture passages are now read as in the evening. In public service the leader again unites the last words, "The Lord your God," with "True" or "Truth" at the beginning of the benediction that follows.

Dropping some of the sixteen synonyms at the beginning, we have:

III. True and established [upright, lovely, majestic, received, good, and fair] is this word to us forever. [Truly, the everlasting God is our King, the Rock of Jacob is our saving shield; in all generations he standeth, his name standeth, and his throne standeth, and his Kingdom standeth, and his faith endureth forever. His words are living and steadfast, true and pleasant, unto everlasting, for our fathers, for us, and for our children, for our generations, and for those of the seed Israel, thy servants. For the first and for the last, the word is good and standeth forever. True and faithful, the ordinance will not pass away. Truly, thou, O Lord, art our God, and the God of our fathers, our King, the King of our fathers, our Redeemer, the Redeemer of our fathers, our Maker, the Rock of our salvation, our Liberator and Saviour; from everlasting is thy name; there is no God beside thee.] [Thou hast been the help of our fathers from all time, a shield and saviour to their children after them in every age. Thy seat is in the eternal heights, thy judgments and thy righteousness go to the ends of the earth. Happy is the man who listens to thy commandments, who takes to heart thy Law, thy Holy Word. Truly thou art a Master to thy people and a mighty King to plead their cause.] [Truly thou art the first and the last, beside thee we have no King, Redeemer, or Saviour.] From Egypt thou hast redeemed us, O Lord our God, and from the house of bondage thou hast ransomed us; *thou didst kill all their first-born, and didst redeem thy first-born; thou didst split the Red Sea; thou didst sink the haughty, and broughtest over the beloved* (Ps. 106: 11): And the waters covered their enemies, there was not one of them left. [Therefore the beloved praised and exalted God, and the beloved gave out music, songs, and hymns, blessings and thanks, to the King, the living and everlasting God; high and exalted, great and fearful, who lowers the proud, and raises the lowly, frees the captives, and redeems the humble; he helps the poor and answers his people when they supplicate to him; praises to God on high, blessed and again blessed.] Moses and the children of Israel struck up a song to thee with great joy, and all of them said (Ex. 15: 11, as in the evening): The redeemed took up a new song to thy name

on the shore of the sea; all gave thanks and homage, and said
(Ex. 15: 18): The Lord will reign for evermore. [Rock of Israel,
arise to the aid of Israel, and redeem according to thy word Judah
and Israel.] (Isa. 47: 4): Our Redeemer! the Lord of Hosts is
his name, the Holy One of Israel; blessed be thou, O Lord, he
has redeemed Israel.[9]

The parts of later growth have been put in brackets.
"True and established" are the initial words given in the
Mishna; the heaping up of fourteen other qualities of the
Law, which is heaping up so many compliments to its
author, is against the rules of taste laid down in the earlier
days.[10] There is also this positive proof of interpolations
in the first part of the benediction, that the West Germans
abridge it very considerably, reducing the sixteen synonyms
to eight whenever "poetry" is inserted on the Festivals and
certain Sabbaths. Several subsequent passages begin with
the word *Emeth*, i. e., truth, true, truly. This word occurs
only once in the *Geulla* of the evening, and very probably
only once in the first draft of that for the morning. The
first of these longer insertions, which so eloquently claims
that our Law is unchangeable, and that God alone is our
Redeemer, was evidently written as a protest against growing and threatening Christianity. The next bracketed part
(Thou hast been the help) is in no way indicated by the
short Talmudic form quoted in the preceding chapter, and
has no bearing on the redemption from Egypt. The next
sentence, in separate brackets, looks like another protest-
against Christianity. "From Egypt thou hast redeemed
us" is of the very essence of the benediction; but the lines
between asterisks, though as a whole indispensable, look
like a poetic expansion. The next bracketed part (Therefore the beloved) is certainly such, of the kind as, in the
oldest time of the liturgy, would have been left to the taste
of each individual leader. Nearly all the rest is old, as the
two verses from the Red Sea Song are clearly indicated
by the Talmudic form. The words, "Rock of Israel," were

strongly objected to as unauthorized as late as the thirteenth and the fourteenth centuries by German as well as by Spanish scholars. They bring in a request for a redemption hereafter, while the benediction should deal only with the redemption in the past,[11] and the *Geulla* in the evening service does not contain a word of request. The verse from Isaiah naturally leads to the close, but has probably taken the place of a short un-Biblical clause; many service books put it in parentheses.

CHAPTER V

RESPONSES—THE KADDISH

It is the custom now, and was such in the earliest time in which the "benediction" made a part of the service, that when it was pronounced in public by a leader, those present would adopt it as their own by answering, "Amen." According to the Mishna, the Jew might respond *Amen* even to the benediction of a Samaritan if he had heard it all.[1] But *Amen* was said only in the Synagogue or at the table, not in the Temple; there the answer was: Blessed be the name of his glorious Kingdom forever and ever.[2]

After the three distinguishing words of the benediction (Blessed be thou, O Lord), spoken by a leader, it has for many centuries been the custom for the hearers to answer: Blessed be he, and blessed his name. This, as well as the response in the Temple, is based on the verse in Deut. 32: When I call on the name of the Lord, give ye homage to our God.[3]

A more important response is that which follows the leader's address by which the evening service and the more essential part of the morning service are introduced. When the assembled worshippers are thus addressed and do thus respond, they are said, in the words of the Mishna, to "break" (or "to cut pieces") on the *Shema*, and this can only be done in the presence of ten men.[4]

It is on the Shema, because the address and response precede its first benediction, which is deemed a part of it. The words of the address are four:

1. *Barechu*, bless ye. 2. *Eth*, the mark of the objective. 3. The four-lettered Name. This would have been enough,

but by stopping here the leader would have excluded himself from those who bless God, and so he adds: 4. *Hammeborach*, the blessed. The whole thus becomes, "Bless ye the Lord, the blessed."

The people answer, and the leader repeats after them (the latter usage seems to be an after-thought), "Blessed be the Lord, the blessed, forever and ever." In the answer the first word is *Baruch*, the second "blessed" as in the address, *Hammeborach*.[5]

The privilege of being thus addressed and of answering thus was deemed almost a sufficient reward for a long walk to the Synagogue. It was not, as with our Catholic fellow-citizens, the sacredness of a priest conferring holiness upon the words spoken by him, but simply the presence of ten men, assembled for the worship of God; ten such men represent the Congregation of Israel; where they meet, the Shechina, or Presence of God, is poured out among them.[6] We say "almost" a sufficient reward only because there came other responsive passages.

These are the *Kaddish* and the *Kedusha*. The former word is the Aramaic form of the Hebrew *Kadosh* (holy); the latter is good, classic Hebrew for holiness, but means here hallowing or sanctification; it can only be explained in the next chapter in connection with the Amida, or Prayer.

The former is, as found in the present service books, a queer compound of Hebrew and Aramaic; Hebrew predominates in the words, Aramaic in the flexions. The Aramaic element was infused into it to make it more readily understood by women and children and, generally speaking, by the most ignorant portion of the people.

The so-called "complete" Kaddish in the modern rituals, German and Sefardic, stands as follows. The parts put in brackets belong to the latter only, and are later interpolations. The responses are shown in quotation marks:

Magnified and hallowed be (see Ezek. 38: 23) his great name in the world which he hath created according to his will, and may he cause his Kingdom to reign [let his salvation grow, and bring on his Anointed] in your lives and days and within the life of all Israel, speedily and in a near time, and say ye, "Amen. Be his great name blessed forever and to all eternity." Blessed and honored and glorified and exalted and raised and beautified and lifted up and praised be the name of the Holy One, "blessed be he." Upwards over all blessings, songs, hymns, and consolations that are spoken in the world, and say ye, "Amen."*

May the prayer and request of all Israel be received before their Father who is in Heaven, and say ye, "Amen."**

Be there much peace from heaven, life [and plenty and salvation and comfort and help, healing and redemption, forgiveness and atonement, room and deliverance] for us and for all [his people] Israel, and say ye, "Amen."

He who maketh peace in his places (Job 25: 2), may he [in his mercy] make peace among us and among all Israel, and say ye, "Amen."

Stopping at the second Amen (*) we have the Half Kaddish of the Germans or *Kaddish Le'ella* of the Sefardim. Leaving out the next paragraph alone, but proceeding with what follows, we have what is now known as the "Kaddish of the Fatherless," or the Mourners' Kaddish, which plays an inordinately great part in modern Judaism.

The complete Kaddish is recited after and with regard to each *Amida*, as is indicated by its words, "the prayer and request." The main office of the Half Kaddish is to introduce the address, "Bless ye," in the morning service; it thus becomes a part of "breaking on the Shema." But it must have some Psalm or Bible passages to precede it, or it must precede them when it is interposed between the Prayer and the complete Kaddish.

The weighty response of the Kaddish is:

"Amen, be his great name blessed forever and to all eternity." This is considered the most solemn part of public worship; though it is undoubtedly much younger than "Blessed be the Lord," in answer to "Bless ye the Lord."

In a Baraïtha of some length, ascribed to R. Jose, a mystic of the second century, the prophet Elijah informs the pious Rabbi that when Israel, in the houses of study and in the Synagogues, answers, "Be his great name blessed," God nods assent and says, "Happy is the King to whom they bring such homage!" And the Talmud says that while a person engaged in study might not interrupt himself for any other purpose, he should do it, in order to respond, "Be his great name blessed." Yet neither the Kaddish as a whole nor the response is mentioned anywhere in the Mishna, a circumstance which throws some doubt on the genuineness of the Baraïtha credited to R. Jose.[1]

The response, we are told above, is heard in the house of study, for there is a species of the Kaddish known as "that of the Rabbis." In this the paragraph as to prayer is omitted, and in its place there is inserted:

Upon Israel and upon our teachers (Rabbis) and upon their disciples, and all the disciples of their disciples, and on all those that study the law, whether at this place, or in any other place, may there be for them and for you, much peace, grace, and kindness, mercy and long life, plentiful nourishment and deliverance, from the presence of the Father of Heaven and Earth, and say ye, "Amen."

When ten or more men have studied the Mishna or its commentary, the Talmud, together, one of them at the close recites the Kaddish of the Rabbis, the others responding, and two or three sections of the Mishna are, in modern times, often read and interpreted at the end or before the opening of the regular services purposely, to give the mourners present an opportunity to recite this Kaddish.

There is yet another species of the Kaddish more solemn than all others. It is spoken at the open grave, also at the house of study when some one of those present has, in his studies, gone through one whole "Order" of the Mishna. In this Kaddish the first paragraph is enlarged so as to take the following shape:

Magnified and hallowed be his great name, which in the future is to be renewed, when he will revive the dead, and raise to eternal life, and build the city of Jerusalem, and finish the Temple in its midst, and uproot the false service from the earth, and restore the heavenly service to its place; and the Holy One, blessed be he, will cause his Kingdom and glory to reign, in your lives and days, etc., and say ye, "Amen."

"Upon Israel" is added in its proper place when this Kaddish is recited in the house of study.

The response, "Be his great name blessed," in two of the four passages of the Talmud which quote it, is given in good Hebrew or nearly so; Abudraham found it so in an old and authentic manuscript. The last paragraph and the latter half of the last but one are still Hebrew; when the rest took their Aramaic guise is uncertain, probably in the sixth or seventh century.

The older authorities on the Prayer Book know nothing about a Mourners' Kaddish by that name; they denote it simply by the opening words of the fourth paragraph, because the third is omitted. They do not intimate that anybody but the regular leader recites it. Maimonides wants Kaddish said seven times a day, i. e., thrice the complete one, four times the Half Kaddish, which leaves none to the mourner. How and when the custom arose that the mourners present at a service recite the body of such a Kaddish, receiving the responses of the Congregation, and when the belief sprang up that the son performs a duty to his departed father and mother by repeating the Kaddish during the year of mourning and on the anniversaries of his and her death, it is hard to tell.

It seems, however, clear, from the legends on the subject, that the custom and underlying belief at first required the son to prove the merit of his parents by "breaking on the Shema."

He would thus in the morning service give out Kaddish and "Bless ye," in the evening service only the latter, and would obtain the responses to both. But this was not always feasible, for a boy under thirteen is not qualified to "break on the Shema," nor can several orphans join in doing so, and when it became the rule for the same man to do this and to lead in prayer generally, many mourners would be found unequal to the task. Then some particular Kaddish (neither the half nor the complete) not wound up with the essential parts of the service, following some Psalm or voluntary devotion, or the Kaddish for the Rabbis after the reading of Mishna or Baraïtha, could be set aside for the mourners. This custom arose among the German and French Jews (probably by way of reflex from their Christian neighbors) long before it found a place among the Sefardim, who grew up under Moslem rule. Abudraham, in his book published shortly before 1340, has no allusion to the Mourners' Kaddish,[8] while the Mahzor Vitry, dated A. M. 4968 (1208), refers to it pretty plainly by the words, "the lad stands up and says Kaddish," and by publishing, probably for the first time among books still preserved, a well-known legend, written for the purpose of bringing orphans who mourn for a father or mother to lead in public worship.

Rabbi Akiba is said to have seen a coal-black man at a grave-yard bearing a heavy load of faggots and running like a horse. He kindly offered to redeem him from bondage to a master imposing such hard tasks, but the answer came, Do not delay me, or my taskmasters will be angry. On further question the stranger told him that he was dead, that while alive he had been a cruel and unjust gatherer of tribute, favoring the rich and murdering the poor, and that there was no help for him, unless, as he heard, something should happen that was clearly impossible, namely, that a son of his would give out "Bless ye" in the Synagogue, and the people would respond. R. Akiba asked for his and his wife's name and for the name of his town; it was Laodicæa. He there found the widow, as wicked as her late husband, and a posthumous son uncircumcised and wholly untaught.

He circumcised, and, with unutterable effort, taught the boy the rudiments, i. e., to read the Shema and to say grace after meals; he stood him up in public, so that he gave out "Bless ye," and the people responded. At that moment the dead man was relieved from his sufferings in Gehinnom, and he informed R. Akiba thereof in a dream.[9] Hence, adds the compiler of the Mahzor, it is usual on Saturday night (when the condemned no longer enjoy the weekly remission of their torments) for some one who has no father or mother to say "Bless ye" or the Kaddish.

The underlying sentiment of the legend is this, that a child, religiously trained by his dead father or mother, may well hope that his acts of worship in the Synagogue reflect credit before God upon those who taught him to be a good Israelite, but the story seeks to impute R. Akiba's merits to a dead sinner, which is Catholic but not Jewish doctrine.

The phrase, "breaking upon the Shema," which in the Mishna means the responsive reading of "Bless ye," or of Kaddish and "Bless ye," before the first benediction, is in modern practice applied to a repetition of these responsive parts after the morning prayer for the benefit of those who may have missed them in the proper place by coming too late to the services. Among the Sefardim this is done as a matter of course, if any belated visitor is present.

In the German Minhag two verses (Num. 14: 17 and Ps. 25: 6) are said silently by the Congregation while the reader chants the words "Magnified and hallowed," and in both rituals the Congregation is directed to whisper a short doxology, while he slowly chants "Bless ye." This embraces in the German Prayer Book Ps. 68: 5, and 113: 2. But the more learned very properly disregard these directions, deeming it more meritorious to listen to the leader than to mumble something else.

CHAPTER VI

THE CONSTANT PARTS OF THE TEFILLA

THE Tefilla, or Prayer proper, is made up on work-days of nineteen benedictions, formerly of eighteen, from which latter number it takes its popular name; on Sabbath and Festivals, and as "Additional," on New Moons and half festivals, it consists of only seven; the "Additional" on the Memorial Day, of nine.

But the first three and the last three of these benedictions are constant for all days, and in their structure and language they show a higher age than almost any of those intervening. Only one of the six has gone through any material change from its first draft, and they undoubtedly date back to the days of the Great Synod.

The first benediction is known as "Fathers" (*Aboth*),[1] and runs thus:

[1]Blessed be thou, O Lord, our God—[2]and God of our fathers, God of Abraham, God of Isaac, and God of Jacob—[3]the great, the mighty and the fearful God—[4]God Most High—[5]who bestoweth goodly kindnesses—[6]and is Owner of all—[7]and remembereth the piety of the fathers—[8]and bringeth a redeemer to their children's children—[9]for the sake of his name—[10]in love. [11]King, helper and saviour and—[12]shield; blessed be thou, O Lord, Shield of Abraham.

We have marked twelve phrases to trace them separately to their Scriptural origin. That of (1) has been shown in a former chapter in speaking of the benediction; (2) is drawn from the vision of the thorn bush, "The Lord, the God of your fathers, the God of Abraham, the God of Isaac, and the God of Jacob has sent me to you;" (3) from the verse in

Deuteronomy, "For the Lord your God is the God of gods, and the Lord of lords, the great, the mighty, and the fearful God," etc.; and the same appellation is found in Neh. 9: 32; (4) and (6) from the words of Melchizedek, "Blessed be Abram to God most high, owner of heaven and earth;" (5) from Isaiah 63: 7, "I will make mention of the loving-kindness of the Lord, according to all that the Lord has bestowed on us;" (7) from the promise in Leviticus 26, "I will remember my covenant with Jacob, even my covenant," or from the statement in Exodus, "And God heard their groans, and God remembered his covenant with Abraham." There is some difficulty about (8), as the belief in a coming Messiah probably did not prevail when this benediction was composed, and it was deemed too sacred for interpolation or change; but the redeemer in the author's mind was in the past, such as Moses, whom God sent to redeem Israel from Egypt, that the promise made to the fathers might be fulfilled, as we are repeatedly told in the opening chapters of Exodus. He brought a redeemer again, say Cyrus or Zerubbabel, in the words of the second Isaiah (59: 20): "A redeemer will come unto Zion."[2] (9) "For the sake of his name" God redeemed Israel heretofore and must always redeem it from captivity; in the words of Ezekiel (36: 23, 24), "And I will sanctify my great name, etc., for I will take you from the nations;" (10) "In love" rests on Deuteronomy 7: 7, 8, where it is said that God chooses Israel not for its merits but from love.

The three words (11), King, Helper, Saviour, are so often applied to God in Scripture that the particular allusion can hardly be fixed; but (12) Shield, and particularly Shield of Abraham, is evidently drawn from God's words addressed to Abraham in Genesis 15: 1: "I am thy shield."

The Talmudic Sages are at one in holding this benediction to be the oldest among all the non-Biblical parts of the service, and they ascribe it with good reason to a very early age of the Great Synod.

8

The second benediction is known as "Powers" (*Geburoth*), also as Revival of the Dead, and runs thus:

II. Thou art mighty forever, O Lord; thou revivest the dead; art great to save. He sustains the living in kindness, he reviveth the dead in abundant mercy, supporteth the falling and healeth the sick and looseneth the captives, and keepeth up his faith to the sleepers of the dust. Who is like thee, master of mighty deeds; and who compareth with thee, King that killeth and bringeth to life, and causeth salvation to grow; and thou art trusted to revive the dead; blessed be thou, O Lord, who reviveth the dead.

The word "Lord" in the first line is not the Tetragrammaton, but *Adonai* in letters as in sound. Some phrases are not Biblical, as the underlying thought, that of the resurrection, is hardly so. "Supporteth the falling" and the two following predicates occur in the Psalms; "killeth and bringeth to life," in the prayer of Hannah.

The third benediction is known as the "Sanctification of the Name" (*Kedushath ha-Shem*), and is very short.

III. Thou art holy and thy name is holy, and the holy ones praise thee every day. Selah [Sefardim add: for thou art a great and holy God and King]; blessed be thou, O Lord, the Holy God.

The holy ones who praise God every day are not heavenly beings, but the saints on earth,[3] referred to in Psalm 16: 3. The word "Selah" (a corruption of the Greek imperative *psalle*, play!) was inserted, as in many Psalms, as a command to the musicians in the Temple Court to strike up.

The word *God* in the close of the benediction is not Elohim, but *El*, the one Divine name oftenest coupled with adjectives, as in phrases (3) and (4) of the first benediction.

In public worship, when the "messenger of the assembly" reads the prayer aloud, he puts in place of all but the closing formula, "Blessed be thou," the Thrice-Holy, popularly known as the *Kedusha*. To hear this spoken responsively and to take part in the responses is one of the objects which the good Jew has in mind in praying in public rather than in private.

The shortest form is the following, employed by the Germans on work-days and also in the afternoon of Sabbaths and Festivals:

(The leader opens): We shall hallow thy name in the world, as they hallow it in the heavens on high; as it is written by the hands of thy prophets (Isa. 6: 3): And one called to the other and said:

(All join): Holy, holy, holy is the Lord of Hosts, full is the whole earth of his glory.

(The leader): Opposite to them, they say blessed [Sefardim: Opposite to them they praise and say].

(All join): Blessed be the glory of God from its place (Ezek. 3: 12).

(The leader): And in Thy holy words it is written:

· (All join): The Lord will reign forever, thy God, O Zion, from generation to generation. Halleluiah (Ps. 146: 10).

(The leader): To all ages we will tell of thy greatness, and to all eternity we will proclaim thy holiness; thy praise, our God, shall never cease from our mouth, [Sefardim begin:] for thou art a great, a holy God and King.

On the morning of Sabbaths and Festivals the words introducing the second and third responses are greatly enlarged in a strongly poetic vein; the authorship of the Psalm verse is assigned to "David, son of Jesse, thy righteous Anointed."

In the "additional" prayer of Sabbaths and Festivals the German *Kedusha* runs thus:

(Leader): We shall revere and sanctify thee, as in the secret whisper of the Holy Seraphim, who sanctify thy name in holiness, as it is written by, etc. (to "the whole earth of his glory").

(The leader proceeds): Of his glory the earth is full, his attendants ask each other, where is the place of his glory? Opposite to them they say: Blessed!

(All join): Blessed be the glory of the Lord from its place.

(The leader): May he from his place turn in mercy and show

favor to the people who give unity to his name; evening and morning, each day, unceasingly, in love they twice cry: Hear!

(All join):   Hear, O Israel, the Lord our God, the Lord is One.

(The leader): One is our God. One our Father, One our King, One our Saviour; he will sound forth to us in his mercy again, in the presence of all that liveth, the words: To be your God.

(All join):   I am the Lord your God.[4]

(The Leader): And in thy holy words, etc.

The Sefardim employ the lines, "We shall revere," on work-days and in the Sabbath morning service, and they introduce for the more solemn occasion of the "additional" on Sabbath and Festivals the following introductory lines (which we render with their inversion in order to bring the leading word to the front):

The crown (*Kether*) [O Lord our God], the angels, the crowds on high, give to thee; also thy people, Israel, who are gathered below, all of them as one sound to thee the Thrice-Holy: as it is written, etc.

The divine names as bracketed above are not found in the oldest liturgies. The *Hasidim* have adopted this form with other parts of the Sefardic ritual, and attach importance to its fervid ejaculation. *Kether* has indeed become their badge of recognition.[5]

On the Day of Atonement the *Kedusha* with five responses is recited, not only in the "additional" prayer, but in all the others, at least among the Germans.

Reserving in thought the figure IV for the variable middle parts of the Prayer, we pass now to the last three benedictions. The first of these is known as "The Service" (*Aboda*). Its present form is the following:

V. Be pleased, O Lord our God, with thy people Israel and with their prayer [and return the service to the innermost of thy House]; and receive with favor the fire offerings of Israel and their prayer; and may the service of Israel thy people be always acceptable. [Sefardim insert: And in thy great mercies thou wilt delight in us and accept us] [and may our eyes behold thy merciful return to Zion]; blessed be thou, O Lord [who restoreth his residence to Zion].

The words above put in brackets, "and return," "and may our eyes," were evidently inserted after the destruction of the Temple; and the close of the benediction, "who restoreth," was at the same time substituted for the original words, which are still employed in the Synagogue when the priests are expected to impart the blessing, viz.: "Thou whom alone we shall serve with fear."[6] The words, "And in thy great mercies," were probably a part of the old benediction; they lead well up to its closing keynote.

The word for residence is *Shechina*, the divine presence, which, in the fond belief of our Sages, left Jerusalem when the Law was no longer discussed by the Sanhedrin in the hewn-stone chamber of the destroyed Temple.[7]

The next benediction is called "Thanks," perhaps more correctly "Acknowledgment" (*Hodaïa*). When it is repeated all join with the leader in the opening words, *Modim anahnu lach*," by the first of which the benediction is popularly known. It runs thus:

VI. We acknowledge to thee, that thou, O Lord, art our God, and the God of our fathers forever and ever; rock of our life, shield of our help! thou art the same from age to age. We thank thee and we tell thy praise, for our lives that are delivered in thy hands and for our souls that are entrusted to thee, and for thy miracles that are with us every day, and for thy wonders and thy kind acts that are of every time, evening and morning and noonday. Thou art good; for thy mercies never end; thou art merciful; for thy kindness is never full; from evermore we trust in thee.

And for all these things may thy name be blessed and exalted, always and for evermore.

And all that live will give thanks to thee, and shall truthfully praise thy [great] name, God, our salvation and help. Selah [Sefardim add: the good God]. Blessed be thou, O Lord, thy name is the Good, and to thee it is fit to give thanks.

The next benediction is that of the "Priestly Blessing" (*Bircath Cohanim*). Before the leader repeats it in the morning or in the additional prayer (on the Day of Atonement in the afternoon also, on the Ninth of Ab only in the afternoon), he speaks this petition:

> Our God and God of our fathers, bless us with the threefold blessing that is in the Tora, which is written by Moses thy servant, that is spoken by Aaron and his sons the priests, thy holy people, that is to say: ¹May the Lord bless thee and keep thee; ²may the Lord let his countenance shine unto thee, and be gracious to thee; ³may the Lord lift his countenance to thee, and give thee peace. [Sefardim add (Num. 6: 27): So shall they put my name upon the children of Israel, and I will bless them.]

After each of the three blessings the people answer: Such be the will.[9]

The last benediction itself in its fuller form runs thus:

> VII. Bestow peace, happiness, and blessing, grace, kindness, and mercy, upon us and upon all Israel thy people; bless us, our Father, even all of us, by the light of thy countenance, for by the light of thy countenance thou hast given us, O Lord our God, the law of life, loving-kindness and righteousness and blessing and mercy, life, and peace; and it is good in thy eyes to bless thy people Israel* at every time and at every hour with thy peace. [Sefardim substitute: *with much strength and peace.][10]
> Blessed be thou, O Lord, who blesses his people Israel with peace.

We find here the priestly blessing thrown into the shape of a prayer, while the close in the Sefardic modification is drawn from the last verse of Psalm 29. Those of the German ritual have deemed this full form fit only for the forenoon services, when that blessing can be delivered, and have contrived for the evening and afternoon prayers a much shorter form, thus:

> VII. Thou wilt bestow much peace forever on thy people Israel, for thou art, O King, the Master of all Peace; and it is good in

thy eyes to bless the people Israel at all times, at every time and every hour with thy peace. Blessed be thou, O Lord, who blesseth his people Israel with peace."

The Sefardim use the full form in the Minha and evening as well as in the morning services.

We find no evidence that the first three benedictions were recited in the Temple in connection with the sacerdotal functions; but the last three were.[12]

From a very early day the Prayer has been introduced by the Psalm verse (51: 17), "O Lord (Adonai), open my lips, and may my mouth tell thy praise," and has wound up with another (19: 15), "May the words of my mouth, the meditations of my heart be acceptable before thee, O Lord, my Rock and my Redeemer." They are well chosen, each for its purpose, and are considered by the Talmud as almost of equal age and sacredness with the Prayer; yet they only belong to the silent devotion, and are not repeated by the leader.

When the *Aboda* (Service) is put back, as indicated above, into the form it bore before the fall of the Temple, it will be found that the six constant parts of the Prayer do not contain a single word of un-Biblical Hebrew, and only one that is used in an un-Biblical sense, *Nes*, which in classic Hebrew means a banner, but stands in the "Thanks" for miracle.

A petition found in the Talmud as habitual with its author has become a pendant to the Prayer when spoken silently. The Sefardim put the verse, Ps. 19: 15, both before and after it, the Germans after it only:

My God, guard my tongue from evil, and my lips from speaking guile (see Ps. 34: 14). May my soul be dumb to those that curse me; be it (humble) as dust to all. Open my heart to thy law; may my soul pursue thy commandments, and as for all who think evil against me, do speedily defeat their counsel, and undo their thought. [Do it for the sake of thy name; do it for the sake of thy right hand; do it for the sake of thy holiness; do it for the sake of

the Law.¹ That thy beloved may be delivered, save with thy right
hand and answer me (Ps. 108: 7)."

The bracketed part is of later origin, flowing probably
from a Cabbalistic source.

The Talmud assigns to this piece no place in the order of
worship. Abudraham, in the fourteenth century, remarks
that some "individuals" recite it after the Prayer. The
great Code of the sixteenth century speaks of some men who
recite petitions at this place. But at present the piece is
found in the service books of all the old rituals, more
through its merits than upon any authority.

After everything else the worshipper steps back with these
words, which are also the conclusion of the Kaddish:

He who maketh peace in his high places (Job 25: 2), may he
give peace to us and to all Israel, and say ye: Amen."

CHAPTER VII

MODIFICATIONS OF THE CONSTANT PARTS

A FEW changes in the six constant benedictions and a few insertions which are made in them on certain days or in certain parts of the year must now be noticed.

First come those which are made on the first ten days of Tishri, that is, on New Year and Atonement Days and the days that intervene. They refer in the main to the heavenly judgment which is expected and to the character of King, which more than at other times is assigned to God at this season.

In the first benediction after "in love" there is inserted:

Remember us for life, O King who delightest in life, and write us down in the book of life; for thy sake, living God.

In Hebrew the adjective comes at the end, and is the same word as life. Thus a petition is made part of what otherwise contains only confession and praise.

In the second, after "causing salvation to grow" is inserted:

Who is like thee, Father of mercy, who remembers his creatures to life in mercy.

In the third, the close of the benediction, "Holy God," is changed into "Holy King."

In the last but one there is inserted before the last paragraph:

"O write down for a happy life all the sons of thy covenant;" again the only petition amid confession and thanks

In the last benediction before the close is inserted:

May we be remembered and written in the book of life, of blessing, and of peace, and of good sustenance, we and all thy people the house of Israel, even for happy life and for peace.

And the close is made to read thus: "Blessed be thou, O Lord, who maketh peace," but only in the German Minhag, though at one time this seems to have been the form in daily use.[1]

In the last service of the Day of Atonement (Neïla), the book of Judgment is, by a lively imagination, conceived as already written in our favor; it only needs sealing, hence the above insertions then become, "seal us in the book of life," "seal for a happy life," "may we be remembered and sealed," instead of "write" or "written" or "inscribed."[2]

Second. On the solemn Days of Memorial and Atonement the following petition for the Kingdom of Heaven is inserted before the close of the "Holiness of the Name," or third benediction:

And now, O Lord our God, put thy fear over all thy works, and awe for thee on all thou hast created; may all thy works fear thee, and all creatures bow before thee, and all become one band, to do thy will with full heart; as we know, O Lord our God, that the dominion is with thee, strength in thy hand, and might in thy right arm, and thy name is fearful over all thy creation. And now, O Lord, grant honor to thy people, praise to thy worshippers, hope to those who seek thee, and a free speech to those waiting for thee; gladness to thy land and joy to thy city; a growing horn to David, thy servant, and a shining lamp to the son of Jesse, thy anointed, speedily in our days. Then the righteous will see it and be glad, the upright will triumph, and the pious will sing for joy; wrongdoing will shut its mouth (Job 5: 16) and all wickedness will end as in smoke, when thou drivest the rule of haughtiness from off the earth. And thou, O Lord, wilt reign alone over all thy works, in Zion, the dwelling of thy glory, in Jerusalem, thy holy city, as it is written in thy holy words (Ps. 146: 10): The Lord will reign forever, thy God, O Zion, from generation to generation. Hallelujah.

The next and closing paragraph has at times been used in the daily service as a substitute for the usual benediction,

in which the phrase "Holy God" is taken from the verse
here quoted:

Thou art holy and thy Name is fearful, and there is no God
beside thee, as it is written (Isa. 5: 16): The Lord of Hosts is
exalted in judgment, and the Holy God is sanctified in righteousness.[3]

The benediction closes: "The Holy King," as on the
other seven days of penitence.

Also, on New Year and Atonement Days, only, however,
in the loud recital, and according to the German custom
only in the Additional service and in Neïla (by the Sefardim
also in the morning service), the following petitions (arranged by the alphabet or a part thereof) are inserted in the
last benediction after the request for a favorable entry in
the book of life and before the very close or "sealing" of
the benediction:

(Deut. 4: 4): Ye who cling by the Lord your God are all alive
this day.
   This day thou wilt strengthen us. (Amen.)
   This day thou wilt bless us. (Amen.)
   This day thou wilt raise our stature. (Amen.)
   This day thou wilt seek us out for food. (Amen.)
   This day thou wilt hear our supplication. (Amen.)
   This day thou wilt hold us up with thy righteous hand.

The first line and the general drift is held in common,
but the number and choice of the lines differ as between
the rituals.[4]

Third. The Jewish year is divided into the "days of the
sun," beginning on the first day of the Passover, and the
"days of rain," beginning with the eighth of the Feast. In
the half year of rain, or of fall and winter, "they mention the
powers of rain;" that is, the power of God to send rain is
acknowledged. This is done by inserting in the second
benediction after the words, "thou revivest the dead; art

great to save," these: "He causes the wind to blow and the rain to descend." Both rituals agree in these words for the winter. The Mishna bears witness: They mention the powers of rain in the Resurrection of the Dead. The Sefardim say in the summer months: "He causeth the dew to descend," as they did in Palestine, where dew is an important source of moisture during the summer. In the northern climates inhabited by those of the German ritual, dew is less important, and this phrase was dropped from the Prayer Book, but is retained in the *Mahzor*, or Festival Order, for the first day of Passover, when poetic hymns and prayers about dew are recited, as there are similar hymns and prayers on the eighth day of the Feast for the blessings of rain.

The mention of dew in connection with the revival of the dead was suggested by the verse, Isa. 26: 19. In the poetic pieces, which, on the solemn days, the Germans insert in the repetition of the Prayer, dew and the revival of the dead are always named in one breath.

In the German ritual, after poetical effusions, the leader, in repeating the Additional Prayer on the first day of Passover, intones:

For thou, O Lord our God, causest* the dew to descend.
For a blessing, not for a curse. (All answer) Amen.
For plenty, not for failure. Amen.
For life, not for death. Amen.

On the eighth of the Feast the course is the same, except that he says in the first line: * the wind to blow and the rain to descend.⁵

Fourth. On New Moons and Middle Days, except in the Additional service, the Prayer is the same as on working-days, only the following petition is inserted in the *Aboda* before "bring back," in translating which we omit some of the synonyms and transpose the verbs and nouns in the first part:

Our God and God of our fathers! May the remembrance of ourselves and of our fathers, and of thy anointed servant, the son of
David, and of thy holy city Jerusalem, and of all Israel thy people,
arise and come, be seen and heard before thee, on this day of the
(New Moon) (Feast of Unleavened Bread) (Feast of Booths)
unto deliverance, happiness, life, and peace; remember us thereon,
O Lord our God, for happiness;¹ visit us for blessings²; save us
unto life³; and with words of help and mercy, spare and favor us,
show us mercy! save us! for to thee our eyes are turned: thou art
the gracious and merciful God and King.

When this piece is read by the leader, the others answer
Amen at the points marked (1), (2), (3).⁶

Fifth. On Hanucca and Purim special thanks are offered,
and inserted in the last benediction but one (*Thanks*) after
the words, "from everlasting we hope in thee."

On both occasions:

For the miracles and deliverance, for the salvation and mighty
deeds and battles, which thou hast wrought for our fathers in those
days at this season.

Then on Purim:

In the days of Mordecai and Esther, at Susa, when the wicked
Haman rose against them, and sought to kill and destroy all the
Jews, young and old, women and children, on one day, the thirteenth day of Adar, the twelfth month, and to plunder their spoil;
but thou, in thy great mercy, didst defeat his plan and upset his
counsel, and requite his deserts upon his head, and they hanged
him and his sons upon the tree.

This account is given on Hanucca:

In the days of Mattathia, son of Johanan, the Hasmonean High
Priest, and of his sons, when a wicked Greek kingdom arose
against Israel, to make them forget thy law and transgress thy
decrees; but thou didst in thy great mercy stand by them in their
distress, plead their quarrel, judge their cause, wreak their vengeance; delivering the strong into the hands of the weak, the many
into the hands of the few, the unclean into the hands of the pure
(etc.); and thereafter came thy children to thy sanctuary, cleared

thy Temple (etc.), and lit lamps in thy sacred courts, and established these eight days of Hanucca, to give thanks and praise to thy great Name.

The account of the Maccabean wars here given is true as far as it goes, except that Mattathia never was a High Priest; but it leaves a false impression. The reader is apt to believe that the re-conquest of the Temple ended the struggle. But, in fact, independence was attained only after twenty-five years of almost uninterrupted fighting, while the result which the feast of Hanucca commemorates was reached in three years.

That Hanucca and Purim are mentioned in "Thanks" is spoken of in the Talmud as a matter of course.[7]

Sixth. It was formerly the custom that the "priests" would, on every morning at the Synagogue, deliver the blessing; on Sabbath and Festivals in the morning service and in the "Additional," too, on fast days in the Minha service. For several hundred years they have done it only on the Festivals and generally in the "Additional" service, though the morning service would be more appropriate, as men should perform a religious duty as early in the morning as they can and *before breakfast.* The change from the first to the second service took place in the eighteenth century and on musical grounds; that is, because a better trained singer would lead in the latter service.

Now whenever the priests are desired to do their sacred work, the leader calls upon them by a pre-arranged and well-known sign. In the *Aboda,* after the words, "acceptable before thee," he proceeds:

May our supplication be pleasant before thee like burnt-offering and sacrifice. O thou Merciful Being, in thy great mercy restore thy presence to Zion and the order of service to Jerusalem. May our eyes behold thy return to Zion in mercy, and there we shall serve thee in awe, as in the days of old and in former years (see Mal. 2: 2).

And then he closes the benediction, as shown in the preceding chapter, "thou whom alone we will serve in fear."

The benediction of thanks follows as usual, and the leader as at other times reads the petition which introduces the blessings; whereupon the "priests" say aloud:

Blessed be thou, O Lord our God, King of the world, who has sanctified us with the sanctity of Aaron, and has commanded us to lovingly bless his people Israel.

The words are given out by the leader from a book before him; the priests repeat them one by one.

To each of the three benedictions those present answer *Amen*. It is needless to copy here the verses which are given to the congregation to read to keep them from staring impertinently at the priests during their high function.[8]

Seventh. In the morning of the Ninth of Ab the priests may not confer the blessing, nor does the reader recite it. But the Sefardim go further. In the evening and morning service for this sad day they cut down the last benediction, based on this blessing, to these few words:

Thou who makest peace, bless thy people Israel with much strength and peace, for thou art the Lord of peace. Blessed be thou, O Lord, maker of peace.

CHAPTER VIII

THE WORK-DAY BENEDICTIONS

THE Mishna teaches that when a public fast is proclaimed
in a time of drouth, the man chosen to pray recites twenty-
four benedictions, "the eighteen of every day" and six more.
And in another passage we find: They recite every day
eighteen benedictions, says R. Gamaliel; R. Joshua says,
an abstract of eighteen. Here is the oldest evidence for the
number eighteen, which is still the most popular name for
the Tefilla, or Prayer.[1]

There being the six constant benedictions at the beginning and end, twelve should be left for the middle. But there
are at present thirteen, all of them in the main petitions for
divine help. We shall see which of them is the late intruder.

I. Thou grantest knowledge to man, and teachest mortals understanding;* grant us from thyself knowledge, understanding, and
prudence; blessed be thou, O Lord, who grantest knowledge.

In the evening service after a Sabbath or Festival there
is inserted at *:

[Thou hast favored us to know thy law, and hast taught us to do
the ordinances of thy will], and hast divided, O Lord our God,
between holy and unholy, between light and darkness, between
Israel and the nations, between the Sabbath and the six days of
work. Our Father, our King, let the coming days begin in peace,
free from all sin, clean from all wrong, and firm in the fear of thee.

R. Akiba proposed to put this Separation (*Habdala*) into
another benediction by itself, but was overruled, because
"our Sages have instituted eighteen," not nineteen. The

bracketed part, a needless repetition, is not found in the oldest service books.[2]

II. Bring us back, our Father, to thy Law; keep us near, our King, to thy service, and cause us to return in perfect repentance before thee; blessed be thou, O Lord, who acceptest repentance.

The Hebrew word for repentance (*Teshuba*), literally "return," means in religious parlance the turning back from a wicked to a God-fearing life. It never, either in the Bible or in the older liturgy, stands for acts of penance or feelings of regret for sins committed; it does sometimes take such a meaning in the later Cabbala, as a sort of reflex from Christianity.

III. Forgive us, our Father, for we have sinned; pardon us, our King, for we have transgressed; for thou pardonest and forgivest. Blessed be thou, O Lord, the gracious, who often forgivest.

The second and the third benediction each contains a non-Biblical root; that of the verb which we render "to return," which is, however, pure Hebrew, and that rendered "pardon," which is rather Aramaic. The first was chosen to avoid a repetition of the root contained in *Teshuba* (repentance); the other to keep up the parallelism of the two half-lines: Forgive—pardon; Father—King; sinned—transgressed, in the style which pervades all the poetical books of the Bible. Between sin and transgression there is, however, a broad distinction; the former being the result of carelessness, ignorance, or weakness; the latter, of defiance.

IV. Look but upon our affliction, and plead our cause, and redeem us speedily for the sake of thy name; for thou art a powerful redeemer; blessed be thou, O Lord, the Redeemer of Israel.

Unlike some great Hebrew scholars, I do not believe that this petition for help in need was not composed or used during the reign of the Hasmoneans, because the country

9

was prosperous, nor in that of Herod, because he would have forbidden it as an aspersion on his government. The best of times leaves room enough for improvement. Samaria at a few miles distance from the capital stood out defiantly, hindering the union of Israel into one people. War threatened from abroad; civil strife from within. There were many short crops, a few famines. The Jews in the dispersion, in Alexandria, on the Euphrates, in Rome, often suffered from persecution. There is no nation nor church that does not, in a like strain, pray to God for help. And Herod would not any more than Czar Alexander III have forbidden such a prayer.

V. Heal us and we shall be healed; save us and we shall be saved; for thou art our praise. (See Jer. 17: 14.) And bring a full healing for all our sores; for thou, God, King, art a true and merciful physician; blessed be thou, O Lord, who healest the sick of his people Israel. (See Ex. 15: 26.)

So far the Sefardic forms differ from the German forms here given only by adding here and there a few expletive words.

VI. Bless for us, O Lord our God, this year and all kinds of its produce for the best; and give (dew and rain for) a blessing upon the face of the earth; fill us from thy bounty, and bless our year that it be as the good years. Blessed be thou, O Lord, who blessest the years.

The words "dew and rain for" are inserted in winter, when, in the old seats of the dispersion, rain was needed to ripen the crops; beginning with the sixtieth day after the autumnal equinox and ending with the Passover. As the equinoxes were for this purpose counted by the Julian year, the sixtieth day is now December 4th. There was much discussion between the Babylonians and Palestinians, and formerly the Jews of several countries were divided in their allegiance. Modern Rabbis, like Dr. Geiger, have sensibly proposed to pray all the year around that God may give dew and rain for a blessing; we do not pray for floods or cloud-bursts. It is natural to ask for rain in this benediction; the Mishna already bears witness: They ask for rain in the Blessing of the Years.

In the Sefardic ritual the prayer which introduces the benediction is different throughout on the days when rain is asked for and those on which it is not. The latter takes the following shape, and contains a request for dew:

VI. Bless us, O our Father, in all the work of our hands, and bless our year with gracious, blessed, and kindly dews; be its end life, plenty, and peace as in good years; for thou, O God, art good and doest good, and blessest the years; blessed be thou, O Lord, who blessest the years.

Here are thirty Hebrew words; the Sefardic benediction for the rainy season contains eighty-five.[3]

VII. Blow the great trumpet (*Shofar*) for our freedom, and lift a banner to gather our exiles, and gather us into one body from the four corners of the earth; blessed be thou, O Lord, who gatherest the outcasts of his people Israel.

The request or introductory part undoubtedly underwent some changes when the Temple was destroyed, when the last shreds of autonomy were taken from the Jews of Palestine, and the great majority of the Jews were in exile. But there could have been such a benediction, closing as this does, while the Temple stood. While the House of David reigned, Isaiah said (Isa. 27: 13): "It shall come to pass on that day, that the great trumpet shall be blown, and they shall come that perish in the land of Assyria, and that are outcasts in the land of Egypt." And Psalm 106, written during the second Commonwealth, says at its close: "Save us, O Lord, and gather us from the nations." Psalm 147 praises God who "gathers the outcasts of Israel." The Jewish settlements in Babylonia and Egypt might have been a cause of pride; outposts of the true faith among the heathen; seed-plants of a universal church; but from these Psalms it is apparent that the Palestinian Sages who wrote Psalms, or admitted them into the Canon, did not look at matters in that light.

The same remark applies to the next benediction:

VIII. Restore our judges as at the first, and our counsellors as at the beginning (Isa. 1: 26), and remove from us grief and sighing; reign over us, thou, O Lord, alone in kindness and mercy, and justify us in the judgment. Blessed be thou, O Lord,* the King who lovest righteousness and justice. (On the penitential days:* the King of justice.)

This benediction may have been drawn up just as it stands, when men in full touch with the most religious and patriotic feeling filled the highest courts; for such men would naturally look back to the days of Moses and his seventy associates, or even to King David and the judges whom he installed, though they exceeded David and his contemporaries both in learning and in the love of justice. Deeply religious men have ever looked up with respect to the heroic age of the fathers, and the prediction of Isaiah, that there should again be judges as in the olden days, became to them a prayer.

The next benediction is found in many forms, due not so much to differing tastes among Jews as to the whims of this or that Christian censor.

IX. May no hope be left to the slanderers; may all wickedness perish as in a moment; may all thy enemies be soon cut off, and do thou speedily uproot the haughty, and shatter and humble them speedily in our days; blessed be thou, O Lord, who strikest down enemies, and humblest the haughty.

This is from a Wilna edition of 1892. A note explains slanderers by the well-known Hebrew word for informers. Such there were in Roman times, who for gain delivered their brethren over to the heartless oppressor, and brought many to a painful death. The invocation against these wretches is the same in all editions.

In a South German Prayer Book of 1821 the second clause is not so liberal; unlike the noble wife of R. Meïr, who wished only that sins, not sinners, would perish, the editor frames it: "May all doers of wickedness perish, etc." On the other hand he is satisfied with humbling the haughty, and leaves off the uprooting and shattering.

The Sefardic service book, printed in Amsterdam in 1658, differs from both by the request for the uprooting of the "kingdom of wickedness." Elsewhere on the Continent that phrase was suppressed by the censorship.

The Sefardic prayer books published in England and America, free from all constraint, have it: "May all *Minim* perish;" they render this word by apostates, and such is undoubtedly the old form.

A Baraïtha in the Babylonian Talmud gives this account of Benediction IX:

"Simeon, the cotton dealer, arranged the eighteen benedictions in order before Rabban Gamaliel (the Second, about 100) at Jamnia; then R. Gamaliel said to the Sages: Who can draw up a benediction about the Sadducees? Then Samuel the Little arose, and drew it up. Next year he had forgotten it."

The Talmud, speaking at a later date, remarks: If the leader makes a mistake about this benediction he is stopped, for they suspect him of being an apostate (Min).[4]

Though all prayer books now agree on "Slanderers" (*Malshinim*) in the first petition, and though there are strong reasons for using such a word, it was originally "Perverts" (*Mumarim* or *Meshummadim*). Both Christians and Mohammedans objected to hearing converts to their faith openly cursed, and the words, "kingdom of haughtiness," were taken as a direct attack upon every government under which the Jews lived, and had to be dropped in many places under outside pressure.

From all these testimonies different inferences have been drawn by modern scholars. Some maintain that there had been a prayer against the Sadducees in earlier times, which had fallen into disuse, and that R. Gamaliel of Jamnia wished to have a similar prayer drawn up against the internal enemies of Judaism of his own time. There is hardly evidence enough to sustain such a position. The Patriarch would have known the old formula, and need not have deputed Samuel the Little to draw up another. The more natural inference is this: During the time of the Patriarchate at Jamnia the Sadducees were still dangerous, and were designated as *Minim* (Sectaries), as they are also called in a section of the Mishna which speaks of "mischievous *Minim* who said there is only one world." Not long afterwards they became few and harmless, and gradually disappeared. Meanwhile Jewish or Ebionite Christians became numerous in Palestine; the word *Minim* was transferred to them. The new faith made much progress among the unlearned, the "People of the Land." Without being changed, the formula was in thought applied to them, for they threatened great danger to Israel's further existence as a religious community. The prayer that they should speedily perish was in one sense fulfilled; for in the third century they were absorbed in the Catholic Church; they became simply Gentiles. Toward such the Jew has never shown any animosity, except when persecuted by them; they were to them in peace friends, in war enemies. The Christians of our day are not *Minim*, that is, Jewish sectaries, and need not take offence at the word, which at one time denoted a part of their religious progenitors.[6]

X. May thy mercies, O Lord our God, be aroused over the righteous, and over the pious, and over the elders of thy people, the House of Israel, and over the remnant of their scribes, and over the righteous converts, and over us; and give a goodly reward to those who truly trust in thy name; and set our share with them forever; and may we not come to shame for that we have trusted in thee; blessed be thou, O Lord, support and trust to the righteous.

The "righteous," named first in the request and alone at the close, are to be understood in a general sense, not as a party or a class. Hence the benediction may have been written before any of the events happened which gave rise to the classes prayed for. The "pious" are those intensely patriotic men who, gathering around Mattathia, bore the brunt of the fight against Antiochus; the "elders" are those who reached that office through learning and piety, not by wealth or priestly descent; the "remnant of their scribes" probably referred to the Pharisaic scholars who escaped the slaughter ordered by Alexander Jannæus, and who were, at the instance of his wife, Salome, recalled to the Sanhedrin. The "righteous converts" are Gentiles who take upon themselves the whole Mosaic Law, while "converts of the gate" only bind themselves to monotheism and to the leading rules of the moral law. As there had been thousands of conversions in Galilee at a very early day, as the Idumeans were converted *en masse* in the reign of John Hyrcanus, and as many of the heathen were converted while the Temple stood, it is hard to say when the reference to the "righteous converts" was inserted.

XI. Return in mercy to thy city [Jerusalem] and dwell in her midst as thou hast spoken; build it speedily in our days as an everlasting structure [and set up speedily therein the throne of David]. Blessed be thou, O Lord, the builder of Jerusalem.

The parts in brackets are omitted in the Sefardic ritual, at least according to the older standards. The petition about the throne of David anticipates the next number.

This benediction is older than the destruction of the city; it is based on the words of Psalm 147, "the Lord buildeth Jerusalem," and it might have been spoken in its earliest days pretty much as in the short form used by the Sefardim. The first clause in the German rendition is, of course, a later addition.

On the Ninth of Ab in the afternoon service the following

sad reflections are inserted in XII before the close of the benediction, and this is also modified:

Comfort, O Lord our God, the mourners of Zion and of Jerusalem, and the mourning, wasted, despised, and desolate city; she mourns for the loss of her children; she is wasted of her dwellings: she is despised and without her glory and desolate without inhabitants. She sitteth and her head is veiled, like a barren woman who has not borne. The legions swallowed her, idol worshippers conquered her, and they took off thy people Israel by the sword, and killed wantonly the saints of the Most High. Therefore Zion weeps bitterly, and Jerusalem lifts her voice; my heart, my heart for the slain! my inwards, my inwards for the slain! But thou, O Lord, hast burned her with fire, and with fire thou wilt hereafter build her, as it is said (Zech. 2: 9): I shall be unto her, says the Lord, a wall of fire round about, and I shall be for glory in her midst. Blessed be thou, O Lord, who comfortest Zion and buildest Jerusalem.

This is the German form; the Sefardic is somewhat shorter. That given in the Talmud begins with the word, "Have mercy" (*Rahem*), not as at present "Comfort" (*Nahem*).[6]

The greatest difficulty hangs over the next benediction:

XII. Let the sprout of thy servant David grow speedily, and may his horn be high through thy salvation; because for thy salvation we hope every day. Blessed be thou, O Lord, who causes the horn of salvation to grow.

The two rituals agree here in every word.

The close of the benediction does not point to an expected Messiah; the first part of the short introduction may be understood in such a sense. As only the closing words were originally fixed, all the rest being liquid and changeable, the antiquity of XII could be maintained on the same ground as that of VII, VIII, and X.

When during the reign of Herod the Messianic idea began to rise in many minds, those full of it may have expressed their hopes and wishes on that subject when about to bless him who raises the horn of salvation, and when

Simeon, the cotton dealer, came to draw up his fixed forms at Jamnia, the prayer for a speedy advent had become a part of this benediction.

There is another ground on which to maintain the place of this benediction in the work-day Amida as first constituted. Though the hope in a world-saving Messiah may have only taken shape in the last years of Herod's reign, yet during much, perhaps during all the time of the second Temple, a feeling prevailed that the restoration of the House of David on the throne would mean the nation's welfare and glory, and be the surest mark of God's favor. The next King of that House need not be a precursor of the millennium, nor an inspired poet like David, but only a righteous man and gallant patriot such as King Josiah was. He would marry and have children; he would die and leave his kingdom to his eldest son. This idea runs through several Psalms that are clearly post-exilic, for instance, 89 and 132. Now the words of request in benediction XII ask for no more than such a King of David's seed, not for a Messiah in the later Jewish or in the Christian sense.

But the Jerusalem Talmud seems in two passages to ignore Benediction XII or to combine it with the preceding one, and an old Midrash gives seventeen as the original tale of benedictions, and rather implies that XII was added after IX.[7]

Still the weight of evidence and reason seems to lie on the side of the common opinion: that the work-day benedictions were originally twelve, and that IX was added at the instance of R. Gamaliel II to these twelve.[8]

XIII. Hear our voice, O Lord our God, spare and have mercy upon us, and receive in love and favor our prayer; for thou art the God who hearest prayers and supplications; and do not, thou our King, send us back empty-handed from thy presence. For thou hearest the prayers of thy people Israel in mercy. (Sefardim say: For thou hearest the prayer of every mouth). Blessed be thou, O Lord, he who heareth prayer. (See Ps. 65: 3.)

After the word "presence" the devout Israelite will bring forward, in the silent Prayer, anything that is upon his heart, and ask God's help, either for himself or his household or for the community. On the public fasts, those who do fast insert in this place the following petition:

Answer us, O Lord, answer us on the day of our fast: for we are in great distress; do not turn towards our wickedness: hide not thy face from us: withhold not thyself from our supplications; be near when we beseech thee; may thy kindness come to comfort us; even before we call unto thee, answer us; after thy promise, wherein it is said (Isa. 65: 24): It shall come to pass that before they call, I will answer; when yet they speak, I will hear. For thou art he that answers in the time of distress, who redeems and delivers at every time of distress and trouble.

When the leader on public fasts repeats the Prayer, he makes of the above a separate benediction, and closes, "Blessed be thou, O Lord, who answerest in the time of distress." It is inserted between those above numbered IV and V, and this addition to the regular order is no infringement of the rule of "eighteen" and no more; for such benediction is, at least by its conclusion, one of the six which were in olden times pronounced on public fasts.[9]

The work-day Prayer thus consists of the first three given in the preceding chapter, the twelve or thirteen benedictions above, and again the last three of that chapter. But an opinion is expressed in the Mishna that "an abstract of the eighteen" is sufficient. This means the first three and last three unchanged; the abstract of the middle benedictions is thus reported in the Talmud:

(1) Give us insight, O Lord our God, to know thy ways, (2) and circumcise our hearts that we may fear thee; (3) and forgive us (4) that we may be redeemed; (5) free us from our ailments, (6) and nourish us from the fields of thy earth, (7) and gather our scattered fragments from the four winds; (8) may the erring be judged by thy opinion, (9) and swing thy hand over the wicked; (10) and may the righteous be gladdened (11) by the upbuilding of thy

city, (12) by the growing horn of thy servant David, and when the lamp of the son of Jesse thy anointed is set in place; (13) before we call thou wilt answer (another reading adds: for thou answerest in all time of distress). Blessed be thou, O Lord, who hearest prayer.

Samuel of Nehardea (about 240) gave this composition for what was meant by "an abstract of the eighteen," and he is the author of this, as he was of other prayers. Its use was discouraged by other Rabbis; but few Prayer Books contain it, and few Jews have ever seen it or come across it otherwise than in their Talmudic studies. It is remarkable that the hope for the coming of the Messiah is here expressed more unequivocally than in Benediction XII when recited in full; and the word Messiah is used in the abstract, but not in the original.

Another reading of Samuel's abstract makes the eighth petition read: "May the erring judge by thy opinion;" i. e., we pray that the judges who now give unjust judgments may hereafter give righteous ones; and for the ninth, another reading has it: "Swing thy hand over wickedness." The abstract given in the Palestinian Talmud differs from Samuel's in almost every petition, but shows a common origin by starting with the same word.[10]

CHAPTER IX

THE MIDDLE BENEDICTION ON DAYS OF REST

THE sixteenth chapter of Exodus tells us that double portions of manna fell on Friday, none on the Sabbath, and thus teaches that on the latter day we should be free from care. The idea is carried into the Prayer Book; on days of rest we do not petition for our daily wants; the twelve (or thirteen) work-day benedictions are left off, and one known as "Sanctity of the Day" takes their place. It differs according to the day, but always closes: Blessed be thou, O Lord, who sanctifies ——, the name of the day follows immediately or mediately.

The Mishna speaks of "Sanctity of the Day" as one of the benedictions on the Day of Memorial; the number seven of the Sabbath benedictions is treated in the Talmud throughout as well-known, and many a well-attested Baraïtha discusses this benediction as recited on other Festivals and on the Sabbath. The pure Hebrew of the more essential parts also indicates an early origin.[1]

I. On the Sabbath (not on a Festival) the introductory part of the "Sanctity of the Day" has four different forms for the four services of the day; the constant part is short and almost literally the same in the two rituals:

Our God and God of our fathers! be pleased with our rest; sanctify us by thy commandments, give us a share in thy law; fill us from thy bounty, and gladden us [or: our hearts] in thy salvation; and cleanse our hearts to serve thee in truth; let us inherit, O Lord our God, in love and favor, thy holy Sabbath, and may Israel who hallow [or: love] thy name rest thereon: blessed be thou, O Lord, who sanctifieth the Sabbath.

(140)

The closing words are meant for a literal compliance with the injunction, "Remember the Sabbath day to hallow it," especially when spoken in the evening, or first, service.

The introductions for the four services are undoubtedly of much later origin, that for Friday evening being the simplest in style, but hardly the oldest:

Thou hast sanctified the seventh day to thy name, the conclusion of the work of the heaven and of the earth, and hast blessed it beyond all days, and hallowed it beyond all seasons; and it is thus written in thy Law (Gen. 2: 1-3): And the heavens and the earth were finished and all the hosts of them. And on the seventh day God finished his work which he had made; and he rested on the seventh day from all the work which he had made; and God blessed the seventh day and hallowed it; for on it he rested from all his work which God created and made.

(The Sefardim here add the following lines, which the Germans have only in Musaf:)

Those who keep the Sabbath feel glad in thy kingdom, and those who call it a delight; the people who hallow the seventh day, *all of them will be filled and delighted with thy goodness; yea, with the seventh day thou hast been pleased, and hast hallowed it, and called it the most precious of days.

A wholly different introduction is found in the oldest sources.

In the morning service the introduction reads thus:

Moses is glad in the gift of his lot; for thou didst call him a faithful servant; thou didst put a crown of glory on his head, when he stood before thee on Mount Sinai; he brought down the two tables of stone on which the observance of the Sabbath was written, and thus it was written in thy Law: "Israel shall keep the Sabbath, to make the Sabbath an everlasting covenant for their generations. Between me and the children of Israel it is an everlasting sign, that the Lord made in six days the heavens and the earth, and that on the seventh day he rested and was refreshed."

And thou didst not give it, O Lord our God, to the nations of the lands, nor make it an inheritance for the worshippers of idols,

nor do the uncircumcised dwell in its quiet; but thou hast granted
it lovingly to thy people Israel, the seed of Jacob, the well-beloved;
*all of them will be filled, etc. (as above), in memory of the work
of Creation.

This piece rests on an Aggadta, according to which the
revelation on Sinai took place on a Sabbath morning, but it
is probably the oldest extant written form of that Aggadta.

Leaving for another chapter the introductory part of
the benediction in Musaf, we come to that in the afternoon
service, which has also a Haggadistic tinge, as it ascribes
to Abraham, Isaac, and Jacob the observance of the Sabbath:

Thou art one, and thy name is one; and what one nation is there
like thy people Israel? Thou hast given to thy people beauty and
greatness, and the crown of salvation; a day of rest and holiness.
Abraham would rejoice, Isaac would sing, Jacob and his sons rest
on the same; a rest of love and free will, a rest of trust and faith, a
rest of peace and calmness and confidence, a perfect rest with which
thou art pleased. May thy sons learn and know, that their rest
comes from thee, and may they for their rest hallow thy name.²

Then each of the services is continued: "Our God and
God," as first shown.

The "abstract of seven," which the leader chants on Friday evening, and its object, to lengthen the service of that
evening sufficiently for early and late comers to meet at
the Synagogue, have been mentioned in Chapter I. Another
motive probably was to have the remembrance and hallowing of the Sabbath sounded forth in loud tones and not
confined to a whispered Prayer.

This "abstract of seven" gives the middle benediction
more than in full and a good part of the first, very little of
the others. After reciting the first three verses of Genesis
2, the leader chants:

(1) Blessed be thou, O Lord our God, and God of our fathers,
God of Abraham, God of Isaac, and God of Jacob, the great and

mighty and fearful God, God Most High, owner of heaven and earth. Shield of the fathers by his word, (2) who reviveth the dead by his command, (3) the holy God, like whom there is no other, (4) who giveth rest to his people on his holy Sabbath; (5) before him we shall worship in fear and awe, (6) and we shall give thanks to his name every day unceasingly, to the fountain of blessings, the God of thanksgivings, (7) the Lord of peace (4) who sanctifieth the Sabbath, and blesseth the seventh day, and giveth a rest in holiness to a people sated with delight, a remembrance of the work of creation.'

Then follows the constant part of the middle benediction, so that the leader pronounces at the end, "Who sanctifiest the Sabbath."

It has been suspected that the words above rendered, "fountain of blessings," mean really "abstract of benedictions," and are the title of the composition, which has gotten into its text by the blunder of some copyist. But this could hardly have happened.

II. On Festivals (including those occurring on the Sabbath) the "Sanctity of the Day" is made up of several paragraphs, the first of which is constant and reads thus:

Thou hast chosen us from all the nations, hast loved us, and wast pleased with us; thou hast lifted us above all tongues, and hast hallowed us by thy commandments, and hast brought us, O our King, to thy service, and hast pronounced upon us thy great and holy name.

The next paragraph contains the name and purpose of the special Feast, and, if spoken on the Sabbath, the name and purpose of the latter before that of the Feast. For the Passover days it reads thus:

And thou hast given us, O Lord our God, lovingly (Sabbaths for rest) set times and seasons for joy, (this Sabbath day, a day of our rest, and) this day of the Feast of Unleavened Bread [Sefardim say here: this Holiday], the season of our enfranchisement, a holy convocation, a memorial of the going forth from Egypt.

This is modified on other Festivals thus:

This day of the Feast of Weeks,—the day when our Law was given.

This day of the Feast of Booths,—the day of our gladness.

This Eighth Day, the rest day of the Feast—the day of our gladness.

The Day of Memorial not being one of a class of days, the paragraph takes on it this simpler form:

And thou hast given us, O Lord our God, lovingly (this Sabbath for rest and) this Day of Memorial, a day of alarm sound, a holy convocation, a memorial of the going forth from Egypt.

And so on the Day of Atonement:

And thou hast given us, O Lord our God, lovingly (this Sabbath for rest and) this Day of Atonement for forgiveness and atonement, and to pardon thereon all our iniquities, a holy convocation, a memorial of the going forth from Egypt.

The next paragraph is the same which on New Moons and Middle Days is inserted in the *Aboda*, the name of the Festival alone being inserted in the proper place, not its purpose; nor is the Sabbath referred to in it. It belongs to all the services except the "Additional."

Our God and God of our fathers! May the remembrance of ourselves and of our fathers, and of thy anointed servant the son of David, and of thy holy city Jerusalem, and of all Israel thy people, *arise and come*, be seen and heard before thee, on this day (of the Feast of Unleavened Bread), (of the Feast of Weeks), (of Memorial), (of Atonement), (of Booths), (the Eighth, the rest day of the Feast) unto deliverance, happiness, life, and peace; remember us thereon, O Lord our God, for happiness, visit us for blessings; save us unto life, and with words of help and mercy, spare and favor us, show us mercy! save us! for to thee our eyes are turned; thou art the gracious and merciful God and King.

The final part of the benediction for the three Festivals of joy contains an introductory petition as compared with that for the Sabbath,* which was formerly inserted also on the two solemn Festivals, as follows:

Let us receive, O Lord our God, the blessing of thy appointed times, for life and peace, for gladness and joy, as thou hast in thy favor promised to bless us; (*on Sabbaths:* Our God and God of our fathers, be pleased with our rest); hallow us by thy commandments, and give us a share in thy law; fill us from thy bounty, and gladden us in thy salvation; and cleanse our hearts to serve thee in truth; let us inherit, O Lord our God (in love and favor), in gladness and in joy, (the Sabbath and) thy holy times; and may Israel, who hallow [or: love] thy name, rejoice thereon; blessed be thou, O Lord, who sanctifieth (the Sabbath and) Israel and the seasons.⁴

It will be noticed that while the Sabbath is "sanctified" before and independently of Israel, being older than the chosen people, the Festivals, called here the "seasons" or times, are named only after Israel, for whose benefit they were instituted.

On the Day of Memorial a petition for the coming of the Kingdom of Heaven is now inserted in the close of this benediction in all the services. It seems that at first the Kingdom was prayed for only in the "Additional Service." Now, however, and probably for a thousand years, the last part of the benediction for all the four services runs thus:

Our God and God of our fathers! reign over all the world in thy glory; arise over all the earth in thy majesty; and shine in thy triumphant power over all the dwellers of thy inhabited earth! May every one that is made know that thou hast made him, and every creature understand that thou hast shaped it; may every one who hath breath in his nostrils say: The Lord, the God of Israel, is King, and his Kingdom ruleth over all.* Sanctify us with thy commandments, and give us a share in thy law; fill us from thy bounty and gladden us in thy salvation,** and cleanse our hearts to serve thee in truth; for thou art God in truth, and thy word is true and standeth forever. Blessed be thou, O Lord, King over all the earth, who sanctifieth (the Sabbath and) Israel and the Day of Memorial.⁵

At * the Germans insert on the Sabbath, "Our God and God of our fathers, be pleased with our rest;" at **, "and

10

let us inherit, O Lord our God, in love and in favor, thy holy Sabbaths, and may Israel, who hallow thy name, rest thereon." So also at the corresponding places on the Day of Atonement, when the benediction reads thus:

Our God and God of our fathers! pardon our iniquities on this (Sabbath and) Day of Atonement; blot out and remove our transgressions and sins from before thine eyes; as it is written (Isa. 43: 25): I, even I, am he that blotteth out thy transgressions for my own sake, and I will not remember thy sins; and it is said (Isa. 44: 22): I have blotted out thy transgressions like a dark cloud, and as a vapor, thy sins; return to me, for I have redeemed thee; and it is said (Lev. 16: 30): For on that day he will atone for you to cleanse you from all your sins; before the Lord you shall be clean.* Sanctify us with thy commandments, and give us a share in thy law; fill us from thy bounty and gladden us in thy salvation;** and cleanse our hearts to serve thee in truth [for thou art forgiving to Israel, and holdest out pardon to the tribes of Jeshurun in every age; and we have no King, Forgiver or Pardoner beside thee]. Blessed art thou, O Lord, King who pardoneth and forgiveth our iniquities and those of all Israel, and removeth our guilt from year to year, King over all the earth, who sanctifieth (the Sabbath and) Israel and the Day of Atonement.

The clause in brackets is not in the older sources; its first part was chosen to lead up to the close of the benediction; the latter part sounds like a protest against Christianity. The conclusion is much longer than any other and for that reason suspicious; but the Mishna speaks of a benediction about the "pardoning of iniquity" which the High Priest pronounced in the Temple, and this is explained in the Talmud to be the one then in use as the "Sanctity of the Day;" hence it is probable that both subjects were named in the conclusion.[6] The Sefardim would formerly insert, "Let us receive," from the benediction of the three Festivals in that of the Day of Memorial, and the prayer for the Kingdom from this in the benediction for the Day of Atonement; but under the authority of R. Joseph Karo's Code, their Prayer Books now agree with those of the

Germans in the former matter, while they still retain the prayer for the Kingdom of Heaven on Atonement Day.

One piece may be inserted in the "Sanctity of the Day," viz., when a Festival (which never happens with the Day of Atonement) is on a Sunday; there is a Separation (*Habdala*) in the Saturday night service, just as in the work-day Prayer; for the Festival is of lower sanctity than the Sabbath. It is made to follow the second paragraph, in which the Festival is named, and it reads thus (some redundancies being clipped):

Thou hast made us know, O Lord our God, thy righteous judgments, and taught us to act by the decrees of thy will [hast given us just rules, true laws, good statutes, and commandments]; hast made us heirs to seasons of joy, sacred set times and generous feasts, possessors of the holiness of the Sabbath and of the glory of the Festival. Thou hast divided between holy and profane, light and darkness, Israel and the nations, the seventh day and the six work-days; also between the holiness of the Sabbath and that of the Feast, and hast sanctified the seventh day from all days, and distinguished and hallowed thy people Israel through thy holiness.

The bracketed sentence is not in the form which the Talmud gives for the occasion.[7]

So much for the benediction in all its present forms. As to its antiquity, it appears that the schools of Hillel and Shammaï already discussed (perhaps in King Herod's days) as to how it should be framed on a day both Sabbath and Festival. Shammaï's school proposed to have two separate benedictions; that of Hillel, which, as usual, prevailed, to have one benediction, begin therein with the Sabbath (as we do now, for the first paragraph refers to neither), then speak of the Festival in the middle, and close with the Sabbath alone. But R. Judah the Patriarch carried the Festival also into the conclusion, which on the Day of Atonement must have always been done.[8]

CHAPTER X

THE "ADDITIONAL," OR MUSAF

THE "Additional" follows the morning service on the days
for which the Law (Num. 28 and 29) prescribes the offerings in addition to the continual, or daily, i. e., on Sabbath,
New Moons, the three Festivals, and the Days of Memorial
and Atonement. The first three and the last three benedictions were always parts of it. On the Day of Memorial
there are three middle benedictions, on other days only one,
a modified "Sanctity of the Day." Its last part (except on
New Moons) is the same as in the other services, but there
is an introductory part, setting forth that we ought to bring
certain offerings on the day, and a petition that we may
again be enabled to do so.

The "Additional" was instituted to stand in place of the
additional offerings, just as the morning and afternoon
Prayer stood in place of the morning and the evening lamb,
before sacrifices had come to an end, as the overwhelming
majority of the people could not witness the offerings in
the Temple Court. The daily lamb is not mentioned in the
morning or afternoon Prayer, hence the additional sacrifices were probably not mentioned in the "Additional" as
first drawn up.

It is within reason that on a day which the law of sacrifice denotes as especially holy a man should pray more or
oftener than on other days; but not that he should in his
devotion refer to that law. As far as the allusions of the
Mishna go at the date of its conclusion, the "Prayer of the
Additionals" may have been only a repetition of the morning Prayer, though for one hundred and fifty years there

had been ground to pray for a restoration of the day's offerings.[1]

Let us begin with the middle benediction of the Musaf for a plain Sabbath, as distinguished from Sabbath and New Moon or Sabbath and a Festival. The Sefardic form is given first as the simpler of the two:

Thou hast delivered to Moses upon Mount Sinai the commandment of the Sabbath: Remember! observe!* and thou hast commanded us, O Lord our God, to offer thereon additional offering according to rule. May it be thy will, O Lord our God and God of our fathers, to bring us in gladness to our land, and to plant us in our borders; there we shall perform before thee the offerings as in duty bound, the daily and additional after their order and rule. Even the additional of this day of rest, we shall prepare and offer before thee lovingly, according to the command of thy will, as thou hast written it for us in thy Law, through Moses thy servant, in these words (Num. 28: 9, 10): "And on the Sabbath day two yearling lambs without blemish, and two tenth parts of fine flour for a meal-offering, stirred in oil, and its drink-offering. The burnt-offering of the Sabbath for the Sabbath, beside the daily burnt-offering and its drink-offering."

May those who keep the Sabbath be glad in thy Kingdom, those who call it a delight, the people who sanctify the seventh day, may they all be filled and delighted from thy bounty; thou wast pleased with the seventh day, and didst hallow it, and call it the most precious of days [Germans add: a memorial of the days of Creation].

In place of the first part to (*) the German ritual (supported herein by the authority of R. Amram and of R. Saadia, which the Sefardim generally follow but here reject)[2] has a labored composition of which the first twenty-two words run in the inverted order of the alphabet. What follows after (*) differs only in grammatic forms, which do not show in English; the rest is unchanged:

Thou hast built up the Sabbath, wast pleased with its offerings, didst command its details, with the order of its drink offering; those delighted by it will forever inherit glory; those who taste it deserve the life; even those who love to speak thereof have chosen greatness. Then they were commanded concerning it from Sinai.'

This request for the renewal of the sacrificial service is fuller in the Musaf of the Festivals and more objectionable to modern thought, because on those days it starts with the assertion that the dispersion of Israel and the destruction of the Temple were caused by "our sins" or the sins of our fathers eighteen hundred years ago, and was not brought about by a wise Providence to substitute the more spiritual worship of the Synagogue for that of the altar. The formula is known by its opening words (*U-mippene hataenu*), and is one of the first banished, wherever men deal boldly with the liturgy:

On account of our sins we have been exiled from our country, and removed from our soil, and we can no longer (add on the three joyous Feasts: go up and appear and) worship and perform our duty before thee in the House of thy choice, in the great and holy house, on which thy Name was pronounced; by reason of the hand that was stretched forth against thy sanctuary. Be it thy will, O Lord, our God and God of our fathers, merciful King, again to show mercy to us and to thy sanctuary, to build it soon and to heighten its glory. Our Father, our King, reveal speedily to us the glory of thy Kingdom, and shine forth and rise over us in the sight of every living creature; bring home our scattered remnant from out of the nations, and assemble our broken parts from the ends of the earth; and bring us to thy city Zion in song, and to thy sanctuary at Jerusalem with everlasting joy; and there we shall prepare and offer before thee, as in duty bound, our sacrifices, the daily and the additional, according to their order and their rules; and the additional sacrifices of this (Sabbath and of this) Feast of Unleavened Bread (or of Weeks, or Day of Memorial, etc.), we shall prepare and offer before thee as thou hast written it for us in thy law, by the hands of thy servant Moses, from the mouth of thy glory, as it is spoken:

Here the Sefardim stop, not quoting the verses from Numbers 28 and 29, in which the sacrifices for each day are set forth, because they have already been read in the

Pentateuch lessons.⁴ On the Sabbath they proceed as above with Numbers 28: 9, 10.

The Germans quote on every Festival the verses for the day, abridging in general words the rules for meal and drink offerings. On Saturday all add, as on a plain Sabbath, "May those who keep," as above.

This ends for the Days of Memorial and of Atonement all reference to the Temple service, but on the three Festivals, on which every male Israelite was bidden to "go up and appear" at the spot which God would choose, this further petition is put up:

Our God and God of our fathers, merciful King, show us mercy; thou, the good and benignant, allow us to seek thee! Return to us in thy manifold mercies for the sake of our fathers, who performed thy will. Build thy house as at the first; set up thy sanctuary on its foundation. Let us live to see when it is built; gladden us in its restoration. Restore the priests to their service, the Levites to their song and their music, Israel to their dwellings; and there we shall go up and appear and worship before thee at the three appointed times, as it is written in thy Law (Deut. 16: 16, 17): Three times in the year shall all thy males appear before the Lord, thy God, in the place which the Lord shall choose; in the Feast of Unleavened Bread and in the Feast of Weeks and in the Feast of Booths; and they shall not appear before the Lord empty. Every man shall give as he is able according to the blessing of the Lord, thy God, which he has given thee.⁵

The last and oldest part of the benediction follows in each case, that is, "Our God, etc., be pleased with our rest," on the Sabbath; "Let us receive," on the three Festivals, and so on the Day of Atonement in the silent Prayer; we shall see what intervenes on the Day of Memorial. On all days the matter of the sacrifices takes the place of, "May the remembrance," in the evening, morning, and afternoon service.

The Musaf for the "Middle Days" is the same as for the feasts proper, and is read even on the Sabbath.

We come now to the "Additional" for the New Moon.

Here we have no "Sanctity of the Day" in the morning
Prayer as a basis, for that is the work-day Amida; the benediction is built up for this service alone. It consists of an
introductory part of later growth, with its regrets for the
departed sacrifices, and an older part, in which we pray for
a blessed month on its first day:

Thou hast given New Moons to thy people, as a time of forgiveness in all those ages, when they brought before thee acceptable
sacrifice and goats for sin-offering to atone for them; may these
be a memorial for them, and a saving to their souls from the adversary. Do thou set up a new altar at Zion; may we offer thereon
the burnt-offering for the new moon, and prepare acceptable he-
goats, and feel joy in the service of the sanctuary, in the songs of
David that resound in thy city, that are sung before thy altar; thou
wilt bring home to the sons everlasting love, and remember to
them the covenant of the fathers. O bring us to Zion, thy city, in
song, and to thy sanctuary at Jerusalem in everlasting happiness;
there we shall offer to thee, as in duty bound, our sacrifices, daily
and additional, according to order and rule. Even the additional
for this day of New Moon we shall lovingly offer before thee,
according to the commandment of thy will, as thou hast written it
for us in thy Law, by the hands of Moses, thy servant, from the
mouth of thy glory, as it is spoken (quoting Num. 28: 11).
Our God and God of our fathers: renew for us this month, for
happiness and blessing,* for joy and gladness,* for salvation and
comfort,* for provision and sustenance,* for life and peace,* for
pardon of sin and forgiveness of iniquity.* For thou hast chosen
thy people Israel from all the nations, and hast fixed for them the
ordinances of the new moon. Blessed be Thou, O Lord, who
hallowest Israel and the New Moons.

When the leader repeats the benediction those present
answer *Amen* after "happiness and blessing,"* and so at
each *.

The introductory part is very slightly changed in the
Sefardic ritual; but in praying for a happy month the further request is inserted, "May this month be the last of all
our troubles, a beginning of our redemption."⁶

Lastly, the Musaf for "Sabbath and New Moon" must be

considered. Here the two rituals differ broadly in a material point. That of the Germans wholly suppresses those short requests which are common to every "Sanctity of the Day," while that of the Sefardim, after asking that "on this Sabbath" the month be renewed for happiness, winds up the benediction as on other Sabbaths, only naming Israel and the New Moon in the very conclusion.

The whole benediction in the German Minhag runs thus:

Thou hast formed thy world of old, and finished thy work on the seventh day;* thou hast loved us, and wast pleased with us; thou hast lifted us above all tongues, and hast hallowed us by thy commandments, and hast brought us, O our King, to thy service, and hast pronounced on us thy great and holy name; and hast given us, O Lord our God, Sabbaths for rest, New Moons for atonement, and because we and our fathers sinned against thee, our city is in ruins, and our sanctuary has been laid waste, our glory has fled, and our abode of life is dishonored; and we cannot perform our duties in thy chosen house, in the great and holy house over which thy name was pronounced, on account of the violence done to thy sanctuary. Be it thy will, O Lord our God and God of our fathers,* to bring us in gladness to our land, and to plant us in our borders; and there we shall (here they proceed as on Sabbath and Festival, including the verses on sacrifice from Numbers 28; then: "May those who keep," as on other Sabbaths; then comes this conclusion):

Our God and God of our fathers, be pleased with our rest, and renew for us on this Sabbath day the coming month for happiness and blessing, for joy and gladness, for salvation and comfort, for provision and sustenance, for life and peace, for pardon of sin and forgiveness of iniquity; for thou hast chosen thy people Israel from all the nations, and hast made known to them thy holy Sabbath, and fixed for them the ordinances of the new moon. Blessed be thou, O Lord, who hallowest the Sabbath and Israel and the New Moons.

The above reads in parts very much like the corresponding formula for the Festivals.

The Sefardim, after praying for a restoration of the Temple and sacrifice, ask for a happy month in the same words as on work-days, stopping short at the close or sealing of the benediction; then say, "May those who keep," and the ordinary last paragraph of the Sabbath benediction, but conclude like the Germans, "who hallowest the Sabbath and Israel and the New Moons."[1]

CHAPTER XI

As the Shema with its benedictions is the same for all the days of the year, and as the constant parts of the Amida with their modifications and the "Sanctity of the Day" for each of the Festivals, among them the Day of Memorial, have been set forth in former chapters, little would remain to be said of the services for that solemn day but for the peculiar construction which has been given to its "Additional Prayer" in connection with the blowing of the alarm-sounds, by which this day is distinguished.

The Mishna, on behalf of one of the lesser Sages, states the order of benedictions thus: 1. Fathers. 2. Powers. 3. Holiness of the Name, and he (the leader) embraces Kingdoms. 4. Sanctity of the Day, and he blows (the Shofar). 5. Remembrances, and he blows. 6. Shofaroth (Ram's-horns), and he blows. 7. Service. 8. Thanksgiving. 9. Blessing of the Priests. R. Akiba corrects this, because Kingdoms and blowing must go together, and the order stands, aside from 1, 2, 7, 8, 9, thus: 3. Holiness of the Name. 4. Sanctity of the Day and Kingdoms, and he blows. 5. Remembrances, and he blows. 6. Shofaroth, and he blows.[1]

By Kingdoms are meant verses or passages from Scripture in which God is recognized as King. Remembrances are similar verses in which God is shown to be mindful of mankind and especially of Israel. Shofaroth are verses in which the Shofar is named either literally as an instrument used in worship, or figuratively, when thunder mimics its notes, or when God himself sounds it as a call to Israel or to mankind.

The opinion that the Kingdoms should be embraced in the "Holiness of the Name" may have left a trace in the insertion therein of "Now set thy terror" (for which see Chapter VII) in all the services of the Days of Memorial and Atonement. The Mishna lays down only general rules for the choice of these verses; there should be not less than ten under each head, it being understood that they should be culled from Tora, Prophets, and Hagiographa; remembrance for evil or the cornet sounding for punishment must not be among them, nor the remembrance of an individual, but only that of Israel or of the righteous or of mankind. The Talmud points out that the Tora really contains only three Kingdom verses, those now in use, to which "Hear, O Israel" may be added as a fourth, and mentions also some of the other verses as already in use.[2]

The Kingdom of Heaven is already prayed for in the fourth benediction as it stands in the morning Prayer, and it concludes, "King of all the earth." The conclusion of the two other benedictions must also have been agreed on as soon as these were named, for the conclusion was never left to the whim of the leader. But the choice of the passages, the following piece which introduces the Kingdoms, and the whole framework of the fifth and sixth benedictions, belong to Abba Areka, known as Rab, and to the first half of the third century:[3]

IV. It is for us to praise the Master of the Universe, to show the greatness of him who formed it in the beginning; that he has not made us like the nations of the land, nor put us with the families of the earth; that he has not set our portion with theirs, or our lot with all their crowd [of those that bow down to vanity and emptiness and pray to gods who cannot help—this has been expunged by the censor from the German ritual]; but we [kneel and] bow down [Sefardim omit: and acknowledge] before the Supreme King of kings, the Holy One, blessed be he; to him who spanneth the heavens and foundeth the earth (see Isa. 51: 13); the throne of whose glory is in the heavens above, and the residence of whose might is in the highest of heights. He is our God, none else; truly our King; there is nothing beside him, as it is written in his law (Deut. 4: 39): "Thou shalt know this day, and bring it home to thy heart, that the Lord is the God, in the heavens above, and on the earth beneath; none else."

Therefore we lift our hope unto thee, O Lord our God, soon to look upon the beauty of thy might, when defilements are driven from the earth, and the idols are wholly cut off; when the world is built up in the *Kingdom* of the Almighty, and all the sons of flesh call on thy name; when all the wicked men of the earth turn to thee: let all the dwellers of the globe learn and know, that every knee bendeth, every tongue sweareth to thee. Before thee, O Lord our God, they shall kneel and fall down, and give honor to thy glorious name; and they shall all receive the yoke of thy Kingdom, and mayest thou speedily reign over them for everlasting. For the Kingdom is thine, and to all eternity thou shalt reign in glory.

Now come the Kingdom verses, three from the Pentateuch, three verses or passages from Psalms, three from Prophets, lastly, "Hear, O Israel," which, though not containing the word, is known as the assumption of the Kingdom:

As it is written in thy Law (Ex. 15: 18): The Lord shall reign forever and ever; and it is said (Num. 23: 21): He has not seen falsehood in Jacob, nor has he beheld mischief in Israel; the Lord his God is with him, and the shouting (or alarm-sound) for the King in his midst. And it is said (Deut. 33: 5): There was a King in Jeshurun; when the heads of the people were gathered, as one the tribes of Israel. And in thy holy writings it is written thus (Ps. 22: 29): For the Kingdom is of the Lord; and he ruleth among the nations. And further (93: 1): The Lord was King; he is clothed in majesty, the Lord is clothed, he is girt in strength; even the world is established, that it cannot be shaken. And further (24: 7-10): Lift up, ye gates, your heads, and be raised, everlasting doors, that the King of Glory may enter. Who is this King of Glory? the Lord, who is strong and mighty; the Lord, who is mighty in war. Lift up, ye gates, your heads, and lift, ye everlasting doors, that the King of Glory may enter. Who is this King of Glory? The Lord of Hosts; he is the King of Glory. Selah. And by the hands of thy servants, the prophets, it is thus written (Isa. 44: 6): Thus saith the Lord, the God of Israel and his redeemer, the Lord of Hosts; I am the First, and I am the Last, and beside me there is no God. And further (Obad. 21): Saviours shall go up on Mount Zion, and they shall judge the Mount of Seir, and the Kingdom shall be the Lord's. And further (Zech. 14: 9): The Lord shall be King over all the earth; on that day the Lord shall be One, and his name One. In thy Law it is written: Hear, O Israel, the Lord, our God, the Lord is One.

After *Alenu* and the Kingdom verses the benediction proceeds: "Our God, etc., be King over us," to "King over all the earth, who sanctifieth Israel and the Day of Memorial."

The piece which introduces the "Remembrances" has given to the Festival almost a new character, that of the yearly day of judgment,[4] which the verses alone do not indicate. The benediction of Remembrances reads thus:

V. Thou rememberest the eternal doings, and visitest the creatures of the oldest past; before thee all secrets are laid bare, and the multitude of hidden things since the creation. There is no forgetfulness before the throne of thy glory, and nothing is hidden before thy eyes. Thou rememberest every deed, and no creature can deny itself from thee. Everything is open and seen before thee, O Lord our God, who espies and beholds to the end of all the ages, when thou bringest a rule and reminder, that every spirit and soul be visited, that many works be remembered, and the multitude of hidden things till there is no end. Thus thou hast made it known in the beginning; long since hast thou revealed it. This day is the commencement of thy works, a memorial of the first day (Ps. 81: 5): For it is an ordinance to Israel, a judgment with the God of Jacob.

And thereon it is judged upon the countries, which is to have war and which peace; which famine and which plenty; and the creatures are visited thereon, to name them unto life or unto death. Who is not visited on this day, when the remembrance of all works cometh before thee: the work of the mortal and his visitation, and the actions and steps of man; human thoughts and devices, and the impulses of man's action? Happy is the man who does not forget thee, and the son of man who findeth courage in thee. For those who seek thee will not stumble, nor wilt thou allow those to blush that trust in thee. For the memorial of every creature comes before thee, and thou searchest into the doings of all. Thou wast even mindful of Noah, and didst visit him with a merciful salvation, when thou broughtest the waters of destruction over all flesh for their evil actions; but his memorial came before thee, to multiply his seed like the dust of the earth, his descendants as the sand of the sea; as it is written in thy law (Gen. 8: 1): And God remembered Noah and all the beasts and all the cattle that were with him in the ark; and God made a wind to pass over the face of the earth, and the waters settled. And it is said (Ex. 2: 24): God heard their sighs, and God remembered his covenant with Abraham, with Isaac, and with Jacob. And it is said (Lev. 26: 42): Then I will remember my covenant with Jacob, even my covenant with Isaac, even my covenant with Abraham, I will remember: and I will remember the land [Sefardim substitute for this verse, Ex. 6: 5]. And in thy holy writings it is written thus (Ps. 111: 4): He made a memorial of his wonders; the Lord is gracious and merciful. And further (111: 5): He giveth gain to those who fear him; he will forever remember his covenant. And further (106, 45): And he remembered to them his covenant, and bethought himself according to his abundant mercies. And by the hands of thy servants, the prophets, it is written (Jer. 2: 2): Go and proclaim in the hearing of Jerusalem. Thus saith the Lord: I remember unto thee the kindness of thy youth, the love of thy bridal state, when thou wentest after me in the wilderness, in a land not sown. And further (Ezek. 16: 60): I shall remember unto thee my covenant with thee in the days of thy youth, and shall keep up with thee an everlasting covenant. And further (Jer. 31: 19): Is not Ephraim to me a darling son or a petted child? for in measure as I speak against him, I remember and think of him the more; therefore my inwards are moved towards him; I shall surely have mercy on him, says the Lord.

[The Sefardim here insert paragraph 3 of the morning benediction: May the remembrance, etc.].

Our God and God of our fathers, remember us with a kind remembrance, and visit us with salvation and mercy from the everlasting heavens; remember unto us, O Lord our God, the oath which thou hast sworn to our father Abraham on Mount Moriah; consider his binding his son Isaac upon the altar, suppressing his love to do thy will perfectly; thus may thy love suppress thy anger at us, and may, through thy goodness, the heat of thy wrath be turned away from thy people, thy city, and thy heritage. Fulfill for us, O Lord our God, the promise made to us in thy Law, written by Moses, as spoken by the mouth of thy glory (Lev. 26: 45): I shall remember unto them the covenant with the men of old, whom I brought forth from the land of Egypt in the sight of the nations, to become their God; I am the Lord. For thou rememberest all things forgotten; and there is no oblivion before the throne of thy glory. Remember to-day the binding (*Akeda*) of Isaac mercifully to his seed. Blessed be thou, O Lord, who remembereth the covenant.

In Western Germany the leader, when he repeats this benediction, intersperses the verses with "poetry," and substitutes several other "Remembrance" verses for those given above, and moreover gives those from the three divisions of Holy Writ in a different order.

This benediction and the burden of the verses is justified by the name Day of Memorial, which the Festival bears throughout the Prayer Book.

But under the Law it is a day of alarm-sound, and this, according to the tradition, must come from the *Shofar* (a prepared ram's horn), which for convenience we may render "cornet." The English Bible renders it in many passages trumpet, which is wrong, for trumpets of silver or other metal were well-known by another Hebrew name. The sound of the *Shofar* always stands in the Bible for a solemn message, either of awe and terror or of freedom and joy.

The benediction *Shofaroth* with its verses runs thus:

VI. Thou wast revealed in a cloud of glory to thy holy people, to speak with them from the heavens; thou madest them hear thy voice, appearing to them in sacred thunderclouds; all the world trembled before thee, and the world-old creatures shook in fear; when thou, our King, wast revealed to us on Mount Sinai, to teach thy people law and commandments. They heard thy majestic voice and thy holy speaking from fiery flames. Thou didst show thyself in lightning and thunder, and didst appear to them in the sound of the cornet. As it is written in thy Law (Ex. 19: 16): And it was on the third day towards morning; there were thunders and lightnings and a heavy cloud on the Mount; and the sound of the cornet was very strong; and all the people in the camp trembled. And further (ib. 19): And the sound of the cornet was waxing

exceedingly strong; Moses would speak, and God answered him
in thunder. And further (Ex. 20: 18): And all the people saw
the thunder, and the lightning, and the sound of the cornet, and the
Mount smoking; and the people saw it and moved, and stood
afar off. And in thy holy writings it is written thus (Ps. 47: 6):
God has gone up in the alarm-sound, the Lord in the sound of the
cornet. And further (98: 6): With trumpets and the sound of the
cornet strike the alarm-sound before the Lord our God. And
further (81: 4, 5): Blow ye the cornet on the New Moon, on the
darkening, the day of our Feast. For it is an ordinance to Israel,
a judgment of the God of Jacob. And further (Psalm 150, see it):
And by the hands of thy servants, the prophets, it is written thus
(Isa. 18: 3): All ye that dwell in the world; all ye that inhabit the
earth, ye shall see when the banner is raised on the hills; when the
cornet is blown, ye shall hear. And further (ib. 27: 13): It shall
come to pass on that day, that the great cornet shall be blown; and
those will come who wander in the land of Assyria, and they who
are cast out in the land of Egypt, and they shall worship before the
Lord on the holy Mount in Jerusalem. And further (Zech. 9:
14, 15): And the Lord will appear over them; his arrow will go
forth like lightning, and the Lord God will blow the cornet, and
go forth in the storms of the South; the Lord of Hosts will shield
them.

Do thus shield thy people Israel with thy peace.

Our God and God of our fathers, blow the great cornet for our
freedom, lift the banner to gather our exiles; bring our scattered
home from among the Gentiles, and assemble our fragments from
the ends of the earth. Bring us in gleeful song to Zion and to
thy sanctuary at Jerusalem in everlasting delight. There we shall
offer our sacrifices, as in duty we are bound, and as it is written in
thy law by the hands of Moses from the mouth of thy glory (Num.
10: 10): On any day of your gladness, on your set times and on
your New Moons, ye shall blow the *trumpets* at your burnt-offerings
and at your peace-offerings, and they shall be unto you for a memorial before the Lord your God. I am the Lord your God. Thou
hearest the voice of the cornet, and listenest to the alarm-sound;
and none is like thee. Blessed be thou, O Lord, who heareth the
alarm-sound of his people Israel in mercy.

Upon Israelites who believe in the truth of the prophets,
the predictions of God's Kingdom on earth, the assurance
of his love to Jerusalem and even to Ephraim, and the

expected sounding of the great cornet which will assemble all their outcasts to the worship of the Lord, exert the most thrilling effect. Among them hardly an eye remains dry when the leader, with proper feeling and expression, reads the Shofar verses from Isaiah.

The old rule for this Prayer was for the private worshipper to read it silently without the Kingdom verses in the fourth benediction and to omit the fifth and sixth altogether, relying for these upon the leader.[5] But since service books have become so cheap, this custom has been forgotten, and every one reads his *Musaf* in full. When the leader in repeating this Prayer has gone through the first paragraph of Alenu and enters on the distinctive part of this service, he prays first that he and his colleagues may do their high task worthily:

I tarry for the Lord, I supplicate to him, I ask from him an answering tongue, him whose might I will sing among the assembled people, pouring out glad songs about his deeds.

Following this and the verses Prov. 16: 1, Ps. 51: 16, Ps. 19: 15,[6] a long and partially rhymed prayer for all the messengers of the Congregations of Israel has been added. Both of them are also spoken in the corresponding prayer of the Day of Atonement at the same point.

After the fourth, after the fifth, and after the sixth benediction, the leader chants:

This is the birthday of the world: to-day he causes all its creatures to stand in judgment; either as children or as servants; if we be like children, be merciful as a father has mercy on his children; if like servants, our eyes are turned to thee, till thou wilt show us grace and bring forth our cause, clear as light, Terrible and Holy God.[7]

Though the *Musaf* of the Day of Memorial is the only striking part in its services, we must here mention the petitions, "Our Father, our King," which it has in common with

the Day of Atonement and with the seven intervening days,
or with six of them, for in the German ritual the eve of
Atonement Day as a day of good cheer is exempt from these
petitions, as well as any Sabbath. They are also spoken on a
public fast other than the Ninth of Ab.

The series is well-known by the two Hebrew words, *Abinu
Malkenu.* They follow immediately upon the morning and
the afternoon Prayer, but are omitted in the latter on Fridays. The number of lines varies from twenty-seven in
the Sefardic to forty-four in the Polish branch of the German ritual. Premising for each the address, Our Father,
our King, the fullest form runs thus:

(1) We have sinned before thee. (2) We have no King but thee.
(3) Act for us for the sake of thy name. (4) Renew (or bless) for
us a good year. (5) Annul all hard sentences against us. (6)
Annul the plans of our foes. (7) Defeat the counsel of our enemies. (8) Remove all our oppressors and adversaries. (9) Stop
the mouths of our adversaries and accusers. (10) Drive pestilence,
the sword, famine and captivity, sin [and apostasy—blotted out by
the censor] from the children of thy covenant. (11) Keep the
plague from thy heritage. (12) Pardon and forgive all our iniquities. (13) Blot our transgressions and sins from thy sight. (14)
Wipe our bonds of debt out in thy great mercy. (15) Bring us
back in sincere repentance to thy presence. (16) Send a full healing to the sick of thy people. (17) Tear up the evil sentence
against us. (18) Remember us for good. (19) Write us in the
book of [at the close of Atonement Day—"seal us in the book of,"
on fasts other than in Tishri—"remember us for"] a happy life. (20)
Write us in the book of redemption and salvation. (21) Write us
in the book of provision and sustenance. (22) Write us in the
book of merit. (23) Write us in the book of forgiveness and
pardon. (24) Let salvation soon grow for us. (25) Lift the horn
of thy people Israel. (26) Lift the horn of thy anointed. (27) Fill
our hands with thy blessing. (28) Fill our storehouses with
plenty. (29) Hear our voice, spare and pity us. (30) Receive our
prayer with mercy and good will. (31) Open to our prayer the
gates of heaven. (32) Do not turn us empty-handed from thee.
(33) Remember that we are dust. (34) Be this hour an hour of
mercy and the time of favor. (35) Have pity on us, our little

ones and our children. (36) Act for the sake of those who were killed for thy holy name. (37) Act for the sake of those who were slaughtered for thy Unity. (38) Act for the sake of those who went into fire and into water to hallow thy name. (39) Avenge before our eyes the spilt blood of thy servants. (40) Do it for thy sake, if not for ours. (41) Do it for thy sake and save us. (42) Do it for the sake of thy great mercy. (43) Do it for the sake of thy great, mighty, and fearful name, that is pronounced upon us. (44) Be gracious and answer us, though we lack in works; act for us in charity and kindness and save us.

It will be seen that many of the petitions of the work-day Prayer are contained herein; hence the omission of *Abinu Malkenu* on the Sabbath.

Among the seventeen lines which the Sefardim lack in their ritual are 36-39, which refer to the martyrs to our faith, and these were not known to the French and Germans at the date of the Mahzor Vitry. They were probably inserted after the persecutions which accompanied the Black Death about the year 1348.

The Talmud speaks of the first two lines as part of a prayer which was spoken by R. Akiba on a public fast, held in a season of drought. The series was transferred from these fasts to such as the Seventeenth of Tammuz and the Fast of Gedaliah. Abudraham knows it only in this light. R. Joseph Karo's Code speaks of it incidentally as in use on the Day of Atonement. Among the Germans its use on the Day of Memorial and the days of penitence generally seems to have been much older than among the Sefardim.[8] It lends itself admirably to slow chanting, and has become a favorite devotion even in radically reformed places of worship.

CHAPTER XII

ALL the parts of the seven benedictions in the *Amida* for the Day of Atonement in each of the five services have been given, including the change from "writing" into "sealing" in the last service, known as Neïla. There is another important element, the confession of sins, which the individual worshipper recites after the seven benedictions, but which the leader, in repeating the Prayer, includes in the Sanctity of the Day, which is also the Pardon of Iniquity. In the Atonement service set forth at length in the 16th chapter of Leviticus, the High Priest "confessed all the iniquities of the children of Israel, and all their transgressions, as to all their sins;" and such a confession, which now everybody makes for himself, is thought to be the first condition of forgiveness.

The three verbs in which the High Priest confessed were, "I have sinned, I have done wrong, I have transgressed;" the guilt rising in intensity from the first to the third. A confession in such words, or even in the first of them, would be enough, but the love for synonyms and for the alphabet has found its way even into the enumeration of sins.

The confession (*Viddui*) in its present form as appended to the Amida for each service runs thus:

O God and God of our fathers, let our prayer come before thee: do not hide thyself from our supplication; for we are not so brazen-faced or stiffnecked as to say before thee, O Lord our God and God of our fathers, that we are just, and that we have not sinned. Nay, we [some add: and our fathers] have sinned. We have been guilty, have deceived, have robbed, have spoken slander, have caused wrong, and done injustice, have acted wantonly, have done violence, have fastened lies, have counselled evil, have failed in promise, have scoffed, have rebelled, have blasphemed, have disobeyed, have done wrong, have transgressed, have oppressed, have hardened our necks, have been wicked, have corrupted, have done abominably; we have erred and led into error.

We have departed from thy commandments and thy righteous judgments; it is not right with us. But thou art righteous in all that has befallen us; for thou hast done truthfully, and we have done wrong. What shall we say before thee, who dwellest on high; what story shall we tell to thee who residest in heaven; dost thou not know all things, both the seen and the hidden?

The Talmud says distinctly that the plain words, "but we have sinned," are a sufficient fulfillment of the Law.[1] In all the services other than the last (Neïla), the confession proceeds:

Thou knowest the mysteries of the world, and the hidden secrets of all that has life. Thou searchest all the inward chambers, and provest the reins and the heart. Nothing is a secret from thee; nor is anything hidden from thy eyes. Be it thy will, O Lord our God and God of our fathers, to forgive us for all our sins, to pardon us for all our iniquities, to atone for all our transgressions.

For the sin that we have committed through—

There are forty-four of such lines, two for each letter of the alphabet,[2] in each of which the causes or occasions of sin are stated after these introductory words, a few in very broad or all-embracing terms, as: 1, "through compulsion or free-will;" 14, "in defiance or in ignorance;" others more specific, as 21, "through lying and deceit;" 23, "by scoffing;" 24, "by the evil tongue;" 25, "in trade" (literally, in buying and selling); 41, "by false swearing;" 42, "by unfounded hatred." At three points the list is interrupted by the petition:

"For all of these, God of forgiveness, forgive us, pardon us, atone for us."

Then come nine lines beginning with the words:

"For the sin by which we have incurred the guilt (or

duty) of ————," beginning with a "burnt-offering," which
was the expiation for a sin of omission, arising from mistake, and ending with the "four death penalties inflicted by
the Court," which must be breaches of the highest moral
or religious prohibitions, done knowingly and defiantly.
This part of the prayer of forgiveness rests on the doctrine
that the infliction of the penalty named in the Tora wipes
out all guilt; hence, as these penalties are not and cannot
be inflicted in our days, there is so much more need for
God's free grace.[3]

The confession then closes:

> For sins of omission or of commission; for those known to us
> and for those unknown: those known to us, we have already named
> them before thee; but those concealed from ourselves are seen and
> known of thee, as it is written: The hidden things belong to the
> Lord our God; but the things revealed belong to us and to our
> children forever, to do all the words of this Law.

The object of those who drew up the confession, "We
have been guilty," and the longer one, "For the sin," in
arranging them by the alphabet, was to aid the memory at a
time when books were scarce. The shorter as well as the
longer list lie under the same objection: the many general
phrases cannot go home to the confessor's heart, but rather
draw his attention away from his own faults, which he is
made to admit only in a few instances. It was left to the
preacher (and there has nearly always been preaching on
this day) to set forth the besetting sin of the time and place.
The general introduction is Talmudic; the double alphabet
is of later date.[4]

A much finer taste has been displayed in the confession
for the fifth or Neïla service, which, after the first three
paragraphs, proceeds thus, in a loftier vein:

> Thou lendest a hand to the transgressor, and thy right hand is
> stretched out to receive the repentant. Thou hast taught us, O
> Lord our God, to confess our iniquities before thee, that we may

cease from our wrongful deeds, and thou wilt then receive us as fully restored in thy sight, as upon fire-offerings and sweet savors. According to thy words which thou hast spoken, there would be no end of the offerings we owe, no counting the sweet savors for our guilt; but thou knowest that our future is the moth and the worm; hence thou hast multiplied forgiveness.* What are we, what is our life, what our goodliness, what our virtue, what our help, what our strength, and what our power? What shall we say before thee, O Lord our God and God of our fathers? Are not all the heroes as nothing before thee; all the men of fame as if they had never been; all the wise as if without knowledge; all the well-reasoning men as if without sense? For their many actions are a waste; the days of their lives are vanity before thee, even the excellence of man over the beasts is nothing; for all is vanity.

Thou hast set man apart from the first, and thought him worthy to stand before thee. For who can tell thee what to do, and if he doeth right, what does he give thee (see Job 35: 7)? And thou hast given us, O Lord our God, lovingly, this day of fast and atonement, an end and pardon and forgiveness for our iniquities, that we may cease from our wrongful deeds, and return to thee to do thy will with a perfect heart. And thou spare us in thy great mercy; for thou dost not desire the destruction of the world, as it is said (Isa. 55: 6): Seek ye the Lord, when he can be found; call him when he is near. And further (ib. 55: 7): Let the wicked forsake his way, and the evil-doer his thoughts; and let him return unto the Lord, and he will show him mercy; even to our God, who will abundantly pardon. And thou, O God of forgiveness, art long-suffering and great in kindness and truth, and doest good abundantly, and thou desirest the return of the wicked, and not their death. As it is said (Ezek. 33: 11): Say unto them, as I live, saith the Lord God, I do not delight in the death of the wicked, but that the wicked turn back from his way, and that he live; return, return from your evil ways; and why will you die, O House of Israel! And further (ib. 18: 23): Do I indeed delight in the death of the wicked, saith the Lord God; is it not, that he turn back from his ways, and that he may live? And further (ib. 18: 32): For I delight not in the death of the dying, saith the Lord God. Return and live.

This reflection is, like the confession proper, read by the leader as part of the "Sanctity of the Day" when he repeats Neila.⁵ But in the night service, when the Prayer as a whole is not repeated, the leader recites the "Order of Confession" alone. In this, as in all the other services, it is then enlarged by Bible verses, short petitions, and, if there is time to spare, by poetic compositions known as "Selihoth" (Forgivenesses), some of which are quite old, reaching nearly back to Talmud times. After every "Seliha" God is besought to remember his thirteen qualities of mercy, thus:

God, the King, sitteth on the throne of mercy; he governs in kindness, he pardons the iniquities of his people, he passeth by the first fault again and again, he multiplieth forgiveness to sinners and pardon to those who transgress. Thou who doest righteously with all flesh and spirit, do not requite them according to their evil way! God, thou hast taught them to recite the thirteen; remember for them the covenant of the thirteen; which thou madest known to the Humble (Moses) of old; as it is written (Ex. 34: 5. 6. 7): And the Lord came down in a cloud, and he (Moses) stood with him there and called on the name of the Lord. And the Lord passed by him, and called: (1) The Lord, the Lord: (2) God, (3) merciful and (4) gracious, (5) long-suffering and (6) great in kindness and (7) truth: (8) guarding kindness (9) unto a thousand (generations); (10) taking away iniquity. and (11) transgression, and (12) sin, and (13) holding guiltless!"

The thirteenth quality is obtained by stopping before the negative, which makes the text read, "and does not hold wholly guiltless." There is a poetical version of this prayer, which in some of the local rituals is used once in each of the services. In the evening service the *Selihoth* are introduced by a long collection of Bible verses, which deal rather with God's wondrous work in nature than with the forgiveness of sins. The verses chosen are not everywhere the same. They are in most well-conducted Synagogues read responsively, the leader reading the odd and the congregation the even numbered verses.

(Ps. 65: 3) O thou that hearest prayer, unto thee shall all flesh come. All flesh shall come to bow before thee, O Lord. (From Isa. 66: 23.)

Then: Ps. 86: 9; 95: 6; 100: 4; 134: 1, 2; 132: 7; 99: 5, 9; 96: 9, then 5: 8 and 138: 2 (changed from singular to plural); 89: 9; 89: 7; 86: 10; 108: 5; 145: 3; 96: 4; 95: 3; Deut. 3: 24; Jer. 10: 7; 10: 6; Ps. 89: 14; 74: 16; 95: 4, 5; 106: 2; 1 Chron. 29: 11; Ps. 89: 12; 74: 17, 15, 14, 13; 89: 10; 48: 2; Isa. 37: 16; Ps. 89: 8, 6; 95: 1, 2; 89: 15; 55: 15; 95: 5.

(Job 12: 10): In whose hand is the soul of every living thing and the breath of all mankind. We have come for thy name; do for the sake of thy name; for the sake of thy glorious name, which is the gracious and merciful God (cmp. Jer. 14: 7). For the sake of thy name, O Lord, thou wilt forgive our iniquity, though it be great. (Cmp. Ps. 25: 11.)

Most of the verses are so chosen that each seems to be suggested by the one next preceding it. But this belongs only to the night service, *Col Nidre*, so-called. Then follow, and in the other services there are first, the *Selihoth*, after each of them the invocation, "God, King that sitteth," then, in the German ritual at least, an aggregate of verses and short petitions, which must have grown out of the "Remembrances" of the Day of Memorial. The verses in the Polish Prayer Book are:

Ps. 25: 6: Remember thy mercies, O Lord, and thy loving-kindness; for they are from everlasting. Then: Ps. 79: 8; 106: 4; 74: 2; then a made-up verse: Remember, O Lord, the affection of Jerusalem; do not forget the love of Zion eternally. Then: Ps. 137: 7; 102: 14; Ex. 32: 13; Deut. 9: 27; Num. 12: 11.

But the next piece, which is recited in every Atonement service, except in Neila, is most characteristic. Every petition is fortified by a verse of promise from the Law or the Prophets; the trustful Israelite taking his heavenly Father at his word. The verses are recited with deep feeling. Only a few of them are copied out below:

Remember unto us the covenant of the fathers, as thou hast said (Lev. 26: 42): I will remember my covenant with Jacob, even my covenant with Isaac, even my covenant with Abraham I shall remember; and I will remember the land. Remember unto us the covenant with the ancients, as thou hast said (ib. 26: 45. etc.). Do with us as thou hast promised unto us (ib. 26: 44): And yet even this; when they are in the land of their enemies I will not reject them, nor will I loathe them, to make an end of them, or to break my covenant with them, for I am the Lord their God. Show mercy to us and do not destroy us, as it is written (Deut. 4: 31, etc.). Circumcise our hearts that we may love thy name (Deut. 30: 6, etc.). Return our captives and show mercy, as it is written (Deut. 30: 3. etc.). Gather our outcasts, as it is written (Deut. 30: 4, etc.). Let thyself be found when we seek thee, as it is written (Deut. 4: 29): And ye will thence seek the Lord your God, and ye will find him, when ye seek him with all your heart and with all your soul. Blot out our transgressions for thy sake, as thou hast said (Isa. 43: 25, etc.). Blot out our transgression as a cloud, as thou hast said (Isa. 44: 22, etc.). Whiten our sins as snow and as wool, as it is written (Isa. 1: 18): Come now, let us reason together, saith the Lord; though your sins be as scarlet, they shall be white as snow; though they be red as crimson, they shall be as wool. Sprinkle upon us clean waters and cleanse us, as it is written (Ezek. 36: 25, etc). Atone for our sins and cleanse us on this day, as it is written (Lev. 16: 30, etc.). Bring us to thy holy hill and gladden us in thy house of prayer, as it is written (Isa. 56: 7).[1]

After a few verses, turned from the singular of Holy Writ into the plural of the congregation at prayer, the leader proceeds:

Do not forsake us, do not reject us, bring us not to shame; do not break thy covenant with us. Lead us to thy Law, teach us thy commandments; instruct us in thy ways; bend our hearts to fear thee; circumcise them, that we may love thee, and that we return to thee truly and perfectly. For the sake of thy great name pardon and forgive our iniquity, as it is written in thy holy words (Ps. 25: 11): For the sake of thy great name, forgive my iniquity, though it be great.

Then the following is read responsively in Neïla as well as in the other services:

Forgive, pardon, atone! for
We are thy people and thou art our God.
We are thy sons and thou art our Father.
We are thy servants and thou art our Master.
We are thy flock and thou art our Shepherd.
We are thy vineyard and thou art our Keeper.
We are thy heritage and thou art our portion.
We are hoping in thee and thou art our Saviour.
We are thy work and thou art our Maker.
We are thy treasure and thou art our kinsman.
We are thy people and thou art our King.
We are thy bride and thou art our lover.
We are vouching for thee, and thou vouchest for us.

(Cmp. Deut. 26: 13.)

We are brazen-faced; but thou art gracious and merciful;
We are stiffnecked, and thou art long-suffering;
We are full of iniquity, and thou art full of mercy;
We—our days are a passing shadow; but thou art the same; thy
days never end.

Then comes the shorter confession as in the silent Prayer.
Then:

Our God and God of our fathers, forgive and pardon our iniquity
on this Day of Atonement; listen to our prayer; blot our iniquities
from thy sight; bend our impulse that we may serve thee; let us
bow our necks to return to thee; renew our reins that we observe
thy statutes; circumcise our hearts to love thy name; as it is
written (Deut. 30: 6, etc.). Thou knowest what is wilful sin and
what is error.

Then follows, "What are we—all is vanity" as in Neïla;
and "What shall we say before thee," leading to the longer
confession.

After this the leader refers to other Bible verses in which
forgiveness and cleansing from guilt are promised. Foremost among them are the three closing verses of the
prophecy of Micah. Here the words, "Thou wilt cast all
their sins into the depths of the sea," are brought into
prominence.[8]

It may be here remarked that the collection of verses,

"Thou who hearest prayer," the *Selihoth* with the interspersed "thirteen qualities," the verses asking God to remember us, and the verses reminding him of his Scriptural promises, together with the shorter confession, are also recited *very* early in the morning before the regular morning service on the days between the Day of Memorial and the Day of Atonement and on a number of days preceding the former, which are hence known as *Selihoth*-days. This is a well-known custom everywhere, but it is not so well-known that in many places in Germany there are still ascetics who carry on a similar service on every work-day of the year not marked as joyous or festive. This service is known as *Shomer labboker* (watchman of the morning).[9]

The "Order of Confession" in the Atonement night service (unless it be on the Sabbath), also on the mornings of *Selihoth*-days, closes with three sets of invocations. The first, "O Lord, do it for the sake of thy name," proceeds through the twenty-two letters of the alphabet (Do it for the sake of thy Truth, etc.), then eighteen invocations, e. g., "Do it for the sake of the children at school," they being according to Talmudic views the part of mankind dearest in the sight of God. Next, "Answer us, O Lord, answer us;" running from, "Answer us, our Father (*Abinu*), answer us," for Aleph, through the twenty-two letters, and then through eleven other attributes to "Answer us, Father of the fatherless, answer us, Judge of the widows, answer us." Lastly, "He who answered our Father Abraham on Mount Moriah, he will answer us;" which runs through twenty lines, in which other Biblical characters and occasions are substituted.

This last series dates back to seven invocations, which were recited in the days of the Temple in times of drought, calling on him who answered Abraham on Mount Moriah, who answered our fathers on the sea, who answered Joshua at Gilgal, Samuel at Mizpah, Elijah on Mount Carmel,

Jonah in the belly of the fish, David and Solomon in Jerusalem.[10]

In the morning and afternoon services the "Order of Confession," enlarged by the leader in his repetition of the Prayer as above indicated, brings us to the last part of the "Sanctity of the Day." But the "additional" Prayer has another feature, the *Aboda*, or Service, i. e., a recital of the manner in which the Atonement service was conducted by the High Priest at Jerusalem, and this precedes the "Order of Confession" as given above.

The leader begins with the first paragraph of *Alenu* as on the Day of Memorial, then chants the petitions for "an answering tongue" and for a worthy ministration by himself and his colleagues, as shown in Chapter XI. Then he launches into a rather dry account of the service, as sketched in Leviticus and in the Mishna. This contains the three confessions of sin which the High Priest pronounced, when he atoned first for himself and his own household, next for himself and his wider household, the whole priestly tribe, lastly for himself and all Israel. Where "the Name" or "the Lord" now occurs, the High Priest uttered the Tetragrammaton. The Hebrew *Anna*, an interjection often used in prayer ("We beseech thee," in the English Bible), is best rendered by "O now." The first confession is given thus:

And thus he would say:

"O now, the Name, I have done wrong, I have sinned, I have transgressed before thee, I and my household; O now, for the Name, atone for the sins, the iniquities, the transgressions, which I have sinned and done wrongfully and transgressed before thee, I and my household; as it is written in thy law (Lev. 16: 30): For on that day he shall atone for you, to cleanse you from all your sins before the Lord."

And when the priests and people standing in the court heard the "plain Name" come forth from the mouth of the High Priest in holiness and purity, they knelt and bowed down and fell on their faces, and said: "Blessed be the name of his glorious Kingdom forever and ever." Even he sought to finish the Name in harmony with those who blessed, and then said to them—"ye shall be clean."

In the second confession "the priestly tribe" is substituted for the household; in the third, "thy people, the house of Israel."[11]

It remains to be told how the Atonement services are begun on the first evening and how closed on the next.

On the first evening, slightly before night-fall, the two most learned and reputable men of the congregation stand up with the leader, and all three say thrice:

"By the opinion of God and the opinion of the assembly, as given in the session on high and in the session below, we give leave to pray with the transgressors."

Formerly this was not an empty form; it meant that the excommunicated might join with the congregation in the devotions of the day. As the leader was not chosen for his musical training, but for his worth and learning, the three formed a sort of Court (*Beth Din*), with power to absolve from the ban.[12]

Next comes the Remission of Vows (*Col Nidre*), which has given much trouble among persecuting Gentiles as well as among our own brethren.

Vowing has been the bane not of the Jews alone, but of men of all races and creeds. The vow might be of some self-infliction, an extra fast, abstention from wine or animal food, or from the enjoyment of anything belonging to a named person; or that a named person should have no enjoyment from the belongings of him that made the vow. The Bible warns against taking vows lightly; the Rabbis discouraged them, and found ways to annul them. They laid down a rule that if, on the first day of the year, a man declared: all the vows I make this year are void, those vows would be void, unless he should, when vowing, think of this declaration, and nevertheless declare: this vow shall stand.[13] This view is best illustrated by an act of an American legislature, which declares: Any charter granted hereafter by this or any subsequent legislature shall be revocable, unless it is in so many words made irrevocable. For a long time men used to make such a declaration on the first of Tishri (New Year) in private or before witnesses. When the custom arose for all to make it in public on the eve of Atonement, the leader singing it to slow music, is not easy to ascertain.

Col Nidre was drawn up with a view to the classification of vows given in the 30th chapter of Numbers and to the rules given in the Mishna. For greater assurance it takes in "by-names," that is, vows made in mutilated words, like *Konam* for *Corban* (sacrifice), because such are valid. Seven synonyms were strung out, not because a gushing heart craved the fullest expression, but simply to meet all possible cases; in short, *Col Nidre* is neither prayer nor praise, but a legal document. It is drawn up in Aramaic, like other documents, except the clause limiting the time for which it is to take effect. It reads thus in the German Ritual:

All vows and prohibitions, and bans, and devotions for sacrifice, and vowings by nickname, and penalties and oaths, which we have vowed, or which we have sworn, or which we have put under ban, or which we have forbidden to ourselves (from this Day of Atonement to the next Day of Atonement, may it come in peace); we have repented of all of them; let all of them be dissolved, abandoned, put at rest, be void, and be annulled; not valid, nor of force; our vows are no vows, our prohibitions are no prohibitions, our oaths are no oaths.[14]

This is *sung* three times. Then the leader and congregation say thrice:

(Num. 15: 26): And all the congregation of the children of Israel shall be forgiven and the stranger that sojourneth among them; for as to all the people it was done unwittingly.

In the Polish ritual Num. 14: 19 is also read, the congregation answering thrice in the verse following: "And the Lord said: I have pardoned according to thy word."

The above is the form and theory of *Col Nidre* as it was settled for the Jews of the German Ritual by Rabbenu Tam in the twelfth century. But the Sefardim define the time of the loosed vows otherwise; they say "from the Day of Atonement last past unto this," as well as from the present one to the next, and justify this on the ground that they need forgiveness for the vows which they have already made, and which, from forgetfulness or weakness, they may have violated. The verbs, "which we have vowed," etc., are all in the past tense, and in Aramaic prose the tenses are hardly ever mixed up. There is a mode pointed out in the Mishna by which three men, acting as judges, may remit a vow for good cause shown; but that would certainly not cover the case of a wholesale remission of all the vows of everybody made during a whole year. According to the Sefardic theory of *Col Nidre*, the verse from Numbers, promising forgiveness for acts done unwittingly, is quoted with a view to the probable violation of vows theretofore made.[15]

According to either theory *Col Nidre* must be recited or at least begun while it is not quite night, as either a declaration regarding vows or a formal remission of vows is not proper on a Sabbath or Festival, being in its nature a judicial act.

When all this has been said, the Day of Atonement is fully on. It is proper then to thank God in the usual way for having spared us to see the Festival, for such the Day of Atonement is. On other Festivals thanks are given over the wine cup; as this cannot be done on a fast day, the leader in the evening service, before beginning it, says the benediction:

Blessed be thou, O Lord our God, King of the world, who hast let us live and kept us up and made us reach this time.

12

Then he addresses the congregation, "Bless ye" (see Ch. V), reads the Shema with its benedictions (Ch. III), and finishes the evening service as explained in Chapters VI, VII, IX, and the present chapter, adding *Abinu Malkenu* towards the end, unless it be Friday night.

Late in the afternoon of the next day *Neïla* is read, and is finished about sundown, followed by *Abinu Malkenu* and the complete Kaddish. Then the sacred names are given out by way of confession of faith, all present repeating them after the leader, "Hear, O Israel" once; "Blessed be the Name" thrice; "the Lord is the God" (1 Kings 18: 39) seven times; this ends the services of the great day.[16]

The modern custom of Europe, Africa, and the Spanish and German Jews of Asiatic Turkey is to spend the whole Day of Atonement with prayers, Bible lessons, and sermons, the afternoon lessons following the "additional" without intermission, a custom which makes fasting easier to those who enter into the spirit of Bible and Prayer Book. But in the old native congregations at and around Bagdad, among the descendants of the Jews who elaborated the Talmud, this is not so. They read their morning Prayer, Bible lessons, and "additional" in the forenoon, go home and return in time for the lessons and Prayer of the afternoon, finishing Neïla with sunset.[17] That the Day of Atonement was not all spent in worship while the Temple stood in its glory is proved by the following account given by Simeon ben Gamaliel, a survivor: "Israel had no such holidays as the Fifteenth of Ab and the Day of Atonement. For on these days the daughters of Jerusalem would go out in white borrowed garments (all borrowed so as not to put those having none to shame). They went out and danced in the vineyards. And what did they say there? Young man (they said), lift now thy eyes and see what thou choosest for thyself. Do not fix thy eye on beauty but on family (good stock)."[18]

NOTE.—Beside the divergencies of the Sefardic from the

German Ritual, already stated in this chapter and in Chapter IX, it may be further said: 1. The following twelve Psalms are, by the Sefardim, added in the morning hymns (see next chapter), Psalms 17, 25, 32, 51, 65, 85, 86, 102, 103, 104, 98, 121. 2. In the complete Kaddish, after every Prayer, a long Hebrew supplication for the hearing and answering of our prayers is inserted before the short Aramaic clause to that effect. 3. The introduction, "It is our duty" (Alenu), to the Kingdom verses, at least its first paragraph, is made part of the Sanctity of the Day in Musaf, not only for the leader in repeating it, but in the silent Prayer. 4. In the "Order of Confessions," as read by the leader, the shorter confession ("We are guilty") is given out twice, with a plaintive piece between, as is customary on the "Selihoth days" and fasts. 5. The Thrice-Holy or Kedusha, for the morning and early afternoon services, is in the shorter form with three responses only, while with the Germans it has five. 6. After the morning, the Additional, and the Minha Prayer, lists of invocations are read, like those which the Germans have at the end of the evening service, and which like these are survivals of the old "Public Fasts." Here also some of the Selihoth are inserted, followed by "God the King" and the thirteen qualities. 7. After the Additional, with its complete Kaddish, the Germans at once proceed with the lessons of the afternoon service, thus running the forenoon and afternoon services into one whole. The Sefardim close Musaf with some of the Talmudic passages, prose pieces, and poetry, with which the Sabbath forenoon services are wound up, and begin Minha with the Psalm verses, etc., of the Sabbath afternoon service, thus leaving open a seam between forenoon and afternoon. 8. The Sefardim recite, "Our Father, our King" after Minha, the Germans after Neïla.

CHAPTER XIII

PSALMS AND BIBLE VERSES IN THE SERVICE

THE Psalms were written as hymns or supplications in public or private worship. Some of them show this in the context; as Ps. 118 in the words: "This is the day the Lord hath made, let us be glad and rejoice therein;" others by the heading, as Ps. 92, a "song for the Sabbath," or 100, "for Thanksgiving," that is, to be sung at the Thanksgiving sacrifice, named in Leviticus 22: 29.

The six Psalms, 113-118, known jointly as "The Praise" (Hallel), are much discussed in the oldest standards. They were probably written for the Feast of Hanucca. "All the nations surround me; in the Lord's name, I shall cut them down," points to a bloody war; "the Lord has sorely chastised me," to a war at first unsuccessful; "open to me the gates of righteousness, I will enter them, and thank the Lord," points to the Temple re-opened for the service of the true God. The scorn of idols and idol-makers poured out in Ps. 115 bears witness to a fierce struggle with idolaters, and, as said above, these Psalms were written for a feast; the many Aramaic forms indicate a late date of authorship; so Hanucca may have been that feast.[1] The Mishna treats them as one composition, and the Halleluiah at the end of four chapters is a choral response rather than a part of the context.[2]

The Hallel was originally recited: 1. On the Passover night, at the meal made of the Paschal lamb, as now it is at the family supper, taking the place thereof; 2, on the first day of the Passover in the morning; this day is doubled "in Exile;" 3, on Pentecost; 4, on the Feast of Booths, including the closing day; the Talmud treats of it mainly in connection with this feast; 5, on the eight days of Hanucca.[3]

On all these days the whole Hallel is read, and in the Sefardic ritual the benediction runs: "Blessed be, etc., who has commanded us to complete the Praise." But later on, it seems after the completion of the Talmud, these Psalms were introduced into the service on the middle and end days of the Passover and on New Moons, except the New Moon of Tishri, the solemn Day of Judgment. The innovators, however, dared not place their ordinance on a level with that of their heroic forefathers; so for the new occasions they clipped the songs of praise. The first eleven verses of the 115th and as many of the 116th Psalm were to be omitted. The 115th then opens with the words: "The Lord has been mindful of me;" the 116th: "How shall I return." These are natural divisions; when the whole Hallel is read the leader rests here as at the end of a chapter. By-the-by, the version, "all men are liars," in Ps. 116: 11, is incorrect. The true meaning is "every man is unreliable." The Hebrew verb used here in the participle means to break promises, not to tell an untruth.

Before the so-called "Half Hallel," the Sefardim bless, as the Germans always do, him "who has commanded us to read the Hallel."[4]

The 118th Psalm is opened with the much older verse, "Give thanks unto the Lord, for he is good; for his mercy endureth forever" (literally, "for forever is his kindness"). This was so well-known by all, even those who understood not another word of Hebrew, that the assembled multitude was called on to shout only this one line in response, after the leader had given out either it or one of the three following verses, Let Israel now say, Let the House of Aaron now say, Let those that fear the Lord now say, and this is still the custom.[5]

The last nine verses, beginning "I will thank thee,"

are spoken twice; that is, the leader gives them out and the congregation says each verse after him. The hemistichs, "O now, O Lord, save now" (Hosianna) and "O now, O Lord, give but prosperity," are repeated separately. The reason commonly assigned is this: in all the preceding verses of the Psalm some words occur twice, which gave an opportunity to alternating choirs, but not in these last verses; hence they had to be sung twice. In the Polish ritual the responsive method has been lost, and every one says twice the verses that should be repeated by way of response.

Hallel is closed with this benediction:

O Lord our God, may all thy works praise thee, and thy saints, who do thy will, and all thy people Israel in glad song bless and honor thy glorious name; for it is proper to give thanks to thee, and pleasant to play melodies to thy name; and from everlasting to everlasting thou art God; blessed be thou, O Lord, the King praised in hymns.

(Six of the synonyms for "bless and honor" have been omitted.)

From the 114th Psalm (When Israel went forth from Egypt) the whole series is sometimes called the Hallel of Egypt, to distinguish it from "the Great Hallel," that is, Psalm 136, and the name of Hallel is also applied to the five last chapters of the Psalter, or at least to Psalms 148 and 150. The Great Hallel is a favorite with the young through the merry ring of its steady burden, *Ki leolam hasdo* (for his mercy endureth forever).

Among the morning hymns for all days the most important is Psalm 145, preceded by two verses (84: 5, and 144: 15): "Happy are they who sit in thy House; they will still be praising thee, Selah. Happy is the people that is in such a case; happy is the people whose God is the Lord;" and followed by this (115: 18): "But we will bless the Lord, from this time forth and for evermore! praise ye the Lord." The whole is known as *Ashre* (Happy), from its first word.

The two grounds for choosing this Psalm are, that it is alphabetic and that it teaches in its sixteenth verse how God nourishes all his creatures.

When and how the other morning hymns gathered round this center it is hard to ascertain. There is a benediction to be read before and after them like grace before and after meals; the Sefardim have denied a place between the two to the latest accretions, keeping them on the outside before the opening benediction, and are followed herein by the *Hasidim*.

The order in the German ritual is this: The opening benediction, next the song ascribed to David, 1 Chron. 16: 8-36, then twenty-two scattering Psalm verses, as follows: Ps. 99: 5, 9; 78: 38; 40: 12; 25: 6; 68: 35, 36; 94: 1, 2; then three end verses used also at other times: (46: 12) "The Lord of Hosts is with us, the God of Jacob is our tower, Selah." (84: 13) "O Lord of Hosts, happy is the man who trusteth in thee." (20: 10) "O Lord, save; the King will answer us, when we call." Then Ps. 28: 9; 33: 20, 21, 22; 85: 8; 44: 27; 81: 11; 144: 15; 13: 6.

The number twenty-two of the verses is that of the letters in the alphabet, and indicates a Cabbalistic origin. Abudraham still objects to the Song from Chronicles as well as to the twenty-two verses as an unauthorized addition to the services, though the former is recommended by the "Treatise of Scribes" (*Soferim*).

The German ritual has, after the benediction, the piece from Chronicles and the twenty-two verses, on work-days the Psalm at Thanksgiving (Ps. 100); but on Sabbaths and Festivals these nine Psalms, 19, 34, 90, 91, 135, 136, (Great Hallel), 33, 92 (the Sabbath Psalm), 93. But the Sefardic ritual has, after the twenty-two verses, Psalms 30, 103 and 19. (Abudraham still objected to the use of 19 on work-days); then on Sabbaths and Festivals Psalms 33, 34, 90, 91; (then on Passover 107, on Pentecost 68, on Feast of Booths 42 and 43, on the Day of Memorial 81, on the Day of Atonement twelve named Psalms); then 98, 121, 122, 123, 124, 135, 136; then the benediction; then, on work-days, 100, on Sabbaths and Festivals, 92, 93. Thereafter the rituals agree, first, eighteen verses analogous to the eighteen benedictions beginning: (104: 31) "Let the glory of the Lord endure forever; the Lord rejoiceth in his works." Then follow verses 2, 3, 4 of 113; then Ps. 135: 13; 103: 19; 1 Chr. 16: 31; then this line made up by the "Treatise of Scribes," of which the latter half is from Ex. 15, "The Lord is King, the Lord has reigned, the Lord will reign forever and ever." Then Ps. 10: 16; 33: 10; Prov. 19: 21; Ps. 33: 11, 9; 132: 13; 135: 4. (94: 14) "For the Lord will not reject his people, and will not forsake his heritage." Then Ps. 78: 38 and 20: 10, which we meet again at the head of the evening services.

Then comes *Ashre* as defined above, then the five Halleluiah Psalms, 146-150; then the doxologies from the ends of three Psalm books:

(89: 53): Blessed be the Lord for evermore. Amen and Amen. (106: 48): Blessed be the Lord, the God of Israel, from everlasting even to everlasting; and let all the people say, Amen, praise ye the Lord. (72: 18, 19): Blessed be the Lord God, the God of Israel, who only doeth wondrous things. And blessed be his glorious name forever; and let the whole earth be filled with his glory. Amen and Amen.

Then the following words of homage, 1 Chron. 29: 10-13:

Then David blessed the Lord before all the assembly, and David said, blessed be thou, O Lord, the God of Israel, our Father, forever and ever. Thine, O Lord, is the greatness and the power and the glory and the victory and the majesty; for of all that is in the heavens and in the earth, thine is the Kingdom, O Lord, and thou art exalted as King over all. Both riches and honor come of thee, and thou rulest over all, and in thine hand is power and might; and in thine hand it is to make great and to give strength unto all. Now, therefore, our God, we thank thee and praise thy glorious name.

This passes imperceptibly into Nehemiah's address (Neh. 9: 6-11), and this leads to the last two verses of Exodus 14

(And the Lord on that day saved), and these introduce the great song of triumph after the crossing of the Red Sea:

(Ex. 15: 1-18). The last verse (The Lord shall reign forever and ever) is followed by three other of the Kingdom verses. (Ps. 22: 29): For the Kingdom is of the Lord and he ruleth among the nations. (Obadiah, 21): And saviours shall go up on Mount Zion to judge the Mount of Esau, and the Kingdom shall be the Lord's. (Zech. 14: 9): And the Lord shall be king over all the earth, on that day shall the Lord be one, and his name one.

Then follows the closing "Benediction of Song;" of this hereafter.

As to the comparative date of the parts which make up the morning hymns, or "musical verses," we have seen that Psalm 145 takes the first rank; Psalms 146-150, or at least 148 and 150, come next; their recital can be traced back to the Talmud, perhaps to the days of the Mishna.[8] Nearly the same rank is held by Psalm 100, and on Sabbath and Festivals by 92 and 93. The scattering twenty-two verses are the latest accretion. The long piece from Chronicles and the Sabbath hymns, which the Sefardim do not admit within the benedictions, are also late additions. This historic order is roughly recognized by the rules found in many prayer books as to the pieces which should be skipped by one who comes too late to the morning service, and wishes to catch up with the congregation.

After the *Amida* in the morning or afternoon comes the "supplication," or penitential Psalm. It is 6 with the Germans, 25 with the Sefardim; it is not recited on Sabbaths, Festivals, Middle Days, New Moons, Hanucca, or Purim, nor in the Passover month, nor, on the other hand, on the Ninth of Ab and a few other days as to which the rituals differ, nor in the afternoon before Sabbaths or Festivals, nor when a "bridegroom" (a man who has married within a week) is in the Synagogue, nor when a circum-

cision takes place in it. Its omission carries with it all its
later accretions and all the plaintive matter written for
Mondays and Thursdays.[7]

The penitential Psalm is followed (mediately or immediately) by these verses:

(2 Chron. 20: 12): But we know not what we should do; for
our eyes are turned to thee. (Ps. 25: 6): Remember thy mercies,
O Lord, and thy loving-kindness; for they are from everlasting.
(Ps. 33: 22): May thy kindness be upon us, O Lord, as we have
hoped unto thee. (79: 8): Do not remember unto us the iniquities
of the forefathers; let thy mercies speedily prevent us; for we are
brought very low. (123: 3): Be gracious to us, O Lord, be
gracious, for too long we have been filled with contempt. (Hab.
3: 2): In anger thou art mindful of mercy. (Ps. 103: 14): For he
knoweth our nature; he is mindful that we are dust. (79: 9):
Help us, O Lord, for the sake of thy glorious name; deliver us
and cleanse away our sins for thy name's sake.[8]

On Monday and Thursday a composition, about 700
Hebrew words in length, is inserted before the penitential
Psalm, full of bitter complaints for the sufferings which
Israel undergoes for its faith, known popularly as "long
Vehu Rahum," from the first words of the opening verse,
"And he is merciful, atoneth sin." A story ascribing its
authorship to three shipwrecked refugees from the sack of
Jerusalem or of Bethar has obscured the true origin of this
collection. It sets out with Bible verses, some as they
read in Scripture, others with the "I" or "thou" of the
Psalmist or Prophet turned into the "we" of the worship-
pers. Thus we have Ps. 78: 38; 40: 12; 106: 47; 130: 3, 4;
103: 10; Jer. 14: 7; Ps. 25: 6; 20: 2, 10; Dan. 9: 15-19;
Isa. 64: 7; Joel 2: 17; Deut. 9: 27; Ex. 32: 12; Dan. 9: 7;
Lam. 3: 40; Ps. 118: 25; Isa. 64: 11.

The verses drop off gradually into post-Biblical matter.
The whole is hardly fitted to express the feelings of American Jews, who cannot be said to suffer for their faith; but
a short poem which, on Mondays and Thursdays, is recited

after the penitential Psalms utters the plaint for such sufferings with even greater bitterness.

After the morning *Amida* and after these "supplications," when these are in place, comes Half Kaddish on work-days, a full Kaddish on days requiring a Musaf Prayer; then (besides the lesson from the scroll and whatever goes with it) the second *Ashre*. Then on days on which "supplications" are made, Psalm 20 ("The Lord will answer thee in time of distress"); then on all work-days a collection of verses from Psalms, Chronicles, and Prophets, which, though not Talmudic, is very old. It is named from its opening words *U-Ba le-Tzion* (Isa. 59: 20, 21).

A redeemer shall come to Zion and to them that turn from transgression in Jacob, saith the Lord. And as for me, this is my covenant with them, saith the Lord; my spirit that is upon thee, and my words which I have put in thy mouth shall not depart out of thy mouth, nor out of the mouth of thy seed, nor out of the mouth of thy seed's seed, says the Lord, from henceforth and forever. (Ps. 22: 4): Thou art holy, dwelling in the praises of Israel. (Isa. 6: 3): And one called unto the other and said: Holy, holy, holy is the Lord of Hosts, full is the whole earth of his glory. (Repeated in Aramaic paraphrase). (Ezek. 3: 12): Then the spirit lifted me up, and I heard behind me the sound of a great rushing: Blessed be the glory of the Lord from his place (Aramaic paraphrase follows). (Ex. 15: 18): The Lord will reign forever and ever. (Aramaic version). (Four verses: 1 Chron. 29: 18; Ps. 78: 38; 86: 5; 119: 142). (Micah 7: 20): Thou wilt perform the truth to Jacob and the mercy to Abraham which thou hast sworn unto our fathers from the days of old. (Ps. 68: 20): Blessed be the Lord day by day; God heapeth upon us our salvation; Selah. (Three verses Ps. 46: 12; 84: 13; 20: 10; see above).

(After two non-Biblical passages, to be given hereafter, proceed):

(Ps. 30: 13): To the end that my glory may sing to thee and not be silent, O Lord my God, I will give thanks to thee forever. [(Jer. 17: 7): Blessed is the man who trusteth in the Lord, and whose hope the Lord is. (Isa. 26: 4): Trust ye in the Lord forever; for in Jah, the Lord, is the rock of ages.] (Ps. 9: 11): Yea, those that know thy name will trust in thee; for thou hast not forsaken those that seek thee. O Lord. (Isa. 42: 21): It pleased the Lord for his righteousness' sake to magnify the Law and make it honorable.

The Sefardim omit two verses from the Prophets and substitute two Psalm verses. The ground for inserting this mosaic given by the old writers is that late visitors at the Synagogue may still have an opportunity to say the Thrice-Holy in company.

This brings us near the end of the morning service. At or very near its conclusion the Psalm is read which was sung on that day of the week in the Temple, the 24th on Sunday, on Monday the 48th, on the following days, 82, 94, 81, 93, and on the Sabbath 92.[9]

From work time on Friday to the sacred rest on the night of Sabbath we are led by six Psalms, 95-99, "Come, let us sing to the Lord," and 29, which closes "with peace," a poem addressed to the Bride Sabbath, and Psalm 92, with the opening words of which each worshipper enters the sacred day; to this Ps. 93 is a pendant. What precedes 92 and thus precedes the Sabbath is now called its "reception." The Psalms and the poem have been set to numberless airs of both old and new style, and seem inseparable from the genuine Friday evening. Yet their use is modern. Not only Abudraham early in the fourteenth century, but R. Joseph Karo, writing his Code in the sixteenth, knows nothing about them, but they speak of a man "receiving" the Sabbath in his evening Prayer; that is, when it is already upon us. The poem of Solomon the Levite (Alkabets) in which he sings to the Bride has gathered round it all these Psalms for her reception.[10]

On all afternoons the service begins with *Ashre*, then on Sabbaths or Festivals the verses and prayers beginning "A redeemer will come to Zion," which have been omitted in the morning; then a Half Kaddish, and on the Sabbath this Psalm verse (69: 14):

"But as for me, my prayer is unto thee, O Lord, in an acceptable time; O God, in thy manifold mercy, answer me in the truth of thy salvation."

After the Sabbath afternoon Prayer come the following three Psalm verses (unless there is besides the Sabbath some occasion for gladness):

(Ps. 119: 142): Thy righteousness is everlasting righteousness, and thy Law is truth. (71: 19): Thy righteousness, O God, is very high, thou who hast done great things, O God, who is like unto thee. (36: 7): Thy righteousness is like the mountains of God, thy judgments as the mighty deep; thou preservest man and beast, O Lord."[11]

In winter on Sabbath afternoons, Psalm 104, that pen picture of moving and living nature, and the fifteen Songs of Degrees (Ps. 120-134) are read, more as a private devotion than as part of the service. The Sefardim substitute Ps. 119 for 104. When it becomes dark, friends at the Synagogue or at home chant together Psalms 144 and 67; the former speaks of health, plenty, and peace; the latter calls on all nations to thank God with us for his blessings, so that the Sabbath may leave a good taste. The 104th Psalm is, however, solemnly chanted by the Sefardim in opening the evening service on New Moons.[12]

On ordinary evenings, including Saturday night (and as late as the fourteenth century on the nights of Sabbaths and Festivals as well), the following two verses are spoken before the first benediction or in public before the leader's address:

(Ps. 78: 38): "He is merciful, atoneth iniquity; and will not destroy, and will often turn back his wrath; and will not arouse all his anger. (Ps. 20: 10): O Lord, save; the King will answer when we call."[13]

But when the evening service is held "in its season," that is, after night-fall, and disconnected from the afternoon

Prayer, it is introduced by Psalm 134 ("Bless the Lord, all ye servants of the Lord, who stand in the Lord's house by night," and the three verses before mentioned (Ps. 46: 12; 84: 13; 20: 10), which make a sufficient basis for a "Half Kaddish;" and such a service is closed with Psalms 24, 8, and 29 as a basis for a Mourners' Kaddish.[14]

We have spoken of a third benediction which has come into use among all "Germans" in the work-day evening service. It is introduced by the following Bible verses, the doxologies already mentioned, Ps. 89: 53; 106: 48; 72: 18, 19. Then:

(Ps. 104: 31): Let the glory of the Lord endure forever; the Lord rejoiceth in his works. (Ps. 113: 2): Let the name of the Lord be blessed from henceforth and for evermore. (1 Sam. 12: 22): For the Lord will not forsake his people for his great name's sake; for it has pleased the Lord to make you his people. (1 Kings 18: 39): And the whole people saw it and fell on their faces and said: "The Lord is the God; the Lord is the God." (Zech. 14: 9): The Lord will be King over all the earth; in that day shall the Lord be one, and his name one. (Ps. 33: 22): May thy mercy be upon us, as we have hoped in thee. (Ps. 106: 47). Save us, O Lord, our God, and gather us from the nations, to give thanks to thy holy name and to triumph in thy praise. (86: 9): All nations whom thou hast made shall come and worship before thee, O Lord, and give honor to thy name. (Ps. 86: 10): For thou art great, and doest wonders, thou, O God, alone. (79: 13): And we are thy people and the sheep of thy pasture; we will thank thee for evermore; from generation to generation we shall tell thy praise.

In analogy to the above verses in the evening service for work-days, other verses have come into use for the nights of Sabbath and Festivals without any Talmudic authority. For Friday night:

(Ex. 31: 16, 17): The children of Israel shall keep the Sabbath, to observe the Sabbath throughout their generations, for a perpetual covenant. It is a sign between me and the children of Israel forever, that the Lord in six days made the heavens and the earth, and on the seventh day rested and was refreshed.

On the evenings of three festivals of joy in the German ritual:

(Lev. 23: 44): "And Moses declared to the children of Israel the set times of the Lord."

While the Sefardim say:

(Lev. 23: 4): "These are the set times of the Lord, holy convocations, which ye shall proclaim in their season."

On New Year's night in the German ritual:

(Ps. 81: 4): "Blow ye the horn on the new moon, the darkening, the day of our feast; for it is an ordinance to Israel; a judgment of the God of Jacob."

The Sefardim say on the same occasion:

(Numbers 10: 10): On the day of your gladness, and at your set times, and on your new moons, ye shall blow the trumpets upon your burnt offerings and upon your peace offerings, and it shall be to you for a memorial before the Lord your God; I am the Lord your God.

On the Atonement night both rituals have here:

(Lev. 16: 30): For on this day he will atone for you, to cleanse you from all your sins; before the Lord ye shall be clean.

On Saturday night after the Amida and Half Kaddish (unless a Festival falls within the coming week) Ps. 91 is spoken, preceded by the last verse of Ps. 90:

"Let the pleasantness of the Lord our God be upon us, and establish thou for us the work of our hands; yea, the work of our hands establish thou it."

Then the collection given above ("A redeemer will come to Zion") is recited, leaving off, however, the first two verses, so as to begin "Thou art holy;" then the full Kaddish. Then follows a collection of blessings and happy prophecies, the two blessings Isaac bestows on Jacob, Gen. 27: 28, 29, and 28: 3, 4; Jacob blessing Joseph, Gen. 49:

25, 26; Moses the people, Deut. 7: 13, 14, 15. (Blessing on Ephraim and Manasseh, Gen. 48: 16; on the people, Deut. 1: 10, 11.) Blessings and predictions of good, Deut. 27: 3-6; 27: 8, 12; 15: 6; 33: 29. (Forgiveness and redemption, Isa. 44: 22, 23; 47: 4.) Joy over God's help, Isa. 45: 17; Joel 2: 26, 27; Isa. 55: 12; 12: 2-6; 25: 9. (Isa. 2: 5; 33: 6; 1 Sam. 18: 14; on redeeming, Ps. 55: 19; 1 Sam. 14: 45; Isa. 35: 10.) (On turning evil into good, Ps. 30: 12; Deut. 23: 6; Jer. 31: 12.) On peace, Isa. 57: 19; 1 Chr. 12: 19; 1 Sam. 25: 6; Ps. 29: 11. (A Talmudic passage, then words of comfort, 1 Kings 8: 57; Deut. 4: 4; Isa. 51: 3; 42: 21. Lastly Ps. 128, a eulogy on the hard-working breadwinner, for the week of toil now begins.)

The parts in parentheses belong only to the Polish branch of the German ritual.

Other Psalms and poetic verses will be referred to in connection with the reading of the Pentateuch lesson; others again, in connection with the meal or retirement to bed. For want of space we cannot treat of the verses which are intermingled with the Selihoth, or poetry on forgiveness, mentioned in Chapter XII.

Many devout men and women read the whole Psalter through once a month, or even once a week, according to divisions made for that purpose. In many Synagogues the whole Psalter is read on the afternoon of the first New Year's day or on the night of Atonement. It is also the second part of the exercises in "staying up" in the night of Hoshana Rabba, the reading of Deuteronomy being the first part. Verses from the Psalms or other parts of Scripture that are quoted in non-Biblical prayers, or intertwined with them, are treated with the latter.

THE words in the second benediction of the evening, "In thy law we breathe by day and by night," are not meant as a figure of speech. He who learned and taught the written and oral law, and placed this occupation above all earthly joys and hopes, was the ideal to the men who have, in the course of two thousand years, elaborated the service book, as he was to the author of the 176 verses of the 119th Psalm.

Many loyal and well-meaning Jews were disabled by poverty, lack of teachers, or lack of talent and taste from deeper study. To these it was thought good to furnish a minimum; they might acquire a substitute for real learning.

The Shema contains the weightiest matter, but its recital is separately commanded, aside from the general duty to learn and remember the Law.[1] Hence the sages of Israel placed in the service book, to be read every day or at stated times, other passages from the Tora and some Mishna and Baraïtha, so that everybody should do some studying.

The first choice was made of such passages, one from each of the sources, which were put in the early morning service after the benediction on rising and dressing, but before the Psalms and hymns: from the Tora the section from Numbers 28, on the daily sacrifice, the verses for Sabbath and New Moon to be also read on those days; from the Mishna, a chapter on the place of the several kinds of sacrifice in the Temple, and the distinctions in offering and eating.[2] Thus the worshipper, while dutifully studying, would also make mention of the daily oblations, the next

13   (193)

best thing to bringing them. For the uncodified oral Law, or Baraitha, R. Ishmael's account of the thirteen rules for expounding the Tora was given as a fit sample. The first two rules are easily understood and remembered, "to reason 1, from the lesser to the greater; 2, by judgment on like words;" the other eleven are rather abstruse.[3]

But these passages are long, dry, and undevotional; something short was needed, something to go to the heart. In a note written late in the twelfth century we come across the new selections, now in daily use.[4] Three verses from the Law are wanted; none are finer than the priestly blessing; better yet the whole section of six verses which embraces it, the command to Aaron and his sons to impart it, and the promise, "they will set my name on the children of Israel and I will bless them."[5] From the Mishna this section:

These things have no (prescribed) measure: The field corner, the first fruits, the appearance-offering (on the Festivals), and charity and the study of the Law.

These are the things of which man eats the fruits in this world, but the capital remains for the world to come; these they are: honoring father and mother, and charity, and going early to the house of study in the morning and evening, and housing travellers, and visiting the sick, and endowing the bride, and devotion in prayer, and escorting the dead, and bringing about peace between man and man; and against all of these (stands out) the study of the Law.[6]

Here we have a daily confession that a good and noble life finds its reward here and hereafter. Thousands who drop or slur over the three longer passages recite these short ones immediately after the benedictions over the duty of studying the Law, which run thus:

Blessed be thou, O Lord our God, King of the world, who has sanctified us with his commandments and commanded us to be busy with the words of the Law. O Lord our God, make the words of thy Law pleasant in our mouth; and may we and our children, and late descendants, and all the descendants of thy

STUDY AS PART OF THE LITURGY

people, the House of Israel, all of us know thy name, and learn thy Law for its own sake; blessed be thou, O Lord, who teacheth the Law to his people Israel. Blessed be thou, O Lord our God, King of the world, who hath chosen us from all the nations and given us his Law; blessed be thou, O Lord, the Giver of the Law.

The latter of these two benedictions is the same which is recited at the reading desk before the open scroll; it renders thanks for the written law; the first acknowledges the honorable but laborious task of studying the traditions and of searching the Scriptures.[7]

So much for every day. On the Sabbath and Festivals after the "Additional" three other Talmudic passages follow the introductory line, "Thou art he before whom our fathers burn the incense of sweet odors." First, a Baraïtha which sets forth by weight and measure the composition of this incense; next, a section of the Mishna, which gives the Psalm for each day as the Levites sang it on the steps of the Temple, not by the numbers of the Psalms, but by their first verses;[8] third, the following eulogy on the men of learning:

Rabbi Eleazar says, said Rabbi Hanina, the disciples of the Wise further peace in the world, as it is written: For all thy sons are disciples of the Lord; and much is the peace of thy sons. (Isa. 54: 13): Do not read *Thy Sons* (Banaich), but *Those That Build Thee* (Bonaich). There is much peace for those who love thy Law; and they find no stumbling block. For the sake of my brothers and friends, may I speak peacefully to thee; for the sake of the Lord, our God, may I seek happiness for thee. The Lord giveth strength to His people; may the Lord bless His people with peace.[9]

On Friday night a chapter of the Mishna is read (by the Sefardim before the regular evening service begins, by the Germans near its end), which deals with the Friday night lamp and other laws of the Sabbath.[10] The above saying of R. Eleazar and R. Hanina is added, so that this lesson also ends with peace.

The chapter on the place of sacrifice, the thirteen rules, the discourse on the Sabbath lights, and the mixture of spices, are always among the things dropped first whenever a progressive congregation takes any liberties with the old service book. Most important among the longer Talmudic passages is the Treatise *Aboth*, in five chapters, to which a sixth chapter of similar strain was added at a later but unknown time; the six being found in every old-fashioned prayer book.[11] At present the Sefardic Jews read one chapter on each of the six Sabbaths between Passover and Pentecost, but the Jews of the German Minhag not only do this, but go over the whole again and again, to the last Sabbath before New Year. The Treatise is known in English as the Ethics.[12] The chapters are not chanted by the leader; any man or woman reads a chapter either at home or in the Synagogue before or after the afternoon service.

At the house of mourning and on anniversaries, or whenever ten Jews, gathered for the common worship of God, wish to "learn," a few sections from one of these chapters are ready to hand. Children whose training does not pass beyond the Prayer Book and Pentateuch are set to study the Ethics, and thus whatever knowledge the unlearned Jew has of the Mishna is drawn from this source.

These comforting words are read before each chapter:

All Israel has a share in the world to come, as it is said (Isa. 60: 21): And thy people, all of them righteous, shall forever inherit the land (? earth), the young tree of my planting, the work of my hands, that I may be glorified.[13]

After each chapter or any selection from the Ethics the following is read:

R. Hananiah ben Akashiah said: The Holy One, blessed be he, was pleased to give Israel merit; therefore he multiplied for them Law and commandments, as it is said (Isa. 42: 21): It pleased the Lord for his righteousness' sake to make the Law great and honorable."

The Treatise *Aboth*, unlike most other treatises in the Mishna, does not deal with some branch of jurisprudence, polity, or ritual law, nor does it lay down any rules of conduct by the authority of the greater number or of the prevailing party among the learned. It reports the opinions of the "Fathers," that is, of individual Rabbis from the days of the Great Synod down to the sons of Rabbi Judah, the Patriarch, on points of morals, faith, and occasionally of worldly wisdom.

The first chapter brings down the chain of tradition from Moses, Joshua, the Elders (or Judges), and Prophets to the men of the Great Synod; from the last of them, Simeon the Just, to his disciple Antigonus, from the latter's disciples to the five "couples," that is, the successive Presidents and Vice-Presidents of the Sanhedrin, including Hillel and Shammaï, contemporaries of Herod the Great; then it names Rabban Gamaliel, who was a late descendant of Hillel, and his son Rabban Simeon, the Patriarchs of their day; and it credits each with one or more favorite sayings. Some of these refer to the duties of the judge alone; but "always judge every man for the best" (literally, towards the scale of innocence) is intended for daily life. Great are Hillel's words, "Who pushes his name forward, his name is lost; he who does not add (to his knowledge) loses, and he who does not teach, deserves to be killed; and let him who makes gain of the crown (religious learning) perish!" Also, "If I am not for myself, who is for me! if I am for myself, what am I?" Shammaï says, "Say little and do much, and receive everybody with a pleasant face."

The second chapter begins with Rabbi (i. e., Judah), and the Patriarch Gamaliel, his son, but then goes back to earlier teachers as far as Hillel. Its gems are, "Study of the law is best when combined with secular work; for in the fatigue over both we forget sin." Or, among Hillel's sayings, "Do not believe in thyself till the day of thy death; and do not judge thy neighbor till thou hast come into his position." Again, "The bashful cannot learn, nor the impatient man teach." Seeing a skull floating in the water he said, "Because thou didst drown thou wast drowned; and those that drowned thee will be drowned." Rabbi Eliezer says, "Return one day before thy death." Rabbi Simeon says, "When thou prayest, do not make thy prayer a fixed task, but mercy and supplication before God; for it is said: For he is gracious and merciful, even long-suffering, and bethinks himself upon the evil." Rabbi Eleazar says, "Be watchful to learn the Law and know how to answer the infidel" (literally, Epicurus). Rabbi Tarphon (Tryphon) says, "Know, the reward of the righteous is given in the world to come."

The third chapter delights in an antithetic style.

Says R. Hanina ben Teradion, "When two men sit together with no talk of the Law between them, that is the seat of the scoffers, of which Scripture says: He does not sit in the seat of scoffers. But two who sit down and talk words of the Law, the presence of God (*Shechina*) is poured out between them, as it is written: Then those that feared the Lord spoke to each other, and the Lord listened and heard, and it was written down in the book of remembrance before him, for those who fear the Lord and think of his name." R. Simeon follows with a parallel as to three who eat at one table and do or do not speak "words of the Law." And another Rabbi sets forth the merits of ten, of five, of three, of two, who study together, and at last of one by himself, having for each number a verse by way of proof, winding up, "In every place where I make mention of my name, I will come unto thee and bless thee." The saintly R. Hanina ben Dosa says, "Whose fear of sin precedes his learning, that man's learning will stand; but if his learning precedes his fear of sin (religious feeling), it will not stand. Whose good works are greater than his learning, that man's learning will stand," etc. R. Eleazar ben Azariah, one of the Patriarchs, enlarges on this by comparing the man whose learning exceeds his good works with a tree of few roots and many branches, which the first storm will tear from the ground and overthrow; the man of more good works than learning, with a tree of widespread roots and few branches that will withstand all the winds in the world unmoved, and quotes for each of them one of the beautiful and well-known verses in the 17th chapter of Jeremiah.

The fourth chapter sets out with Ben Zoma's rules, "Who is wise? he who learns from everybody; who is mighty? he who represses his passions, as it is written: The long-suffering man is better than the mighty, and he who rules over his own spirit, than one who takes a city; who is rich? he who is glad with his portion, as it is written: When thou eatest of the labor of thy hand thou art happy, and it goes well with thee. Happy (he adds) in this world, and it goes well with thee in the world to come." Rabbi Jannai says, "We have no means to understand either the happiness of the wicked or the sufferings which befall the just." An otherwise unknown R. Mathia says, "Be a tail to the lions rather than a head to the foxes." R. Jacob says, "This world is like a vestibule before the next world; prepare thyself in the vestibule, that thou mayest enter the banquet hall" (triclinium). R. Meïr says, "Do not look at the jar, but at what there is in it; there is many a new jar full of old wine, and old jars that hold not even new wine" (old men wholly ignorant).

The fifth chapter is almost throughout arranged by numbers. First the number ten: the generations from Adam to Noah; from Noah to Abraham; ten temptations of Abraham, the ten plagues of Egypt, ten at the Red Sea, ten times the Israelites tempted God in the wilderness, ten wonderful things bordering on the miraculous were noticed in the Temple. But the most noteworthy decade comes last, "Ten things were created on the eve of Sabbath during the twilight, namely, the mouth of the earth (which swallowed Korah), the mouth of the well (from which the Israelites drank in the wilderness), the mouth of (Balaam's) ass, the rainbow, the Manna, the rod (of Moses), the Shamir (an insect said to have been used in cutting the stones for Solomon's Temple), the alphabet, and the writing (on the tables), and the tables (of the covenant)." Here is an evident effort to reconcile the belief in the miracles of Scripture with the orderly progress of the world according to laws implanted in it from the beginning; on the same lines as that of Babbage, the inventor of the calculating machine, in this nineteenth century. Next come sevens; the first and best known is:

Seven things are known in the stupid fellow and seven in the wise man: the wise man has nothing to say in presence of one who is more learned and has a greater following; and he does not interrupt the words of another; and is not overhasty in answering; he asks according to the subject-matter; and answers (questions of religion) according to the established Law (not what he thinks ought to be the Law); and speaks of things in their order from first to last; and of what he has not heard, he says, I have not heard it, and he admits the truth; and the opposite to all these denote the stupid fellow.

After the sevens come the fours, of which the following is the best example:

There are four qualities in giving alms: One who is willing to give, but does not wish others to give, he begrudges the wealth of others; willing that others shall give, but unwilling himself to give, he begrudges his own; willing to give, and that others give, is pious; unwilling to give, or for others to give, is wicked.

After a short prayer, which originally marked the end of the chapter and treatise, we find:

Ben He-He (quære: the son of Hillel the Great) used to say: According to the trouble is the reward. He also said: One five years old should begin to read (the Bible), at ten years, study the Mishna, at fifteen years, Gemara (that is, discussion on the Oral Law); at eighteen, he is ready for the bridal chamber; at twenty to pursue (his trade); at thirty, he is in his strength; at forty, he reaches understanding; at fifty, he reaches wisdom; at sixty, old age; at seventy, the hoary head; at eighty, might (cmp. Ps. 90: 10); at ninety, to bend down low; at one hundred, as if he were dead, and had passed from the world.

The sixth chapter was compiled probably after the completion of the Talmud as a supplement to these five chapters. It is weaker than the Treatise Aboth, and made up mainly of praises of the Tora and of those who study it. Among the forty-eight qualities, efforts, and habits by which the crown of the Tora must be acquired, the last is:

One must tell everything in the name of him who said it before him; for we learn from Scripture, that one who says a thing, giving the proper credit, brings salvation into the world; for it is written (Esther 2: 22): "Esther told the King in the name of Mordecai."

We may lastly mention a highly interesting passage from the Babylonian Talmud, which in the Polish ritual is recited on Saturday nights:

R. Johanan says: At every place where thou findest the greatness of God, thou wilt also find his condescension. This is written in the Law, repeated in the Prophets, and put for the third time in the Holy Writings. First in the Law: For the Lord, your God, he is the God of gods, and the Lord of lords, the great, the mighty, and the fearful God, who does not respect persons, and who takes no bribes. And right thereafter it is written: He worketh the cause of the fatherless and of the widow, and loveth the stranger, to give him bread and raiment. Repeated in the Prophets, where it is written: For thus saith he who is high and exalted, who dwelleth eternally, and whose name is holy: I dwell on high and holy; also with the contrite and the humble in spirit; to quicken the spirit of the lowly and to revive the heart of the contrite. Thirdly, it is written in the Holy Writings: Sing unto God, play on strings to his name; make a road to him who rides through the spaces; in his name, the Lord; and shout ye before him. And right thereafter: A father of the fatherless and the judge of the widows is God in his holy dwelling.[15]

Other selections from the Mishna in the service books are of less import. The *Tikkun*, or Arrangement, for the first night of Pentecost contains the first and last section in each treatise of the Mishna. This is read in a perfunctory way, and has done little if anything towards the spread of Rabbinic learning. The Sefardic Prayer Book used in the East contains the Treatise Rosh Hashana as a proper reading for the supper table on the first night of the New Year; lastly, it is usual for men of learned tastes to take the Mishnic Treatise Joma to the Synagogue on the Day of Atonement and to read it rather than take part in the recital of the less attractive "poetries."

CHAPTER XV.

THE LESSER AND THE DOUBTFUL BENEDICTIONS

A PASSAGE in the Babylonian Talmud, given in the names of the Rabbis who flourished early in the fourth century, sets out the different benedictions which the Israelite ought to recite, when he rises in the morning, thanking God for each of the several operations which lead from sleep to the work of the day. Considering that it was thought improper to pronounce God's name before washing hands and face, these words cannot be suited to the act; all must wait for the morning ablution; the present custom for those who attend the Synagogue each morning is to recite them all as the first part of the service.[1] All of the benedictions are introduced with the words, "Blessed be thou, O Lord our God, King of the world;" only what follows need be stated. We omit here what one should say when he goes to bed, but when one awakes he says (without the introductory words):

My God, the soul which thou hast placed within is pure; thou hast formed it, thou hast breathed it into me, thou guardest it within me, and thou wilt hereafter take it from me, to return it to me in the later future; as long as the soul is within me, I confess before thee, O Lord my God and God of my fathers, Master of all worlds, Lord of all souls. Blessed,etc., who returneth the soul to dead bodies.

Here is an assertion of the resurrection of the flesh not found elsewhere in the liturgy. An old authority however suggests, "Blessed be thou, O Lord our God, King of the world, who revivest the dead," as a substitute.[2]

The Talmud proceeds: When he hears the crowing of the cock, let him say—

"Blessed, etc., who hast given understanding to the cock, to distinguish between day and night" (alluding to Job 38: 36, where the common version however renders "mind" the word which the Rabbis interpret "cock").

When he opens his eyes, "Blessed, who makest the blind to see." When he sits up, "Blessed, who loosest the captives." Its temporary substitute. "Blessed, etc., who settest the lowly on high," soon fell into disuse.

The benedictions over the study of the Law have been given in the preceding chapter. When he has put on his garment, let him say, "Blessed, who clothest the naked;" when he sits up straight, "Blessed, who raisest up them that are bowed down." When he comes down on the ground, let him say, "Blessed, who stretchest the earth over the waters" (Ps. 136: 6). When he steps out, "Blessed, who directest the steps of man." When he fastens his shoe, "Blessed, who hast provided for all my wants." When he binds his girdle around him, "Blessed, who girdeth Israel with strength." When he spreads his kerchief on his head (making his turban), "Blessed, who crownest Israel with beauty." When he wraps himself in the fringed shawl, "Blessed, who hast sanctified us with his commandments, and hast commanded us to wrap ourselves with the fringes." When he puts the phylacteries on his arm, he should say, "Blessed, who hast, etc., and commanded us to put on phylacteries." When he puts them on his head, "Blessed, etc., and commanded us about the duty of phylacteries." When he washes his hands, "Blessed, etc., and commanded us about the washing of hands." When he washes his face, he should say:

Blessed be thou, O Lord our God, King of the world, who removest the bonds of sleep from my eyes and slumber from my eyelids (cmp. Ps. 132: 4). Be it thy will, O Lord my God and God of our fathers, that thou mayest lead me in the path of thy Law, keep me fast to thy commands, and bring me not into sin or iniquity, *nor into temptation*, nor into scorn; bend my impulse into subjection to thee; let me be far from evil men and evil companions; let me hold fast to the good impulse and to a good companion in thy world, and let me find to-day and every day grace, love, and mercy in thine eyes, and in the eyes of all that see me, and deal with me in kindness. Blessed be thou, O Lord, who dealest kindly with his people Israel.

Since these benedictions were transferred from the bedside to the house of worship, and are given out by the leader to be answered by the *Amen* of those assembled with him, the singular in the last of them has been turned into the plural, "Our God, lead us; bring us," etc. For a few hundred years the benediction, "He who crowns Israel with beauty," was neglected in Christian countries,[3] because the Jew did not wind his handkerchief into a turban, or actually walked about bare-headed, but in the fifteenth century it became again universal.

Another passage of the Talmud recommends three benedictions, "who hast not made me a Gentile," "who hast not made me a bondman," "who hast not made me a woman," which are in our service books placed among those given above. The Israelite here thanks God for his duties, he being bound by all the commands of the Law, the Gentile by very few, the bondman and the woman by only a part. In another passage the first of these benedictions says plainly, "who hast made me an Israelite," "not made me a woman," "not made me quite ignorant." But the former version has prevailed.[4] The motive assigned in the Talmud for these expressions of thanks is that each Israelite may have occasion for blessing God one hundred times each day.

Another benediction, very proper after a good night's rest, is found in the German prayer books, "who givest power to the faint" (cmp. Isa. 40: 29); but it is wholly rejected by the Sefardim, because it has no support in the Talmud.

A half homiletic, half mystical book of the ninth century recommends the recital of "Master of all worlds," which was probably then in daily use by the more devout, in the following words:

"Let every man fear Heaven in secret as in public, confess the truth, speak the truth in his heart, and rise early and say." This is also found in R. Amram's liturgy, which, if the passage is authentic, would be the older source. In the Sefardic and in the Polish Minhag the above injunction is read along with the piece that follows:

Master of all worlds! we cast our supplications before thee, not by reason of our righteousness, but of thy abundant mercies. (Dan. 9: 18): What are we (etc., as in Ch. XII, in Neïla, to "all is vanity").

(After this deep wail over the nothingness of man before infinite time comes the answer, that though plain man be nothing, the Israelite is something):

But we are thy people, the sons of thy covenant, children of Abraham, thy friend, to whom thou sworest on Mount Moriah, the seed of Isaac, his only child, who lay bound on the altar, the congregation of Jacob, thy first-born, to whom in love and in rejoicing thou gavest the names of Israel and Jeshurun. Therefore we are bound to thank, to praise, and to glorify thee, and to hallow, to honor, and to sanctify thy name. Happy we are, how goodly is our share, how pleasant our lot, how fair our heritage; happy we who early in the morning, and when the evening sets in, twice every day, say:

Hear, O Israel, the Lord our God, the Lord is One.

(Blessed be the name of his glorious Kingdom for evermore.)

Thou wast before the world was made; thou art since the world is made; thou art the same in this world; the same in the world to come; hallow thy name in those who sanctify it; hallow it in thy world; lift and raise our horn through thy salvation. [Blessed be thou, O Lord, thou who hallowest thy name among many].

This conclusion is given in the German prayer books, in the second person throughout. The Sefardim have never admitted that a competent authority has drawn up or recommended this benediction so as to justify the use of God's name in the close; they wind it up, "Blessed be he who sanctifieth his name among many."

Maimonides ignores it in enumerating the obligatory morning benedictions, but gives it in a slightly modified form without the divine name at the close in his "Order of Prayer for the Whole Year." Abudraham more than a hundred years later rejects it all as unauthorized.

A prayer beginning "Master of the Worlds" is spoken of in the Talmud as one of those drawn up to introduce the confessions on the Day of Atonement, but it can never be known how far it coincides with the above; probably only as far as "All is vanity."[5]

We have next in the morning service the "hymns," which carry with them two "Benedictions of Song," one at or near the beginning, the other at the end.

The first of these is peculiar by the many starts taken with the word "Blessed" before "Blessed be thou, O Lord" is reached:

Blessed be he who spoke and the world was; blessed be he; blessed the maker at the beginning; blessed be he who saith and doeth; blessed be he who decideth and carries out; blessed be he who hath mercy on the earth; blessed be he who hath mercy on his creatures; blessed he who payeth a goodly reward to those who fear him; blessed he who liveth forever, and lasteth into the infinite; blessed he who redeemeth and delivereth; blessed be his name.

Blessed be thou, O Lord our God, King of the world, the God, the merciful Father, who is praised by the mouth of his people, lauded and glorified by the tongue of his pious worshippers; in the songs of thy servant David we shall praise thee, O Lord our God, with hymns and melodies; we shall exalt and praise thee; we shall give thee glory and homage; we shall make mention of thy name, and give thee homage, our King, our only God, who liveth for evermore. Blessed be thou, O Lord, the King, who is praised in hymns.[6]

The closing benediction of song which follows the Psalms and other, morning hymns is quite short on work-days, but it is introduced on Sabbaths and Festivals by a long half-poetical introduction, of which a good part at least is very old, known from its first word as *Nish'math:*

May the soul of all that liveth bless thy name, O Lord our God, and the spirit of all flesh steadily glorify and exalt thy memorial, our King.
From everlasting to everlasting thou art God, and beside thee we have no King, Redeemer, or Saviour, no Deliverer, no merciful Provider; in all times of trouble and distress we have no King but thee. God of the first and of the last, Lord of all generations, praised in numberless hymns, who guideth his world with kindness and his creatures with mercy. And the Lord slumbers not, nor sleepeth; he who rouseth the sleeping, and them who are sunk in stupor he waketh; he causeth the dumb to speak, he looseth the bound, he supporteth the falling, and raiseth them that are bowed down; to thee alone we give thanks.

This part is of later date than what follows next, and sounds like a protest against the Christian belief in a Redeemer other than God. The Talmud, in speaking of the benediction after a copious fall of rain, denotes it, "Were our mouth full." We proceed here:

Were our mouth full of song like the sea, our tongue of gleeful airs like its numberless waves, our lips of praise like the wide expansion; were our eyes shining like sun and moon; could our hands reach out like the eagles of the sky; were our feet swift as the hinds; yet we could not thank thee, O Lord our God and God of our fathers, nor could we bless thy name one thousandth of what is due. Thousands of millions, myriads of myriads are the kind things which thou hast done for our fathers and for us. Thou hast saved us from Egypt, O Lord our God, and redeemed us from the house of bondage; hast fed us in famine, and supported us through plenty, hast delivered us from the sword, made us to escape the plague, and kept us from evil and malignant sickness. So far thy mercy hath helped us, and thy kindness hath not forsaken us; then do not, O Lord our God, reject us forever. Therefore, the limbs which thou hast distributed through our bodies, the spirit and breath which thou hast breathed into our nostrils, the tongue which thou hast placed into our mouth; all these shall thank and bless and praise and glorify and exalt and hold in awe and hallow thy name and do to it homage. For every mouth giveth thanks to thee; every tongue sweareth allegiance; every knee bendeth, and whatever is erect, boweth down before thee. And all hearts fear thee; all inwards and reins sing to thy name. As it is written (Ps. 35: 10): All my bones shall say: O Lord, who is like thee, who deliverest the poor from one stronger than he; the poor and needy from him that robbeth him.

So far, perhaps not quite so far, we have the thanksgiving spoken after a longed-for rain. The suggestions in the Talmud, that thanks should be given "for every single drop," accounts for the vast numbers; it does not take long for a thousand million drops to fall. It explains also the reference to famine and to plenty. What is given below has nothing to do with the thanks for rain:

The Almighty (El), the great, powerful, and fearful, God Most High, the owner of heaven and earth. We will praise and glorify thee and bless thy holy name. As it is written by David (Ps. 103: 1): Bless, O my soul, the Lord, and all my inwards his holy name. The Almighty, in the strength of thy power, the great, in the glory of thy name, the powerful for victory, and the fearful in thy terrors; the King sitting on a high and exalted throne; who inhabiteth eternity, high and holy is thy name (cmp. Isa. 57: 15) [for all this the Sefardim substitute: Thou hearest the supplication of the lowly; thou listenest to the cry of the poor man and savest him].

As it is written (Ps. 33: 1): Rejoice in the Lord, O ye righteous; praise is comely for the upright.

Be thou praised by the mouth of the upright; be thou blessed in the words of the righteous; be thou exalted by the tongue of the pious, and be thou sanctified in the heart of the saints.

And in the numerous assemblies of thy people, the house of Israel, thy name is glorified in song in every age; for such is the duty of all creatures before thee, O Lord our God and God of our fathers, to give thanks and praise, to glorify and exalt, to honor and to bless, to raise on high and to adorn with all the songs and praises of David, the son of Jesse, thy servant, thy anointed.

On work-days the benediction begins here:

14

May thy name be praised forever, our King, the great and holy King and God, in the heavens and on earth; for there are due to thee, our Lord, our God and God of our fathers, songs and hymns, praise and music, might and dominion, triumph, greatness, power, honor, magnificence, holiness, kingship, blessings, and thanksgiving from now for evermore. Blessed be thou, O Lord, God, King who art great in praises, God of thanksgivings, Lord of wonderful deeds, who hast chosen musical songs, King, God who liveth eternally.

The latter parts of the composition for Sabbath and the benediction proper betray accretions when acrostics had crept into the liturgy. The initials of Upright, Righteous, Pious, Saints, spell J-Tz-H-Q, i. e., Isaac, and the words were probably put into this order to bespeak the merits of Father Isaac on his seed. The words, Exalted, Blessed, Sanctified, Praised, are arranged thus on the solemn days, to make up R-B-Q-H, i. e., Rebekah, and the very seal of the benediction in clauses yields A-B-R-H-M. The fifteen nouns from Songs to Thanksgiving in the last paragraph were (it is believed) suggested by the fifteen Songs of Degrees.

The sealing of the benediction for rain was at first "God of many thanksgivings;" that of the benediction after song, as of the benediction before it, "King honored in praises," or, if you so choose to render it, "King praised in hymns." The longer sealings now in use in both rituals probably took their shape in the seventh or eighth century.[7]

Another doubtful benediction is the third one after the Shema in the evening service. We have in Chapter XIII given the Bible verses which introduce it. It proceeds thus:

Blessed be the Lord by day; blessed be the Lord by night; blessed be the Lord when we lie down; blessed be the Lord when we rise. For in thy hands are the souls of the living and of the dead (Job 12: 10): In whose hands is the soul of every living thing and the spirit of all mankind. (Ps. 31: 6): In thy hand I commit my spirit; thou hast redeemed me, O Lord, God of truth. Our

God in Heaven, give unity to thy name; establish thy Kingdom, and reign over us forever.

May our eyes behold, may our heart be glad, and our soul rejoice, in thy true salvation; when they say to Zion, thy King reigneth. The Lord is King, the Lord has reigned, the Lord will reign for evermore (see about this line, Ch. XIII). For the Kingdom is thine, and to all eternity thou wilt reign in glory; and we have no King but thee. Blessed be thou, O Lord, the King, who in his glory will always reign over us and over all his works.

The original of the benediction cannot be traced to any certain source. The Sefardim for a long while disputed its lawfulness, and have finally rejected it. In the German ritual it is used on all work-day evenings. It is said to be in some way a counterpart of the eighteen benedictions of the Amida, intended at first as a substitute for this.[8]

Lastly we have a benediction which precedes the performance (by the speaking of certain words) of a Scriptural command. The twenty-third chapter of Leviticus bids us count the days "from the morrow of the rest day," seven times seven days, nine and forty days between Passover and Pentecost. The command is performed during the services of the evening with which the day to be counted begins. Thus, on the thirty-third day, for instance, they say, "This is the thirty-third day, being four weeks and five days of the 'Omer (sheaf)." But first they give thanks on these forty-nine evenings.

Blessed be thou, O Lord our God, King of the world, who hast sanctified us by thy commandments, and hast commanded us about the counting of the 'Omer.[9]

CHAPTER XVI

OTHER PROSE COMPOSITIONS

RABBI JUDAH, the second Patriarch of the name and grandson of the compiler of the Mishna, is reported as sending up the following petition after the Prayer:

> May it be thy will, O Lord my God and God of my fathers, that thou mayest deliver me to-day and every day from the hard-faced and from hardfacedness (i. e., the impudent and impudence), from an evil man, an evil companion, an evil neighbor, and evil happenings, from the destroying adversary (Satan), from a hard cause and a stubborn litigant, be he a son of the covenant, or be he not a son of the covenant.

This "litany" has been received into the early morning service right after the bed-room benedictions set forth in the preceding chapter. In modern prayer books of the Sefardic ritual (not yet in Abudraham's commentary) the utterly unauthorized words are added, "and from a sentence to Ge-Hinnom," i. e., "from damnation." The "litany," or prayer for deliverance from named or unnamed evils, is undoubtedly much older; the filling up, in which the impudent, that is, undutiful subordinates and stubborn litigants are prominent, may have been suggested to the Patriarch by his troubles with the Rabbis and scholars, who often revolted against his measures.[1]

Next comes the doubtful benediction, "Master of the Worlds" (see the preceding chapter), then the following pendant thereto, written in very pure Hebrew:

> Thou art, O Lord our God, in the heavens and on the earth and in the highest heaven of heavens (cmp. 1 Kings 8: 27). Thou art the first and thou art the last, and beside thee there is no God.

Gather those that hope for thee from the four ends of the earth; may all those that come into the world learn and know, that thou art alone God for all the kingdoms of the earth. Thou hast made heaven and earth, the sea and all that is therein (Ex. 20: 11); and who is there among the works of thy hands, above or below, who can tell thee what to do. *Our Father who art in Heaven!* Deal kindly with us for the sake of thy great name, which is pronounced over us, and fulfill for us, O Lord our God, what has been written (Zeph. 3: 20): In that time I will bring them in; even in the time when I gather them; for I will set them up for a name and praise among all the peoples of the earth; when I return your captivity in your sight, says the Lord.[2]

Omitting for want of space the non-Biblical parts of "long *Vehu Rahum*," as read on Monday and Thursday mornings (see Ch. XIII), we are brought to a short prayer for these days after a Half Kaddish and before the taking out of the scroll, drawn up in two varying forms:

(1) God, long-suffering and great in kindness and truth, do not chastise me in thy wrath; spare, O Lord, thy people, and save us from all that is evil; we have sinned against thee, O Master; forgive, in thy abundant mercies, O God.
(2) God, long-suffering and great in kindness and truth, do not hide thy face from us; spare, O Lord, thy people Israel, and deliver us from all evil: we have sinned, etc.

This prayer is omitted on all holidays, such as Middle Days, New Moons, Hanucca, Purim, and on the Ninth of Ab. It is not noticed by Maimonides in his Code. Abudraham gives both forms to be recited consecutively as a fully accepted part of the service.[3]

Reserving for another chapter whatever is closely related to the "lessons," we come next to these petitions which the Germans read on Mondays and Thursdays—the Sefardim, however, on the Sabbath preceding a New Moon—while the scroll is on the desk:

Be it the will of our Father who is in Heaven, to set up our House of Life and to restore thy Presence to our midst; soon in our days, and say ye, Amen.

Be it the will of our Father who is in Heaven, to show mercy to us, even to our remnant, and to keep the destroyer and plague away from us and from all his people Israel, and say ye, Amen.

Be it the will of our Father who is in Heaven, to keep alive among us the wise men of Israel, them, their wives and sons and daughters and disciples, and the disciples of their disciples, in all their dwelling places, and say ye, Amen.

Be it the will of our Father who is in Heaven, that we may hear and receive good tidings of salvation and comfort, and may he gather our outcasts from the four corners of the earth, and say ye, Amen.

To which the Germans add:

Our brethren, all the children of Israel, who are placed in distress and captivity, who abide either on the sea or on land; may God have mercy on them, and bring them forth from distress to enlargement, from gloom to light, from bondage to redemption, this year, soon, and at a near time, and say ye, Amen.[4]

We come next to the un-Scriptural part of the collection, "A redeemer will come to Zion," of which the Scripture verses have been given in Chapter XIII:

Blessed be our God, who has created us for his glory, and has separated us from the erring; who has given us the Law of Truth, and has planted within us eternal life. May he open our heart to his Law, and may he put therein the love and fear of him, that we may do his will and that we may serve him with a full heart; to the end we may not labor in vain, and be not born for the hurrying moment. Be it thy will, O Lord our God and God of our fathers, that we may observe thy statutes and precepts in this world, and that we may merit, and live to see and inherit, happiness and blessing [in the days of the Messiah and] in the life of the world to come.

The words in brackets are not in the Sefardic Prayer Book.[5]

A composition written for the Day of Memorial, *'Alenu* ("It is our duty") (see Ch. XI), wherein Israel takes upon itself the yoke of God's Kingdom, and hopes that all men alike will soon acknowledge it, comes next.

The Germans recite the two paragraphs as Rab composed

them, for an introduction to the Kingdom verses, and here
they formerly stopped;[5] but modern prayer books subjoin
these two verses:

As it is written in thy Law: the Lord shall reign forevermore;
and it is said, the Lord shall be King over all the earth: on that
day the Lord shall be one and his name One.

The latter verse, the embodiment of Israel's faith, is best
known to old and young from its recital here. Every choir
solemnly sings the closing words, "The Lord shall be one
and his name One."

'Alenu was formerly recited only in the morning, the
complete Kaddish preceding, the Mourners' Kaddish following it.[6] It is now recited after every service in order
to give the mourners an opportunity to say "Kaddish."

The Sefardim have but very lately (say in the sixteenth
century) adopted *'Alenu* in the daily liturgy, and only its
first paragraph. They put it at the very end, after the
Psalm for the day, without even a Kaddish to follow it.

On the Sabbath, after reading the lessons from the Law
and from the Prophets, but without any reference to them,
four blessings are spoken in the German ritual, two in Aramaic, two in Hebrew. The former have become quite a
stumbling block, partly because the language once chosen
to make them more easily understood is now least known,
partly because the first of the two has long since been out of
date, and a "vain prayer," and as such unlawful: they are
known as *Yekum Purkan*.

May deliverance arise from heaven, grace and kindness, long-
continued mercy and plentiful provision, heavenly assistance, bodily
health, and the higher light, live and lasting seed, a posterity
which will not cease nor drop out from the words of the Law*; to
our Masters and Rabbis, the holy companies that are in Palestine
or in Babylonia; to the heads of the assemblies, the heads of the
exile (*Resh Gelutha*); the heads of the colleges, and the judges of the
courts, to their disciples, and to the disciples of their disciples, and
to all who study the Law.** May the King of the world bless

them, extend their lives, make their days many, and give length to their years; may they be saved and delivered from all trouble and from all grievous sickness; may our Master in Heaven be their support, at every time and season, and say ye, Amen.

According to the rubric in the prayer books an individual should recite this even at his home. But in the Synagogue this formula is repeated, substituting now for the words between * and ** the following:

"to all this holy congregation, the great and the small, women and children."

In what follows, the words "you" and "your" are substituted for "they" and "their."

Thus modified this blessing is very proper.

The language is the eastern Aramaic; the word for assemblies (*Calla*) denotes the half-yearly meeting addressed by the Babylonian Rabbis; the word for colleges (*Methibatha*), those of Sura and Pumbeditha. The heads of these colleges must have sent these compositions to the Western world, that they might have the benefit of the prayers of all Israel, perhaps after, perhaps before the days of R. Amram.[7] The mention of the Palestinian schools was an honor paid to the sacred soil on which they stood; for at the time but little learning was left at Tiberias and Cæsarea.

The Sefardim in lively correspondence with the Babylonian authorities were probably the first to receive *Yekum Purkan* into their liturgy. Being the first also to learn of the downfall and extinction of the schools, they discontinued the recital of words which had become a "vain prayer," while the Jews of the German Minhag, from sheer inertia, went on praying for dignitaries for from four hundred to eight hundred and fifty years after their extinction.[8]

Next comes an appropriate prayer in Hebrew for those of our own day:

He who blessed our fathers, Abraham, Isaac, and Jacob, may he bless all this holy congregation, with all other like congregations;

them, their wives, their sons and daughters, and all that is theirs; those who set aside synagogues for worship, and those who enter them to pray; those who give lamps for lighting them, and wine for *Kiddush* (consecration) and for *Habdala* (separation), bread to travellers, and alms to the poor; and all those who faithfully attend to the needs of the community. May God pay their reward, remove from them all sickness, heal their bodily ailments, and forgive their sins, and send blessing and prosperity unto all their undertakings, and so with Israel, their brethren, and say ye, Amen.

It is an outgrowth of the blessings that are pronounced at the reading of the lessons (see next Book). It is neither found nor mentioned in the older standards of the German ritual, such as the Mahzor Vitry, and dates probably from the sixteenth century.

The Sefardim have combined parts of this blessing with a part of the second *Yekum Purkan* into a curious compound of Hebrew and Aramaic.

A well-known passage of the Mishna tells us to pray for the welfare of the government imposed on Israel by the Gentiles, "for were not men afraid of it, they would eat each other alive;" i. e., the worst government is better than none at all.[9]

However, no prayer for government is found in the old liturgies, nor any direction to recite one at any named time in the old standards. Abudraham, however, after speaking of the lessons, says, "It is the custom to bless the King and to pray to God, that he may give him victory," and after justifying this custom he proceeds, "And then he blesses the congregation." He does not give the form of either blessing. In Spain, where the intercourse between Christians and Jews was close, and where many of the former understood Hebrew, the government probably saw to it that the Jews performed a duty enjoined on them by their own Sages. Hence the formula below was elaborated, and when Spanish and Portuguese Jews about the year 1600 took refuge in Holland, they brought this formula with them; it is printed in the Amsterdam prayer book of 1658. When the German princes found the Jews of Amsterdam praying for their government, they made their own Jewish subjects do likewise, and these adopted the Sefardic form less its astrological part. Thus *Hannothen Teshua* came into the German ritual, but after the blessing of the congregation.

Here it is:

He who giveth salvation to kings and dominion to anointed rulers; his Kingdom is everlasting; he who delivered his servant David from the cruel sword (cmp. Ps. 144: 10); who maketh a way in the sea and a path in mighty waters (Isa. 43: 16); may he bless, keep, guard, and help, exalt, and raise higher and higher our lord, the king, N. N., high be his glory; may the great King of kings preserve him alive, and deliver him from all trouble and harm [Sefardim add: from all unlucky influences of the stars], subject nations to him, overthrow his enemies, and let him prosper wheresoever he turneth; may the great King of kings put mercy into his heart and that of all his counsellors and grandees, to deal kindly with us and with all Israel, our brethren; in his days and in ours may Judah be saved, and Israel dwell securely; and may a redeemer come to Zion; so mote it be; and say ye, Amen.

On the Sabbath before a New Moon the congregation join in the following prayer for the coming of a happy month:

Be it thy will, O Lord our God and God of our fathers, to renew for us this month unto happiness and blessing; give us long life, peaceful life, happy life; a life of blessings; a life of good provision, a life of bodily health; a life full of fear of God and fear of sinning; a life without shame or blushing; a life of wealth and honor; a life with love of the law and fear of God; life in which our wishes may be fulfilled for good. Amen. Selah.

The above is given in the Talmud, without the words, "to renew for us this month unto happiness and blessing," as the private devotion of Rab of Sura, but has been adopted in the German Minhag for this purpose; the prayers in use among the Sefardim for "sanctifying the month" have been noticed above.

Then the leader lifts up a scroll and chants:

He who did miracles for our fathers, and who redeemed them from bondage unto freedom, may he redeem us soon and gather our outcasts from the four ends of the earth, all Israel as companions, and let us say, Amen.

The new moon of —— will happen on the ——day (or days) of the week, coming to us and all Israel for good.

May the Holy One, blessed be he, renew it for us and all his people, the house of Israel, for life and peace, for joy and gladness, for salvation and comfort, and say ye, Amen."

In the German ritual a requiem for the souls of Israel's martyrs is read on Sabbath mornings right before the second *Ashre;* in Western Germany only on the Sabbaths before Pentecost and before the Ninth of Ab; under the Polish Minhag on all Sabbaths except when the day, if a week-day, would displace the penitential Psalms, and except also when the coming New Moon (other than Iyar or Sivan) is announced:

Father of mercy, who dwelleth on high! May he in his powerful mercy turn to the saintly, the upright, the perfect, to those holy communities who gave up their lives for the glory of his name. "They were lovely and pleasant in their lives, and in their death they were not parted; they were swifter than eagles; they were stronger than lions" (cmp. 2 Sam. 1: 23), to do the will of their Master, the wish of their Rock. May our God remember them for good with the other just men of the world, and avenge [before our eyes] the vengeance of the spilt blood of his servants (cmp. Ps. 79: 10); as it is written in the law of Moses, the man of God (quoting Deut. 32: 43). And by the hands of thy servants, the prophets, it is written thus (quoting Joel 4: 21). And in thy holy writings it is said (quoting Ps. 79: 10; Ps. 9: 13; Ps. 110: 6, 7).

On four days of the year, viz., the eighth of Passover, the second of Pentecost, the Day of Atonement, and the "Eighth a rest," the Jews of the German ritual "remember the souls" of deceased parents and relatives. Those whose parents are still alive take no part in the exercises, but generally leave the Synagogue for the time. Each prays by himself thus for a dead father:

May God remember the soul of my respected father (naming him) who has gone to his eternal home; on whose behalf I vow alms; by way of reward, be his soul bound up in the bundle of life (cmp. 1 Sam. 25: 29) with the souls of Abraham, Isaac, and Jacob, Sarah, Rebekah, Rachel, and Leah, and of all other righteous men and women that are in the garden of Eden, and let us say, Amen.

A similar prayer is spoken for a deceased mother, one more comprehensive for deceased grandparents and other relatives, and especially for such as may have become martyrs for the faith, the only change being in the designation of those whose souls are prayed for. In many congregations a list of names is read out of persons who have left money to the Synagogue for that purpose, or for whom their surviving relatives make donations, and prayers for their souls in a different form are pronounced by the leader. The above *in memoriam* for the martyrs forms a fitting conclusion.

The prayer that the soul of the parents or other dead kindred and those of the martyrs for Israel's faith may be remembered and for their eternal happiness, is traced back to the Pesikta, that is, to the seventh century. The Mahzor Vitry testifies that in all Germany, at the beginning of the thirteenth century, they did not "set aside alms for the dead," that is, remember them with vows of almsgiving, except on the Day of Atonement. But in going over the services for the last day of the Passover the same Mahzor says that they only "set aside alms for the living," alluding to the words, "according to the gift of his hand," in the lesson for the day, showing that he meant to include his part of France with Germany in the custom of remembering the dead only on the Day of Atonement.[11]

We have lastly, after the Additional Prayer on Sabbaths

and Holidays and after the full Kaddish that follows it, a very pretty short piece, standing half way between prose and poetry (*En Kelohenu*):

None is like our God! none is like our Lord; none is like our King; none is like our Saviour. Who is like our God? Who is, etc. We give thanks to our God; we give thanks, etc. Blessed be our God! blessed be our, etc. Thou art our God; thou art our Lord; thou art our King; thou art our Saviour; thou art he, before whom our fathers offered the compound of incense.

From the last line it appears that the whole is an introduction to Talmudic pieces which follow. The first of them treats of the composition of the incense, as shown in a former chapter. But the first five lines alone have been set to simple music, and are in all progressive Synagogues and in Sabbath schools the hymn best liked because most easily and readily learned.

Some of the "minor benedictions" and late prose prayers must be much older than the Talmudic sage who first appears as their sponsor; and if not in the same form, at least with the same contents in slightly different phrase. The prayer which our Christian neighbors call the Lord's Prayer professes to be an abridgment of devotions then current among the Jews, these being deemed too long and too full of tautologies, with the exception of the fifth petition, which the author claims as new. We have found the invocation, Our Father who art in Heaven, in two compositions, both of which are given in this chapter; the Kaddish contains, with slight expansions, Hallowed be thy name, and thy Kingdom come; Lead us not into temptation, is in a morning benediction; Deliver us from evil, in the first prayer in this chapter, and the doxology, For thine is the Kingdom, etc., very much expanded in the closing "Benediction of Song." It is therefore highly probable that the germs of all these compositions were well-known among the Jews at as early an age as the reign of Tiberius, perhaps in a form not greatly differing from that now in use.

CHAPTER XVII

In the fifth or sixth century, while Greek was still the ruling language in Palestine, the Greek title of *Poietes* (poet) was taken by Jews who wrote hymns for public worship, generally men who led in prayer, and wished to enrich the service by their own compositions. We have found in the morning benedictions of the *Shema* and in the Benediction of Song matter which, by wealth of metaphors and alphabetic order and rhyme, indicates a conscious intent to write poetry. But the matter has been so thoroughly embodied in the old liturgy that in the eye of the Jewish masses it is deemed as sacred and obligatory as the first groundwork of the benedictions.

But it is very different with later productions written or coming into vogue after the two Rituals had taken form, and perhaps with some compositions of even older date.

Poietes took in Hebrew and Aramaic the form Paietan, and by treating this word as if the *t* was a part of the root, the noun *Piyut* (plural *Piyutim*) was formed, after the laws of Hebrew grammar, to denote those parts of the service which share in the following properties:

1. The recital is not obligatory; it is well-known that those in the German are wholly different from those in the Sefardic ritual; that even those used in Poland differ often from those of Western Germany. In the early morning service (*Hashkama*) for Sabbath and joyous Festivals they are omitted; in any emergency all Piyutim are dropped rather than a line of the old service. Yet a few of these pieces have by their contents, or by the story of their

origin, or by a striking tune, become dearer to the unlearned than the oldest and most solemn devotions.

2. There is generally an alphabetic arrangement, very often ending with an acrostic of the author's name and having either a rhyme or a phrase recurring in each line. Often the task of poetical form is made still harder by working into each stanza running parts from Scripture with which the author's lines have to rhyme. The style is marked by a preference of rare over common words. Instead of the old parallelism in which the Bible poets clothe each thought in two garbs, the later poet may find as many as twenty-two forms for it.[1]

3. The *Piyutim*, in the narrower sense, are not written for every day or every Sabbath, but for the Festivals or for certain named Sabbaths of the year. There are also the *Selihoth*, or Forgivenesses (see Ch. XII), the *Kinoth*, or Dirges, for the Ninth of Ab, the Hosannas for the Feast of Huts. Yet some of the best of the medieval hymns have found their way into the daily or weekly service.

The Jews of the German ritual have in their *Siddur* or *Tefilla* the services for week-day, Sabbath, and New Moon and the Prayer for Festivals, with the devotions for the home. Beside this they have their Mahzor, which contains the old parts of the service, the "lessons," and the *Piyutim* for all the Festivals, which, translated and conveniently arranged, will run up to from five to nine octavo volumes. The "poetries" for particular Sabbaths are found in the *Col Bo* ("all-in-it") editions of the *Siddur*.

The Sefardim follow a different plan. Though men of their branch of the Jewish race have written most of our religious poetry, they have adopted but few pieces into their liturgy; for the Feasts of Passover, Weeks, and Huts, so few, that these can be put conveniently into the daily Prayer Book. On the other hand, everything pertaining to the Days of Memorial and Atonement is left out of it, and the second and third parts of their service book contain all the exercises for these days, both the old, or obligatory, and the new and poetic parts.

There was at first much misgiving about introducing this poetry into the body of a benediction, of those which precede and follow the *Shema* or of those forming the *Amida*, for, unless the piece is fully akin to the matter of the benediction, it is an interruption, and all interruptions are here strictly forbidden.   The Sefardim have lived pretty well up to this principle; most of their Piyutim are inserted among the morning hymns (*Zemiroth*) or after the lessons.   Only the Selihoth, or poetic prayers for forgiveness of sin, and a rhymed account of the Temple Atonement service have been received with common consent into the "Sanctity of the Day," on the Day of Atonement, to which they are undoubtedly germane.   The few other "poetries" that have penetrated into the Amida still meet with protest from the editors of the service book in the remark: It would be better to read all this *after* the Prayer is over.

The Germans on the contrary have thrown aside all scruples on the subject, inserting the greater part of such matter in the Prayer (morning or Additional) when repeated by the leader, mostly as an introduction to the Thrice-Holy; and much of the other poetry for Festivals or special Sabbaths is worked into benedictions before and after the *Shema*.

There is quite a system by which these "poetries" are wrought in.   First, in the ten evenings, counting double days, of Passover, Pentecost, and Succoth, unless it be a Friday night, there are a few poetic lines before the close of the first and second benediction; again, a little before the verse, "Who is like thee," and before "The Lord will reign," and again before the close of the benediction, which is modified "King, Rock of Israel and his Redeemer," and lastly before "Blessed be thou, etc., who spreadest," etc. Too much respect was paid to the services of the Solemn Days to break them up in this way.   In the morning all festive days fared a little more alike. After the first sentence of the first benediction (see Ch. IV), "Who formest (Jotzer) light," etc., there is a poetic piece known as *Jotzer;* after the Thrice-Holy and before the *Ofannim* (Wheels) say their "Blessed" there is another piece, the *Ofan*. In the next benediction (*Ahaba*, or Love) a piece is inserted near the end, known as *Ahaba*. In the benediction which follows the *Shema* the word "beside" (*Zulath*) at the end of a paragraph gives its name to the piece there inserted; last, on the Passover and the Sabbaths between it and Pentecost there is *Geulla* (redemption), so named because it comes right before the closing words, "Blessed, etc., he has redeemed Israel." But on the Solemn Days the Shema and the Prayer are so far respected that the service goes on without interruption between the former and the latter.

The German Mahzor has also poetic pieces on all Festivals in the repeated morning Prayer, except on the first of the Passover and eighth of the Feast (because of the long prayers for Dew and Rain in the Musaf of those days) and except on the "Joy of the Law," when all spare time is given to the lessons. It has them in the Additional service on the Solemn Days, and on the two days named in the second benediction, where dew or rain are dwelt on, and on Pentecost, where the 613 precepts are set forth in a sort of doggerel in the fourth benediction. On the Atonement Day there are a few short Piyutim in the two afternoon services.

The pieces inserted in the Prayer are known as *Keroboth,* being "Approaches" to the Thrice-Holy, and are arranged according to a pretty steady plan. After chanting the first benediction to a point near its end the leader opens thus:

Out of the secret lore of the learned and wise and from the knowledge taught by the well-informed, I will open my mouth, etc.,

varying the last words according to the character of the feast. Then there are a few rhythmic lines, which, on the

Solemn Days at least, refer to Abraham. Near the end
of the second benediction there are other lines which on
these days refer to Isaac, and connect the resurrection of
the dead with the summer dews. As the *Kedusha* takes the
place of the third benediction, the poetical pieces follow at
once after the close of "Powers," and the first of these
generally refers in some way to Jacob, the simple man.
Then the verses, "The Lord will reign forever" (Ps. 146:
10) and "Thou art holy" (Ps. 22: 4), follow; and then a
greater or lesser number of detached pieces, the last of
which is known as the *Silluk*, or ascent, from the line which
introduces it, "Now may the sanctification ascend to thee,
for thou, our God, art King."

This leads directly to the words of the *Kedusha:* As it is
written by the hands of thy prophets (see Ch. VI, p. 119).
On the Day of Atonement, in three of the services, the *Silluk* is preceded by pieces referring to angels, who sing
"Holy" while Israel cry out "Blessed."

On the three Festivals the *Kedusha* and the benedictions
which follow it are no further interspersed by poetry. But
on the Solemn Days there are pieces to be recited between
the responses, and other pieces after the *Kedusha* and before
the close of the benediction "The Holy King." The former
are a serious interruption, leading to great disorder, and
have in late years been dropped in many highly orthodox
communities.

In the fourth benediction of the Day of Atonement there
are for each of the services a number of *Selihoth*, among
them the *Pizmon*, with its burden. Those for Neïla are
fixed, as well as for the preceding night service; those for
the three other services are given to choose from according
to the time on hand. In most Russian congregations none
are said in these services. In *Musaf* of Atonement Day the
account of the Temple service which comes before the *Selihoth* is very dry and prosaic, having nothing but its alphabetic arrangement in common with these "poetries;" but a

number of short and deeply melancholy pieces lead over from the "Service" to the *Selihoth*. The dirge about the Ten Martyrs is inserted in the "Order of Confession" by the Poles in *Musaf*, by the West Germans in *Minha*. Poetry has also been written to introduce the Kingdom, Remembrance, and Shofar verses on the Day of Memorial; these have on account of the great obscurity of the language and style lately fallen into disuse.

For the early morning service on the days between Memorial and Atonement and on a few mornings before the former, Selihoth are said, partly the same as on the Day of Atonement, partly other compositions of similar import; and there are again others on the public fasts other than the Ninth of Ab.

On the Feast of Huts, right after the "Additional Prayer," alphabetic hymns ending with *Hosha'na* (save now!) are chanted, a special one for each of six days, with a second common to all days. There are seven like hymns (embracing most of the six) recited on the seventh day; also the common second; also other poems, which gradually turn off into Messianic hopes and desires, and which culminate in the burden, "A voice brings news, brings news, and says!"

For the first seven *Hosha'na* hymns we find in the Mahzor Vitry a wholly different set from that now in use; the other ones are about the same as now. The common second was always distasteful to the writer for what seemed to him its Christian tinge; it brings out boldly how God went with Israel into exile, and how in delivering Israel from exile he also delivered himself; but this hymn is of undoubted antiquity, and based on a passage of the Palestinian Talmud.

There is a *motif* pervading the "poetry" for each of the Festivals, or some parts of it. Thus, on the first two days of the Passover and on the Sabbath in its middle days, that in the benedictions of the Shema is based on the Song of Songs, in its allegoric meaning of the love between God and the community of Israel. On the seventh and eighth of the Passover, the Red Sea Song is the underlying text; on the Feast of Weeks, the Ten Commandments; on the first two days of the Feast of Huts, the Hut, the Hallel Psalms, and the four species of trees (citron, palm, myrtle, and willow) are combined into one theme. On the Eighth of the Feast there is very little poetry besides the prayer for rain; the few longer pieces on the Ninth (Joy of the Law) are based on the lesson of the day, Moses blessing the tribes.

On the Days of Memorial and Atonement the most striking note is that of the Judgment, which is believed to be prepared on the former and sealed on the latter. God as King, who is greeted with the sound of the cornet, and who himself blows the great cornet, runs through many compositions of the former day; God setting mercy above judgment, through many of the latter. Several pieces on the quality of justice and the Day of Judgment belong to both days.

One of the oldest and most fertile writers of poetry for the Festivals is R. El'azar, surnamed Kalir.[2] His compositions are full of manifold self-imposed difficulties, and through his disregard of grammar, use of rare words, elliptic style, and running allusions to the Aggadta, they can hardly be understood by even good Hebrew scholars except after careful study. They are thus far from edifying. Kalir lived in the ninth century, but in an unhistoric age his admirers turned him into a Sage of ante-Mishna times; and thus the French and German Jews felt justified in disobeying the rule of the Talmud, that no one should ask for his needs in the first three benedictions; for how could the Babylonians forbid the recital of hymns which the foremost disciple of Rabban Johanan ben Zaccai had composed?[3] Thus not only his "poetries" but those of his successors were crowded into Festival Prayers to such an extent that the "Sanctity of the Name" in the Atonement morning service takes up nearly an hour and a half, and even on Pentecost or the Memorial Day half an hour or three-quarters.

Much of the so-called "poetry" for the Day of Atonement is free from obscurity, but it is bare of meaning, and shows on its face that the only object of the writer was to fill out time. Thus the Silluk in the morning service of that day begins with a line for which a good English equivalent would be, Who can tell the terror of thy truth? followed by twenty-one other lines, of which the next has three words beginning with *s*, instead of tell, terror, truth, and so back to three words with *a*. There are however compositions of much higher value, some of them true poetry touching the finest chords of the human heart. Jehuda Hallevi, writing in Arabic Spain in the middle of the twelfth century, takes the highest rank, especially by his elegy, "Zion," for the Ninth of Ab, which is however not now in use in either ritual. Solomon Ibn Gebirol is famed mainly by the "Song of Unity," for the seven days of the week, with many fine passages, but rather too much of Aristotelian reflection on the infinite. The "Song of Glory," ascribed to Samuel ben Kalonymos, is rather too bold in its anthropomorphism. There are fine stanzas in the *Selihoth*, many of which are very old; the gems are collected in Neïla.

Some of the best known Piyutim will be given as samples in the next chapter in whole or in part. Other passages here and there are quite inspiring to the Israelite who is thoroughly versed in the Aggadta, and who is acquainted with the chips of Cabbala afloat among the uninitiated; but they fall flat on the ears of those for whom it all has to be translated and explained. Thus, when the poet speaks of men from whom God accepts praise, weak mortal men who breathe out their soul, and he gives to that soul its five names in the rising scale (*nefesh, ruah, haïa, neshama, jehida*) before he lets it die through justice, only to live again through mercy, he thrills the heart of the well-posted Jew, for whom these words have a meaning and a familiar sound; but to all others it is *vox et praterea nihil*. Of the Selihoth some are sublime, most of them expressive of deep feeling, and they are all written in plain, intelligible speech. In the different rituals the same Seliha may be employed on different occasions. Thus, "Judge of all the earth," of which the burden is "like the burnt offering of the morn, which is for a daily offering," is in the German ritual the last Seliha in the morning service of the Day of Atonement, while the Sefardim have it on New Year after the morning hymns.

There are some Hebrew and some Aramaic hymns closely bound up with the reading of the "lessons" which will be mentioned hereafter in connection with those lessons.

CHAPTER XVIII

SAMPLES OF POST-BIBLICAL POETRY

SOME unknown hand at a date unknown turned the thirteen articles of the creed as drawn up by Maimonides into measure and rhyme. Denoting full vowels by -, the *Sheva mobile* by ⌣, each half line runs: - -⌣ - - - ⌣ - - -.

One rhyme, at the end of the whole line of twenty syllables, runs through all thirteen of these lines. This poem (*Yigdal*) is often sung at the end of services to a well-known air. Mrs. Henry Lucas renders it thus in her *Songs of Zion:*

> The living God we praise, exalt, adore!
> He was, He is, He will be evermore.
>
> No unity like unto His can be,
> Eternal, inconceivable, is He.
>
> No form or shape has th' Incorporeal One,
> Most holy beyond all comparison.
>
> He was, ere aught was made in heaven or earth,
> But His existence has no date or birth.
>
> Lord of the Universe is He proclaimed,
> Teaching His power to all His hand has framed.
>
> He gave His gift of prophecy to those
> In whom He gloried, whom He loved and chose.
>
> No prophet ever yet has filled the place
> Of Moses, who beheld God face to face.
>
> Through him (the faithful in his house) the Lord
> The law of truth to Israel did accord.

This law God will not alter, will not change
For any other through time's utmost range.

He knows and heeds the secret thoughts of man,
He saw the end of all ere aught began.

With love and grace doth He the righteous bless.
He metes out evil unto wickedness.

He at the last will His anointed send,
Those to redeem, who hope and wait the end.

God will the dead to life again restore,
Praised be His glorious name for evermore.[1]

Adon Olam has ten lines, each hemistich built thus: ◡ -
--, ◡---; a single rhyme runs through it. It is read or
sung in the Synagogue at the beginning or end of services;
also spoken in the night prayer on going to bed.
The version below is pretty faithful:

Lord of the world, enthroned as King.
Before each creature had its frame.
    When by his word he fashioned all.
    His works did him as King proclaim.

And when all things fade into naught.
The fearful still will reign the same.
    It's he that is; it's he that was;
    He will be in eternal light.

And he is one, there's second none
With him to liken or unite.
    Without beginning, without end.
    His is dominion, strength, and might.

He is my rock, my Saviour lives;
Rock of my strength, in trouble's night
    He is my banner, my retreat;
    My blissful cup midst bitter cries.

Into his hand I trust my soul,
When I lie down, and when I rise.
    And with my soul my body too;
    I fear not when I close my eyes.

The last line is rendered somewhat freely and with a view to the use of this poem as part of the night prayer.[2]

The "Reception of the Sabbath" in its modern sense by eight Psalms (see Ch. XIII) arose from a modern poem round which the Psalms gathered. The author's name is signed in acrostic, SH-e-L-oM-o-H H-a-L-e-V-I, to eight out of the nine quatrains. He wrote at Safet in Palestine about 1500, but was born in Granada. His fame rests on the one couplet and nine quatrains. Mrs. Lucas thus renders the burden and four of the nine stanzas, extending each to five lines:

> Come forth, my friend, the bride to meet;
> Come, O my friend, the Sabbath greet!
>
> "Observe ye" and "remember" still
> The Sabbath—thus His holy will
> God in one utterance did proclaim.
> The Lord is one, and one His name
> To his renown and praise and fame.
> > Come forth, etc.
>
> Greet we the Sabbath at our door,
> Well-spring of blessing evermore,
> With everlasting gladness fraught,
> Of old ordained, divinely taught,
> Last in creation, first in thought.
> > Come forth, etc.
>
> Arouse thyself, awake and shine,
> For, lo! it comes, the light divine.
> Give forth a song, for over thee
> The glory of the Lord shall be
> Revealed in beauty speedily.
> > Come forth, etc.
>
> Crown of thy husband, come in peace,
> Come, bidding toil and trouble cease.
> With joy and cheerfulness abide
> Among thy people true and tried,
> Thy faithful people—come, O bride!
> > Come forth, my friend, the bride to meet,
> > Come, O my friend, the Sabbath greet!

The last words of the last stanza, "Come, O Bride," are as old as the third century.[3]

Solomon Ibn Gebirol, who lived in Arab Spain in the eleventh century, wrote Hebrew rhymed poetry in easy and flowing language. His "Crown of Kingship" (*Kether Mal'-chuth*), a long, poetic reflection on man's weakness before God, was not written for the Synagogue, though it is read by many persons of both rituals on the night of Atonement. The following specimens are taken from the "Song of Unity," written by him for the Sabbath; he wrote similar songs for the other days of the week. These are read in German and Polish congregations at the end of the morning service. The translation is pretty literal:

> On the seventh day thou tookest rest:
> The Sabbath hence by thee was blessed.
> Glory o'er all thy handiwork is spread:
> Hence by thy saints thy praise is always said.
> Blessed be the Lord, who shaped and formed each thing,
> The living God and everlasting King.
> Upon thy servants from the days of old,
> Thy kindness and thy grace were manifold.
> Thou didst begin in Egypt to make known,
> How great thy power, and how high thy throne
> Above their gods, when thou didst strike
> Their rulers and their feeble gods alike.
> When thou didst part the sea, thy people saw
> Thy mighty hand, and they were filled with awe.

> With light of countenance bless thy people still!
> Who ever anxious are to do thy will.
> And in thy will, do with our wish comply,
> We're all thy people; always to thee nigh.
> Hast thou not chosen us for thine own treasure?
> Pour on thy people blessings without measure.

But few poems of the greatest of Hebrew medieval poets, Jehuda Hallevi, are in the liturgy. There is, however, a little gem, written to be sung on the first (or the seventh) morning of the Passover, before the words, "the redeemed sang a new song" in the Geulla. It is also sung on a Sabbath morning when a circumcision takes place at the Synagogue. Mrs. Lucas renders it thus:

When as a wall the sea
  In heaps uplifted lay,
A new song unto Thee
  Sang the redeemed that day.

Thou didst in his deceit
  O'erwhelm the Egyptian's feet.
While Israel's footsteps fleet
  How beautiful were they!

Jeshurun! all who see
  Thy glory cry to thee:
"Who like thy God can be?"
  Thus even our foes did say.

O! let thy banner soar
  The scattered remnant o'er,
And gather them once more
  Like corn on harvest-day,

Who bear through all their line
  Thy covenant's holy sign,
And to Thy name divine
  Are sanctified alway.

Let all the world behold
  Their token, prized of old,
Who on their garment's fold
  The thread of blue display.

Be then the truth made known
  For whom, and whom alone,
The twisted fringe is shown,
  The covenant kept this day.

O! let them, sanctified,
  Once more with Thee abide,
Their sun shine far and wide,
  And chase the clouds away.

> The well-beloved declare
> Thy praise in song and prayer:
> "Who can with Thee compare.
> O Lord of Hosts?" they say.
>
> When as a wall, etc.

The *Hosha'na* hymn for the third day of the Feast is highly prized by the *Hasidim* as representing in its first part Israel as a woman faithful to God and suffering cheerfully for his sake. There is neither rhyme nor meter, only the limitation of the alphabet.

Om ani Homa may be rendered thus, representing the Hebrew letters by those corresponding in English. (The change of person is as in the original.):

> Am firm as brazen walls,
> Bright as the midday sun!
> Gone into exile, she's
> Daring as tallest palm.
> How death she meets for thee,
> When she's to slaughter borne,
> Zealous foes around her!
> Held fast in thy embrace,
> Toiling beneath the yoke,
> In love she acclaims thee One.
> Kept down in foreign lands, she
> Learns to fear thee more.
> Maltreated sore by men,
> Nor free from pain and blows,
> Still under heavy loads,
> On steps the tempest tossed;
> People freed by Tobiah (Moses),
> Celestial flock of lambs.
> Quick hosts of Jacob's seed
> Resounding with thy name.
> Shouting Hosha'na loud.
> Thy help they lean upon,
> Hosha'na!

The hymn shows very little literary skill, but every word and letter of it were felt and meant. There is no clue to the

author. Another hymn takes its place in the Mahzor Vitry;
hence, it probably was the product of persecution in the
fourteenth century.

Of the *Piyutim* in the narrower sense the most proper is
the "Ascent" (Silluk) to the Thrice-Holy in the Additional for the New Year, composed by R. Amnon of Mainz
(Moguntia) in the twelfth century; not only on account of
its stirring contents, but on account of the sad fate of its
author, who read it, when it was heard for the first time,
while bleeding to death from cruel wounds.

After the introductory words:
"To thee ascends holiness, for thou, O God, art King,"
U-nethanne tokef (so it is named from its initial words),
begins:

We will tell the powerful praise of the day, which is dreaded
and fearful; on it thy Kingdom will be exalted, and thy throne
laid firmly in kindness; and thou wilt sit thereon in truth. Truly
thou art the judge, he that rebukes, he that knoweth; thou art the
witness, the writer, and he that sealeth, and telleth, and counteth.
Thou wilt bring all that is forgotten to mind, and open the book of
remembrance; it reads itself; the hand and seal of every man attests
it. The great cornet is blown; and the still small voice is heard;
then the angels are frightened; trembling and terror takes hold of
them; they say, this is the day of judgment, to visit justice upon
the hosts on high; for they are not pure in thy sight in the judgment. All that come into the world thou passest before thee like
lambs; as the shepherd examines his flock, and lets his sheep pass
under his staff, thus thou bringest them along, telling and counting,
and thou visitest the soul of all that liveth, and cuttest out the
destiny of every creature, and writest the sentence of each

On the New Year they are inscribed, and on the Fast of Atonement the seal is affixed: how many shall pass away, and how many
shall be born; who may live, and who must die; whose end has
come, whose end is not yet; who is to perish in fire, and who in
water; who by the sword, and who by famine; who through earth-
quake, and who through pestilence; who shall rest, and who shall
move; who shall be quiet, and who shall be torn along; who shall
have peace, and who shall be chastised; who shall be high, and

who shall be humbled; who shall grow rich, and who become poor.

But repentance and prayer and charity—turn the evil sentence. For as thy name, so is thy excellence; hard to provoke and easy to please; for thou dost not desire the death of him that is guilty; but that he may turn from his ways and live. Even to his dying day thou waitest for him; when he turns back, thou receivest him at once. Truly thou art their creator and thou knowest their nature, even that they are flesh and blood; as for man, his foundation is in the dust, and his end is dust; with his life he earns his bread; he is likened to the broken potsherd, to dried-up grass, to the withering blossom, to the passing shadow, to the cloud that has vanished, to the wind that is stilled, to the whirling dust, to the winged dream:

But thou art the King, the living, everlasting God.

Thy years have no goal, thy lengthened days no end; none can measure the chariot of thy glory, nor explain the mystery of thy name; thy name is proper to thee, and thou befittest thy name: and our name thou hast called after thy name.

There is no trifling with the alphabet, no acrostic of the author's name, no attempt at measure, and but a few rhymes in the first few lines.

In the Polish ritual R. Amnon's composition is recited also in the Additional of the Day of Atonement instead of the very weak "Ascent" which the congregations of Western Germany have retained for that occasion.

Among the dirges for the Ninth of Ab in the German ritual, the one best known, mainly on account of its plaintive but highly rhythmical air, is *Eli Tzion*, written in short couplets, the first of which, rendered pretty faithfully in the original meter, reads thus:

Cry loud for Zion and her towns, like women in their sore travail,
Or maid, who for her murdered swain sets up her bitter, piercing wail.

Both rituals have a long composition showing how sad the difference between exodus and exile.

Of the thirty odd couplets (each of which is here drawn out into six lines) the first, second, and last follow:

Fire is kindled in my breast
At the thought of times so blessed,
When from Egypt land I start.
But I raise my saddest lay
At the thought of that dire day,
When from Salem I must part.

Moses sings on sacred spot,
Song that ne'er shall be forgot.
When from Egypt land I start;
Jeremy his woeful dirge,
Wherein sighs and moanings surge,
When from Salem I must part.

God, of heavenly hosts the Lord,
Will unsheath anew his sword,
As on Egypt's fertile plain;
Will return his Presence bright
Unto Zion, and his might
Unto Salem's hills again.

Without trying to follow the measure or rhyme of the original, we put here in English some of the "gems" of the *Seliboth* as they are gathered in the last Atonement service. Each is the burden of a longer piece, which is recited in the matins of the Seliboth days:

(1) Remember the covenant with Abraham and the binding of Isaac, and return the captivity of the tents of Jacob, and save us for the sake of thy name.

(2) Israel is saved by the Lord in everlasting redemption; may they be helped this day also, by thy word, dweller in boundless heights; for thou art rich in forgiveness and full of mercy.

(3) May he hide us in the shadow of his hand beneath the wings of the Presence; show his grace when he proveth the crooked heart, to right it; arise, our God, my strength, show might, do now! O Lord, do listen to our fond beseeching!

(4) May he that dwelleth hidden and most high tell us: I have forgiven; may a people, down-trodden and poor, find aid in his saving arm; when we humbly pray to thee, thou answer us in solemn tones of acquittal; O Lord, be thou the helper at our side.

(5) I think of it, O God, and am troubled, when I see every town rebuilt on its ruins; but the city of God is laid low, deep

down as the pit; and yet we are the Lord's and to the Lord are our eyes.

(6) I have firmly set my stakes upon the thirteen words of mercy and on the gates of tears that never are locked; on these I set my trust, and in the merit of three fathers.

(7) Be it thy will, thou who hearest the sound of weeping, that thou wilt gather our tears into thine own flagon; and do thou deliver us from all cruel decrees; for on thee alone our eyes are fixed.

The following piece in the Monday and Thursday service after the penitential Psalm has hardly any poetic form, but is classed as a *Pizmon* (French Pseaumon), and deserves attention as being, along with the prose pieces for those days (see Chs. XIII and XV), one of the few parts of the service in which the sufferings of the Jews in exile are dwelt on:

O Lord, God of Israel, turn from thy burning anger, and bethink thyself of the mischief to thy people. Look from heaven and see that we are for sport and contempt among the nations; we are counted as sheep carried to slaughter, to kill, to destroy, to smite, and to disgrace. Yet with all this we have not forgot thy name; O do not forget us. Strangers say: there is no prospect nor hope; show grace to a people trusting in thy name. Pure One, bring on thy salvation; we are weary, we have had no rest; may thy mercies suppress thy anger against us. O return from thy anger and show mercy to thy chosen treasure. Spare us, O Lord, in thy mercy; put us not in the hands of the cruel; why should the nations say: where then is their God? deal for thy sake kindly with us; do not delay. Hear our voice, show grace, do not cast us off into the hands of our enemies, to blot out our name; remember what thou swarest to our fathers: I shall multiply your seed as the stars of heaven; yet now we are left few of so many.

The last remark renders this piece (written probably in the tenth century) rather inapplicable in our times.

CHAPTER XIX

CABBALISTIC INTERPOLATIONS

In the later middle ages and in still more recent times, many passages from Cabbalistic sources have crept into the Prayer Book. Some of these contain on their face nothing that is mystical or seems to belong to a special school of thought. Such is a supplication taken from the Bahir and falsely ascribed to Nehonia ben Hakkana, one of the earlier Sages of the Mishna. It is placed among the passages from Bible and Talmud in the early morning service (see Ch. XIV *supra*), and begins thus:

(1) Oh, now, by the force of the greatness of thy right hand, loose her that is bound.

(2) Receive the singing of thy people, set us on high, cleanse us, fearful One.

(3) Oh, thou strong One, guard those who seek thy Unity, like the pupil of the eye, etc.

There are seven lines; each is made up of six Hebrew words, and at its end the initials are reproduced; those of the second line spell out *Kera' Satan*, tear the adversary! Thus this otherwise harmless looking composition seems to be intended rather as an incantation than a devotion, and it has fallen into deserved disuse.

Lastly, every prayer book of the German ritual copies from the Zohar a prayer to be read by every one when the scrolls are taken out, against which no objection of any kind can be raised.

Blessed be the name of the Master of the world; blessed be thy crown and thy residence. Be thy favor ever with thy people

Israel. Show the help of thy right hand to thy people in thy
Temple; let the gift of thy light reach us, and receive our prayer
in mercy. Be it thy will to lengthen our lives in happiness; may
I be reckoned among the righteous; have mercy on me and guard
me and mine and all that belong to thy people Israel. Thou art
he that feedeth all, and provideth for all; thou art he that ruleth
over all; and the Kingdom is thine. I am the servant of the Holy
Blessed One; before whom and before the glory of whose law I
kneel at every time. I do not trust in man; nor do I lean on any
son of God; but I trust in the God of Heaven, who is God in
truth, whose Law is truth, whose prophets are true; and who
worketh abundantly kindness and truth. In him I trust, and I
speak praises to his holy and glorious name. Be it thy will to
open my heart to thy Law and to fulfill the cravings of my heart
and of the hearts of all thy people, for happiness, life, and peace.[1]

We have seen also a collection of twenty-two verses or
one with twenty-two repetitions of the name of God; in all,
the Cabbalistic purpose is hidden, and does not interfere
with the edifying effect of the words or of the thoughts
and feelings which they express.

Very different are a number of petitions and declarations
which have crept into many prayer books since the days
of Isaac Luria, and are built upon the peculiar theology
taught by him and other Cabbalists, which, in the opinion
of the writer and of many strict and law-observing Jews,
runs counter to every principle of Israel's religion, for it
recognizes phases, almost persons, in the deity.

Here is an example as short as any that could have been
chosen. Before reciting the morning hymns the worshipper
is advised to say:

Behold, I prepare my mouth to thank, to praise, and to honor
my Maker, for the purpose of unifying the Holy One, blessed be
he, and his Presence (*Shechina*), by means of that Name which is
hidden and secret in the name of all Israel.

Before the performance of any ceremony ordained by the
Law, such as the putting on of the fringed shawl, the Cabbalists and those who accept their interpolations in the

Prayer Book offer a petition to be rewarded therefor in a special way, which is introduced thus in Aramaic:

"To the end of uniting the Holy Blessed One and his Presence (*Shechina*) in love and fear in the name of all Israel."

The "love and fear" is evidently borrowed from Christian sources; the phrase is unknown in all the older, in all but the Cabbalistic literature of Jewish prayer.

Even worse are the petitions ("Be it thy will") found in small print in the New Year's service book, to be read between the alarm sounds in which certain angels otherwise unheard of are supposed to "proceed" from the sounds of the Shofar; and perhaps worst of all, a petition to be devoutly said by the people while the priests in the blessing ring out Peace (Shalom), wherein arbitrary combinations of letters are palmed off on the innocent worshipper as names of God that "proceed" from the priestly blessing.[2]

Among the *Hasidim* sect of Poland and the Sefardic Jews of Turkey these almost idolatrous interpolations, none of which is even four hundred years old, stand very high, and their service books are full of matter of the same kind. A true conservatism among the Jews of the sixteenth and seventeenth centuries would have kept our liturgy clear of them. They are gradually being weeded out in our own times, and the learned quietly ignore them, while the ignorant believe in the merit of reading and pronouncing whatever they find in print.

Much as the writer dislikes to acquaint the general reader with the very existence of these excrescences, he cannot pass them over without being guilty of implied falsehood. Altogether, the Jewish liturgy has perhaps lost more than it has gained by the additions made to it since the days of Rab and Samuel in the first half of the third century. There are some beautiful gems imbedded in vast masses of ore of medieval poetry; the very prayer quoted from the Zohar in this chapter is almost sublime; but it seems that these gems are bought at too high a price, if all the inert and all the poisonous matter must be taken into the bargain; and if the daily and Sabbath services are to be swollen to such length that leader and people feel tempted to shorten them by slurring.

Setting aside the "Reception of the Sabbath" by Psalms and hymns, due to Solomon the Levite, which is less than four hundred years old, but is worth preserving on intrinsic grounds, all steps in the line of shortening the Jewish services might safely be taken in the reverse order of time, that is, by lopping off and dropping first what has been added last.

BOOK III

The Desk and the Pulpit

CHAPTER I

THE WEEKLY PENTATEUCH LESSON

WHATEVER the higher criticism may say about the comparative age of Biblical writings, for the observing Israelite the five Books of Moses, known as the *Tora*, or Instruction, hence as the Divine Law, occupy a much higher rank than anything else, and a Scroll of the Law, written according to precept "in the Hebrew tongue and Assyrian character," is in his eyes the most sacred of all implements; as much so almost as the Ark of the Covenant was before it disappeared in the sack of Solomon's Temple. Children, at least boys, are expected to study the Pentateuch (Chumash) before and above everything else; grown men, to keep up their acquaintance with it by reading it through every year, and it has been divided into fifty-four sections, one (or if there are not enough Sabbaths, then occasionally two) to be read on each Sabbath of the year. The section for each week is called by the Germans the *Sidra*, by the Sefardim the *Parasha;* the former apply the latter name to the shorter divisions into which the *Sidra* is divided when publicly read.

To the Jews raised and taught in the old-fashioned way the division of the Pentateuch into sections is much more familiar than that into chapters, which came to them only from the Septuagint through Christian channels. Every

section is named after its first striking word. Thus the first
in Genesis is known as *Bereshith* (In the beginning), the
second as *Noah*, etc. There are twelve sections in Genesis,
which begin as follows:

I, 1: 1; II, 6: 9; III, 12: 1; IV, 18: 1; V, 23: 1; VI,
25: 19; VII, 28: 10; VIII, 32: 4; IX, 37: 1; X, 41: 1; XI,
44: 18; XII, 47: 28.

There are eleven sections in Exodus, beginning as follows:

XIII, 1: 1; XIV, 6: 2; XV, 10: 1; XVI (*Beshallah*, containing the Red Sea Song), 13: 17; XVII (*Jithro*, containing the Ten Commandments), 18: 1; XVIII, 21: 1; XIX,
25: 1; XX, 27: 20; XXI, 30: 11; XXII, 35: 1; XXIII,
38: 21.

There are ten sections in Leviticus:

XXIV, 1: 1; XXV, 6: 1; XXVI, 9: 1; XXVII, 12: 1;
XXVIII, 14: 1; XXIX, 16: 1; XXX (*Kedoshim*, containing the Moral Law), 19: 1; XXXI, 21: 1; XXXII, 25:
1; XXXIII, 26: 3.

There are ten sections in Numbers:

XXXIV, 1: 1; XXXV, 4: 21; XXXVI, 8: 1; XXXVII,
13: 1; XXXVIII, 16: 1; XXXIX, 19: 1; XL, 22: 2; XLI,
25: 10; XLII, 30: 2; XLIII, 33: 1.

There are eleven sections in Deuteronomy:

XLIV, 1: 1; XLV (*Vaethhannan*, containing the second
version of the Ten Commandments and Hear, O Israel),
3: 23; XLVI, 7: 12; XLVII, 11: 26; XLVIII, 16: 18;
XLIX, 21: 10; L, 26: 1; LI, 29: 9; LII is chapter 31;
LIII is chapter 32; LIV, chapters 33, 34. This section is
read on the "Joy of the Law," the ninth day of the Feast of
Huts.

In a year of twelve months (353, 354, or 355 days) there
are at most 51 Sabbaths. But some of these fall upon Festivals or upon the middle days of the Feasts, when the regular lesson of the week is displaced. But even in a year of
thirteen months, which has generally 55 Sabbaths, these

interruptions leave less than 54 of them for weekly les-
sons. Thus it is always necessary to combine some of the
weekly portions into doublets. This is done according to
rules, which we need not discuss in all their details, with
XXII and XXIII (both about setting up the Tabernacle);
XXVII and XXVIII (about leprosy and like matters);
XXIX and XXX (Day of Atonement and Moral Law);
XXXII and XXXIII; XXXIX and XL; XLII and
XLIII; and lastly LI and LII (the last doings of Moses).

The earlier doublets are always arranged in such a manner that *Debarim*, the first section in Deuteronomy, is read
before the Fast of the Ninth of Ab; *Vaethhannan* on the
Sabbath after the Fast; hence the joining or separating of
LI and LII depends only on the question whether or not
New Year and the Day of Atonement are both on week-
days, or whether one of them is on a Sabbath. In the
former case one more weekly lesson is needed, and these
sections are read separately.[1]

Both Josephus and the New Testament speak of the public reading of the Law on every Sabbath as a well established custom by means of which "Moses" is well-known
to every Israelite. There are many Talmudic passages tracing the weekly readings, including those on Mondays and
Thursdays, back to the days of Ezra; but there is no contemporary testimony earlier than the Gospels and the Acts.
The Books of the Maccabees (as stated in a former chapter)
never speak of a Synagogue, but of a place of prayer. It
is, however, most probable that the habit of these public
readings grew with the multiplication of books and of persons capable of reading, and if during the procuratorship
of Pontius Pilate there were a scroll of the Law and seven
men capable of reading it in every village, even in the less
cultured district of Galilee, two hundred years earlier copies
of the Law and men able to read it in public could be found
at least at the places dedicated to public instruction in
Jerusalem and in the larger towns. That there were already

many books of the Law in the time of Antiochus Epiphanés
seems clear from his attempt to destroy them in order that
the Law might be forgotten in Israel.[2]

But the Tora was not, while the Temple stood, nor in
Palestine for a long time thereafter, read in the course of a
single year. To trace this matter we must look first to the
Scriptural command.

The only command which the Law itself gives as to its public reading is found in Deuteronomy 31, "At the end of seven
years, in the set time of the year of release, is the Feast of
Huts, etc.; thou shalt read the law before all Israel in their
hearing. Assemble the men and the women and the little
ones," etc. It might be hence inferred that the first cycle
would have been one of seven years; that is, a small portion,
about sixteen verses, might be read on every Sabbath for
seven years till the 5,845 verses were gone through with,
and then the whole Tora would be read at the Feast of the
year of release. But there is no historic evidence that this
was ever done. There was perhaps at one time a division of
the Pentateuch into 175 parts, which would point to a
cycle of three years and a half; but otherwise there is hardly
any historic evidence that such a cycle was ever used.[3]

All Hebrew Bibles of the present day state at the end of
each of the five books how many divisions named "Seder"
it contains, and of these there are 154, just enough to supply a cycle of three years; and the Babylonian Talmud says
distinctly: in the West (i. e., in Palestine) they finish the
Tora in three years, while on the Euphrates it was read
through in one year, so that the same section always came
around at the same season.[4] The Sefardim took their
ritual from Babylonia, and naturally fell into the yearly
cycle; and it seems that the Jews of France and Germany
acted in the same way. It appears that the Palestinians
simply held to their custom in the belief that it was unworthy of the dwellers in the Holy Land to follow the lead
of the men of the dispersion; while Jews in all other parts

of the world, after the downfall of the Patriarchate at Tiberias, obeyed in this as well as in all other matters the only central authority remaining, that is, the schools of Sura and Pumbeditha. The three-years cycle cannot have disappeared altogether till after the expulsion of the Jews in Spain, when the complete Sefardic ritual was introduced in the Holy Land.[5]

But it seems that the three-years cycle cannot have taken hold even in Palestine without a struggle. For a Baraïtha sets up the tradition that Ezra had ordained to read the "blessings and curses" in Leviticus before Pentecost, those in Deuteronomy before New Year. The former (Lev. 26) are now read on the second Sabbath before Pentecost, the latter on the second Sabbath before New Year. This must have been the custom, or at least the custom of some party or school at Jerusalem, otherwise no one would have claimed Ezra as authority.[6]

The ordinary Jew is more familiar with the first subsection than with other parts of the portion, for on Sabbath afternoon and again on Monday and Thursday the first part of the coming Sabbath's portion is read.[7]

Monday and Thursday were the days on which the courts met in all the towns of Palestine for the dispatch of civil causes. On these days the farmers came into town for legal and other business, and dropped in at the Synagogue; it was deemed the best time for obtaining an audience for a short lesson from the Law. The Talmud distinctly claims that Ezra instituted as well the court sessions as the Bible readings on these two days of the week, and there is no reason for denying that he established the former, though it is highly improbable that the week-day readings are so old, when so high an age cannot be proved even for the Sabbath lessons.[8]

The movement in modern times towards a three-years cycle, which prevails in many otherwise quite conservative congregations, arose from the lessened interest in the

Pentateuch, especially its drier portions, those in attendance finding it irksome to listen for from fifteen to twenty-five minutes consecutively to names and numbers, orders of sacrifice, laws of clean and unclean, or, what is worse, simply to Hebrew words which they do not understand at all. Hence a return to a custom which was probably universal till the establishment of the Babylonian schools in the third century of the Christian era, and which was kept up in Palestine during all or most of the middle ages, was naturally suggested; strange though it seems to a Jew raised in the "Babylonian" style, by whom the Sidra is felt as much a part of each particular Sabbath as the ram's horn is of New Year or fasting is of the Day of Atonement. Hence, by way of compromise, many modernized congregations retain the one-year cycle, but read in each year only about one-third of the Sidra, thus finishing the whole Tora in three years.

That the one-year cycle is made to end on the closing day of the Feast of Huts seems naturally suggested by the Biblical command to read the whole Tora on that feast in the seventh year, and from the intimation of the Babylonian Talmud, that sections XXI and XXII were read shortly before the first of Adar, it is clear that the cycle was begun and closed then as it is now.[9] But there is some evidence to indicate that the three-years cycle began early in the Passover month.[10]

It is well-known that throughout the Bible there are a number of double readings, one being "written" (*Kethib*) in the text, the other being handed down by tradition as more correct, which latter in vowelled books is indicated by its vowel points, while its letters are marked in the margin as "to be read" (*K'ri*). Among these double readings are several in which the *Kethib* is not set aside as a corrupt text, but simply deemed indelicate; and a word of the same meaning, but not so coarse, is substituted in reading. Such corrections are made as well in the prophetic books as in the Tora, and are marked in the copies from which the former are generally read. Those in the Tora the reader must know by heart."

CHAPTER II

ON all the Biblical holidays, that is, on the Festivals which require rest, on the middle days of the Feasts, and on the New Moon, also on Purim, the public fasts, and on Hanucca, which is wholly un-Scriptural, passages from the Pentateuch are read in the public service with the same solemnities as on the Sabbaths or on Mondays and Thursdays.

At present the order is the following:

On the first day of the Passover the narrative of the departure from Egypt, beginning with verse 21 of the 12th chapter of Exodus and ending with the last verse of the chapter. When it is on a Sabbath the Sefardim begin at verse 14.

On the seventh day of the Passover, the crossing of the Red Sea, beginning with section XVI (Beshallah) in the 13th chapter of Exodus and closing with the 26th verse of chapter 15.

On Pentecost, the 19th and 20th chapters of Exodus, giving the narrative of the revelation on Mount Sinai and the Ten Commandments as part thereof.

On the first day of the New Year, the 21st chapter of Genesis, containing the birth of Isaac.

On the second day of the New Year, the 22d chapter of Genesis, the "binding of Isaac."

On the Day of Atonement, in the morning, the sixteenth chapter of Leviticus, which sets forth the Temple service of that day.

On the same day in the afternoon, the 18th chapter of Leviticus, containing the laws against incest.

On the first day of the Feast of Huts, the 23d chapter of Leviticus, in which all the festivals are prescribed, and as an introduction thereto the last eight verses of chapter 22d.

On the *ninth* day of the same feast, that is, on the double of the "Eighth," in other words on the "Joy of the Law," section 54 of the Pentateuch, and as soon as it is ended, the first chapter of Genesis with three verses of chapter 2, that is, the Elohistic account of creation.

The lesson for the second day of the Passover and of the Feast of Huts is the same as on the first day of the Feast of Huts.

On the eighth or double of the seventh day of Passover, on the second day of Pentecost, and on the "Eighth" in the Feast of Huts, the account of the three Feasts in Deuteronomy is read. On the two former of these days, when on a work-day, the lesson begins at ch. 15, v. 19; on the last-named Festival and always on the Sabbath at ch. 14, v. 22, and it always ends with the weekly portion, section XLVII, Deut. 16: 17.

These lessons displace that of the week though the day be a Sabbath. So also, when one of the middle days of the Passover or of the Feast of Huts is on a Sabbath, the weekly portion is not read, but a part of section XXI beginning at Exodus 33: 12, and closing with 34: 26, which contains a short reference to the three Festivals.

On the middle days of the Passover when not on the Sabbath, the following small portions are read: On the first middle day (the third of the feast), Ex., ch. 13: 1-16; on the second middle day, Ex. 22: 24 to 23: 19; on the third middle day, Ex. 34: 1-26; on the fourth, Num. 9: 1-14 (about the second Passover). All of these contain references to the three Feasts or at least to the Passover.

On the middle days of the Feast of Huts the sacrifices

for the particular day are read from Numbers, ch. 29, counting both from the first and from the second day.[1]

On Purim the last nine verses of the 17th chapter of
Exodus are read, proclaiming the everlasting war against
Amalek.[2]

On public fasts passages from the 32d and 34th chapters
of Exodus (11-14 of the former and 1-10 of the latter), telling of God's forgiveness of the sin of the golden calf and
teaching the thirteen qualities of mercy. These passages
are read both in the morning and in the afternoon.[3] But
in the morning of the Ninth of Ab the lesson is from
Deuteronomy, chapter 4, verses 25-40, which are full of
warning.

On Hanucca are read three of the paragraphs in the
seventh chapter of Numbers, in which the chiefs of the
tribes bring their gifts at the dedication of the Tabernacle,
progressing according to the day.

On New Moons Numbers, ch. 28, vv. 1-15, is read, which
contains the public sacrifices for every day, for the Sabbath,
and for the New Moon; about all appertaining to the day
that could be found in the Pentateuch.[4]

Purim and the fasts are never celebrated on a Sabbath.
and the New Moon or Hanucca lessons do not displace
the weekly lesson, but are read in addition thereto; that for
the New Moon being begun at Num. 28: 9, and that for
Hanucca being confined to the verses for the particular
day. But all these lessons displace the reading from the
current Sidra for Mondays and Thursdays. Nothing but
the Day of Atonement displaces the Saturday afternoon
reading. Thus when the first and eighth days of the Passover come on Saturday, the first subsection of the lesson for
the Sabbath which follows after these two is read on the
afternoons of three Saturdays, two of which are also Festivals.

On all Festivals, also on the middle days of the Passover.
two scrolls are read from; the portions named above are

read first from one scroll, then the paragraph from the 28th or 29th chapter of Numbers, which sets forth the duty and the sacrifice of the particular feast, are read from the other. The second days of the Festival are treated for that purpose as if they were the genuine first days. On the middle days of the Feast of Huts (except on the Sabbath) only one scroll is read from, because the lessons are entirely from the 29th chapter of Numbers.

On Sabbath and New Moon or a Sabbath in Hanucca there are two scrolls, for the reason given above; but if the New Moon of Tebeth is a Sabbath, three scrolls are needed, one for the portion of the week, one for the reading of the sacrifices for the Sabbath and the New Moon from Numbers 28, and the third for the Hanucca lesson from the 7th chapter of Numbers.

Lastly the four extra lessons must be explained. During the subsistence of the Temple a poll-tax of a half-shekel was paid in pursuance of Ex. 30: 11-16 by every full-grown Israelite on the first day of the eleventh month, the anniversary of the day when like contributions were made to the Tabernacle in the wilderness. Hence to remind men of their duty, this passage (known as *Shekalim*) was read on the Sabbath next before or coinciding with the first of Adar. Next, on the Sabbath before Purim, the last three verses of Deut. 25 were read (Remember what Amalek did unto thee) on the supposition that the wicked Haman was an Amalekite by descent. On the Sabbath after Purim it was fit that men should take the proper steps to become Levitically clean for the Passover; hence the law about the ashes of the red heifer (Numbers, ch. 19) was then read. Lastly, as the first command given by Moses to the children of Israel refers to the consecration of Nisan (then called Abib) as the first month of the year, the "portion about the month," Ex. 12: 1-20, was read on the Sabbath before or coinciding with the New Moon of Nisan, that this duty and the events upon which it rests might be impressed on the

17

minds of the hearers. Thus arose the institution of the four
Sabbaths known as *Shekalim* (Shekels), *Zachor* (Remember), *Para* (Heifer), *Hodesh* (Month). The short lessons
are read from a second scroll after the weekly portion.
Shekalim and *Hodesh* may happen on a New Moon, and then
three scrolls are used, one for the weekly portion, one for
the New Moon from Numbers 28, and one for the lesson
due to the season.

This is the modern custom in nearly all of its details, and
it seems to agree pretty well with the statement of the Babylonian Talmud as to the custom in the days of Abbaye, who
flourished in the middle of the fourth century, and this custom purports to rest upon the teaching of Sages of the
Mishna, such as Rabbi Meïr. The Babylonians only add
further readings for their second holidays, which were unknown to the old Sages, and where these were divided in
opinion as to the proper lesson, they follow both views,
assigning one lesson to the first, the other to the second day.
However, the lesson for the eighth of the Passover, the
second of Pentecost, and eighth of the Feast is in the Talmud given only in its shorter form, beginning in the fifteenth chapter of Deuteronomy, v. 19, and omitting the
provisions about the tithe for the poor, the year of release,
and the manumission of bondmen.[5]

But the Mishna differs very much from the modern custom thus delivered to us by the Babylonians. Only for the
Day of Atonement it prescribes the reading of Lev. 16,
which was already read by the High Priest in the Temple,
and could not be passed by; on all other festivals it puts us off
with parts of the "lesson of feasts" (i. e., ch. 23) in Leviticus
or a short paragraph about Pentecost in Deuteronomy; it
thus robbed that day of its peculiar holiness as the feast of
revelation, and did not associate New Year with the youth
of the world, the age of Abraham and Isaac.[6]

It is not clear from the list of the lessons as given in the
Talmud that the paragraphs as to sacrifices from Numbers

28 and 29 were read from a second scroll on those days when a lesson elsewhere was prescribed; in other words, on any days but the middle days of the Feast of Huts. There is however a hint that such was already the custom in Talmudic times, conveyed in the legendary saying that Abraham anxiously asked God how the sins of Israel would be forgiven when their Temple was destroyed, and they should have no place where to bring their sacrifices, and he was told that to read the duty of these sacrifices from the Tora would be accepted as a full equivalent.[1]

CHAPTER III

ABOUT the distribution of the lesson from the Pentateuch the Mishna teaches the following:

"On Mondays and Thursdays and on Saturday afternoon three read, neither more nor less; on New Moons and Middle Days, four, neither more nor less; on (other) festivals five, on the Day of Atonement six, on the Sabbath seven; never less, but they may have more; none should read in the Tora less than three verses."[1]

It is the part of the leader (generally under the secular head of the congregation) to call these 3, 4, 5, 6, 7, or more men to the desk, and for many centuries each read his allotted part aloud in the hearing of the congregation.

The "Hazan," or overseer, or other person skilled in the knowledge of the text might prompt him, but those present expected to hear the lesson from the person called, and as there might not always be the seven men on hand capable of reading, it was lawful to call boys under thirteen or women to the desk.[2]

When a man of the priestly tribe (a Cohen) is in the Synagogue, he is called first; after him a Levite; thereafter those making up the smallest required number (seven on a Sabbath) should be plain Israelites, and a woman should rather be called to make up the seven than that one priest after another should read a portion.[3]

When the reading by from three to seven laymen was first instituted, the "companions still held aloof from the unlearned people of the land;" moreover, vowel points being unknown, whoever could read Hebrew at all read as well from the scroll as from any other book; lastly, those accents which give to each verse a different tune had not yet been set to the texts in books other than the scroll; hence no need of a long preparation for studying these tunes. When the bars against the ignorant were thrown down, when the use of vowel points in ordinary books had raised the reading of the bare scroll into an art, and when chanting by accents had come into vogue, say as early as the tenth century, the men called to the desk felt unequal to the task of reading aloud; they left it to a permanent official, themselves reading with the eye only, at most, articulating inaudibly, as in the silent Prayer. That such a course was already taken in olden times, that R. Akiba himself once refused to read his Parasha for lack of preparation, is asserted in the younger Aggadta, but is not very probable.[4] But it was always the rule that only one must read, either the official or the person called, never both of them together. The sixteenth century Code of R. Joseph Karo with its later annotations still recognizes the distinction between persons who can and those who cannot read; it still speaks of women and children being preferred to men unable to read. But when these men were only expected to read with the eye, the distinction became untenable, especially when it was hoped that those called to the desk would make offerings to the fund of the Synagogue. Such aid could not well be refused for a lack of skill that would not be tested. Thus anyone was called to the desk, and hardly anyone read. Another change naturally followed. According to the Mishna, whether three or seven were called to the desk, only the first one spoke a benediction, which covered the day's lesson, and the last again another benediction covering it retrospectively.[5] The first benediction is introduced in the way heretofore described as "breaking on the Shema," and runs thus:

"Bless ye the Lord, the highly blessed. Ans. Blessed be the Lord, the highly blessed, forever and ever. Blessed be thou, O

Lord, our God, King of the world, who hast chosen us from all the nations and given us thy Law. Blessed be thou, O Lord, the giver of the Law."

The benediction after reading is, "Blessed be thou, etc., who hast given us the Law of truth, and planted within us eternal life. Blessed be," etc., as above.[6]

The Talmud speaks of some passages to be honored as if they were complete books by having these benedictions recited before and after them, namely the Red Sea Song, the Ten Words in Exodus, the Ten Words in Deuteronomy, the last eight verses of the Pentateuch.[7] But at a later time, during the growth of the Talmud, it became the custom for every man called to the desk to bless before and after his subsection; hence those stepping on the platform had something to say, while otherwise they must have gone through a dumb show.[8] Thus, under the present usage, a man is called to the desk to pronounce a benediction before and after his subsection and not to read it. To read is now the exception. It takes place, *first*, when the official reader is honored with an "Ascent" (Aliya) in his own right; *second*, when this official wishes to honor some scholar who likes to read from the scroll, and invites him to do so; *third*, when a Bar Mitzva, a boy who has just attained religious full age, having passed his thirteenth birthday by the Jewish Calendar, is called to the desk for the first time. But it is deemed more meritorious that such a boy should study up the whole Sabbath portion, and be the Baal Kore for the day, reading for the others as well as for himself.

The Bar Mitzva celebration has its benefits and its drawbacks. When a boy is trained to study the whole section for the week together with the prophetic lesson thoroughly, so that he can read both as correctly as the regular reader, he obtains some valuable training, such as most boys will gladly undergo for the pleasure of showing their achievements in public. But the boy's time may be wasted in learning to chant the lessons rather than understand them.

A greater drawback is the early age at which this induction into manhood takes place; to many parents it seems the proper season at which the son's religious studies should come to an end.

The ostensible ground for solemnly calling the boy to the desk as a Bar Mitzva (son of, that is, bound by, the Law) is that learning and teaching the Tora is the one great duty at the base of all others; but this cannot be the true reason, for all the standards, from the Mishna down, hold that boys under thirteen are competent to read the Tora in public; and as to the prophetic lesson, it is still quite common to allot it to such boys.[9]

The custom of the Bar Mitzva is hardly three hundred years old, and may have been suggested by the confirmation of Christian children at nearly the same age. Reform congregations are more frank in their borrowing, for they have taken over the name and form and season along with the general idea of "confirmation."

The Pentateuchs published by Jews for private use have the subsections marked in them, and the two rituals disagree as to this subdivision only in a few places. The Talmud lays down the rule that as far as possible each subsection should begin and end with pleasant or honorable words. Thus a part of the blessings in Leviticus 26 is read by (or · for) him who has the "rebuke," or prediction of evils, in his portion. In the 48th of Genesis a subsection closes, "For thy salvation I hope, O Lord." Subsection four of XVI, which embraces the Red Sea Song, goes on to the words, "I, the Lord, am thy physician." But there is one weekly portion, the last but one in the cycle, Deut. 33, which includes the farewell of Moses, of which the Talmud itself marks the dividing points; this leads us to believe that the subdivision of the other portions is not much younger.[10]

When two sections are read together, for instance 51 and 52, near the end of Deuteronomy, the fourth man called to the desk reads across from the first to the second section.

The books for use in the service mark the divisions thus, "Seventh, fourth when united," or "Second, fifth when united."

When only one scroll is used, as on an ordinary Sabbath, a small passage at the end, say three or six verses, are read by or for the Maftir, or "leave-giver," by way of repetition after the whole portion has already been read by or for the seven or more persons called to the desk. When there is a second scroll the lesson from that belongs to the Maftir. On the middle days of the Passover three men read from the special lesson for the day, and the fourth from the 29th chapter of Numbers. This reading by the Maftir is clearly of Talmudic age.[11]

The lesson for Saturday afternoon and Monday and Thursday is generally the same as the subsection which on the following Sabbath is read to the *Cohen*, or first man called. Only in Ki Tissa (XXI) this subsection is inordinately long, and much less is deemed sufficient, while in Behar Sinai (XXXII) and in the four last Sidras the first subsection has less than ten verses, and therefore is too short. Even in subdividing these small portions among three men, pains are taken to give to each, if possible, a pleasant or solemn ending. Where paragraphs are marked by breaks in the line, the divisions of either the whole section or subsection should either coincide with them or differ from the break in the line or the paragraph by at least three verses.[12]

It is seen that everything connected with the reading of the lessons is minutely looked to, and all contingencies are provided for.

CHAPTER IV

THE LESSON FROM THE PROPHETS

In the Hebrew Bible eight books are classed as "Prophets;" four "earlier Prophets," that is, Joshua, Judges, Samuel, and Kings; and four "later Prophets," Isaiah, Jeremiah, Ezekiel, and the Twelve. It was never proposed to read the whole of these books in the Synagogue; on the contrary, the Sages of the Mishna indicate some passages which should not be read publicly for fear of misunderstandings. But at an early day, probably during the Maccabean wars, it became customary to read lessons from these eight books, at first perhaps as a substitute for those from the Pentateuch, when no copy of this could be obtained, but soon in addition to them, after them. It seems that while now the prophetic lesson is only the last exercise of the desk, being followed by *Musaf*, it was formerly the very last of all the Sabbath morning services; hence it obtained the name of *Haftara* (leave-giving, or dismissal), whence many think the *Missa* (the meeting is dismissed), or Mass, of the Christians derives its name; and he who read it was said to be "giving leave" (*Maftir*) in the Prophet.[1]

There are at present two classes of Haftaroth for the Sabbaths of the year, one chosen with a view to the season, the other, and much larger one, with regard to the lesson in the Law. There are twelve of the former class, the three "Punishments" for the three Sabbaths before the Fast of the Ninth of Ab, the seven "Comforts" for the seven Sabbaths which follow it, then one or two "Repentances," according as one or two open Sabbaths intervene between the Day of Memorial and the Feast of Huts. As the event around which ten of these lessons cluster is the day of the destruction of the Temple by Titus, it is clear that they cannot have been read in this order while the Temple stood.

The first of the "Punishments" is Jeremiah, from ch. 1: 1 to ch. 2: 3; the second, in the same book, ch. 2: 4-28, to which the Germans add by way of comfort ch. 3, v. 4, the Sefardim ch. 4: 1, 2; the third, in Isaiah, in chapter 1, verses 1 to 27, known as *Hazon* (The Vision), from its first word, and so celebrated for the scorn with which the prophet speaks of sacrifice and ceremony.

The "Comforts" are all from the second part of Isaiah, beginning with "Comfort ye, comfort ye, my people," for the Sabbath after the fast, ch. 40: 1-26. On the next following Sabbath, "But Zion said, the Lord has forsaken me," from ch. 49: 14 to 51: 3; on the third, "Thou afflicted, tempest-tossed," from ib. 54: 11 to 55: 5; on the fourth, "I, even I, am your comforter, ib. 51: 12 to 52: 12; on the fifth, "Sing, O thou barren," ib. 54: 1-10; on the sixth, "Arise, shine, for thy light has come," ib. 60: 1-22; on the seventh, "I will greatly rejoice in the Lord," ib. 61: 10 to 63: 9.

As to the "Repentances" the rituals differ. The Sefardim read on the Sabbath before the Day of Atonement, "Seek ye the Lord when he may be found," Isa. 55: 6 to 56: 8, which the Germans set aside for fast day afternoons; the Germans, "Return, O Israel, to the Lord, thy God," from the last chapter of Hosea, to which "Blow ye the horn in Zion," Joel 2: 15-27, is added when there is no free Sabbath after the Day of Atonement, but the last three verses of Micah, when there is; while the Sefardim reserve "Return, O Israel" for fast day afternoons.

For a Sabbath between the Day of Atonement and the Feast the Haftara is Ezekiel 17: 22 to end of ch. 18, a complete treatise on the right of the individual to earn divine favor by a return to righteousness.[2]

For the other Sabbaths of the year the Haftaroth are

chosen as shown hereafter: For Section I, the Creation, "Thus says God the Lord who created the heavens," Isaiah 42: 5-21 (or to 43: 10). For II, the Deluge, lesson from Isa. 54: 1-10, with the words, "Is not this for me like the waters of Noah," the same as the fifth "Comfort." Section III, the call of Abraham from the east, Haftara, Isa. 40: 27 to 41: 16, with the words, "Whom has he aroused from the east," applying to Cyrus. For Section IV, the late birth of Isaac and his escape from death, 2 Kings 4: 1-37 (or 23), the son born to the lady at Shunem brought back from death. Section V, Abraham getting old, David becomes old, 1 Kings 1: 1-31. Section VI, the birth of Jacob and Esau and their blessings; Malachi 1: 1 to 2: 7, God's preference for Jacob. Section VII, Jacob goes to Laban wooing, "Then Jacob fled to the plain of Syria, and Israel served," etc., Hosea 12: 13 to the end of the book, for which the Sefardim substitute Hosea 11: 7 to 12: 12, referring to Jacob's later life. Hence with VIII, the friendly meeting of Jacob and Esau, some of the Germans read Hosea 11: 7 to 12: 12; others and all Sefardim read the book of Obadiah, a rebuke to Edom, the descendants of Esau. IX, Joseph sold by his brethren, "When they sell the righteous for money," etc., Amos 2: 6 to 3: 8. X sets out with Pharaoh's dreams; hence, unless it is read during Hanucca, "And Solomon awoke and behold it was a dream," leading to his wise judgment, 1 Kings 3: 15 to 4:1. Section XI begins with Judah's plea before Joseph and their drawing together; the Haftara, Ezekiel 37: 15-28, predicts the reunion of Judah with the House of Joseph, led by Ephraim. Section XII tells of Jacob's death; the Haftara, 1 Kings 2: 1-12, of David's death; unfortunately the latter does not die with only blessings on his lips like the former. So far in Genesis.

Exodus begins with Section XIII, the call of Moses, also the great increase of the children of Israel; hence the Sefardim read the call of Jeremiah, the same Haftara as the first of the "Punishments" above; the Germans read from

Isaiah, "In coming days Jacob will drive roots," etc., 27: 6 to 28: 13, adding the comforting verses, ch. 29: 22, 23. In Section XIV Moses is sent with a threatening message to Pharaoh; the counterpart, Ezek. 28: 25 to 29: 21, predicts the sufferings of Egypt under Nebuchadnezzar. In Section XV Moses is again told to "go in unto Pharaoh" with threats; this is coupled with Jeremiah's prophecy against Egypt, ch. 46: 13-28, with the two beautiful verses at the end, assuring Israel that it is indestructible. In Section XVI the main feature is the Song on the Red Sea; the Song of Deborah (Judges 5) is the proper counterpart; the Germans begin with chapter 4, whereby the Haftara becomes inordinately long. Section XVII, the revelation on Mount Sinai, calls for the vision of Isaiah; chapter 6, in which the Seraphim utter their Thrice-Holy. The Germans add, rather awkwardly, ch. 7: 1-6, and the two apparently Messianic verses, 9: 5, 6. XVIII begins with the law requiring the discharge of Hebrew bondmen after a service of six years; hence the narrative, Jer. 34: 8-22, on this subject, with the comforting verses, ibid. 33: 25, 26, added. The next two sections, XIX and XX, contain the commands as to the building of the Tabernacle and all its vessels; these are matched from 1 Kings 5: 26 to 6: 13, as to the building of Solomon's Temple, and Ezek. 43: 10-27, about the ideal Temple of the prophet Ezekiel. In XXI the Golden Calf and the zeal of Moses against the idolaters are spoken of; Elijah is introduced (1 Kings 18: 1 or 20 to 39) as overthrowing the Baal worship of the Northern Kingdom. The two next sections (XXII and XXIII) relate how the Tabernacle was built and set up, the Haftaroth are taken from 1 Kings, ch. 7 and 8; that for *Pekude* (XXIII) ends with ch. 8: 21, where Solomon dedicates his finished Temple.

We now come to Leviticus. The first two sections (XXIV and XXV) give detailed laws as to all kinds of offerings; both of the Haftaroth, Isa. 43: 21 to 44: 23, and Jer. 7: 21 to 8: 3, with 9: 22, 23 added for comfort, make rather light of sacrifices. The former dwells mainly on the folly of idolaters; the latter opens with the plain words, "Add your burnt-offerings to your peace-offerings and eat flesh." In XXVI the two elder sons of Aaron die by fire from heaven for improperly handling holy things; the same fate befalls David's friend Uzza in the Haftara, 2 Sam. 6: 1-19 (or to 7: 17). The next two sections (XXVII and XXVIII) deal with leprosy; the two prophetic lessons are both from the story of Elisha in the 2d book of Kings; the first speaks of Naaman the Syrian (4: 42 to 5: 19) whom Elisha cured; the other (7: 3-20) of the four lepers who, during the siege of Samaria, sat in the gate and were the first to learn of the flight of the besiegers. XXIX deals with incest; for this and other vices Israel is reproved by Ezekiel, chapter 22: 1-19. Section XXX (Kedoshim) also rebukes gross vices; and the Sefardim accompany it with a kindred lesson from Ezek. 20: 2-20, while the German Haftara for this week, "Are ye not unto me like children of the Ethiopians," Amos 9: 7-15 has no visible relation to the lesson from the Tora. Section XXXI, about the duties of the Aaronide priesthood, is illustrated by Ezekiel's prophecy (ch. 44: 15-31) as to the position of the "Priests, the Levites, sons of Zadok," in his ideal commonwealth. Then XXXII, on the Jubilee and redemption of land, is illustrated from Jeremiah 32: 6-27, where the prophet, under God's command, redeems with money his cousin's field, while the Chaldean army is encamped upon it. For XXXIII, with its promises of good and evil, a good side-piece is found in Jeremiah 16: 19 to 17: 14, in which the man who trusteth in human strength and the man who trusteth in God are contrasted.

Next for the book of Numbers. Its first section with the census of the tribes is met by Hosea's prophecy, "The number of the children of Israel will be like the sand of the sea," ch. 2: 1-22. In XXXV is the law of the Nazarite;

the Haftara, Judges 13: 2-25, tells the miraculously announced birth of Samson, the life-long Nazarite. The next
section (XXXVI) begins with the seven-branched candlestick; Zechariah's vision of the candlestick with its seven
pipes and lamps (2: 14 to 4: 7) follows it. In XXXVII
Moses sends his scouts into the Holy Land; in the Haftara
(Josh. 2: 1-24) the spies sent out by Joshua to Jericho are
saved by Rahab. In XXXVIII Moses, in view of Korah's
revolt, avows his disinterestedness; Samuel does so in
almost the same words (1 Sam. 11: 14 to 12: 22), when the
people ask him to give them a king. In XXXIX the con-
quest of part of Ammon's territory by the Emorites is told,
and how this land was conquered from the latter by Israel;
in the lesson from Judges 11: 1-33, we read how the children
of Ammon sought to reclaim this district, and how Jephtha
fought and defeated them. Section *Balak* (XL) tells how
Balaam was forced to bless Israel, whom he sought to
curse; this is mentioned by Micah in the Haftara (5: 6
to 6: 8), which winds up with the summary of man's duty,
"but to do justice and to love mercy and to walk humbly
with thy God."

The next section (*Phinehas*) is read either within or before
the three weeks preceding the fast of the Ninth of Ab;
in the former case the first of the "Punishments" is read
with it, for which see above; in the.latter case, as Phinehas
was zealous for the Lord, the Haftara (1 Kings 18: 46 to
19: 21) introduces Elijah's words, "I have been truly zealous for the Lord the God of Hosts."[3]

This disposes, with the Punishments, Comforts, and Repentances already enumerated, of all the sections except
the last, which is read on the "Joy of the Law," and has for
its Haftara what follows next in the Bible, the first nine (or
twenty-one) verses of the first chapter of Joshua.[4]

When two sections are combined on a Sabbath, the Haftara belonging to the second prevails. On the Sabbaths
which have short readings from a second scroll, this reading

determines the prophetic lesson. It is for *Shekalim* the account of King Joash gathering money contributions for the repair of the House (2 Kings 12: 4-17); for *Zachor* (Remember Amalek), the death of Agag (1 Sam. 15: 1-34); for *Para* (the Red Heifer), a spiritualized cleansing, "I shall sprinkle upon you clean water, and ye shall be clean, I shall cleanse you from all your sins" (Ezek. 36: 16-38); for *Hodesh* (the Month), Ezekiel's predictions as to the service on Sabbaths and New Moons, Ezek. 45: 16 to 46: 18. On the Sabbath before the Passover, known as the "Great Sabbath," though there is no reading from a second scroll, there is still a special Haftara: Malachi, ch. 3: 4 to end; on account of the verse, "I will send you the Prophet Elijah before the coming of the great and fearful day of the Lord." On a Sabbath in Hanucca the same Haftara is read as for section XXXVI, the vision of the candlestick. If there are two Sabbaths in Hanucca, they read on the second from 1 Kings 7: 40-50—the dedication of Solomon's Temple.

On a "Sabbath and New Moon" the 66th chapter of Isaiah is read, by reason of the verse (last but one, but repeated as the last), "It shall come to pass that every month on its new moon and every week on its Sabbath, all flesh shall come to bow before me." When the Sabbath is not, but the next day (Sunday) is a New Moon, a passage from 1 Samuel is read (20: 18-42), beginning with the words, "And Jonathan said unto David, to-morrow is new moon." But these two last-named lessons yield the place not only to Hanucca, to *Shekalim*, and to *Hodesh*, but also to the "Punishment" on the first of Ab.

The lessons for the Festivals remain, and all of these are enumerated in the Talmud. On the first day of the Passover, the celebration of the Passover in the Holy Land (Josh. 5: 2 to 6: 1); on the second day the celebration as restored by King Josiah, 2 Kings 23: 1-9, 21-25; on the Sabbath in the middle days, Ezekiel's vision of the Valley of Bones (36: 37 to 37: 14), for which the reason is not clear. On the seventh day of the Passover, as the lesson from the Tora contains Moses' thanksgiving song on the Red Sea, the great thanksgiving of David (2 Sam., ch. 22). On the eighth of the Passover, Isaiah 10: 32 to the end of chapter 12, perhaps because the last chapter is also a song of joy; but the Talmud gives another and not very apparent reason.

Although the Mishna by a majority of voices forbids the public reading of the "Chariot,"[5] Ezekiel's vision (ch. 1, also 3: 12) nevertheless has become the Haftara for the first day of Pentecost—a vision cf heavenly things as against visible revelation; the choice of the third chapter of Habakkuk, which is a Psalm, for the second day, seems to rest either on the word *Shebuoth*, which it contains, or on the opening, "O Lord, I have heard thy report, and have feared," as reminding of the thunders of Sinai.

On the fast of the Ninth of Ab the very sad passage from Jeremiah 8: 13 to 9: 23. is read in the morning.

On the first day of the New Year, the birth of Samuel and the prayer of Hannah, because Samuel, like Isaac, was, according to the legend, born on the first of Tishri; on the second day, Jeremiah 31: 2-20, because the closing verse, "Is Ephraim my darling son," is deemed the most impressive among the "Remembrance" verses.

On the Day of Atonement in the morning Isaiah is read from ch. 57: 14 to the end of 58; the true manner of making the fast acceptable before God is here taught, and in the afternoon the Book of Jonah is read, because it teaches that repentance to lead to forgiveness must be real ("and God saw their works, that they turned from their evil ways").

A fit lesson for the first day of the Feast is found in the 14th chapter of Zechariah, where it is predicted that all nations will have to celebrate the Feast of Huts. On the second day the dedication of Solomon's Temple by prayer, on the "Feast in the seventh" month, 1 Kings 8: 2-21; and on the "Eighth" from the same chapter, verses 54-66, in which the eighth day (though of a second week of feasting) is specially named.

Meanwhile, on the Sabbath falling into the middle days, they read from Ezekiel the prediction of the wars, in which Gog of the land Magog, prince of Rosh, Moshoch, and Tubal, is to succumb in the Holy Land (Ezek. 38: 18 to 39: 16). With the Haftara for the "Joy of the Law" already named, this disposes of the whole year.[6] There are a few days when the two rituals disagree, a few when the Haftara is longer in one (generally the German) than in the other; but on the whole the agreement is very close, and indicates a high antiquity for the selection. An Aggadic work of the seventh century, the Pesikta, restored from scattered fragments by the labors of Rapoport and Zunz, is written as a commentary upon eleven of our present Haftaroth, which must then have been in undisputed use.[7] Those for the Festivals are indicated in the Talmud just as we read them now, except that a prayer by Solomon from 1 Kings 8 is there named, for which the beginning of Joshua as the continuation of the last chapter of Deuteronomy was substituted afterwards, the dispute not being fully settled in the thirteenth century. The first chapter of Isaiah, which now serves for the last Sabbath before the fast of the Ninth of Ab, seems in Talmudic times to have been read a week earlier.[8]

A Haftara ought to have twenty-one verses, three for each man called to the desk to read in the Law; one of the Sages says, when an interpreter is employed, they should stop at ten verses, in order not to become irksome to the public, though the subject-matter is not finished; when it is, ten verses always suffice; and one Haftara in the German ritual (for Sec. XXX) has only nine verses.[9]

Another somewhat later authority says that when the lesson is translated or made the subject for preaching, from three to seven verses are enough without benedictions.[10]

That the German Haftara is so often longer than the Sefardic happened probably because the Germans dropped the habit of translating the lessons much earlier than the Sefardim.

Altogether the Haftaroth cover a little more than one-fifth of the eight books that are classed as Prophets. Most Jews and Jewesses of the old stripe know very little of these books but what, in the course of every year, they read again and again in these lessons, which contain very little history, but much of the ennobling and comforting sentiments of the second Isaiah and of other prophets. There are no less than thirteen Haftaroth from Isaiah, chs. 40-66, and thirteen from the "Twelve." The selections were made more for the heart than for historic learning.

It has been noticed that in many Haftaroth one or more verses are added from a later chapter, and the Maftir even skips from the last chapter of Hosea to Joel or Micah. This skipping is expressly authorized in the Mishna, while forbidden to those who read from the Law.[11]

Something must be said about the prophet lessons which went with the Palestinian cycle of three years. They were naturally shorter than those which go with the one-year cycle. The Gospel of Luke, ch. 4, v. 17, tells how Jesus was called to the desk as Maftir at Nazareth, as any man of note coming into the Synagogue at his old home would be in our own days. He finds his place in the Book of Isaiah; he reads two verses (61: 1, 2), rolls up the book and returns it to the Shammash, and then preaches upon what he has read. The lesson seems strangely short, but it might have been no longer had he stood at the desk of a Synagogue in Galilee fourteen hundred years later. A manuscript in the Bodleian Library gives a list of the Haftaroth for about one-half of the three-years portions. They vary from two verses to twenty-one; some of our present Haftaroth are in the list allotted to other portions of the Pentateuch, e. g., the lesson from Micah ending, "and to walk

humbly with thy God," which we read with the story of
Balaam, goes with Jacob's flight to Haran. Some lessons
in the list allotted to one-third of a full section are a part of
that which now goes with the whole; thus about half of the
German Haftara, "In future Jacob will take root," for the
first section in Exodus, is allotted here to a "Seder" within
that section. But lessons of only four or five verses are not
unusual. Some of the portions of the Tora for which Haftaroth are here chosen, such as Genesis 21, seem to be not
Sabbatic but Festival lessons. Among the forty-five prophetic lessons for Genesis there are twenty-nine from Isaiah,
one each from Jeremiah and Ezekiel, seven from the Twelve,
six from the historic books, one in doubt.[12] There are other
sources, disclosing in part the Haftaroth for the three-years
cycle, which do not fully agree with what is found in this
manuscript.[13]

The Talmud refers occasionally to a Haftara on Sabbath
afternoon, and it is believed it was taken, not from the
Prophets, but from Hagiographa.[14] The usage has however
wholly gone out; the only Haftaroth for afternoons at present are those for the Day of Atonement and for other fasts.

CHAPTER V

THE LITURGY OF THE DESK

THE benedictions before and after each subsection having of necessity been given and explained heretofore, we need speak here only of the additional thanks to be rendered when one who is called to the desk falls within the four classes who are to render them under the teachings of Psalm 107, namely: One who arises from grave sickness; or who is released from prison; or who has crossed the sea; or the desert; such a one adds to his benediction after reading the following:

Blessed be thou, O Lord, our God, King of the world, who bestowest favors on the guilty, and who hast bestowed on me all that is good.

The by-standers answer:

He who has bestowed good on thee, may further bestow good on thee. Selah.[1]

He who "gives leave in the prophet" reads beside the benedictions over his portion from the Pentateuch the following:

Blessed be thou, O Lord, our God, King of the world, who hast chosen goodly prophets, and wast pleased with their words, that were truthfully spoken; blessed be thou, O Lord, who hast chosen the Law and Moses, his servant, Israel his people, and true and righteous prophets.

And after the prophetic lesson:

Blessed be thou, O Lord, our God, King of the world, Rock of all ages, righteous in all generations, the faithful God, who says and doeth, who decrees and carrieth out; all of whose words are truth and righteousness. Thou art faithful, O Lord, our God, and thy words are faithful, and not one of thy words will return unfulfilled. Blessed be thou, O Lord, thé God, faithful in all his words.

(Among the Sefardim the congregation chimes in with the words, "truth and righteousness," *cmeth vatzedek*):

Have mercy on Zion, which is the home of our lives; save her, whose soul is grieved, speedily in our days. Blessed be thou, O Lord, who gladdenest Zion in her children (an older reading: who buildest Jerusalem). Gladden us, O Lord, our God, with Elijah, the prophet, thy servant, and with the kingdom of David, thy anointed; may he soon come, that our heart may rejoice, and may no stranger sit upon his throne, nor let others inherit his glory; for thou didst swear to him by thy holy name, that his seed shall never come to an end. Blessed be thou, O Lord, Shield of David.

In the service for fast days and on the afternoon of Atonement there are only these three benedictions.[2] On the Sabbath they proceed:

For the Law, and for the service, and for the prophets, and for this Sabbath day, which thou hast given us, O Lord, our God, for holiness and rest, for glory and beauty; for all this we thank and bless thee; be thy name blessed by the mouth of all that live, always and for evermore. Blessed be thou, O Lord, who sanctifiest the Sabbath.

On Festivals this benediction is modified like the last part of the "Holiness of the Day" in the Amida. It concludes on the Day of Memorial thus:

Thy word is true, and standeth forever. Blessed be thou, O Lord, King of all the earth, who sanctifiest (the Sabbath and) Israel and the "Day of Memorial" (or "the Day of Atonement" on that day).

We have to go back now to the very beginning of the ceremonies which are bound up with the lesson. But very lately, first probably on some Cabbalistic ground, but now mainly as a text for singing, the Germans have introduced the recital of the following lines before the Ark is opened to take out the scroll:

(Ps. 86: 8): There is none among the Gods like thee, O Lord, and none like thy works. (Ps. 145: 13): Thy Kingdom is the Kingdom of all ages, and thy dominion lasts for all generations. The Lord is King, the Lord has reigned, the Lord will reign forever and ever. (Ps. 29: 11): The Lord giveth strength to his people, the Lord blesseth his people with peace. Father of mercy, deal after thy will kindly with Zion; build the walls of Jerusalem. For in thee alone we trust, King, high and exalted God, Lord of Eternities.

When the Ark is opened the Germans on all occasions, except on the "Joy of the Law," say:

(Numbers 10: 35): It came to pass when the ark moved forward, Moses would say: Arise, O Lord, and thy enemies will scatter, and those that hate thee will flee before thee. (Isa. 2: 3): For from Zion the Law shall go forth, and the word of the Lord from Jerusalem. Blessed be he who gave the Law to his people Israel in his holiness.

The Sefardim begin on Sabbaths and Festivals with the verse:

(Deut. 4: 35): Unto thee it was shown that thou mightest know that the Lord is God, there is none beside him.

Other verses follow; among them, "There is none," etc., and "It came to pass," etc., as above. But on work-days they say nothing to accompany the opening of the Ark, unless it be the prayer from the Zohar, given in Book II, ch. XIX, and "God, long-suffering, etc." (See ch. XVI.)

On the "Joy of the Law," when the taking out of the scrolls is the very center of the day's celebration, the leader gives out separately and the congregation repeats after him the verses cited above, beginning, "Unto thee it was shown," and several other verses from the prayer of Solomon in the 8th chapter of 1 Kings. These had become stereotyped and well remembered as early as the eleventh century, and poetry of easy grasp gathered round them, shutting out later accretions, which came into use for other Festivals or for the Sabbath.

For example: On all other festive days it has within the last two or three hundred years become customary with the Germans, right after the scrolls are taken from the Ark, to sing three times the "thirteen qualities" (Ex. 34: 6, 7; see chapter on Day of Atonement). The custom came in by the Cabbalistic door, as is shown by a prayer, "Be it thy will," which follows; but at present its main strength is musical.

The leader in prayer carries the scroll from the Ark to the platform; when more than one scroll is needed, the task of taking it out and carrying it to the platform is conferred as an honor on some member of the congregation. When the platform is reached, the leader, holding up his scroll, proclaims:

(Ps. 34: 4): Ascribe greatness to the Lord with me, and let us exalt his name together.

Such is still the Sefardic custom, and was but recently that of Western Germany. But within the last fifty or sixty years a not much older Polish usage has altogether on musical grounds become general among all the Germans; that on Sabbaths and Festivals the leader first gives out:

"Hear, O Israel, the Lord our God, the Lord is One," which the congregation or choir repeats after him. Then he says:

"One is our God; great is our Lord; holy is his name," which is repeated in like manner. Then he adds as above, Ascribe greatness, etc. This is answered in the German ritual with the verse (1 Chron. 29: 11), "Thine, O Lord, is the greatness," etc., which has been set to beautiful music; and the two verses, "Exalt ye," etc., from Psalm 99. The Sefardim answer with these latter verses, to which they add many others. They proceed then to the *Hagbaha*, or "holding up high;" that is, the leader partly unrolls the scroll, and holding it up high turns around with it, so that all present can see the written part. While doing so he says aloud:

"This is the law which Moses has set before the children of Israel." With the Germans the Hagbaha follows the reading, and they add to the above the words, "from the mouth of the Lord, by the hand of Moses."

With the Sefardim thereupon the reader of the lesson or the leader in prayer simply calls, "Cohen come near and do thy duty," while the Germans introduce this call thus:

May thy Kingdom appear and be revealed. May he show grace to our remnant, to the remnant of his people Israel, for happy life and peace. All of you ascribe greatness to God, and show honor to the Law! Cohen come near. Let—— son of——, the Cohen, stand up.

Then in both rituals two verses from Ps. 19, in praise of the Tora, are spoken. Also (Ps. 18: 31), "The God whose way is perfect; the word of the Lord is tried; he is a shield to all that trust in him." On Sabbath the seven who are to read are addressed in the seven Hebrew words (Deut. 3: 4), "But-ye, that-cleave to-the-Lord, your-God, are-all alive this-day." Whereupon the first man called says his benediction and the reading begins.

If no Cohen is present, an Israelite is called with an explanatory remark. After each subsection an official invokes on the man called to the desk this blessing:

He who has blessed our fathers, Abraham, Isaac, and Jacob, may he bless —— son of ——; because he has come up in honor of God, of the Law, and of the Sabbath (or Festival or Day of Judgment); may the Holy and Blessed One for this merit bless and preserve him, send happiness and success into all his undertakings, together with all Israel, his brethren, and say ye, Amen.

If the person called wishes to "offer" money to the Synagogue or a charity, the same official will, at his request invoke a similar blessing by name or description upon others, and state what offering is made. When the blessing is invoked on women, "He who blessed our mothers, Sarah, Rebekah, Rachel, and Leah," is named.

The names used in calling to the desk and when invoking blessings are the Hebrew names, such as Moses, the son of Eleazar (Moshe ben El'azar), with *Hac-Cohen* or *Hal-Levi* added, when such addition fits the party. Not all Biblical names are now in use among Jews; and there are a few Aramaic and Greek ones that are fully recognized as "holy names," Akiba and Sheragga (Lamp) of the former, Alexander and Kalonymos among the latter. Among women fully one-half have not Hebrew names, but for religious purposes only old German names, handed down from grandmother to granddaughter or greatniece without change; and the Sefardim use for their daughters current Spanish or Italian names, by which they are blessed in the Synagogue. About the only Hebrew names for women still in common use are Sarah, Rebekah, Rachel, Leah, Deborah, Hannah, Hadassah, Esther, also Malca (queen), Haïa (the living), which are not Biblical.

These "vows" take the place of the contribution box in Christian churches, as it is not deemed lawful to actually handle money on the Sabbath or Festivals.

When the portion is finished the reader recites the Half Kaddish; among the Germans only after the portion from the first scroll (or after the first and second, when there are three); among the Sefardim after each scroll, except in the afternoon service, when the Half Kaddish before the Prayer is supposed to rest on the lesson or lessons.

A number of prayers which are spoken before the scroll is returned, but not connected with the lesson, have been given in Book II, ch. XVI; on Sabbath and Festivals among the Germans, with the Sefardim on all days. *Ashre* is also recited while the scroll remains out. Before returning it to the Ark the leader, standing on the platform, lifts

it up and sings from Ps. 148, "Let them praise the name of
the Lord: for his name alone is exalted." The congregation or choir continues:

His majesty is above earth and heaven. He has lifted the horn
of his people, to the praise of all his saints, of the children of
Israel, the people near unto him. Halleluiah.

Next in order on Sabbath mornings, when seven men are
called and the divine law is thus heard seven distinct times,
is the 29th Psalm with its seven times recurring, "Voice of
the Lord." On all other occasions the 24th Psalm is spoken,
with its question, "Who may ascend the mount of the Lord"
(that is, the platform from which the Law is read), and the
answer, "He who is clean of hands and pure in heart."
Meanwhile the scroll is slowly carried back to the Ark, and
when this is opened the Germans speak the verse following
upon and corresponding to the one spoken when the scroll
was taken out, viz.:

(Num. 10: 36): And when it (the ark) rested, he would say:
Return, O Lord, with the myriads of thousands of Israel. (Then
Ps. 132: 8, 9, 10; Prov. 4: 2.) (Prov. 3: 18): She is a tree of life to
those who take hold of her, and those who grasp her firmly are
happy. (Ib. 17): Her ways are ways of pleasantness, and her
paths are peace. (Lam. 5: 21): Draw us back unto thee, O Lord,
and we will return, renew our days as of Old.

The Sefardim recite only the first and last of these verses,
introducing them with two un-Biblical lines.

Other verses and petitions are found in the prayer books
as accompanying the scroll on its travels between the Ark
and the desk, some of which are omitted in one or the other
place; some are slurred over. Those copied above, and some
that are not, are found in the Treatise of Scribes, and this
alone contains the benedictions over the prophetic lesson,
a little longer than the one now in use and with parts of it
still in dispute.[3]

The formula for calling up by name must reach back at

least into the twelfth century, for the Mahzor Vitry already contains its poetic enlargement, by which on the "Joy of the Law" the "Bridegroom of the Tora" (he who reads the closing chapter) and the "Bridegroom of Genesis" (he who reads ch. 1: 1 to 2: 3 from Genesis) are called to the desk, after the most gushing compliments to the Law and to them, with a threefold: Stand up! Stand up! Stand up! and blanks for the name of the groom and of his father.

CHAPTER VI

THERE are five small books, composed at very different dates, which are comprised under the name of the Five Rolls (*Megilloth*): the Song of Songs, Ruth, Lamentations, Ecclesiastes, and Esther. These have been allotted to five seasons of the year, the Song of Songs to the Passover, as the time when winter passes away, because of the verse, "Behold the winter is gone;" Ruth to the Feast of Weeks, as the time of the first-fruits, though it is really the time for early wheat, and in the book of Ruth they are harvesting barley; Ecclesiastes to the Feast of Huts (give a share to seven, also to eight); and what is more natural and more important, Lamentations to the Ninth of Ab and the Book of Esther to Purim.

The three former books are read at the Synagogue on some day of the respective Feasts, generally on a Sabbath, without any benediction or ceremony, though it seems that formerly a benediction used to precede them. Every man reads from his own copy; no parchment scrolls are prepared; the reading takes place after the morning Prayer and before the scrolls of the Law are taken out.

With Lamentations there is more ceremony. On the night of the Ninth of Ab the leader chants them slowly and plaintively; the last chapter is repeated with certain interjections of woe and glosses which lead up to the dirges that follow. In the Sefardic ritual the book is read again in the morning service. The benediction, which is recommended by the "Treatise of Scribes" for Lamentations, as well as for Canticles and Ruth, has long been dropped; it would be too hard to give thanks for the occasion which calls for such a lesson.[1]

But it is altogether different with the Book of Esther. This is written out on a parchment roll with lamp-black ink, in square characters, without vowels or accents, like the Pentateuch; this roll is well-known as *the* Megilla.[2] It is read on the night of Purim after the evening service and again in the morning after the "lesson" of the day from the same desk. The reader says these benedictions before he begins:

Blessed be thou, O Lord, our God, King of the world, who hast sanctified us by thy commandments, and hast commanded us to read the Mégilla. Blessed be thou, O Lord, our God, King of the world, who hast done wonders for our fathers; in those days, at this season. Blessed be thou, O Lord, our God, King of the world, who hast let us live, and hast kept us up, and made us reach this time.

The first and second (though not the third) of these benedictions are again spoken in the morning before the book is read.[3]

To render the recital of this book more solemn the people break in at the following verses, reading them before the reader: At verse 5 of chapter 2, in which Mordecai is named for the first time[4]; at verse 15 of chapter 8, telling of Mordecai's triumph, and again at the following verse: "The Jews had light and gladness and joy and honor;" then at verses 7, 8, 9, 10 of chapter 9, with the names of Haman's ten sons; and at the last verse of the whole book, as they do at the close of the Pentateuch.

After the book is finished the reader and the others present join in this benediction:

Blessed be thou, O Lord, our God, King of the world; who strives in our quarrel, and who judges our cause, and wreaks our vengeance, and requites to all our enemies their just deserts, and punishes our enemies. Blessed be thou, O Lord, who dealest out punishment to Israel's enemies, the God, the Deliverer.[5]

This benediction and the following short piece (not yet enriched by the fourfold rhyme) are found in the Treatise of Scribes:

The lily of Jacob rejoiced and was glad, when all beheld the rich blue of Mordecai. Their salvation was everlasting; their hope reached through all generations. It was made known, that men hoping to thee shall not be put to shame; nor shall those who trust in thee ever have to blush. Cursed is Haman, who sought to undo me; blessed be Mordecai, the Jehudi; cursed Zeresh, wife of him who troubled me; blessed Esther, my shield and shading tree! Even Harbona be mentioned for good!

The reading of Canticles on the Passover and Ruth on Pentecost is witnessed by the Treatise of Scribes as being then a well-known custom, but they were read at night at the home rather than in the Synagogue. Phrases from Ecclesiastes are found in some of the Piyutim for the Eighth of the Feast, and the Song of Songs is woven all through those for the Passover; a good proof of the age of these compositions. In the thirteenth century men were yet divided, whether to read Ecclesiastes in the Hut or in the Synagogue, nor had the proper time for Canticles been fully decided.

The Book of Lamentations must have become the chief lesson for the Ninth of Ab very soon after the last Temple was destroyed. It had been written on a similar sad occasion at a time when the Hebrew language and the poetic genius of the Jewish people were at their highest. No one could write anything more sublime or soul-stirring than the dirges ascribed to Jeremiah.

A Baraïtha, which by its pure Hebrew seems to prove its antiquity, says: On the Ninth of Ab it is unlawful to read the Law, the Prophets, or the Holy Writings; but one reads in the Lamentations, and in Job, and the sad parts of Jeremiah. As the former book is so short, when the habit to read "in it" was once established, it must soon have extended to reading the whole of it. To read Job is still the custom among the Sefardim, but only chapters 1, 2, 3, and 42 are read aloud at the Synagogue.[6]

While the Mishna is silent about the public reading of the other four rolls, a whole treatise is named Megilla, after the Book of Esther; the lessons from the Law and the Prophets are treated in the latter part of the treatise as if they were of lesser importance. In Jerusalem and other cities that were already fortified in the days of Joshua, the son of Nun, Purim is, as in Susa, kept on the 15th instead of the 14th of Adar.[7] When the month of Adar is doubled, Purim is celebrated in the second month of that name.[8] The benediction after the reading of the Megilla is said to be a matter of custom; it should be recited or omitted according to the usage of the country or town.

CHAPTER VII

THE INTERPRETER, OR METHURGAMAN

NEHEMIAH speaks in his last chapter of his efforts, which must have been vain, to keep up among his compatriots the classic idiom of Judea against the inroads of dialects from the Philistian and Phœnician coast. Yet these dialects were at least Hebrew. Three hundred years later, in the days of the Maccabees, the people of Judea no longer spoke Hebrew; they used it in prayer, in the study of their sacred law, and in writing poetry. Aramaic, infiltrated to some extent with Hebrew and with Babylonian, in which about one-half of the Book of Daniel is written, seems in those days to have been the spoken language of Judea. Legal documents, such as marriage contracts and bills of divorce, were drawn up in Aramaic. In Galilee the Phœnician dialect of Hebrew may have held its own a little longer, but the Aramaic of Syria crowded it out. In the time covered by the Gospel narrative it seems that Aramaic was the common language of intercourse, both in the north and in the south, though many of the wealthier folk spoke, and all men of education understood, the Greek language also.[1]

Thus the Methurgaman, or Interpreter, came into the Synagogue. The Mishna, in speaking of a person reading the Law or Prophets at the desk, says: He gives out only one verse at a time to the Methurgaman from the Law and not more than three from the Prophets; where a verse treats of a separate subject, then only that one verse; and it names several passages from both which are "read but are not translated."[2]

The Methurgaman was not allowed to read from a book, in order to keep the difference between the sacred text and a translation clear in the minds of his hearers; but there seems to have been no rule against his having a book at home from which to study up the day's lesson. His rendering followed the tradition; it was governed by the Rabbinic schools, and it was a ready means for keeping in the people's memory the accepted meaning of obscure passages. Thus we find in the "Targum (translation) Onkelos," which is the authorized version, that the four species named in Leviticus 23, to be handled on the Feast of Huts, are "citrons, palm leaves, myrtles, and willows."

"Onkelos" is corrupted from Akylas, the Greek for Aquila. A convert from Pontus by that name turned the Bible into either Greek or Aramaic, while R. Akiba taught, but long after public readings were in use. The older writers always speak of Onkelos as the convert, identifying him with Akylas; many modern writers believe that the Targum which goes by his name is only the old tradition put into writing by one or more unknown hands and not earlier than the third century.[a]

The version is pretty literal, but in seeking to prevent all misconceptions about God it gives him practically but one name, placing the mark of the double or treble Jod, which is read Adonai, not only for the Tetragrammaton, but for Elohim. Where the latter word is used in a profane sense, such as "the gods of Egypt," Onkelos turns it into "the errors," that is, the idols. Where the Bible speaks of God somewhat boldly, as if he came down or appeared bodily, Onkelos interposes "the Word of" (*Memra d'*) before the Sacred Name. Only a few passages are paraphrased in a poetic vein, as by giving an allegoric meaning to geographical names. The rule for the observant Jew is during every week to read the portion at home twice in text and once in Targum; hence the latter is published in most

19

Jewish editions of the Pentateuch, and it serves as a basis for all commentaries.

A Targum of the eight prophetic books, ascribed to Jonathan ben Uzziel, a survivor of the Temple, is more paraphrase than version; it is full of legend, and it accommodates older events to the spirit of his own time. This, as far as we can see, was used to accompany the prophetic lessons while these were read with Targum, as shown by examples in the Mahzor Vitry.

The lessons from the Law and the Prophets were thus for centuries interspersed with an Aramaic version in all those countries in which Greek was not the common tongue, even when Aramaic was no longer spoken, and was understood less than Hebrew. One of the Talmudic Sages protested, saying: Let us have Hebrew and Persian in the East, Hebrew and Greek in the West (i. e., in Palestine).[4] The Grand Rabbis, bearing the title of Gaon, however, insisted to the last (1040) on reading with Targum, though at their own home Arabic had for centuries been the only language of conversation. They claimed that Onkelos taught the traditional meaning of the Tora, and was indispensable on that ground. In many places an unreasoning conservatism holding on to usages that have outlived themselves sustained the Gaons. In Yemen, at the date of this writing, a boy stands by the desk, turning every verse as it is read into the Aramaic of Onkelos.[5] The Talmud itself does not treat the reading of the Targum as obligatory in all cases, as is seen by the rule already quoted from it, that shorter prophetic lessons may be read where time is spent in translation than where they proceed without it. The Code of R. Joseph Karo flatly declares the public recital of an Aramaic version as out of date, on the ground that the people no longer understand it.[6]

In the thirteenth century the Jews of France, to judge by the Mahzor Vitry, still heard the paraphrase of Jonathan read with the Haftara on Festivals in the old-fashioned way after each verse of the original.

Attempts to introduce a running translation of the lesson into some language other than Aramaic were made from time to time, but these never led to a general or permanent custom. Only within living memory congregations have undertaken to read the Haftara in German, English, French, etc., either in addition to or as a substitute for the Hebrew text. The publication of printed copies of the Bible has enabled those who are ignorant of Hebrew to understand the lessons much better by perusal than they could from listening to a Methurgaman. The Mishna teaches that the Book of Esther may be read to "women speaking another tongue" in that tongue, and the man who reads it to them thus has discharged his own duty, although he understands Hebrew and knows the square writing.[7] The modern standards follow the Mishna herein, but a somewhat bigoted attachment to the old-fashioned roll has nullified this permission. The women generally preferred to hear the Book of Esther read from that roll and get at the story at some other time by reading it or hearing it read in an embellished paraphrase. Indeed, such a paraphrase of the Pentateuch did for several hundred years supply to them the place of a translator of the five Books of Moses.

There have been and are some curious survivals of the Methurgaman. We find from the Mahzor Vitry that at its date it was the custom in France on the Pentecost to give out the Targum after each of the Ten Commandments, and moreover to introduce this rendition by a poem in the same tongue. Thus to treat the most solemn part of God's word looks to us like blasphemy, and we are glad that the custom has gone out. But it has left its trace in the long Aramaic poem (*Akdamoth Millin*), which is still chanted in Synagogues of the German ritual on the first day of Pentecost after the first verse of the Law lesson, and in a short poem in the same language, which is read in many Synagogues on the second day after the first line of the Haftara.[8]

Again, the Sefardim still read on the Ninth of Ab, after every Hebrew verse of the Haftara (Jer. 8: 13 to 9: 23), a Spanish version of the Aramaic paraphrase known as the Targum Jonathan. Herein Jeremiah's thrilling words are made to fit the second rather than the first destruction of Jerusalem. His lament that "they have cast down our dwellings" is turned into the complaint, *destruyeron los enemigos todas las Sinagogas y lugares de estudio* (the enemies have destroyed all the Synagogues and houses of study), which Nebuchadnezzar's soldiers could not have done, as there were then none to destroy.

Greek stood on its own footing. The Alexandrians read their services and lessons therein, most of them knowing little or no Hebrew. A Greek scroll was as sacred to them as that in holy tongue and character was elsewhere. A Patriarch who held it unlawful to write versions of the sacred books in other tongues held Greek editions to be lawful. While versions of Esther in Coptic or Median might be read only to those speaking the particular language, a Greek text might be read to the general public.[9]

But all this is ancient history without bearing on later times. The great settlements of Greek-speaking Jews were broken up, North Africa and Palestine became Arabic, and the language of Homer and Plato, so much admired by the Sages of Tiberias, became flat and stale in the mouth of monks, pedants, and rabble, and was disfigured by Latin and Slavonic admixture. Later Jewish writers would no longer recognize in the Romaic of their time the language of poetry, of learning, and of deep thought which their ancestors had so highly prized.[10]

CHAPTER VIII

PREACHING

THE Hebrew word for preaching means literally to search, that is, to search the Scriptures. A sermon is called *Derasha*, an act or the result of searching; a professional preacher of the old stripe was known as a *Darshan*, sometimes a *Maggid*, that is, one who tells, who strings out what has in former chapters been defined as Haggada or Aggadta. But there has been preaching of dry law to the exclusion of legendary lore and of sentimental interpretation. Only in very modern times some preachers have faithfully undertaken to draw good instruction and ennobling sentiment from the true and natural sense of Scripture and from the highly poised moral teachings of the Mishna.[1] With many even in our days to preach means to interpret Scripture in an ever new and ever varying and vanishing fashion.

"The Sages teach that Moses already laid down the rule that they should inquire and preach about the business of the day, the rules of the Passover on the Passover, the rules of Pentecost on the Pentecost, the rules of the Feast (of Huts) on the Feast."[2]

As the lesson for the festival touched upon its laws, it formed the readiest text for a sermon upon them, and if the preacher was inclined rather to moralize, to rebuke, to comfort, or to inspire with hopes, he could bring before his hearers the legends and the free handlings of Scripture connected with the sacred day. On the Sabbath he had no special laws to discuss, but he found a new text every week in its portion from the Law or in the lesson from the

Prophets. Here again the incident told in the Gospel of Luke is instructive. When Jesus had finished the lesson from Isaiah he immediately preached on the verses which he had read. And an authority of the seventh or eighth century (already quoted) speaks of shortening the Prophet lesson when it is translated or preached upon. The *Midrash Rabba*, that great store-house of Jewish homiletic lore, is in the main a collection of sermon heads, many of which are available to this day.[3]

The usual time for preaching is in the Synagogues of the German ritual still, as it was when the Gospels or when the "Treatise of Scribes" was written, either immediately after the Prophet lesson with its benedictions, or a little later, after the scroll has been returned to the Ark and before the Additional. With the Sefardim the sermon is generally put off till after the Additional, that is, to the very end of the forenoon services. The wonder-working "Rebby" of the *Hasidim* delivers his talks generally to a crowd gathered round his table, and his talk is full of Cabbalistic lore; he does not disdain the presence of outsiders (Misnagdim, i. e., adversaries). In the night of Atonement Day it has been usual for the Rabbi to rebuke sin and to preach repentance, but never on Friday evening or in the night service of the Festivals; and this for two reasons, first, the women did not attend; secondly, the men were not to be delayed from the Sabbath or Festival supper, which was deemed religiously more important than the exercises of the Synagogue.

The great meetings held near the Babylonian schools on the Sabbath before the Passover and a Sabbath before the Day of Atonement have already been mentioned; they have survived in the rule that a Rabbi ought to preach on the "Great Sabbath," i. e., the one immediately preceding the Passover, and on the "Sabbath of Repentance," if he does not at other times. And many Jewish communities have been satisfied with such a scant allowance of the "living word." Even when preaching at stated intervals was thought proper, a sermon once in each lunar month, on the Sabbath on which the next New Moon is announced, was deemed sufficient. The almost universal ability of men and widespread ability of women to read books made preaching less indispensable than it was among the more illiterate Christians of the middle ages. In comparatively modern times the travelling *Maggid* often attracted great crowds of men only when his programme was "sharpness," that is, hair-splitting discussion of Talmudic problems; of both men and women, when he proposed to speak in the way of the Aggadta. The discourses of a speaker of this class would run on for two hours or more at a stretch, and could not be wedged in between the two forenoon Prayers; the audience would come on purpose in the afternoon to hear him.

The problem, how to find proper preachers, confronted the Jews of Germany and Austria (and to some extent of England and America) most seriously in the first quarter of the nineteenth century. Many Jews in commerce or in professional life and their wives and daughters had the advantages of modern culture; they spoke the language of their country with purity, often with elegance; they had some slight knowledge at least of history and of science, and expected the truths of religion to be illustrated from these fields of human endeavor. But the Rabbis who should have instructed them or kept religious feelings alive in their breasts spoke nothing but an uncouth jargon, knew nothing but Bible and Talmud, not even Hebrew Grammar, and for that reason did not know even the Bible and Talmud correctly. The old-fashioned *Derasha* would not suit the leading members, but the Rabbi, or Maggid, was unable to furnish any other mental food.

This difficulty has been in a great measure overcome in

all those parts of Europe in which laymen and women in any great number are posses ed of the culture of the day and country.   Rabbis and preachers are found who share it in a like or even higher degree.

BOOK IV

Incidents and Ceremonies

CHAPTER I

POSTURE, SOUND, THOUGHT

THE ordinary posture at worship is to sit. With a partial exception in countries east of Palestine affected by Moslem habits, the Synagogues are and ever have been fitted with seats.[1] The word "Amida" (Standing), applied to the eighteen benedictions, and the term "seated," denoting certain acts of worship outside of it, prove this, and stray passages of the Mishna attest it.[2] But while the congregation sits, the leader in prayer, the reader of the lesson, those who are "called" to the desk and virtually read their portions, the presiding officers who are at the desk during the reading, and the preacher during his discourse, stand, as do the priests, with hands uplifted before them, when they impart the blessing.[3]

While some ascetics remain on their feet as long as they stay in the House of God, the worshipper is required by rule to stand only: *first*, while reciting the *Amida*, and while the leader repeats the first three benedictions, including the Thrice-Holy; *second*, while he gives out the responsive parts of the service (Bless ye," etc., and the Kaddish), and the mourners stand at their Kaddish; *third*, at the Psalms of Praise on Feasts, New Moons, and Hanucca; *fourth*, at the confession of sins; *fifth*, whenever the Ark is open, as at the taking out and return of the scroll; but especially on the Festivals some passages, deemed more impressive, are honored by the opening of the Ark, that the congregation may stand up.[4] Standing at a few other passages is usual and enjoined by some of the standards, but it is not deemed important enough for special mention.

During the lesson from the Law the people stand only when the following passages are read: The Red Sea Song (Exodus 15), the first version of the Decalogue (Exodus 20), the second version (Deuteronomy 5), the last three verses of Deuteronomy; at these last all rise, reciting them in chorus before the reader.[5]

When the worshipper stands in the Prayer, he turns his face towards Jerusalem (at least if the Synagogue is built with the Ark in that direction), in accordance with King Solomon's words, "They will pray towards this House." The Mishna, speaking of one who is journeying in a boat or on a raft, says, if he cannot turn his face towards the Holy of Holies, he should turn his heart towards it. In the Prayer the worshipper also stands in the most respectful attitude, his feet close together; at its conclusion he steps backward, like a servant in the presence of his master.[6]

He is guarded against disrespect from others; no one is to sit down within four cubits; none should pass before him.[7]

Though the first verse of the *Shema* is the weightiest part of the service, yet the worshipper need not rise when he reaches it, but retains any respectful position he then occupies. Shammai's school thought that to fulfill the words of the Law, "when thou liest down, and when thou risest," we should read the Shema at night lying down and standing up in the morning; but the school of Hillel, which prevailed, relied on the words, "when thou sittest in thy house, and when thou walkest by the way." (A deep moral underlies this view; religion must be in and with us whatever we do.)[8]

Kneeling (unless for a few moments) does not now belong to Jewish worship; it did when the Book of Daniel was written, for its hero prays thrice a day on his knees, and the

Talmud speaks of some great Rabbis who, when praying in private, knelt and prostrated themselves.[9] In the Temple, when the High Priest three times, in the three confessions of sin, pronounced the otherwise unpronounceable Name, the people "knelt and bowed down and fell on their faces," which is still done among the Jews of the German and Polish ritual when the Atonement service is recited. They also suit the action to the word when, on Memorial Day and the Day of Atonement, the words, "We kneel and bow down," are reached, while the Sefardim on both occasions are satisfied with a curtsy.[10]

Bowing the head forward seems natural to a man in devout supplication. But our Sages feared that frequent bowing would degenerate into mock humility, and restricted the habit, so that one reciting the eighteen or seven benedictions of the Prayer should bow the head only at the beginning and close of the first (Fathers) and of the last but one (Thanks); following therein the warning in Isaiah 58, "Is it to bend the head like a bulrush?"[11]

When the penitential Psalm is recited in public, men sit and lean forward with the head resting on one arm, as a mark of sorrow and remorse, much as they do in American churches.[12]

The Jews all over the world have long had the habit (only broken in upon by modern culture) of swaying the body backward and forward at their devotions, justifying it by the Psalm verse (35: 10), "All my bones shall say, my Lord, who is like thee!" Among the several explanations of the rise of this habit the most rational is found in the nervous temperament of the Jew, who likes to speak with his whole body, not only to God, but to his fellow-men.[13]

The covering of the head may be here mentioned. The Bible tells us that the priests within the Tabernacle wore miters and head-tires; in fact, the High Priest could hardly be thought or even dreamed of without his miter.[14] To the people at large, men and women, as with the dwellers of

Western Asia now, the head-cover was a matter of course. A woman with uncovered head was deemed immodest; a man in like guise was in undress, like a European when in shirt sleeves, or worse. If once in the Talmud the covered head is spoken of as conducive to piety, it is simply because the uncovered head was deemed slovenly and indecent. A Jew would always put on his turban, made of a kerchief, when he got out of bed, along with his belt and shoes or sandals.[15]

But to the Romans it was a matter of pride to brave sunshine and rain with uncovered head. When they invaded the Holy Land, the covered or uncovered head became a badge of distinction between the Jew and the invading foreigners; and so it was in Jewish settlements elsewhere. The Romans also demanded of their Asiatic subjects that they should, as a mark of respect, doff their headgear when addressed by the representatives of the Emperor.[16]

Hence when Paul of Tarsus set forth his views to churches made up of Jews and Gentiles, intending to fuse both elements into a new communion rather than a Jewish sect like that over which James presided at Jerusalem, he demanded that the men should sit in church with uncovered head as the surest method of breaking the lingering tie between the Church and the Synagogue.[17] From this command in Paul's Epistle comes the Christian custom, by which the bare head alone is admissible in worship, or wherever else respect is to be shown to anyone; probably the lifting of the hat in salutation had its rise when Christians meeting each other took it off as a mark of recognition.[18]

Modern standards of Rabbinic law, written in or for Christian countries, naturally forbade the performance of any religious act or the reading of the Law with uncovered head as being an imitation of Christian custom. Perhaps the writers did not know how this custom originated in hostility to the Synagogue, but they could not have been more severe if they had known it.[19]

Bare feet have always been a mark of humility, proper for those who stand on sacred ground, as is known to all readers of the Bible; to this day Mohammedans always enter the Mosque without shoes. But such is not the custom of the Synagogue. Shoes are removed on the Day of Atonement and on the Ninth of Ab, only because this is one of the inflictions which belong to the fast.[20] Indeed, in old times to say prayers in bare feet was deemed suspicious as the badge of a sect which looked on the "flesh" as depraved, and sought to mortify it on all occasions.[21]

From posture and array we come to sound. The early Sages assume that the words of the services are articulated, not merely thought over, or read with the eye;[22] but these words need not be uttered loud enough for even the utterer himself to hear them. In the *Shema*, the weightiest part of the service, a sound loud enough for the reader's own ear and a clear separation of the words are deemed meritorious,[23] while for the Prayer the conduct of Hannah is quoted as a precedent, "Her lips were moving, but her voice could not be heard;[24] yet God answered her." In the Synagogue the obligation of each person present not to disturb the others is an additional reason for speaking the Prayer in the lowest possible tones; the standards however make some allowance for the supposed irrepressible warmth of feeling on the Days of Memorial and Atonement.[25] The responses, such as, Amen, the answer to "Bless ye," the Thrice-Holy, etc., should of course be given heartily by all who attend public worship; "in assemblies I will give thanks to the Lord," "the Majesty of the King is in the multitude of people," are the words of Scripture. The oldest line in our service of which the continuous use can be traced, "Give thanks to the Lord, for he is good," etc., was always sung or shouted by all the people. Each of the five paragraphs of the Kaddish ends, "Say ye, Amen," showing that a loud response was expected.[26] Among the majority of the Jews, those of the Polish branch of the

German ritual, responsive reading of the Psalms from the prayer book has fallen into disuse through a fear that the people might not listen attentively enough to the odd numbered verses, which fall to the leader; everyone reads each Psalm for himself, and lets the leader chant the closing verses; the Germans proper have kept up the old and beautiful custom.

This brings us to musical treatment. Leaving modern chorals out of consideration, there are great local differences. The old, always Oriental congregations of Bagdad and Cairo are satisfied with the simple chant of antiquity, easily learned and rendered by any man with sound organs; they do not care for a professional to lead them in prayer. The Sefardim of Europe and America would employ a Hazan, and ask from him some proficiency, but as the congregation chimes in, and the phrasing is highly monotonous, this proficiency could be readily acquired. But the Jews of the German ritual soon changed the simple old sing-song of Asia into something more European and more melodious; distinct airs were developed for different parts of the service on the Sabbath and on all the feasts and fasts, which airs could not be rendered well except by men with good voices and some musical training.[27] The Hazan borrowed from his Christian antitype the name of Cantor, or "Vorsänger;" the profession of the leader in prayer became more and more musical; good Hazanim would travel from place to place to attract crowds like opera singers or violinists. Old established tunes were carefully handed down from age to age, and the invention of a new tune for some passage in the service (especially for the "Fearful Days") became a source of pride and fame. The skill to "arouse"[28] was especially valued; a good Hazan must have the capacity to make his congregation weep in anguish or shed tears of joy.

In the east of Europe, in Poland and Hungary, the

standard of good singing was higher, and the desire to hear
the best performers more widespread and intense than in
Germany. The ways of these artists were in many respects
deplorable. While slurring over those parts of the service
which both for their contents and according to the Rabbinic law should never be spoken without devotion, they
dwelt with unending trills and roulades on some single
word or on unmeaning sounds between the words. The
peculiar chorus, made up of the so-called Meshorerim and
led by a "singer," or high tenor, and a base, did not sing
responsively, but only helped the Hazan in his coloratura,
and thus aggravated the abuse, and the remonstrances of
the learned, supported by the Shulhan Aruch, could not
repress them till the modern choir rescued the services of
the German and Polish Jews from their musical excrescences, perhaps to lead to some new abuses worse than the
old.[29]

Now as to the frame of mind during services. Prayer,
praise, or thanks addressed to God should of course never be
put forth without devotion or at least without attention to
the words spoken and to their meaning. But can the worshipper keep his mind fixed upon all parts of the service
when it grows in length to one or two hours? If so, what is
the minimum of attention demanded from him? The
Mishna distinguishes between the reading of the Shema and
of the Prayer. One may recite the former while "walking
by the way," except the first two verses, which must be "on
thy heart," or matter of devotion; but a man must not even
enter upon Prayer but out of a serious mood.[30] An old
maxim is recorded that Prayer should not be a fixed duty,
but a seeking for mercy,[31] and the hours for Prayers are
more extended than those for the Shema, to give the worshipper time to reach the proper mood.[32] And if he cannot
keep his attention alive throughout, he must hold it at least
while reciting the first benediction (Aboth), in which God's
attributes of mercy and his love for Abraham and his seed
are remembered.[33]

20

Even the dry words of the written law require attention to certain parts of the service. "That thou mayest remember the day of thy going forth from Egypt," is not satisfied by uttering words concerning it thoughtlessly. "Remember the Sabbath day to keep it holy," is not obeyed if in the Kiddush or the night service we say, "Blessed be the Lord who sanctifies the Sabbath," without thinking of the Lord or of the Sabbath.

All this was well weighed when the Sages declared that (the reading of) the Shema, the Prayer, and Grace after meals might be recited in any language, for there can be no devotion or thought in words which the speaker himself does not understand.[34]

The worshipper is not in the frame of mind for prayer when he is the worse for drink; in the words of our Sages, who probably were thinking of heathen orgies, one who prays while drunk is no better than an idolater.[35] Nor should one perform acts of worship while he feels the calls of nature, nor while within the sight or smell of anything which is filthy or indecent to behold.[36]

But aside from attention to the context there are "attentions" (Cavvanoth) of a subtler sort. Thus, in the "Hear, O Israel," the word *Ehad* (One) is drawn out long, to give the worshipper time to think of the One as filling and animating the earth and heavens and the four regions around him. In the next verse, "with all thy heart" means with thy lower as well as thy higher impulses; "with all thy soul," even if it costs thy life; "with all thy might," with all thy wealth or means. Such and a few similar "plain meanings" are found in the Talmud, and though our taste may reject them as dry and undevotional, they can do but little harm.[37] It is not worth while to speak here of the still subtler "Cavvanoth," which are found in prayer books published by masters of the Secret Lore.

The worshipper is not to interrupt his devotions by a single word which does not belong there; the oldest

standard lays down the rule thus as to the Reading of the
Shema: In the middle (of a paragraph or benediction)
· one may salute from fear, and return a greeting from respect
(to a superior); between the parts one may salute first from
respect, and may return any one's greeting.[38] But as to the
Prayer the rule was more severe; for of the pious of olden
times it is said: Even if the King should greet one (while
at Prayer) he would not answer; a rule so harsh that the
Talmud in its comments upon it seeks to soften it in the
interest of security of life and limb.[39]

The modern codes have not lowered the rule against
interruptions; certainly talking in the Synagogue is not
good orthodoxy. In fact, the tenor of the services, not to be
broken by an outside word, has been much lengthened
since the hymns and Psalms for the morning were prefixed
to the Shema and cast into one recital with it, while the
joining of "Redemption" to "Prayer" leaves no gap where
to edge in a word during the greater part of the lengthy
morning service.[40] And while the lesson from the scroll or
from the Prophets is read there is the same requirement of
silence and attention.[41]

CHAPTER II

THE TROPE

THE Greek word τροπή (tropé) for melody, sounded
"Tropp," has come in the jargon of the German Jews to
denote the musical reading of the Bible lessons from the
platform, while the Sefardim know only the Hebrew word
Negina (melody). The accents on which this melody
depends were invented two hundred years or more after
the vowel points, and are carefully attached to the whole
text of the Hebrew Bible upon a uniform system, only the
three poetic books, Psalms, Proverbs, Job, having their
own system, with which we are not here concerned. The
accents are found in almost every printed edition of the
Bible or of any part; not however in the parchment scrolls
made for use in the Synagogue. Most of them are put
under or over the tone-syllable of the word, and thus aid in
the right pronunciation. But their main office is performed
in other languages by punctuation. They are divided into
disjunctives of several degrees and conjunctives. Words
belonging very closely together are connected by a hyphen
(*Makkif*); only the last of the words thus joined has any
accent; thus the *Makkif* binds more closely than any conjunctive. Of the disjunctives the strongest are the *Sof
Pasuk*, or *Silluk*, at the end of the verse. The division into
verses is well-known to the Mishna; hence, is much older
than the accents. Next in power is the *Ethnah(ta)*, put under
the last word of half the verse. Next in power comes the
Segol, rather rare, marking off the first one-third of a verse;
the *Zakef Katon*, which cvts the two halves of a verse into
shorter clauses; when a single word is such a clause, it has

Zakef Gadol; the *Tifha* is a divider near the end of the half or whole verse.

The weaker dividers are Rebia, Pashta (which on a single word may become Jethib), Zarka (only before Segol), and Tebir (only before Tifha). Still weaker are Pazer, Telisha, Geresh (which takes three shapes and names), and a conjunctive accent with a vertical stroke (*Pesik*) after the word. The conjunctives are *Munah, Mahpach, Mer'cha, Telisha Ketanna, Kadma* (the strongest conjunctive), and *Darga.* Including four very rare marks there are twenty-six in all.[1]

If the men who invented and applied this system were right in their understanding of the text, they have, by placing these accents as they did, contributed much to teach later generations a correct interpretation of the sacred books. A good illustration of this may be given from the opening verse of Ezekiel's vision of the valley of bones (Ezek. 37: 1):

"The hand of the Lord was upon me; *Va-iotzieni* (there took me out) with a conjunctive mark, *Beruah* (in spirit) with a weak disjunctive, *Adonai* (the Lord); i. e., the Lord carried me out in spirit, not in the flesh. The common English Bible mistranslates, "and carried me out in the spirit of the Lord," which conveys no sense.

The names of the accents have been strung together with some repetitions in something like the order in which they might occur in a long verse, except that *Jethib Pesik* are put near the end to denote the cadence at the end of a lesson or subsection.[2]

Each accent indicates a musical phrase, and when grouped they make up something like a tune. And when a verse is read by such tune, the grouping of the words according to the sense strikes the ear naturally.

They are, however, read musically in different ways. The first distinction is between that of the Sefardim and that of Germans and Poles. The former is very much like the old

Oriental chant; it moves mostly within five tones, often by chromatic intervals, while the latter moves over a wider compass, is livelier, and more akin to European music.

Again, each branch of the Synagogue has its "trope" for the Pentateuch, which is simple and does not express much, if any, feeling; and a modification thereof for the Haftara, or Prophet lesson, which is richer and somewhat pathetic. The German Jews modify the prophetic trope still further into a very sad air for the Book of Lamentations and for the Haftara of the Sabbath preceding the Fast of the Ninth of Ab. There is another variation for the Book of Esther, brisk and defiant; and yet another among the Germans for the Pentateuch lessons on the morning of the Solemn Days. Some passages of the Pentateuch are read to marching music: part of the Red Sea Song, the tribes and their princes with their marching order in Numbers 10, and the journeys and stations in Numbers 33.

The music for the accents in the conventional order is given in a note as chanted in the German ritual to the Pentateuch lesson and to the Haftara; in the Sefardic ritual as applied to the Haftara; also the first verse of Lamentations in the Sefardic chant.[3]

The benediction before the Haftara is read so as to fit in with its "trope;" many service books fit accents to it as if it were a Bible verse. On the Solemn Days the benedictions before and after the reading from the Pentateuch are chanted so as to fall in with the tune of the lesson.

The "trope" is generally learned by Jewish boys when they are nearing their thirteenth birthday, and are to celebrate their Bar Mitzva (see Bk. III, ch. III) by reading the Sidra and Haftara for the first and alas! often for the last time.

The accents are not noticed in reading any part of the Bible except the Pentateuch, the lessons from the Prophetic books, and the Books of Esther and Lamentations.

The time and place of the invention of the accents are

shrouded in obscurity, as much so as the time when the vowel signs were contrived. But while the vowels are a product of Galilee, the accents seem to have originated among Jews who read Hebrew in the Sefardic style, if we may judge by the secondary word-accent known as *Metheg*, which is part of the system, and which helps to distinguish the long from the short *Kametz* and thus to read correctly from the Sefardic standpoint.[4]

But while the details are comparatively late, the general habit of chanting the Bible rather than reading it in declamatory style is probably as old as the use of Scripture in public service. An early Talmudist said, "Whoever reads (Bible) without pleasantness and teaches oral law without song, of him Scripture says (Ezek. 20: 25): I also gave them statutes that were not good."[5]

In fact, there is a particular sing-song in which Mishna and Gemara are studied, wholly different from the trope in any of its forms, but quite as characteristic.

CHAPTER III

THE fringed shawl and the phylacteries are a sort of uniform which the good Israelite dons in the service of God. According to the tradition the wearing of the fringes (*Tsitzith*) as well as of the phylacteries is required only in daytime, and as women are not bound by positive commands which apply only to some given time, they do not wear either the fringes or the phylacteries.[1]

Towards the end of the 15th chapter of Numbers the children of Israel are told that they make a fringe upon the corner of their garments in their generations, and that they put upon the fringe of the corner a thread of blue. The Hebrew word, which is here rendered blue, does not mean that color in general, but a blue dye stuff, which the Tyrians used to obtain from a shell. This shell is no longer found, perhaps only because it is no longer sought, and the latter part of the command is in our days wholly neglected.[2] In Deuteronomy 22: 12 the people are told: "Thou shalt make to thee cords on the four corners of thy garment." The two passages being construed together, it was inferred (1) that no garment is bound to have either cords or fringes unless it has four corners, neither more nor less; (2) that every such garment should have both cords and fringes at each corner, i. e., the four woolen threads which are run through a hemmed hole near the corner are first wound and knotted into a cord, and the eight ends are then allowed to hang down loose as a fringe. The avowed object of the observance is, that upon looking at the fringe with its blue thread we should be reminded of God's commands, and not spy after our eyes and our hearts, and be holy to our God, as is recited twice a day in the third paragraph of the Shema.[3]

A shawl with the fringes is known as *Talith* (a word probably derived from the Greek *stole*); it is worn in the morning service by every man present, among the Sefardim also by small boys; and though some worshippers may not be provided with it, those having any functions, as the leader in prayer, he who reads the lesson, the preacher, the officers who stand by the desk, etc., always wear it. Before putting on this shawl, the benediction is spoken, "Blessed, etc., who hast sanctified us, etc., and commanded us to wrap ourselves in the fringes."[4]

It seems that, with the disappearance of the proper dye stuff of which to make the thread of blue, the wearing of fringes for a while fell into partial disuse before the Rabbinic Jews adapted themselves to the new condition of wearing the fringed shawl without blue threads, as they were justified in doing under the teaching of the Mishna; but ever since the eleventh or twelfth century such a shawl has been generally worn. The Karaites have solved the problem otherwise, by placing among the white woolen threads a thread dyed in some common vegetable blue.[5]

It appears from the Mishna that while the distinction between "Companions" and the "People of the Land" remained, the latter were not in the habit, or at least not in the constant habit, of wearing fringes on their garments. But it does not appear that any sect or school denied the obligation to wear them. The failure to do so was simply the result of indifference.[6]

The word phylacteries, found in the New Testament, is only a Greek corruption of the Hebrew Tefillin. The Greek word means "things that guard," as much as talismans or amulets, which the phylacteries are not and never were. The Hebrew word is derived from Tefilla, i. e., prayer, because they were worn mainly during the morning devotions. The wearing of the Tefillin is commanded by four passages in the Pentateuch, Exodus 13: 1-10, ib. 11-16; Deut. 6: 4-9; 11: 13-21, all of which contain the words, "thou shalt bind them for a sign on your hand, and they shall be as frontlets between your eyes." The word for "frontlets" is *Totafoth* in Hebrew, which is also applied (in later writings) to bands worn by women round the forehead by way of ornament. Any derivation from African or other outlandish tongues is fanciful and unscientific.[7] The four passages, including in each the above command, are written on strips of parchment, or continuously on one strip; one copy is enclosed in a leather box, which is put on the left arm above the elbow, the other in a similar box, to be placed high up in the middle of the forehead. For this purpose a loop is attached to each box, through which long leather straps are drawn. The strap for the arm is wound seven times round the arm below the elbow and then round the hand and fingers; that for the head is tied into a peculiar knot at such a distance as to fit the head, and its two ends hang down behind. There is some dispute as to the order in which the four pieces for the phylactery of the head should be arranged; in the phylactery for the arm the four passages are written upon one strip in the same order in which they follow each other in Scripture.[8]

Phylacteries are not worn on the Sabbath or the Festivals, because these are "signs" between God and Israel, and no further sign is needed; the Sefardim and the sect of *Hasidim* extend the same reasoning to the middle days of the Passover and Feast of Huts, as the Unleavened Cake and the Hut are sufficient signs.[9]

In "laying Tefillin," that for the arm is put on first, after a blessing, "who hast commanded us to lay Tefillin;" then those for the head, with the blessing, "who hast commanded us about the duty of Tefillin." Then the strap of the phylactery for the arm is put about the fingers in a conventional way, while the verses from Hosea are recited, "I shall

betroth thee unto me forever: I shall betroth thee unto
me in righteousness and justice, in kindness and in mercy:
I shall betroth thee unto me in faithfulness; and thou shalt
know the Lord."[10]

It is maintained by the Karaites and by many modern
Bible students that the commands to put or to bind certain
words upon hand or forehead were meant in a figurative
sense, and mean simply that these words should govern our
actions and our thoughts. This is however on two grounds
very improbable. Many of the nations which surrounded
Israel wore talismans inscribed with what were supposed
to be powerful charms, and these were well-known to the
Israelites. Hence they would naturally understand a command to have certain words upon the hand or between the
eyes literally, and whoever wrote the passages in Exodus
or Deuteronomy must have known that they would be thus
understood. In the next place, in the two latter passages
it is also commanded to write the same words upon the
door-posts, and it is impossible to give a figurative sense
to this precept.

The author does not mean to say that the Biblical passages in their natural sense mean that the whole of each
paragraph, including the very command to make it a sign
or to bind it, should be written out in full. It is admitted
that the duty "to speak of them," enjoined in the second
paragraph of the Shema, may be fulfilled by reading the
Ten Commandments, because they also teach the doctrine
of rewards and punishments; and similar substitutes might
be found for the duty of phylacteries as for the daily recital.
Nor does the Tora demand the wearing of these signs and
frontlets with any regularity at stated times. But those who
would otherwise have carried about them talismans inscribed with incantations expressive of trust in subordinate
beings or invocations of heathen deities (as most men probably did), were here directed: Turn your thoughts wholly
to the God of Israel, and let every scrap of writing that

you carry about you be witness to your undivided faith. And in this sense the fourfold command may have been fulfilled long before the modern phylactery (say in the Maccabean age) was developed.[11]

The religious leaders in Israel, being once convinced that the two passages in Exodus and the two in Deuteronomy ought to be observed, and finding men here and there who observed them, naturally sought to so interpret the words of the Law as to establish a uniform custom. They had to determine therefore how much is to be written of each passage, whether only in the Hebrew text, or whether it might be written also in Greek or in some other tongue; in what characters, on what material; whether the phylacteries should be placed on the hand or on the arm, between the eyes or higher on the forehead, and many other like particulars.[12] The Mishna denounces those who have round instead of cubic phylacteries, those who gild them, who bind them on the sleeve instead of the bare arm, etc., as sectaries hostile to the traditions. A well authenticated Baraïtha speaks of those who do not wear phylacteries while reading the morning service as bearing witness against themselves when reciting the very command which they break. This indicates that in olden times already the Tefillin were worn mainly at prayer.[13]

However, as long as the schism between the "companions" and "the people of the land" prevailed, the latter cared very little for the institution, and the former often wore phylacteries all day.[14]

The Talmud claims immemorial custom (Halacha of Moses from Sinai) for almost every feature of the Tefillin, but admits that the black straps had, within times of memory, not been universal, as a noted Sage of the Mishna tied his own Tefillin with purple ribbons.[15]

No contemporary writer earlier than those who furnished the facts for the Gospel history speaks of the wearing of phylacteries at all. But after the Talmud had once regulated the mode of making them, and enjoined the duty to wear them, the custom seems to have taken firm ground among all otherwise law-observing Jews, and there is no proof that it ever fell into disuse for any length of time in any great part of the dispersion except among the Karaites, who reject the literal meaning of the four Biblical passages.[16] If it ever fell into disuse elsewhere, it was at any rate fully re-established by Rashi, according to whose views the writing in the phylacteries for the head has been arranged since his days. The diverging opinion of his grandson Jacob, known as Rabbenu Tam, has not prevailed any further than that some over-scrupulous men "lay" Tefillin of both kinds every day, to be sure of having done their whole duty.[17]

To the Talmudists the fringed shawl and phylacteries, enforced by the writing on the door-post, appeared like a heavenly uniform; how can a man thus surrounded by all that reminds him of God come to sin? Alas, he often does.[18]

CHAPTER IV

CEREMONIES ON YEARLY OCCASIONS

AMONG the yearly or great occasions the priestly blessing, given in form, must now be reckoned, for it is in our days imparted only on the seven Biblical festivals doubled into thirteen; and in many Synagogues not on one of these days when it happens on a Saturday, lest more honor be shown to a festival than to the Sabbath.

A *Cohen* who has ever killed a human being, or has ever worshipped idols, or who has on that morning drunk wine or strong drink in sufficient quantity to affect him, must not stand among those who bless; nor a cripple or hunchback, nor one whose hands are swollen or crippled or dyed a sharp blue, lest the attention of those present be distracted. Otherwise every Cohen over thirteen years of age is competent. Those who are incompetent for the above reasons, or who deem themselves unworthy, should leave the Synagogue before the leader gives the signal in the benediction Aboda (see Bk. II, ch. VII); for otherwise they would violate the positive command of the Law (Num. 6: 23), "Thus ye shall bless the children of Israel."[1]

The "priests" take off their shoes. A basin and pitcher are provided, and the Levites, or if there are none, the firstborn who are present in the Synagogue, step with the "priests" into an anteroom or court, and pour water over their hands. The latter step upon the platform before the Ark, say the benediction prescribed for them (Bk. II, ch. VII) with their faces towards it, and then, with their fringed shawls over their heads, turn to the congregation with their hands held before their faces in a traditional manner; that is, the two thumbs brought tip to tip, the second and third fingers of each hand held straight up and together, and the fourth and fifth fingers separate from these and likewise joined. Each word is sung out for them by the leader from a book before him; they sing it after him in his tune, which differs according to the festival; the last word in each of the three blessings is dwelled on pretty long to give time to repeat a prayer recommended in the Talmud to those who are troubled by a dream.[2]

The leaders, in the "Additional" on the first day of the Passover who pray for fertilizing dew, and on the Eighth of the Feast who pray for rain, are supposed to plead before God as on the Day of Judgment; hence they put on the white shroud with linen cap to match as on the Solemn Days, the days of judgment, and they chant the Half Kaddish with which the Additional service begins in a tune borrowed from the Solemn Days.[3]

On the Day of Memorial we have the most striking of all the ceremonies, the blowing of the Cornet. The Cornet, or Shofar, is a ram's horn without metal mouthpiece; it must be sharply bent at the broad side near the base of the horn so as to double the column of air. Putting this horn obliquely to the lips and blowing with sufficient force brings out a clear, deep note, something near the A on the top line of the score in the base clef; blowing with greater effort gives the fifth above. Only these two notes are used.

In speaking of the silver trumpets Scripture distinguishes "blowing," or rather "sounding," simply and producing alarm sounds. By tradition the former, or *Teki'a*, means two long notes, the lower first, then its fifth, each sustained for at least two seconds. The "alarm sound" requires notes of only one-third of this length; each of these is supposed to be equal to three of the shortest notes that can be blown. Each alarm sound has been always introduced and followed by a *Teki'a*. It was thought that there should be three alarm sounds; this would make nine soundings altogether, and Mishna and Talmud speak throughout of the duty to hear nine soundings from the cornet in the indicated order.

Afterwards doubts arose whether slow "breaks" (*Shebarim*), like A e A e A e, each note about two-thirds of a second, or a greater number of much shorter notes (A A A A A A A A e), the latter being called *Teru'a* in the narrower sense, were the truest alarm sounds; and to solve all doubts the following scheme was adopted, in which the combination of both alarms is put first:

Teki'a	Shebarim-Teru'a	Teki'a
Teki'a	Shebarim	Teki'a
Teki'a	Teru'a	Teki'a

These were still considered to be only nine soundings.

The Mishna and Babylonian Talmud, in speaking of the Shofar-blowing on the Day of Memorial, always connect it with the fourth, fifth, and sixth benedictions in the "Additional" (Bk. II, ch. XI); the "second (i. e., the leader in the Additional) causes the blowing;" and the more learned, knowing this, consider the "standing cornet sounds," that is, those emitted during the Prayer, as the most solemn and important. In the Sefardic and West German Minhag they are rendered as in the above scheme, with Shebarim-Teru'a after the "Kingdoms," Shebarim after the "Remembrances," and Teru'a after the "Shofars;" while in Eastern Germany and Austria-Hungary Shebarim-Teru'a is sounded after each benediction.[4]

But from a passage of the Jerusalem Talmud, now lost, though attested by several medieval writers, it appears that the whole scheme was at an early day felt to lack one element: there was no opportunity to render thanks in the common form for the performance of duty, nor for the good luck of having lived to reach the occasion; for the Prayer could not be interrupted for such a purpose; hence the "sitting cornet sounds," that is, blowing outside of and before the additional Prayer, were introduced. The man chosen to blow the cornet, after the Prophet lesson and after a Psalm (such as 47) or appropriate verses have been read, chants slowly:

Blessed be thou, O Lord, our God, King of the world, who hast sanctified us by thy commandments, and hast commanded us to hear the sound of the cornet. Blessed be thou, O Lord, our God, King of the world, who hast let us live, and kept us up, and hast made us reach this season.

And he then blows each of the three lines above given three times, upon words of command given by some prominent member.

The form of the benediction was still in doubt in the twelfth century—should it be "to hear" or "to sound?" It was settled as above by R. Jacob Tam; his decision is approved by Maimonides, who speaks of these "sitting sounds" as a fully established custom.[5]

The last command given is "Great Sounding" (*Teki'a gedola*), and in response the performer brings out louder and longer notes; he then says the verse:

(Ps. 89: 16) "Happy the people who know the alarm sound, O Lord, they walk in the light of thy countenance." The people repeat this after him, and the ordinary service proceeds. Thus the Synagogue fulfills the command to make the first of the seventh month a day of alarm sound. In the Temple the two silver trumpets were sounded along with the ram's horn; hence (or by reason of) the verse, "With trumpets and the sound of the cornet make a joyful noise to the King, the Lord."

The performer on the Shofar must, to satisfy the feeling of the community, be a man of piety and good conduct; a very correct principle, which, however, has its drawbacks; first, because it leads to much ill-natured criticism of those chosen to blow the cornet; second, because it throws the task often on men ill-qualified to perform it, who, by their unsuccessful efforts to get the right notes or any notes out of the Shofar, bring into ridicule a ceremony which is intended to be solemn and awe-inspiring.

The Day of Atonement is brought to an end in the German ritual with a single *Teki'a*, among the Sefardim with the four soundings of the first line. This is nowhere prescribed as a duty, but is simply a reminiscence of the cornet sounds which in the year of Jubilee proclaimed liberty to the land.[9]

The feature of the services on the Feast of Huts is based on a verse in Leviticus 23, which, rendered according to its traditional meaning, reads thus:

"Ye shall take unto yourselves upon the first day the fruit of the citron tree and branches of palms, and the twig of a myrtle tree and willows of the brook, and ye shall be glad before the Lord your God."

The tradition also teaches that there is one citron (*Ethrog*), and one palm leaf in its natural folded state (*Lulab*), three twigs of myrtle of the species which has the leaves in whorls of three, and two willow branches. The citron is held separately in the left hand, the branches are tied together with strips of palm leaf. Scripture speaks only of the first day, but there is a custom which has come down from the days of the Temple of shaking the *Lulab* (the word is applied for short to the four elements) on the seven days of the Feast of Huts.

But the Shofar is not blown and the Lulab is not handled on the Sabbath, for reasons which it would lead us too far to explain. When the first day of the New Year and of the Feast of Huts is on Saturday, both of these ceremonies are adjourned to Sunday.

The festive bunch is to be coupled with gladness before God, hence with reading of the Hallel Psalms (Bk. II, ch. XIII). The "first," i. e., the leader in the morning Prayer and whoever beside him is in possession of a *Lulab* and *Ethrog* say, before beginning Hallel, the following benedictions:

Blessed be thou, O Lord, our God, King of the world, who hast sanctified us by thy commandments, and hast commanded us about the handling of the Lulab. (Adding on the first day) Blessed be thou, O Lord, our God, King of the world, who hast let us live, and kept us up, and made us reach this season.

To fulfill the command every one who has a Lulab and Ethrog then moves them up and down to the right and left and to the fore and aft, in acknowledgment of God's omnipresence. Hallel then proceeds; the same motions are made again at the first four verses of Psalm 118 ("for his mercy endureth forever") at the line, "We beseech thee, O Lord, save now," and again at the last verse, "Give thanks unto the Lord, etc., for his mercy."

The command as to the four species has been carried out in substantially the same manner as it is now as far as any tradition or testimony reaches back; the Karaites, however, point to Nehemiah 8: 15 as showing that the four species should be employed in building the Hut, and not handled separately, as they are by the Rabbinical Jews.

Those who have no "four kinds" of their own, borrow them from others or from the congregation; but on the first day every man ought to have a proprietary interest in those which he handles.[7]

The Hosanna hymns on the Feast of Huts have been mentioned among the later poetry (Bk. II, chs. XVII and XVIII). Right after the repetition of the Additional the leader takes a scroll from the Ark with the invocation *Hosha'na;* those who have a Lulab range themselves behind him in procession, and they walk slowly round the platform, singing the Hosanna hymn for the day. On a Saturday he makes the circuit alone, or stands still. On the seventh of the Feast (the Great Hosanna, or *Hosha'na Rabba*) all the scrolls are taken out, and seven circuits are made through the whole Synagogue, a separate hymn being sung each time, and different men carrying the scrolls on each circuit. The Cabbalists have, in modern times, taken hold of the seven circuits by choosing a verse with the appropriate *Sephira* to recite after each of six, while the verse, "Thine, O Lord, is the greatness," from 1 Chron. 29, is recited after the seventh circuit as embodying all of the seven lower *Sephiroth*. The older standards, such as the Mahzor Vitry, know nothing of all this.

After these circuits a new implement, peculiar to this day, comes into play, the willow bunch, made up of five small willow twigs, familiarly known as the *Hosha'na*. Like everything else that distinguishes the seventh day from the other middle days of the Feast of Huts, this bunch, made of five small twigs, tied together with strips of willow bark or palm leaf, cannot be traced to any Biblical source. The celebration is drawn from the great national holiday of the second Temple, the "Joy of the Water Fetching," which the Mishna describes as having exceeded all other entertainments of the world in its intensity of delight. In this celebration those who made circuits around the altar carried willow bunches. As little as is left of all this, we cannot forget that the authors of the Calendar laid so much store by this holiday that they would push all the feasts forward by one day rather than let it fall on a Sabbath, and thus interfere with the exercises.

The willow bunches are tied up the night before; in the morning they are taken to the Synagogue. After the seven circuits with the scrolls and palm leaves round the platform, a few more poetical prayers are recited, among them one full of Messianic hopes: "A voice brings news, brings news and says" (see Bk. II, ch. XVII). At last, with a petition for forgiveness of sins, each worshipper strikes his bunch a few times on the desk before him and throws it away; a poor remnant, indeed, of the merry processions of the "Water Fetching House." The Cabbalists have given this day a new meaning: the judgments enrolled on New Year and sealed on Atonement Day are sent out by divine messengers into the world. This is certainly a very different character from that which the Willow Day bore in old Jerusalem.[8]

On the last day of the Feast, the "Joy of the Law" is often celebrated in a rather boisterous manner. In the countries of the Polish Minhag the scrolls are taken out near the end of the evening service, which is contrary to all rules observed at other times. They are carried about in procession, all the little boys following with paper flags representing the twelve tribes, singing as prescribed for the next morning, while the ladies in the gallery throw nuts and candies among them. As a further deviation from sober rules, a scroll is sometimes opened, and any passage at random that is flattering to children (e. g., the blessing of Ephraim and Manasseh) is read, "all the boys" in unison saying the benediction.

In the morning it is regular to take out the scrolls of the Law, leaving a candle in their place in the Ark. A procession is formed by the leader, the men carrying scrolls, while all sing:

> We beseech thee (Anna), O Lord, save now!
> We beseech thee, O Lord, give success now!
> We beseech thee, O Lord, answer us when we call!

This is varied by an alphabet of names for God, put in the place of, "We beseech thee, O Lord," with the same three petitions. When the procession has walked round the platform, other men are called with profuse compliments to carry a scroll during the next circuit (Hakkafa), and the merry song goes on. When the song is ended, all but three of the scrolls are replaced, and the regular reading begins. A Cohen is first called "with all the priests;" they all come to the platform and say the benedictions together; then a Levite is called "with all the Levites." Then others are called, have short passages read to them in chapter 33 of Deuteronomy; these same passages being read over and over again, until none are left uncalled but the three needed to finish Deuteronomy, to read in Genesis, and to act as Maftir, or until the patience of the meeting is exhausted. The last called before these three is requested to "stand up with all the boys," and all the boys under thirteen come as near as they can to the desk, and join with him in the benedictions.[9] At the last three verses of Deuteronomy all rise and read them before the reader; and so again in Genesis all chime in, "There was evening and there was morning," six times, and again in the three verses about the Sabbath of Creation.

BOOK V

The Jewish Home

BOOK V

CHAPTER I

MINIAN AT THE HOUSE

The liturgy which has been analyzed in the Second Book, excepting only the responsive parts, such as, "Bless ye," or the "Kaddish," or the "Thrice-Holy," and some of the lesser prayers for "this congregation," are just as much intended for the individual at his home as for those who meet at a common place of worship; in fact, taking all the days of the year together, much more is recited in private houses than in the Synagogue.

But there is an occasion when services must be, another when they are likely to be, carried on at the house; the former is the week of mourning, the latter the anniversary of a father's or mother's death. The former is known as *Shib'a* (Seven), the latter among the Jews of the German ritual as *Jahrzeit* (anniversary), no Hebrew term having ever been contrived for it; among the Sefardim, as *Nahala* (inheritance). Deep mourning is kept for father or mother, son or daughter, brother or sister, husband or wife. The observance of the anniversaries of death is a very modern institution, in all likelihood not quite three hundred years old.[1]

Deep mourning, or "sitting *Shib'a*," involves staying at home, generally in the house in which the death took place, for nominally seven days after the burial. It is carried on in honor of father or mother, husband or wife, son or daughter. (Before the burial the kindred on whom the duty to bury rests are absolved from reading the Shema and the Prayer, and from the observance of all ceremonies whatever.)[2] The part of a day counts for a whole day, and the Sabbath is free. Thus, if a funeral takes place on Wednesday, the mourners "sit" during the afternoon service of that day, the evening service that follows, all Thursday, Friday during morning and afternoon services; attend at the Synagogue on Friday night, and Saturday in the morning and afternoon; they "sit" again on Saturday night, all Sunday and Monday, and Tuesday morning during the services, and for one hour thereafter. We deal here only with the length of time during which the mourners are confined to the house, not with the customs which they otherwise observe. While they cannot go to the Synagogue, it becomes the duty of their friends and neighbors to come to them, to "make up Minian," that is, the lawful number of ten adults, at the home; so that they may have the privileges of a responsive service, above all that of reciting the Kaddish, which in the last three or four hundred years has taken such strong hold of the Jewish heart.[3]

The services at the house during the "seven days" differ from those on other occasions; thus, Hallel (on Hanucca or New Moons), the outbreak of exultant joy, is omitted as unbefitting the newly bereaved widow and child or parent. Nor is the lesson from the Law read; for the study of the Tora is a pleasure in which those in deep mourning may not join.

For a similar reason the Psalms for the days of the week (see Bk. II, ch. XIII) are omitted, and in the place thereof some Psalm of comfort to the weary (16 or 49) is read. The old custom was also to leave out the Red Sea Song from the morning hymns and to substitute for it Moses' Song of Warning (Deut. 32); and this is still the rule with the Sefardim, as well on this occasion as on the Ninth of Ab.

On the other hand, the penitential Psalm, with all its incidents and surroundings (including those for Mondays and Thursdays), is omitted; for the grief of the mourners is not to be aggravated by the sorrow of the community for its sins, nor by its plaints over undeserved sufferings. Lastly, in the Kaddish after the Prayer, which elsewhere is read complete, the third paragraph (May our prayer, etc.) is omitted, so that it does not differ from the Mourners' Kaddish (Bk. II, ch. V). In fact, the latter has probably grown out of this omission.

The shorter period of seven days is met with in the 50th chapter of Genesis, where Jacob's descendants weep near his grave for his loss; the longer period of thirty days is prescribed as a rule in Deut. 21: 13, and found illustrated, Deut. 34: 8, in the mourning of all Israel for Moses. The Mishna recognizes both periods, but hardly anything other than shaving is forbidden during the "thirty." While the Sabbath only interrupts the "seven," the three Festivals, if they happen three days or more after the funeral, stop both the "seven" and the "thirty," and at all events the former. The Eighth of the Feast counts as a new Festival for this purpose. The Sages, though prescribing seven days, thought that really three days of deep mourning were enough, and according to Scripture perhaps even one day.[4]

The Days of Memorial and Atonement, though at first treated like a Sabbath, as only interrupting the "seven," by the rule now in force put an end to them.[5]

The prayer meeting on anniversaries stands on wholly different ground. Those who honor the memory of a father or mother at such a time may go to the Synagogue; if "Minian" is gotten up at a private house it is either as a mere matter of convenience, or because one of those concerned would like to act as leader in prayer, and might not be allowed that privilege in public. But the order of service is exactly the same as at the Synagogue. Nothing is left out, nothing added. If a scroll is at hand, the lesson is read;

if it is New Moon, they read Hallel. It is usual, either after or before the service, to read and translate a few sections of the Mishna, in order to give occasion for the Kaddish of the Rabbis (see Book II, ch. V).

Another occasion for services at the home is a wedding, when celebrated in the afternoon. If there are ten men present, *Minha* is read before the ceremony. It being an occasion of joy, the penitential Psalm is of course omitted. As those present are supposed to be impatient, the service is shortened as much as possible; the Prayer is at once read aloud by the leader as far as the Thrice-Holy, the rest of it silently by all.

A Jewish wedding in its modern form is made up of two parts, which anciently might be separated by days, months, or years—the betrothal and the marriage proper. The former, whether by ring or by written contract, is a legal act, not a devotion or service; the marriage proper consists only of this, that groom and bride, standing together under a canopy which represents their future home, drink a cup of wine together.

The following seven benedictions are spoken before they drink it:

Blessed be thou, O Lord, our God, King of the world, Creator of the fruit of the vine. Blessed be thou, etc., who hast created everything to thy glory. Blessed be thou, O Lord, etc., Maker (literally, shaper) of man. Blessed, etc., who hast shaped man in thy image, in the image of thy likeness, and prepared for him perpetual succession out of himself: blessed be thou, O Lord, Maker of man. Let the barren one rejoice and shout, when her children are gathered with her in gladness: blessed be thou, O Lord, who gladdenest Zion with her children. Gladden, O gladden the beloved friends, as thou didst gladden of old thy first-made man in Paradise: blessed be thou, O Lord, who gladdenest groom and bride. Blessed be thou, O Lord, our God, King of the world, who hast created joy and gladness, groom and bride, rejoicing, song, mirth, and pleasure; love and brotherhood, peace and friendship; may soon, O Lord, our God, (Jer. 33: 11) be heard in the cities of Judah and streets of Jerusalem the voice of the groom and the voice of the bride, the jubilant sound of grooms from their chambers and of young men from their feasts of song; blessed be thou, O Lord, who gladdenest the groom with the bride.

These benedictions are found in the Talmud substantially, but not literally, as they stand now.[6]

About the services at death we need state only one feature, which is common to all Israel; it is the desire of every good Israelite to die with the words, "Hear, O Israel, the Lord our God, the Lord is One," upon his lips, and those who surround him join him therein, and repeat the words when he can do so no longer.

Rabbi Akiba, when put to death amid horrid tortures, expired with these words in his mouth. Before the seventh century this custom must have become general among the Jews of Syria and Arabia, for from it the Moslems learned to die with the words, "I am witness that there is no god but God."

CHAPTER II

THE Mishna teaches that children should, at the age of five, begin to read the Bible. This rule is still carried out literally in the training of hundreds of thousands.[1]

One of the first verses learned by the child as soon as he can talk is Deut. 33: 4, "Moses commanded us the Law, a heritage to the congregation of Jacob." "Hear, O Israel" goes with it, or soon follows,[2] and a few short benedictions, among these that upon washing the hands either on rising from bed in the morning or that before meals, then the short grace before eating bread:

Blessed be thou, O Lord, our God, King of the world, who bringest bread forth from the earth (cmp. Ps. 104).

Also similar benedictions before eating fruit, "Blessed, etc., Creator of the fruit of the tree;" before partaking of milk or other animal food and all beverages other than wine, "Blessed, etc., by whose word all things came into being." But where a meal begins with a morsel of bread, the benediction over that covers everything else. It is not worth while to enumerate here all the other benedictions before varying articles of food or enjoyments.

The Talmud seeks in vain for any Biblical passage that requires us to bless God *before* partaking of food, and contents itself at last with resting the duty to do so, which was already fully accepted, on grounds of reason or natural religion.[3]

Children also learn to speak their benediction at lightning and thunder, which helps to keep them from superstitious fears, and to bless God when they get new clothes, in the words in which a festival is received (Who let us live, and kept us up, and made us reach this time).[4]

Children are also taught separately some of the Bible verses in the "Reading of the Shema at the Bed," such as Ps. 31: 6 or Ps. 121: 4 and Gen. 49: 18, but are at an early age led to recite the whole or a great part of it. It follows here in full, except as far as reference is made to Bible passages or to earlier parts of this work.

A passage of the Talmud, already quoted for the benedictions upon awaking and rising, recommends the following devotion upon retiring to bed:

The first paragraph of Shema (Deut. 6: 4-9) and this benediction:

Blessed art thou, O Lord, our God, King of the world, who layest the bonds of sleep on my eyes and slumber on my eyelids [and who givest light to the pupil of my eye]. Be it thy will, my God, to let me lie down in peace;* [lead me in the path of duty, not in the path of law-breaking; do not lead me into sin, into wrong, into temptation, or into contempt]; [may the good, not the evil impulse rule over me, and deliver me from evil happenings and from grave sickness]; may evil dreams or evil musings not disturb me. May my couch be perfect in thy sight; and illumine my eyes, lest I sleep the death. Blessed art thou, O Lord, who lightest up the whole world with thy glory.[5]

The Germans leave out the parts in brackets, and only say, "and let me rise in peace" at *. The second bracketed passage is omitted in the Sefardic Prayer Book also. In practice the benediction is placed before the verses from Deuteronomy, in analogy to the evening service.

In the older Prayer Books of the Sefardim the night prayer is made up only of these pieces and of the last verse of Ps. 90, followed by all of Ps. 91, as in the Saturday evening service (Bk. II, ch. XIII), and Psalm 3, without the title heading, which, being taken from the history of David, would here be out of place. Both Psalms are highly appro-

priate, Psalm 91 by reason of the verse, "Be not in fear of
the terrors of the night or of the arrow that flieth by day,"
the other for the line, "I lie me down and sleep; I awake,
because the Lord holdeth me up."

The German ritual adds further the benediction, "Let us
lie down," from the evening service (see Bk. II, ch. III),
but without the "sealing," as to repeat this here would be
deemed a "vain benediction;" next, the third benediction
("Blessed be the Lord by day"), which the Germans add in
the work-day evening service (Bk. II, ch. XV), also without
the sealing, or close. The important part here is the verse
(Ps. 31: 6), "In thine hand I commit my spirit; thou hast
redeemed me, Lord, God of truth;" a verse which is especially recommended in the Talmud as a sufficient night prayer
in itself.⁰ Then come a few verses from different books,
the first of which has, in Germany proper, obtained the
undeserved prominence of being about the first thing for
children to learn and to repeat (Gen. 48: 16), "The Angel
who has redeemed me from all evil bless the lads! etc."
Exodus 15: 26, which follows next, is more appropriate;
Zech. 3: 2 (And the Lord said to the Adversary), not so;
while Cant. 3: 7, 8 (Behold the litter of Solomon) seems
especially ill-chosen; for Solomon, as here said, relied
upon sixty armed soldiers rather than on divine help
"because of the fear in the night." Next comes the priestly
blessing (Num. 6: 24, 25, 26), which children thus learn to
memorize while very young, and then the two most important lines of all (each to be said thrice):

(Ps. 121: 4) Behold he that keepeth Israel shall neither
slumber nor sleep.

(Gen. 49: 18) For thy salvation I have hoped, O Lord.
(This makes three words in Hebrew.)

At this point the Cabbalists left their mark, first, by following up the given order 1, 2, 3 of these words, with the
inversions, 2, 3, 1 and 3, 1, 2; next, by this invocation:

In the name of the Lord, the God of Israel! at my right hand is Michael, at my left hand Gabriel; before me Uriel, and behind me Rafael; and over my head the presence (Shechina) of God.

Then follows Ps. 128, the praise of labor and contentment, and lastly a verse also recommended in the Talmud (Ps. 4: 5), after which there should be no further talking:

Stand in awe, and sin not.
Speak to your own heart upon your bed, and be still. Selah.[7]

In many prayer books the poem, "Lord of the World" (see Bk. II, ch. XVIII), is either reprinted or referred to at the end of the devotions on retiring to bed, its last couplet being drawn from the Psalm verse, "In thine hands I commit my spirit."

Pious Jewish parents take particular pains in training their children to say, "Blessed be he and blessed his name" (*Baruch hu u-baruch Shemo*), whenever the father has pronounced the first three words of a benediction, and "Amen" at its close, for which occasion will be shown in the following chapters.[8] And as the youngest child at the table has to ask "the questions" on the Passover night, they naturally form one of the first reading lessons.

The lighting of the lamps or candles on the eight nights of the Hanucca also belongs here, as it is quite usual in old-fashioned homes to furnish to each boy his own set of them, one for the first night, two for the next, and so on to the eighth, beside the "servant," with which the others are lit. The lamps or candles are set near a window, where people on the street may see them, soon after dark before the streets are deserted, all to "publish the miracle." Before lighting them the following benedictions are chanted, the third naturally only upon the first night:

Blessed be thou, O Lord, our God, King of the world, who hast sanctified us by thy commandments, and commanded us to light the lamp of Dedication (Hanucca). Blessed, etc., who didst work

22

miracles for our fathers, in those days, at this season.   Blessed, etc., who hast let us live, and kept us up, and made us reach this time.[*]

A song (*Ma'oz Tzur*) follows to a well-known tune, which for lack of space is here omitted.

CHAPTER III

THE important acts of Jewish home life cluster round the meal; the short blessing before it has been noticed, but Grace after Meal takes a higher rank, as its obligation is drawn from the written Law.

Moses, in his great farewell discourse, tells the children of Israel (Deut. 8: 7-10), "For the Lord thy God bringeth thee into a good land—a land of wheat and barley, of vine and fig tree and pomegranate, a land of the oil-olive and of honey (i. e., palm syrup)—a land wherein thou shalt not lack anything. When thou hast eaten, and art full, then thou shalt bless the Lord thy God for the good land which he hath given thee."

From these words the Sages of Israel infer the duty of saying grace after a meal which, in whole or in part, consists of any of the seven fruits for which the land is praised. This grace is fuller when bread made of wheat and barley (which embrace also spelt, rye, and oats) forms part of the meal; in modern usage a piece of bread the size of an olive is deemed the leading element, all the rest being only side dishes. The grace after bread contained at first only three benedictions. A fourth was added from gratitude for the poor boon which the Emperor Antoninus gave, to bury the bones of the brave defenders of Bethar, the last national stronghold in the days of Hadrian.

We consider first the address and response when three or more men (or three or more women) take a meal together. Two men and a boy old enough to have ideas about God are also deemed sufficient.

The leader, after asking leave ("By leave of the master of the house—or of my father—and the gentlemen"), proceeds: "We will bless him from whose wealth we have eaten."

The others respond:

"Blessed be he from whose wealth we have eaten, and through whose goodness we live."

When there are ten at table God's name is employed in the address and response:

"We will bless our God, from whose wealth we have eaten."

"Blessed be our God, from whose wealth we have eaten, and through whose goodness we live."

When there are ten at a wedding meal, after "our God" the words, "in whose dwelling is joy," are inserted in both address and response. The leader in every case repeats the response after the others.

Every word and almost every letter of the address and response are thoroughly discussed in the Talmud, the reading now in use being in each case claimed as that of the learned, and some variant denounced as the badge of ignorance. There is also a probable story told of Simeon ben Shetah opening grace after dinner with this address after a word skirmish, when seated at table with King Jannæus and Queen Salome.

For the purpose of intertwining religious with home feelings, the love of God with the love of parents, this short address and response have been invaluable. Father and sons are held together at the scantiest and coarsest meal, if it but embraces a crust of bread.[1]

Of the benedictions that follow, the first is fitted for men of any creed or race, if only they believe in God. It reads in the German ritual thus:

I. Blessed be thou, O Lord, our God, King of the world,* he who feedeth the whole world in his goodness with grace, kindness, and mercy, he (Ps. 136: 25) "giveth food to all flesh, for his mercy endureth forever." And with his always great goodness, we have

not lacked, and may we not lack food forever. For the sake of his
great name, for he feedeth, and taketh care of all, and doeth good
to all, and prepareth food for all his creatures that he hath made.**
Blessed be thou, O Lord, who feedeth all.

The Sefardim insert at * "who feedeth us, not from our
own wealth, who provideth for us, not from our own work,"
and at ** quote,"As it is written (Ps. 145: 16): Thou openest
thy hand, and fillest the desire of all that liveth." Both
these additions are rather modern, being unknown to Abudraham.

The second benediction is meant as a literal compliance
with the law in Deuteronomy. At an early date it was, however, held obligatory to thank not only for the possession of
the promised land, but also for the deliverance from Egypt,
for the gift of the Law, and for the covenant with Abraham. The benediction has now with the Germans the following form:

II. We thank thee, O Lord, our God, for that thou gavest as a
heritage to our fathers a delightful, good, and spacious land, that
thou hast brought us forth from Egypt, and redeemed us out
of the house of bondage, for thy covenant which thou hast sealed
on our body, for thy law which thou hast taught us, and thy ordinances wherein thou hast instructed us, for the life, grace, and kindness which thou hast bestowed on us, and for the food to eat; for
thou art our feeder and provider; every day, at every time, at each
moment.*

For all this, O Lord, our God, we give thanks to thee and bless
thee. Be thy name blessed in the mouth of all that liveth, always
and for evermore; as it is written: "When thou hast eaten, and art
full, thou shalt bless the Lord, thy God, for the good land he hath
given thee." Blessed be thou, O Lord, for the land and for the
food.

The next benediction, which ends in a prayer for the
building of Jerusalem, is, by the fullest testimony which
Mishna and Talmud can give, much older than the destruction of the city by Titus; but it may have been considerably
modified by that event:

III. Show mercy, O Lord, our God, to Israel thy people, and to thy holy city Jerusalem, and to Zion, the camp of thy glory, and to the kingdom of David, thy anointed, and to the great and holy House, over which thy name was pronounced. Our God, our Father, be thou our shepherd, feed us, take care of us, sustain us; and give us breathing room speedily, O Lord, our God, out of all our troubles; and put us not in dependence on the gifts or loans of flesh and blood [Sefardim add: for their gift is small, and the disgrace great], but only on thy full, thy holy, thy wide-open hand, that we may not be put to shame or to blush for evermore.*

And build Jerusalem, thy holy city, speedily in our days. Blessed be thou, O Lord, who in thy mercy buildest Jerusalem. Amen.

This is the only benediction which he that pronounces it himself closes with "Amen." The word was put there, when the less obligatory fourth benediction was added to "Grace," as a hint to busy servants or workmen that they might leave the table and go to their work.

At the point * the Sabbath is thus noticed:

Be pleased and strengthen us, O Lord, our God, through thy commandments, even through the commandment of this great and holy seventh day, the Sabbath; for this day is great and holy to rest and stop from toil according to thy command; and in thy favor thou wilt give us such rest, O Lord, our God, that there be no distress or trouble thereon. Let us see the comfort of Zion and the upbuilding of Jerusalem, thy holy city; for thou, O Lord, art able to save and able to give comfort.

On New Moons and all Festivals and Middle Days the petition, "May our remembrance," given in Book II, ch. VII, and again in ch. VIII, is here inserted (on a Sabbath after the above petition for the Sabbath) with this change in the closing words, "thou art a gracious and merciful God and King," the last word, "King," is omitted. And herein lies a curious protest against Christian dogma; the Kingdom of David and the Kingdom of God are not to be mentioned in the same benediction, for they are widely different in their scope and meaning.

On a Sabbath the Sefardim leave out the last petition,

"Build Jerusalem," and wind up thus, "Blessed, etc., who comforts Israel by building Jerusalem. Amen." The idea is not to ask for anything on the Sabbath that is prayed for in the work-day Prayer.

The insertion for the Sabbath, while not set out at large in the Talmud, is treated by it as well-known and highly imperative; a short, separate benediction for the Sabbath, New Moon, or Festival is prescribed for those who should forget to insert it at the proper place.[3]

The gist of the fourth benediction is in these words, "Blessed be thou, O Lord our God, King of the world, who art good and doest good," which were spoken for a long time before the war of Bethar upon the receipt of good news. But it must at an early day have grown into much greater bulk, otherwise the hint would not have been given to workmen to leave the table by the "Amen" which precedes it. It is in full:

IV. Blessed be, etc., the God, our Father, our King, our (a) Majestic, our (b) Creator, our (g) Redeemer, our (q) Holy One, the Holy One of Jacob, our (r) Shepherd, the Shepherd of Israel, the King, "good and doing good" to all, who on every day does and has done and will do good to us. He has bestowed, and does and will forever bestow upon us in grace, kindness, and mercy, enlargement, deliverance, and prosperity, blessing and salvation, provision and sustenance, life and peace, and every good thing; and may he never let us lack all that is good.*

(1) The Merciful shall reign over us forever.

(2) The Merciful shall be blessed in the heavens and on the earth.

(3) The Merciful shall be praised in all ages, shall be glorified through all changes, and honored to all eternities.

(4) May the Merciful give us honorable support.

(5) May the Merciful break the yoke of exile from our necks, and lead us in erect gait to our land.

(6) May the Merciful send plentiful blessing into this house and upon this table at which we have eaten.

(7) May the Merciful send us the Prophet Elijah of happy memory, who will tell us good news, of salvation and comfort.

(8) May the Merciful bless (a child of the family says: my hon-

ored Father and Mother) the Master and Mistress of this House (the *pater familias* says: me and my wife), them and their household and their seed (us and ours), as our fathers were blessed, Abraham in all things, Isaac of all things, Jacob as to all, thus may he bless us all together, and say ye, Amen.

[May they in heaven find merit in him and in us, to bring us lasting peace; may we receive a blessing from the Lord and justice from the God of our salvation, and let us find grace and kind attention in the sight of God and man].

(On the Sabbath) May the Merciful give us for our heritage a day which is all rest and quiet in eternal life.

(On New Moons) May the Merciful renew this month for happiness and blessing.

(On New Year) May the Merciful renew this year for happiness and blessing.

(On other Festivals) May the Merciful give us for our heritage a day which is wholly good.

(In the Succa) May the Merciful raise for us the fallen hut of David.

(9) May the Merciful give us the merit to reach the days of the Messiah and the life of the world to come.

(Ps. 18: 51): He gives great deliverance to his King, and showeth kindness to his anointed, to David, and to his seed forever. He who maketh peace in his heights, may he make peace among us and among Israel, and say ye, Amen.

(Ps. 34: 10, 11; 118: 1; 145: 16; Jer. 17: 7.) (Ps. 37: 25): I have been young, and have also become old; but I have never seen the righteous forsaken, nor his children begging bread. (Ps. 29: 11): The Lord giveth strength to his people; the Lord blesseth his people with peace.[4]

The letters (a), (b), (g), (q), (r) denote the Hebrew initials of the words so marked; probably a full alphabet has been abridged into the few words now remaining.

The words "in all things, from all things, all" refer to the terms employed in Genesis as to the wealth, blessings, or contentment of Abraham, Isaac, and Jacob.

The reference to father and mother (only found in the German ritual) is literally "my father, my teacher; my mother, my instructress." But probably "Mori, Morathi" are only the Hebraized forms for the Aramaic *Mar* and

Martha, Sir and Lady, and *Immi Morathi* is "my lady mother." The bracketed lines are not in the Sefardic ritual; but it has three other petitions, "May the Merciful put peace among us. May the Merciful heal us with a perfect cure. May the Merciful open to us his wide hand."

On Sabbaths, New Moons, and Festivals the verse from Psalm 18 is read as in II Sam. 22. "The tower (*Migdol*) of deliverance," etc. After each petition to "the Merciful" comes the answer, "Amen."

The second benediction is known as "Thanksgiving." The thanks for the miracles (if such they may be termed) that were done for our fathers on Purim and Hanucca are inserted in this, as they are in the "Thanksgiving" of the Prayer and in the same words (see Bk. II, ch. VII).[5]

As the Mishna teaches that three who eat at one table without "words of the Tora" among them are like idolaters eating from the "offerings to the dead,"[6] it is usual to recite or sing a Psalm at the table. The Sefardim have Psalm 23 (The Lord is my Shepherd) at the beginning of the meal; the Germans recite Ps. 137 (On the Rivers of Babylon) on work-days, on Sabbath, New Moons, and the Feasts, Ps. 126, one of the Songs of Degrees, or Ascents (When the Lord returned the captivity of Zion). A number of hymns have also been written during the middle ages to be sung at the Sabbath meal. The most popular of these refers to the "cup of blessing," which is drunk after grace. At least, it was the custom of our fathers when they lived in Western Asia to drink a cup of light wine mixed with water at almost every meal; and when they had only one cup, to hold it in the hand during grace and to drink it after grace with the words, "Blessed, etc., Creator of the fruit of the vine."[7]

At a wedding supper (and such is counted every meal within seven days of the ceremony at which the groom and bride are present, and at which there are ten men ready to say grace together), the seven benedictions set out in Bk. V, ch. I, are recited before the "cup of blessing."[8]

We here subjoin in part a rhythmic version of "Rock from whose wealth we have eaten:"

> Our Rock with loving care,
> According to his word,
> Bids all His bounty share,
> Then let us bless the Lord.
>
> His flock our Shepherd feeds
> With graciousness divine,
> He satisfies our needs
> With gifts of bread and wine.
> Therefore with one accord
> We will His name adore,
> Proclaiming evermore
> None holy as the Lord.
> Our Rock, etc.
>
> Thy city fill once more,
> Thy temple-walls upraise,
> There will we Thee adore
> With joyful songs of praise,
> Thee, Merciful, Adored,
> We bless and sanctify,
> With wine-cups filled up high,
> By blessings of the Lord.
> Our Rock, etc.

But by the side of all this elaboration for solemnly closing and blessing the meal, we read of one of the Babylonian worthies, Benjamin the Shepherd, whose grace was made up of five Aramaic words, "Blessed-be the-Merciful (Rahmana), the-Master of-this bread," and it was held to be a sufficient compliance with the Biblical command.[9]

After drinking wine (as much as the contents of a fair-sized hen egg and a half), after eating food made of the five grains other than bread, or after grapes, dates, figs, olives, or pomegranates, otherwise than at a meal, an abstract of the benedictions of grace is spoken. We give it here in the form it takes after drinking wine; else the words, "sustenance and food" or "tree and fruit of the tree" take the place of "vine and fruit of the vine," and "sustenance" or "fruits," of the words, "fruit of the vine." Those who are not observant enough to recite this benediction at any other time, do so perhaps in the Passover night service:

Blessed be thou, O Lord, our God, King of the world, for the vine and the fruit of the vine and the produce of the field, and for the delightful, good, and wide land which thou gavest to our fathers to eat of its fruit and to be filled from its bounty. Have mercy, O Lord, our God, on Israel thy people, and Jerusalem, thy city, and bring us into it, and gladden us therein, that we may eat of its fruit and bless thee therefor in holiness and purity (and strengthen us on this Sabbath) (and gladden us on this Feast of Unleavened Bread, etc.); for thou art good and doest good to all. Blessed be thou, O Lord, for the land and for the fruit of the vine."

CHAPTER IV

SANCTIFICATION AND SEPARATION

THE first line of the Fourth Commandment truly rendered reads, "Remember the Sabbath day to hallow it!" It is thus the duty of every Israelite, as soon as Sabbath comes in on Friday at night-fall, to name, to think of, and to feel its holiness. We have heretofore seen how this is done in the middle benediction of the Prayer; but our fathers knew that the true spirit of the Sabbath could be caught only in the home circle, where husband and wife, parents and children meet at the meal.

"Thy wife as a fruitful vine at the sides of thy house,
Thy children like olive branches around the table."

And they instituted the Sanctification (Kiddush, whence the Christian Sacrament) over the cup of wine at the place of the meal, in short, over bread and wine, as Melchizedek blessed God in the days of Abraham.

Before darkness sets in on Friday, the housewife lights in the dining room extra candles or a special lamp in honor of the Sabbath, first giving thanks thus:

Blessed be thou, O Lord, our God, King of the world, who hath sanctified us by his commandments, and commanded us to light the Sabbath lamp.[1]

When the husband and sons come back from the Synagogue (women were not wont to attend it on Friday night), they find the table laid with a clean table-cloth, and where the head of the family sits, two loaves of bread (generally baked for the occasion), in memory of the double portion of manna that was gathered on Fridays, lie covered with a napkin, and next to them stands a cup and by it a jug or bottle of wine to fill it.

The husband chants the praises of "the woman of force" (Proverbs 31: 10-31), each man fondly believing that she is reproduced in his own wife. If he has a Cabbalistic tinge, or if he "says" everything that the Cabbalists have crowded into the Prayer Book, he will, however, first greet the "messengers in attendance, messengers of peace."

The Kiddush itself begins with the verses in Genesis 2, which tell of God's rest on the Sabbath day; but it is usual to start a few words further back, thus:

It was evening and it was morning, the sixth day.

And the heavens and the earth were finished and all their host. And God finished on the seventh day all the work which he had made, and rested on the seventh day from all the work that he had made. And God blessed the seventh day and hallowed it; for on it he rested from all the work which God had created and made.

These verses are spoken though the Sabbath be also a Festival. The master of the house then holds up the full cup and proceeds:

Blessed be thou, O Lord, our God, King of the world, the creator of the fruit of the vine.

Blessed be thou, O Lord, our God, King of the world, who hast sanctified us by thy commandments, and wast pleased with us, and hast given us for a heritage, in love and favor, thy holy Sabbath, a memorial of the work of creation. For it precedes all the holy convocations, in memory of the going forth from Egypt. For thou hast chosen us, and hast hallowed us above all nations, and hast given us, in love and favor, thy holy Sabbath for a heritage. Blessed be thou, O Lord, who hallowest the Sabbath.[3]

The master then drinks from the cup and hands it to his wife, and she passes it to the children and other persons at the table, and all drink from it. Then they wash their hands, the master thanks for the bread, cuts one loaf, takes a morsel for himself, and distributes pieces to the others.

If no wine is available, they wash their hands first, and substitute the benediction over bread for that over wine, and the bread is cut and distributed at once. To each benediction those present answer "Amen."

On the nights of the three Festivals, the hallowing of the feast (say the Passover) takes the following form:

> Blessed be thou, O Lord, our God, King of the world, who hast chosen us from every tribe, and lifted us over every tongue; thou gavest us, O Lord, our God (in love, Sabbaths for rest), set times for gladness, feasts and seasons for joy; this (Sabbath day and this) *day of the Feast of Unleavened Bread, the season of our liberation, in memory of the going forth from Egypt; for thou hast chosen us, and hast hallowed us, and hast given us (in love and favor) in gladness and joy the (Sabbath and thy) holy set times for a heritage; blessed be thou, O Lord, who hallowest (the Sabbath and) Israel and the seasons. Blessed be thou, O Lord, our God, King of the world, who has let us live, and kept us up, and made us reach this season.

The proper changes are made on Pentecost, Feast of Huts, and the Eighth, as shown in Bk. II, ch. IX, in the paragraph, "Thou gavest us." On the last days of the Passover the thanks for reaching the season are omitted.

On the night of the New Year the benediction proceeds at *:

> "This Day of Memorial, a day of alarm sound, a holy convocation, in memory of the going forth from Egypt, and thy word is true and standeth forever. Blessed be thou, O Lord, King over all the earth, who hallowest (the Sabbath and) Israel and the Day of Memorial."

Then the thanks for having lived to see the day.[3] But how is a festive day consecrated upon a Saturday night? To those who keep single days this can happen only on the first nights of Passover and Pentecost; but with double days, also on the second and last days of the Passover, on the second of the New Year, on the Feast of Huts, and on the Joy of the Law.

Wine seems indispensable. After two benedictions, one over the cup, the other for the sanctity of the day, follows one over the light, which on the Sabbath just ended it was unlawful to produce from fire:

"Blessed be thou, O Lord, our God, King of the world, Creator of the light-rays of the fire."

Then this "separation" (compare Bk. II, ch. IX):

"Blessed be thou, O Lord, our God, King of the world, who distinguishest between holy and profane, between light and darkness, between Israel and the nations, between the seventh day and the six work-days; between the holiness of the Sabbath and the holiness of the holiday thou hast distinguished, and thou hast distinguished and sanctified thy people Israel in thine own holiness. Blessed be thou, O Lord, who distinguishest between holy and unholy."

Then the thanks for living to see the day.

On Festivals, as on Friday night, the meal proceeds right after the Kiddush, but two loaves are not required.

The five benedictions for a Festival on Saturday night are a combination of the Kiddush with the Habdala or Separation.[4]

The Talmud says quaintly: When the children of Israel were poor, it was ordained to "separate" in the Prayer; when they got to be rich, to separate over the cup; then they got poor again, and again separated in the Prayer. But it is the custom to do both, first to say the evening Prayer with the "separation" or "distinction" in the fourth benediction; afterwards to recite the Habdala over a cup of wine, a lighted wax candle, and a spice box. Including the verses with which the ceremony is introduced in the German ritual the whole of it runs thus:

(Isa. 12: 2, 3): Behold the God of my salvation, I trust and do not fear; for my strength and song is Jah the Lord; and he hath become my salvation. And ye shall draw water with joy from the springs of salvation.

(Ps. 3: 9): Salvation is with the Lord, thy blessing over thy
people. Selah!
(Ps. 46: 12): The Lord of Hosts is with us, the God of Jacob is
a fortress for us. Selah.
(Esther 8: 16): The Jews had light and gladness and joy and
honor (be it thus with us!). (Ps. 116: 13): I lift the cup of salvation, and call on the name of the Lord.
Blessed be thou, O Lord, our God, King of the world, Creator
of the fruit of the vine.
Blessed be thou, O Lord, our God, King of the world, Creator
of the light-rays of the fire.
Blessed be thou, O Lord, our God, King of the world, Creator
of many kinds of spices.
Blessed be thou, O Lord, our God, who distinguishest between
holy and profane, between light and darkness, between Israel and
the nations, between the seventh day and the six work-days.
Blessed be thou, O Lord, who distinguishest between holy and
profane.'

The wine is then drunk, and the wax candle is put out
with drops from the cup.

The first and fourth benedictions are spoken also on the
nights after a festival; the fourth unchanged, though the
distinction to be made is not between the seventh day and
the other days of the week. The formula introduced for
the Sabbath was deemed sufficient for all cases. On the
night of the Day of Atonement the "light-rays of the fire"
are also mentioned, as lighting fires is forbidden on that
day as on the Sabbath.

Hymns are next in order, each of which has its well-
known tune. There is one common to the German and to
the Sefardic rituals, recited right after the separation, in
eight quatrains, the first of which is thus rendered by Mrs.
Lucas:

> May He who sets the holy and profane
> Apart, blot out our sins before His sight,
> And make our numbers as the sand again,
> And as the stars of night.

The third line of the Hebrew text is here slightly idealized, for it reads, "multiply our seed and our money like the sand."

Every verse ends with the word *Laïla*—night.

In another hymn they pray to God to send speedily Elijah the Prophet, Elijah the Tishbite, Elijah the Gileadite, and the Anointed King. Another gathers in an alphabet for the first part of the line short clauses from Scripture about Jacob, such as:

(Alef) "God said unto Jacob," (Beth) "The Lord hath chosen Jacob," while the second part of each of the twenty-two lines remains (Jer. 46: 28), "Do not fear, my servant Jacob." The most pathetic of these hymns, more so by its air than by its words, is made up of eleven triplets, beginning:

> Honored, awful, and terrible one,
> In my distress I call to thee,
> The Lord is with me; I do not fear.

The first two lines in each triplet run through the alphabet; all three rhyme together.

It has ever since Talmudic times been the usage for the leader in prayer at the Synagogue to "sanctify" over the cup at the Synagogue except on the first two nights of the Passover. He does not drink himself, but lets some children take a few drops from the cup. The usage is rather irregular, as the Kiddush ought to be performed at the place of the meal. It was justified on the ground, that poor travellers were in olden times entertained in a room adjoining the Synagogue; but the true reason was that even with the abstract of seven benedictions (see Bk. II, chs. I and IX) the night service for Sabbaths and Festivals was too short, there being then no introductory hymn or Psalms, nor *Alenu*, nor Mourners' Kaddish at the end.

The Habdala is also recited in the Synagogue, and as this is not connected with the meal or table, quite properly.

The two ceremonies here described are among the oldest

23

in the service. True, the Talmud says that the duty to hallow the Sabbath with bread and wine is not Scriptural, but it takes this ground only because every man is supposed to have already hallowed the Sabbath in his Prayer before the evening meal. Yet the sanctification with bread and wine was probably the older of the two, as service by acts and words is always older than service by words alone. The Sabbath lamp, the companion of the Kiddush, was one of the badges of the Pharisaic sect, who, in the benediction, as it is seen, claimed for it divine authority. The Kiddush for the Festivals is intertwined with the four cups of the Passover night (see next chapter), and is as old as these.

The aim of Habdala is to keep men from gradually shortening the Sabbath at its latter end. One must deliberately declare that the night has set in before he can return to his work-day routine. The "first Hasidim," or Saints of early Maccabean days, may have instituted the Habdala in their zeal for the Sabbath, first as an insertion in the Prayer, and when the war was happily closed, with cup and spices.

There is a "Great Kiddush," so called by way of irony, because of its slight importance. Before breakfast on Sabbath and Festivals verses appropriate to the day (Fourth Commandment and Ex. 31: 16, 17 for the Sabbath; Lev. 23: 44 for the three Festivals; Ps. 81: 4, 5 for the New Year) are spoken; then the benediction over a cup of wine or strong drink; all before the meal is begun with the benediction over bread.

The ceremony of blessing the moon may be mentioned here, as it is by preference performed on Saturday night soon after Habdala; the moon is blessed once a month while growing and when it is seen. The benediction as given in a Baraïtha runs thus:

Blessed be thou, O Lord, our God, King of the world, he who by his command created the skies, and all the host by the breath of his mouth.

He implanted in them fixed law and time, and commanded the moon to renew itself; a crown of beauty to those burdened from birth, who will in future be renewed, and will honor their Maker, for the glorious name of his Kingdom. Blessed be thou, O Lord, who renewest the months.

A later authority has added to this simple blessing a great deal of half-Cabbalistic trifles, which need not be noticed here, and which it is best to omit.[6]

On the first (and second) night of the Feast of Huts, or on a Friday night within its middle days, the Kiddush is performed at "the place of the meal," hence in the Hut (or booth). After the benediction for the bread with which the meal begins, not only at these more solemn suppers, but at every meal taken within the Hut, the head of the family proceeds:

Blessed be thou, etc., who hast sanctified us, etc., and commanded us to sit in the Hut.[7]

CHAPTER V

THE Mishna lays down the following programme for
the first night of the Passover, supposing that the Temple is
restored, and that the roasted Passover lamb is the principal
dish. The change from this programme to the one followed
in our days is very slight:

Even the poorest Israelite should not eat supper without
reclining (across a cushioned bench), and none should
have less than four cups of wine. When the first cup is
mixed (with water, as all wine was then drunk), he blesses
first for the wine, then for the day. When they bring (the
herbs) before him, he dips with (i. e., dips and eats) the
horse-radish before he comes to the bread wafers. They
bring before him unleavened bread, horse-radish, and a mixture (of apples and nuts), and two kinds of meat, and in the
times of the Temple the Passover lamb itself. They mix
the second cup, and now the son asks of the father, and if
the son has not the sense, the father teaches him to say:
Why does this night differ from all other nights, for in
other nights we eat either unleavened or leavened bread,
to-night unleavened; in ordinary nights we eat other herbs,
to-night bitter herbs; in other nights we eat meat boiled,
broiled, or roasted, to-night all roasted; in other nights we
dip perhaps not once, to-night twice? And according to
the son's intelligence the father teaches him, beginning
with matters of reproach and ending with those to be proud
of, and discusses the text, "My father was a wandering
Syrian" (Deut. 26: 5), until he goes through that passage.
Rabban Gamaliel used to say, Whoever does not on the

Passover pronounce these three words. *Pesakh, Matza, Maror* (Passover, unleavened bread, bitter herb), has not done his duty; Passover, because God passed over the houses of our fathers; unleavened bread, because our fathers were delivered from Egypt; bitter herbs, because the Egyptians embittered the lives of our fathers in Egypt. In every generation a man should look on himself as if he had himself gone forth from Egypt, as it is written (Ex. 13: 8), "Thou shalt tell thy son on that day, saying: For the sake of this the Lord did it for me, when I went out from Egypt." Therefore we are bound to thank, to praise and glorify, etc., him who did for us and for our fathers all these wonders; who brought us from bondage to freedom, from grief to joy, from mourning to holiday, from gloom to the fullest light, from subjection to deliverance; let us say before him, Halleluiah (i. e., Psalms 113-118). How far do they go? To "the flint to a pool of water" (i. e., to the end of 114). Then the benediction, "Blessed, etc., who redeemed our fathers from Egypt." Thus may our God and the God of our fathers bring us to other festivals and seasons, that come to meet us, in peace, glad through the upbuilding of thy city and joyful in thy service, and may we there eat of the sacrifices and Passover lambs, etc.; "blessed, etc.; he has redeemed Israel." They mix the third cup, and say with it the grace after the meal; then the fourth, and with it he finishes the Hallel Psalms and adds the benediction of song; between the other cups he may drink if he chooses, but not between the third and the fourth. After the Passover lamb they do not close (or take leave) "with Epikoma."[1]

So far the Mishna. The last is clearly Greek; it may stand for *Ephikomenon* (what comes later, i. e., dessert, or Epikōrnon, or Epikómon), whatever that may mean. At all events, a hundred years after the date of the Mishna neither the Rabbis of Tiberias nor those of Babylonia knew it; the former doubting between a dessert of sweetmeats and merry music; the latter between the dessert and merry visiting from house to house.

In our days the Epikomen is the part of one Matza which, early in the evening, is laid aside, and which is broken and handed around at the supper to be eaten as the last morsel.

At present "they (the women of the house) bring to" the head of the family the following articles: On the supper table is the *Seder*-dish (the whole service is called Seder, or Arrangement) with three heavy unleavened cakes, made for the purpose, wrapped up in napkins; on top they lay a roasted bone to represent the Passover lamb, and an egg boiled hard, to denote the free-will sacrifice of the Feast (Hagiga);[2] horse-radish in two forms, green tops and roots, a bunch of parsley, a saucer with salt-water, and a cup with a mixture of apples and almonds or nuts (Haroseth). Wine is on the table with drinking cups for each person present, big or little, and an extra cup stands ready filled for Elijah the Prophet, should he come in an unbidden guest to honor the feast; though the old standards say nothing about this cup. Cushioned armchairs are provided for the master and mistress of the house.

The programme is put into sixteen Hebrew words, thus:

(1) Sanctify.	(9) Bitter.
(2) Wash.	(10) Wraps.
(3) Greens.	(11) Table, he sets.
(4) Divide.	(12) Table, he sets.
(5) Tells.	(13) Hidden.
(6) Washing.	(14) Blesses.
(7) Brings forth.	(15) Hallel.
(8) Unleavened.	(16) Accepted.[3]

1. The head of the family with a glass of wine before him reads the Kiddush for the evening as on other Festivals, taking due notice of Friday or Saturday night, if the Festival should fall on either.

2. The master of the house, to qualify him as a priest for the occasion, then pours water over his hands; but as this

washing is not prescribed by old Rabbinical law, he says no benediction.

3. He dips the parsley in salt-water, blesses as in other cases before eating vegetables, "Blessed, etc., the Creator of the fruit of the earth," and hands tufts of the bunch around to all present, and all eat. This is a deviation from the Mishna, which speaks of horse-radish alone and of no other herb. The parsley dipped in salt-water is to represent the hyssop dipped in blood, mentioned in Exodus 12.

4. He breaks the middle of the two cakes in two, puts one of the halves away and leaves the other in its place on the dish.

5. "He tells," i. e., now the story is told for the instruction of the children. A "Haggada," or story of the Passover, is attainable in both Hebrew and English, with wood-cuts at that, for 25 cents or less, and it is therefore not worth while to reproduce it here in full. First, all that take hold of the Seder-dish or of the napkin on which it rests, lift it up, and chant (in Aramaic):

This is the bread of affliction which our fathers ate in the land of Egypt; whoever is hungry, come and eat; whoever is in need, come and make the Passover with us [this year here, next year in the Holy Land; this year as subjects, next year as free men]!

The first part of this formula undoubtedly reaches back to the days of the Temple.[4]

Then the youngest child at the table puts the questions nearly as given in the Mishna, though the intention is there conveyed that a child of sufficient intelligence should ask in words of his own choice. But he leaves out the question about the meat being all roasted as out of date, there being now no Passover lamb "roasted in the fire," and puts in place thereof, after the other three, one nearly as obsolete, "On other nights, while eating, we all either sit or recline, to-night we all recline." Couches on three sides of a banquet table, the guests reclining across the couch and leaning on their left elbows, must needs be out of fashion, since we eat our food with knives and forks, and this question has thus become unmeaning. The father answers the question in the words of Deut. 6: 21:

"We were bondmen unto Pharaoh in Egypt, and the Lord brought us out thence with a strong hand and an outstretched arm," proceeding in post-Biblical language to say, the more we talk of the departure from Egypt the better, and telling of R. Akiba and four of his noted colleagues, who talked about it all that night till the scholars came to call them to the morning service; and quotes the section of the Mishna, in which Ben Zoma proves that the departure from Egypt should be mentioned in every night.

Then come the four answers which Scripture gives for four kinds of sons:

The wise (or learned) son asks (Deut. 6: 20): What are the testimonies, statutes, and judgments which the Lord, our God, has commanded you? Thou also tell him, according to the rules of the Passover (as far as): They do not after the Passover lamb leave off with an Epikomen.

The passage quoted is nearly the last (probably was the last) in the treatise on Passover; the meaning is, when your son wishes to know all the law on the subject, teach him all.

The wicked son asks (Ex. 12: 26): What is this service to you; to you, not to him, he takes himself out of the generality, and shows his unbelief; hence you should blunt his teeth by saying (Ex. 13: 8): For the sake of this the Lord did it for me, when I went forth from Egypt. Had he been there, he would not have been saved.

The point is good, but the Bible does not give that answer to that question:

The simple boy asks (Ex. 13: 14): What is this? And thou shalt tell him: With a strong hand the Lord brought us forth from Egypt, from the house of bondage.

And he who cannot yet ask, begin thou with him and tell him: For the sake of this, etc. (as above), which does not apply until the hour when the unleavened bread and bitter herb are lying before thee.

In short, the Passover table is to serve the children of tenderest age as an object lesson. This apologue or parable of the four sons is due to R. Hiya, a disciple of R. Judah the Saint, and is thus later than the Mishna.[5]

Next, in conformity with the rule first given, to begin with matter of reproach and end with matter of pride, the master of the house reads from Joshua 24 how our fathers before Abraham were idolaters, but he was chosen, etc., and how God (Gen. 15: 13, 14) "said to Abram, thou shalt surely know that thy seed shall be strangers in a foreign land, etc., and thereafter they shall come forth with great wealth."[6]

Now comes the discourse on the four verses (Deut. 26: 15), "A wandering Syrian was my father, and he went down to Egypt, and he sojourned there with a few men, and he became there a nation, great, strong, and numerous." The first clause seems to be misinterpreted, as if it read, "A Syrian (Laban) was ruining my father." After that almost every word is taken up separately and expounded by reference to some other verse in Exodus or in other parts of Scripture. At last "another idea" is applied to the last of these four verses, namely, "Mighty hand is two, outstretched arm two, terrors two, signs two, wonders two;" here are the ten plagues, which are slowly named, first being "blood," and last "the smiting of the first-born." Next come three curious specimens of Midrash, ascribed to R. Jose the Galilean, R. Eliezer, and R. Akiba, all Tannaïm of the highest rank, in which it is figured out that there were fifty plagues in Egypt, and two hundred, or even two hundred and fifty, plagues on the sea.

Now comes the enumeration of the benefits bestowed on our fathers at the exodus, with the refrain, *Dayenu* (enough for us), in which the children gladly join: Had he brought us forth from Egypt and not executed judgments upon them—*Dayenu!* And so on: not executed judgments on their gods—not killed their first-born—not given us their wealth—not torn the sea for us—not brought us through on dry land—not drowned our enemies therein—not provided our needs in the wilderness for forty years—not given us the manna—not given us the Sabbath—not brought us to Mount Sinai—not given us the Law—not led us into the land of Israel—not built for us his chosen temple—Dayenu!

But how much more are we under double and manifold obligation to God, when he brought us forth from Egypt, etc., and built for us his chosen temple, to atone for all our iniquities.

Next comes R. Gamaliel's saying on the necessity of pronouncing the three words, Passover, Matza, Bitter Herb; each is spoken slowly, and the two latter objects as they lie before the company are pointed to. Each is supported by the proper verse, Ex. 12: 27; 12: 39; 1: 14.

Then follow the words of the Mishna, stating the duty of every man to look on himself as if he had come out of Egypt, quoting, however, another verse, namely (Deut. 6: 23), "He brought us out from thence, in order to bring us in, and give us the land which he swore unto our fathers." Then two Hallel Psalms (113 and 114) are read; then the benediction, "who hast redeemed us," etc., as in the Mishna; then the blessing before wine, and the second cup is drunk.

6. All wash their hands for supper in the usual way.

7 and 8. The head of the family breaks pieces off the first and second cake for himself and each person at table, so that each has a piece of each; before eating he pronounces two benedictions, which all repeat:

Blessed, etc., who hast brought bread forth from the earth.
Blessed, etc., who hast sanctified us by thy commandments, and commanded us about eating unleavened bread.

9. He next takes a bunch of the bitter herbs (horse-radish tops) for each person present, dips it in the *Haroseth*, and hands it around with the benediction, "Blessed, etc., who hast sanctified, etc., about the eating of bitter herbs."

10. The head of the family breaks up the third cake, cuts the horse-radish into slices, folds each slice between pieces of the cake, and distributes the sandwiches thus made, saying:

> In memory of the Temple like Hillel. Thus did Hillel, when the Temple stood. He would wrap together pieces of Passover Lamb, Matza, and Bitter Herb, and eat them together, so as to carry out what is written: upon unleavened cakes and bitter herbs ye shall eat it.[1]

11, 12. Supper is brought in and eaten.

13. The half cake laid aside under 4 is brought out, broken, and handed around and eaten.

14. That is, they all say grace, each having his "cup of blessing," which is the third cup of the evening, before him. If there are three or more, the head of the family, or he who acts as such, makes the address. Of course the proper parts for the Festival are inserted, and if it be Friday night, those for the Sabbath. They then say the benediction over the third cup and drink it.

The door is then opened while the following verses are spoken:

> (Ps. 79: 6, 7): Pour thy wrath out on the nations which do not know thee, and over the kingdoms which have never called on thy name. For they have eaten Jacob up, and wasted his dwellings. [The Germans add: Ps. 69: 25; Lam. 3: 66.]

15. "Hallel of Egypt" is finished, that is, Psalms 115, 116, 117, 118, are read in addition to the two which were read before supper; also the introductory part of the benediction after Hallel, but not the closing words (Blessed, etc., the King praised in hymns). Next the Great Hallel, i. e., Psalm

136. Next the "Benediction of Song," or Nishmath, as given in Book II, ch. XV, to the end.

After this, in the Sefardic and formerly also in the German ritual, they bless and drink the fourth cup, and speak after it the "one benediction, the summary of three," given in a previous chapter, by way of thanks for the wine that has been drunk.

16. Accepted. This meant originally, and with the Sefardim still means only, the service is at an end. But the Germans now express this by a little rhyme, about thus:

> The order of the Passover is ended; according to all that is right and prescribed; as we had the privilege to order it, may we have the privilege to work it out. Pure dweller in thy heights; raise up thy numberless assembly; lead up speedily the young shoots of thy plant redeemed to Zion with glad song.

Going back to the preceding number, the Germans insert a *Piyut* on the first night, based on the words in Exodus 12: 29, "It was in the midst of the night," each line of the twenty-two (from Alef to Tav) ending with the word *Laïla* (night). On the second day a similar *Piyut* is chanted, based on the words, "Ye shall say, it is the sacrifice of the Passover," each line ending with the word *Pesakh*.[8] Next comes an indescribable jingle (*Ki lo naë*), which also runs through the alphabet. After the last cup and the little rhyme given above under 16, the Germans have perhaps the merriest time of the whole evening in three songs, which many of them sing in the German tongue or rather in a Jewish jargon.

The first is:

> "Almighty (the word is chosen because like its Hebrew counterpart it begins with the first letter) is he; he'll build his house very soon; speedily, speedily, speedily; in our days very soon; God build; God build; build thy house very soon.

The other letters of the alphabet, "Blessed is he, great is he, etc.," are, to save time, combined into four groups, the rest goes on as above, "he'll build, etc." The air is very simple and thoroughly German.

The next piece begins, "One who knoweth? One I do know," and runs up to thirteen; the last verse shows the contents of the whole:

> Thirteen who knoweth? Thirteen I do know: thirteen are the qualities; twelve are the tribes; eleven are the stars (in Joseph's dream); ten are the words (commandments); nine are the moons of birth; eight are the days of circumcision; seven are the days of the week; six are the orders of the Mishna; five are the parts of the Law; four are the mothers; three are the fathers; two are the Tables of the Covenant; one is our God, who is in heaven and on the earth.

The last and best known of these poetic enlargements is "One Kid! One Kid!" written in Aramaic mixed with Hebrew, in the same progressive manner as the preceding and as "The House that Jack built." Its last and all embracing part runs thus:

> Then came the Holy and Blessed God, and killed the Angel of Death, who killed the butcher, who slaughtered the ox, who drank up the water, which quenched the fire, that burnt the stick, which beat the dog, that bit the cat, that ate the kid, which my father bought for two shillings, one kid! one kid!

The meaning is well-known. Our Father in Heaven bought the kid Israel with the blood of circumcision and the blood of the Passover. The Kid was swallowed by the cat, Egypt. Egypt was conquered by Babylon (the dog); both by the Medes and Persians (the stick); these by the fiery Alexander; Alexander's empire by Rome, which like water overspread the whole world; Rome as mistress of Palestine was supplanted by the ox, the Saracens. So far there is no dispute. It seems that the butcher stands for the crusaders; that the angel of death, who was to put an end to their cruelties, was only hoped for; and that the piece was written while the Latin Kingdom ruled at Jerusalem. It is objected that "One Kid" (*Had Gadyo*) is not found in service books older than the sixteenth century,[9] but it could easily have been handed down by oral tradition.   The Sefardim in Palestine recite a number of legends connected with the Haggada in Spanish to this day without publishing them in their service books.

The Jews of Yemen enrich their Haggada by an insertion at the beginning rather than at the end, i. e., in the Kiddush, with which the ceremony begins.   Poor and oppressed as they have been for the last 1200 years, they feel the joy of the great national holiday sufficiently to congratulate themselves in the following grandiose words inserted after "he has chosen us" in the regular form:

He was pleased with us and beautified us; separated us as a holy gift from every nation, made us inherit a precious land, sanctified his name in the world for the sake of the fathers who did his will, did mighty deeds for his own sake; his wonders are past finding out.   He called us the community of the saints, a precious vineyard, a pleasant plantation; he called them (us) his own property, took them from all the nations of the earth; for they are compared to the host of heaven, and set like the stars in the firmament; and they were the uppermost in the world, and honored above all tribes; the beaming of their faces is like the radiance of the sun, and the looks of their likeness like that of the ministering angels. Kings look to them and rise; princes bow low, on account of the Lord of Hosts who has chosen them.[10]

Here we have the pride of Israel in its divine mission carried to the verge of burlesque, if not beyond it.   But setting aside this extravaganza, which the religious teachers of Israel in other countries than Southern Arabia have wisely rejected, the prevailing tone running through the Jewish service book for the Sabbath and Festivals, and to a great extent through all our services, is one rather of exultation over our lot, that we are God's children, always at home and welcome in our Father's house, than of grief for our sufferings, deserved or undeserved, or of contrition for our sins.

I have, however, no reflections of my own to add. Let the reader draw his own conclusions. Following the custom of Jewish commentators and editors, I now close with the short epilogue:

Tam Ve-nishlam Shebah la-El Boré Olam.

COMPLETE AND DONE, PRAISE BE TO GOD, CREATOR OF THE WORLD.

NOTES

BOOK I

GENERAL AND HISTORICAL INTRODUCTION

CHAPTER I

DIVISIONS OF THE JEWISH BODY

(Pp. 11-18)

[1]Curious to say, this latter identification is approved, or at least spoken of as plausible, by such profound and earnest scholars as Lenormant and Chevallier, in their History of the East. The Spanish writers of the twelfth, thirteenth, and fourteenth centuries speak of those of the Northern ritual as Tzarfathim, i. e., French, France outside of Provence being then the chief seat of that ritual. The Jews of England were but a colony from France.

[2]Here are some proofs: (1) The vowel marks were made at Tiberias in Galilee, and agree better with the German than the Sefardic style; for in the former Kametz is always *o*, in the latter *a* or *o;* in the former the Sheva is always no vowel, in the latter either none or a light and short one; ב and ת, the letters which oftenest take the *Dagesh lene*, are to the Germans changed by it in sound, to the others not. (2) The guttural ע has been lost by the Germans, as according to Talmudic testimony it was lost by the Galileans. Late Phœnician inscriptions also show confusion between א and ע; that is, the heathens of Galilee had unlearnt the sound of the latter. (3) The German distinctions in ב and ת remind of the Aramaic dialect, the Syriac, spoken in the provinces bordering on Galilee; while there is nothing similar in Arabic, spoken in those bordering on Judea. (4) The Syriac also differs from South Aramaic dialects in the change between *a* and *o*, just as it would, if spelled with Hebrew letters and vowel points, differ between Germans and Sefardim. (5) In Phœnician, the Hebrew of Galilee, as we know through Greek and Latin, the sound of Kametz was mostly *o;* the letter name *Iod*, Greek ἰῶτα, Latin *iota*, is the Hebrew ׳; *Carthago*, Καρχηδών, the Hebrew *Kart-hadasha* (New-

(371)

town); Dido is דִּידָה; *ãwµús* is בכה. And the Holem was not a pure *o;* to the Romans it sounded *u;* e. g. *Suffetes* (the Consuls of Carthage) were שופטים ; *jubilare* comes from יובל, the ram's-horn. The Phœnician Shurek is rendered by Roman *y,* which recalls the sound of this vowel in eastern Europe. By the by, the better schools in Poland and Russia now teach the true sound of the צ, the short vowel value of the Sheva, and the correct word-accent. Maimonides (Hilchoth Tefilla, ch. 8, § 12) shows the exclusiveness of the Sefardim by disabling one who stammers, or "confounds א and ע " as a leader in public worship.

²The כרר of R. Amram was in modern times known only from fragments quoted in medieval works; in 1865 an edition was printed from the only MS. extant; but it is on its face thoroughly "corrupt." It contains passages belonging exclusively to the German Minhag, and many compositions by Spanish poets of the twelfth century. The book would yet have great historic value, if we could be sure that the transcribers have only added, and not omitted. For the German ritual the Mahzor Vitry, dated in 1208, is the highest authority. It does, however, contain some passages which at present belong not to the German, but only to the Sefardic Minhag. In 1892 it was published in print from two MSS. at London and Oxford. A ritual, dated London, 5047 (1287), of which many extracts are given in the *Jewish Quarterly Review* for October, 1891, is also instructive as to the old state of the German ritual. The Jews of Egypt, Palestine, and Arabia formerly had a ritual differing from the German and the Sefardic; but the authority of Maimonides during his stay in Egypt and the inflow of Spanish fugitives carried these countries (except Yemen) into the fold of the Sefardic ritual. In the nineteenth century a vast immigration from Poland, Russia, and Roumania has established synagogues of the German ritual in Palestine and Egypt.

³Pesahim, ch. 4, §§ 1-5; Megilla, ch. 2, § 2. The phrase, "all according to the custom of the country," is often met with.

⁴See an account given by Benjamin, of Tudela, quoted by Zunz, in his *Gottesdienstliche Vorträge.* Ed. 1, p. 439; ed. 2, p. 424.

⁵A peculiar difference between the Sefardic and German service books has arisen since the beginning of the nineteenth century by the labors of Wolf Heidenheim, who revised all those of the German Minhag, of all kinds, daily, Festival, and Fast, correcting the spelling in both letters and vowels, and occasionally the grammatical forms, so as to make the text conform as nearly as possible to the Hebrew of the Bible. The Sefardic books have never undergone such a revision; in fact, the greatest Hebrew scholar among the Sefardim

of the nineteenth century, S. D. Luzzatto, objected to Heidenheim's work as obscuring the history of the Prayer Book.

⁷The writer owes what he says in this work about Yemen to two pamphlets of Dr. H. Barnstein and Dr. W. H. Greenburg, published in 1896. As to pronunciation, the former quotes a book written by Jacob Saphir (Lyk, 1866, אבן ספיר) from his own knowledge. The Yemenites use an over-line set of vowel signs, which has long been called the Babylonian, but must, like our ordinary under-line vowel marks, have come from Galilee. For the Babylonians were Judeans, *sang pur*, reading Hebrew in Sefardic style, and could not contrive a notation in which the same mark is used for long *a* and short *o*, differing from those for short *a* and long *o;* and this is so in the over-line, just as in the under-line system.

⁸Mr. S. Schechter has written a sketch of the life-work of Ba'al Shem Tob, which has been published with other essays from his scholarly pen by the *Jewish Publication Society* (S. Schechter. *Studies in Judaism.* Philadelphia, 1896). In many towns of Southern Russia, the Jews opposed to Hasidism have also adopted the half-Sefardic liturgy of the Hasidim. One of these opponents (Misnagdim) being asked by the writer wherein they differed from the Hasidim, seeing they used the same ritual, answered: That they believed in the "Rebby"—the miracle-working spiritual head of a society of Hasidim—while he and his set did not.

CHAPTER II

HISTORIC BACKGROUND—LIFE-CENTER IN PALESTINE

(Pp. 19–32)

¹Ezra 3: 11; Jer. 33: 11 (with a slight variation).
²Neh. 8. Some critics hold that this chapter only duplicates a similar event told in Ezra 3; but if it does (which it is needless to assume), the later date—that in Nehemiah—should be preferred as the true one.
³Simeon (or Simon) the Just is well known to the Christian world; his ministrations as High Priest are glowingly described at the close of Ecclesiasticus (Ben Sira). Only a few hundred years after his death so little was known of the times between Ezra and him, that he was taken for a younger contemporary of the former. This error in chronology, making the time between the destruction of Jerusalem by Nebuchadrezzar and that by Titus only 490

years, instead of 658, appears first in T. B. Aboda Zara, 9a. The late guess at 120 as the number of the men (T. B. Megilla, 17b; see also T. J. on Berachoth, ch. 2, § 4) coupled with this statement, making them nearly contemporaries (see Bartenoro on Aboth, ch. 1, § 1), is worthless.

⁴T. B. Baba Bathra, 15a. Whenever and by whomsoever Canticles was written, the heading, "Song of Songs which is of Solomon," must have been by the Great Synod, or other Sages at Jerusalem. The heading has the Judaic אשר, while in the poem "which" is always expressed by the Galilaic ש.

⁵Aboth, ch. 1, § 2.

⁶Berachoth, ch. 1, § 1. "From what time on do they read the Shema in the evening? From the hour when the priests come in to eat their tribute (הרומה)." The answer means: From the first appearance of stars. Priests, becoming defiled, had, according to the law in Leviticus, to wait till "evening" before they could become clean, and thus qualified to eat their sacred food. Custom had established, that for this purpose evening meant the appearance of stars, about twenty-five minutes after sunset. So when the question as to the reading of the Shema was first discussed, it could be thus answered by referring to a rule already well-known.

⁷Ecclesiasticus, written soon after the death of Simeon the Just, speaks of his time as one of peace and splendor; of its own time, as beset by troubles and dangers.

⁸Aboth, ch. 1, carries the tradition down from Simeon to Antigonus of Socho, and leaving a gap, says that José ben Joëzer and José ben Johanan received it of *them* (i. e., some disciples of Antigonus). It names as the next couple Joshua ben Perahiah and Nittaï from Arbela (near Babylon); as the next, Judah ben Tabbaï and Simeon ben Shetah (who plays quite a part in history); as the next, Shemaïah and Abtalion (said to have been converts); the next are Hillel and Shammaï. The first named in each couple (זוג) is the Patriarch, literally Prince (נשיא), or President of the Sanhedrin; the other, the Father of the Court (אב בית דין) or Vice-President. Menahem is named as the first colleague of Hillel; he took a political office under King Herod, and made room for Shammaï (Hagiga, ch. 2, § 2). Maxims are ascribed to the bearers of the tradition in Aboth, ch. 1, § 1; little else is known of any of them before Hillel and Shammaï, except Simeon ben Shetah; and few names are found in the Mishna that certainly belong to older times. Tanna (תּנא) is the noun of agent in Aramaic, of a verb equivalent to Hebrew שנה, he did secondly, i. e., he taught *secondary* learning, he taught Mishna.

⁹Jadaïm, ch. 3, § 4. The House of Shammaï rejected Ecclesiastes (Eduïoth, ch. 5, § 3. "Ecclesiastes does not defile the hands"); the Hillelites counted it in the Canon.

¹⁰See Talmuds on Sanhedrin, ch. 10, § 1, for the dispute on the resurrection; on retaliation or damages in money, see T. B. Baba Kamma, 83b. See also the chaffing between Pharisee and Sadducee in Mishna, Jadaïm, ch. 4. As to refinements against capital punishments, see *inter alia*, Sanhedrin, ch. 8, §§ 1-4; as to stoning and burning, ib., ch. 6, § 3 and ch. 7, § 2. Dr. Jost, in his *Geschichte des Judenthums*, says that the Sadducees did not deny all traditions, as they took part with the people in public worship; but only those which run counter to the written letter. But this was a thing of necessity; cutting loose entirely from established usage is almost impossible. Dr. A. Geiger, in his *Urschrift*, seeks to trace the warring sects back to King David's reign, deriving the name of the Sadducees from his High Priest Zadok, and treats the two sects as but another form for the old parties of the hereditary priesthood and of the prophetic schools; but his view has not been generally received.

¹¹Horaïoth, ch. 4, § 8.

¹²Sanhedrin, ch. 2, § 4, says: The king commands in a voluntary war decreed by the Council of 71. The number was made up from Numbers 11: 24. As to the High Priest, see Joma, ch. 1, §§ 3-6.

¹³Matt. 15: 2. Berachoth, ch. 8, gives disputed points on washing for the meal; Jadaïm treats mainly of washing the hands. The salt custom is based on Lev. 2: 3. נוטל "he washes," as applied to the hands, is literally "he lifts." The hands are not dipped in water; it is poured on them.

¹⁴Benedictions at hand-washing, kindling the Sabbath, Festival, or Hanucca lights, reading the Book of Esther, reading the Hallel Psalms.

¹⁵Sicarii in Latin; hence סיקריקון (cmp. Gittin, ch. 5), many of them Gentiles. Jost, in *Geschichte des Judenthums*, pt. 2, p. 14, shows how after Herod's death Rome placed all power in the hands of its tool, the High Priest. It is said that forty years before the destruction the Sanhedrin left the Hewn-stone Hall; the Shechina (God's Presence) went into exile. The Gospels confirm this: there was no regular court, nor regular trial of Jesus; only a political discussion before the High Priest as to the expediency of denouncing him to the Romans. Aboth, ch. 2, § 8, indicates the interregnum after Hillel and Shammaï, by calling Johanan ben Zaccaï their successor in the traditions, though he opened his school only after the fall of Jerusalem.

[16]"Sota, ch. 7, § 5. where Agrippa is told, "Thou art our brother."

[17]Isa. 9: 6, 7; 11: 1-5; Micah 5: 2-4; Zech. 9: 9; Ps. 2; Hab. 2: 3. The great millennial predictions are Isa. 2: 2-4; Micah 4: 1-4.

[18]This point was made in a later age; see next chapter.

[19]E. g., Theudas, mentioned in Josephus and in the Acts.

[20]Much of Eduioth and Berachoth, ch. 8, states many points on which the schools divide; as to divorce, see Gittin, ch. 9, § 10; as to tithing cumin, Eduioth, ch. 5, § 3. Jesus takes ground on both points against Hillel. Hillel's school generally prevailed; see in Berachoth, ch. 1, § 3, the reproof to R. Tarfon for acting against it. Sometimes the Hillelites gave in to the better reason of the Shammaïtes, as in T. B. Berachoth, 53b: "If a man leaves the table forgetting to say grace, must he go back to the place of his meal to say it? Shammaï says yes, Hillel no. Would you, ask the Hillelites, send a man back to the top of a tower to say grace? Would he not, say the others, go up, if he had forgotten a jewel? Thereafter the school of Hillel taught like that of Shammaï." Shammaï's school was generally the stricter.

[21]T. B. Pesahim, 47. Other expressions of hatred are given on like authority.

[22]The treatise Demaï deals with this mistrust about tithing. In T. B. Berachoth, 47b, several Rabbis give their definitions of the Am ha-aretz: (1) He who does not eat profane food in cleanness (i. e., who does not, on Pharisaic principles, extend to his daily food the rules which Holy Writ lays down for sacrificial food, or the Teruma). (2) Who does not tithe rightly. (3) Who does not read the Shema evening and morning. (4) Who does not lay phylacteries. (5) Who has no fringes on his garment. (6) Who has no Mezuza (parchment copy of Deut. 6: 4-9, and 11: 13-21) on his door. (7) Who does not bring up his sons to the study of the Law. (8) R. Meïr says, even if one studies Bible and Mishna, he is an Am ha-aretz, unless he attends upon a disciple of the wise. In this passage it is also conceded that a Samaritan may be a companion (Haber). See above, Note 13.

[23]Ecclus., ch. 38. The sick man should pray, the physician should heal.

[24]בנה׳ is the Hebrew name.

[25]Mishna, Sanh., ch. 10, § 3. "The ten tribes will never return," says R. Akiba. He is said to have travelled to the upper Tigris that he might see the descendants of Shalmaneser's exiles for himself.

[26]Neither Roman nor Jewish sources give a clear and connected account of the rebellion, or series of rebellions. They began in

Trajan's time, the hard fighting was against Hadrian, and it is said that an Antoninus (Pius) gave the Jews permission to bury their dead.

²⁷T. B. Aboda Zara, 10*a*, seems to fix his time. He was intimate with an emperor going by the name Antonine, which must have been Elagabalus, as he speaks of Severus as his son; Severus was such by adoption.

²⁸The unnamed (סתם) Mishna is ascribed to R. Meir. A first Mishna and a Mishna of R. Akiba are mentioned together in Sanhedrin, ch. 3, § 4. The Patriarch is always quoted as "Rabbi" simply: "R. Judah" means an earlier sage, the son of Il'ai. The treatise Eduïoth (testimonies) looks like a first attempt at a collection of disputed points.

²⁹Many believe that "Rabbi" did not write his collection, but only made his scholars learn it by heart, but admit that two of these reduced it to writing within twenty-five years after his death. The close agreement between the Mishna embodied in the Jerusalem and that in the Babylonian Talmud makes one think that it was all written down under his direction. The six orders are: (1) זרעים (Seeds), that is field-corner, tithes, and other charges on agriculture, to which is prefixed treatise ברכות (Benedictions), the most important for our purpose. (2) מועד (Set time) about Sabbath, Feasts, and Fasts. (3) נשים, (Women), about marriage laws and vows. (4) נזיקין (Damages), or civil and criminal law; also two treatises of collected sayings, one of which, אבות (Fathers), is reprinted in the Prayer Book. (5) קדשים (Holy things), mainly, but not wholly, about sacrifice. (6) טהרות (Cleanness) about Levitical purity.

³⁰Mechilta on Exodus, Sifra on Leviticus, Sifri (or Sifre) on Numbers and Deuteronomy; additions to any one treatise are known as Tosifta.

³¹Most of the fifth and sixth orders; also about King and High Priest, Sanhedrin, chs. 2 and 3; the latter's ministrations on Atonement Day, nearly all through Joma.

³²Sanhedrin, ch. 10, § 1.

³³The Talmud seldom doubts the authenticity of the Mishna, but Baraïtha is often quoted in two or three conflicting forms. It tells many fairy tales about R. Akiba, R. Simeon ben Johai, and other early sages, foreign to the sober character of these men, and naturally attributes to them late superstitions.

³⁴Baba Metzia, ch. 4, § 2; Baraïtha in T. B. on same, 58*b*; Aboth, ch. 3, § 11.

²⁴ Civil law forms as in Kethuboth, ch. 4, §§ 8, 10, and popular saws, as Aboth, ch. 1, § 13, are given in pure Aramaic.

²⁵Hor. Sat. L. I, Sat. 9, v. 63 (*trigcsima Sabbata*).

²⁷Jos. Ant. Bk. 20, ch. 2. Monobazes, King of Adiabene, and his mother Helen are mentioned, Joma, ch. 3, § 10. The churches addressed by John in Revelations and by Paul in his Epistles were all made up in part of Jews, or "converts of the gate," i. e., Gentiles acknowledging the truths of Scripture, but not submitting to the yoke of the Law.

²⁸ מינים may be good Hebrew for kinds or species, hence sects; מי, more probably a contemptuous shortening of מאמין believer; or may come from the root כאן, to refuse, and mean recusants.

²⁹Berachoth, ch. 9, § 5. "Since the Minim made mischief, saying there is only one world," could not apply to Christians.

CHAPTER III

HISTORIC BACKGROUND—CENTER NO LONGER IN PALESTINE

(Pp. 33-43)

¹For R. Simlaï's discourse on the 613 precepts, see T. B. Maccoth, 23, 24. Jost, in his *Geschichte des Judcnthums*, thinks that the enumeration must be older; but as there is great latitude in the way of counting, this is by no means certain. The two masters of legend are important, as Palestine hereafter was less the land of dry legal discussion, than of free exegesis, parable, and legend. The two last Geonim, Sherira in the tenth century and Hai in the eleventh, are the main chronologers of this period, the former giving the dates of the Palestinian and Babylonian sages by the Era of Seleucus.

²E. g., T. B. Berachoth, 50a, we find the Resh Gelutha well versed in the forms of after-dinner grace.

³The "two colleges" (כהיבתא) always claimed to set the standard for the liturgy; see R. Amram *passim* in his Seder, and his quotations of his predecessor, the Gaon Natronaï.

⁴A book of the twelfth century, called Kerithoth, followed by later historians, draws the chain of tradition in East and West from the two Talmuds, to the end of כברא (opinion).

⁵T. B. Sanhedrin, 99b; but the Palestinian Rabbis here quoted show the same forgetfulness or lack of learning. The ignorance of Rab and Samuel, both men of Western education—T. B. Megilla, 11a—about the location of הרו and כוש and of Gaza and Thap-

sacus, is assumed for the sake of an argument. The real ignorance in Persian history, shown in Aboda Zara, 9a, which puts the Temple under Persian dominion for only thirty-two years, the Rabbis shared with their Neo-Persian masters, who mixed up the first Darab (Darius) with the last, who was conquered by Alexander. The notions about medicine, which Abbaye, a Chief Rabbi of the fifth Babylonian generation, holds and teaches, are very crude; and the philology of the Babylonians is wild and vile; but hardly worse than that of Plato in his Kratylos, or, considering the times, than that of Noah Webster in the dictionary as he wrote it. Astrology is gotten rid of by the maxim אין מזל לישראל, "The constellations have no power over Israel." T. B. Shabbath, 156b.

⁶T. B. Berachoth, 58b, and T. J. on Samuel, ch. 9, § 3. He made this claim, because the Patriarch at Tiberias pretended to have some secret knowledge of astronomy, enabling him alone to regulate the calendar; though he admitted that the orbit of comets was beyond his powers. His wisest saying is: All the prophets have prophesied only as far as the Messianic age; but the future world "no eye has seen, O God, but thine" (Isa. 64: 4); i. e., the world beyond the grave transcends human conception (T. B. Berachoth, 34b).

⁷T. B. Sanhedrin, 98b, 99a.

⁸T. B. Baba Metzia, 59a, and T. B. Pesahim, 87; see also T. B. Jebamoth, 62 and 63, as to the forlorn condition of the wifeless man.

⁹T. B. Sanhedrin, 28a, where a criminal was sentenced to have his eyes put out, and ib., 25a, where we are told that a Cohen's daughter was burnt for adultery.

¹⁰T. B. Sanhedrin, 99, 100a. What is the use of the Rabbis? They cannot forbid pigeons, nor permit us to eat ravens.

¹¹The Calla is best known from the prayer יקום פורקן, in which the chiefs of the assembly are blessed. Most notices about it come in post-Talmudic times. In Succa, 26a, we read of a large crowd on the banks of the Sura River, to attend the discourse on the Sabbath of the Feast itself.

¹²T. B. Pesahim, 56.

¹³Both Biblical Aramaic and that of the Bab. T. are nearer than Syriac to the Hebrew conjugations; they contain many Assyro-Babylonian elements, both in roots and flexions, do not suppress letters as freely as Syriac, etc. and, of course, they lack Greek, and contain Persian elements.

¹⁴Jost, in *Geschichte des Judenthums*, declares that everything as to time, place, and names of this branch of the Masora (textual tradi-

tion) is unknown. He points out that the "Treatise of Scribes" is still silent on vowels; but no one knows when that book was written. Graetz and more modern writers know no more. The discovery of the over-line vowelling system has contributed nothing to solve the mystery. The identity of one vowel name with the Syriac (Patah and Pethokho) and the aspiration or lack of aspiration in בג״ד כפ״ת in analogy to the קוּשָׁא׳ וְרוּכָא׳ in Syriac, are the only solid starting points, and these only to the place of the invention, not to the time. The history of the accents, in a later century, is as obscure as that of the vowels.

[14]These treatises are generally printed in editions of the Talmud at the end of the fourth Order. For most of what follows in this chapter we refer to the ordinary histories of the Jews, especially that of Graetz (*History of the Jews.* H. Graetz. 6 vols. Am. Ed. Jewish Publication Society of America. Philadelphia, 1898). The codes and literary works named prove themselves.

[15]Some modern prayer books of the German ritual, e. g., that of the "Rabbi of Lissa," put over every benediction the number of words contained, excluding everything which was not numbered in the eleventh or twelfth century; e. g., in the *Geulla* of the morning service the line "Rock of Israel, arise, etc." Other books simply put it in brackets. The motive may have been superstitious, the benedictions being looked on rather as charms and enchantments than as an outpouring of the soul; but the result was good. In this way Cabbalistic interpolations were kept out of the more important parts of the service.

[17]See article on *Rosh* in the Encyclopædia Britannica.

CHAPTER IV

MIDRASH AND AGGADTA

(Pp. 44-49)

[1]Beside the works which bear this title, among which that upon Genesis, ch. 1-44, is the oldest, the Targum, or Aramaic paraphrase, ascribed to Jonathan ben Uzziel, upon the books of the Prophets, and the very late Pseudo-Jonathan on the Pentateuch, deserve mention, and the fragmentary Targum of Jerusalem is a treasure house of "Midrash."

[2]The derivation of this word from the verb הגיד, to tell, has been lately denied, but it seems is clearly right. The learned W. Bacher, in the *Jewish Quarterly Review* for April, 1892, shows that this verb

in the Mishna is predicated of a clause in Scripture which gives or "tells" something not obvious at first sight. Hence the noun הגרה.

[3]The last three pages of the T. B. on treatise Berachoth are made up of such interpretations. Sometimes two on the same verse are frankly connected by the words דבר אחר (another idea), words so common in the Midrash as to be abbreviated ד"א.

[4]Jadaïm, ch. 3. § 4.

[5]The personification of the heavenly bodies in the benediction יוצר אור is not Aggadta; for the Psalms make Sun, Moon, and Stars, and the Firmament, too, praise God (Ps. 19 and 148).

[6]T. B. Rosh Hashana, 8a and 8b.

[7]Rosh Hashana, ch. 1, § 2. On this day all creatures pass before God כבני כרון, like "sons of sheep (?);" the word occurs nowhere else. The phrase is copied into the best known of all the "poetries" for the Festivals. The Mishna proceeds: "and on the Feast (Tabernacles) the world is judged as to rain."

[8]One bullock is sacrificed on this day, seventy bullocks are offered on the seven preceding days; the latter represent the seventy nations, the former Israel, whose time will come on that day; see T. B. Succa, 55b. In T. B. Rosh Hashana, 11a, opinions are divided, whether the final redemption will take place in Nisan or in Tishri. The latter idea was the more popular, as is shown by the song in the service for the Joy of the Law: "The Scion will come on the Joy of the Law," i. e., the double of this eighth day.

[9]The passage in the Day of Atonement service about the "ten martyrs," עשרה הרוגי כלכות, or a dirge in the Sefardic service for the Ninth of Ab on the same subject, is probably the oldest version of the story; for the death of four of the ten is not mentioned in the Talmud.

[10]Bereshith Rabba, ch. 38.

[11]T. B. Berachoth, 6a.

[12]T. B. Menahoth, 35b.

[13]From the Hymn of Glory by Samuel ben Kalonymos, written about 1200.

[14]T. J. on Pesahim, ch. 10, § 1. The other reasons are: Pharaoh's cups are mentioned four times in the account of the cup-bearer's dream; the four kingdoms, i. e., the Babylonian, Medo-Persian, Babylonian, Roman; four times in the Bible the enemies of Israel are threatened with an evil cup; four times a cup of joy or salvation is mentioned.

[15]Will be shown in the chapter on the Passover Night Service.

[16]כניד,דרשן: these are the "nouns of agent" of the verbs to which כדרש and הגרה are the nouns of action. Many a Maggid

has earned a reputation all over Poland and Hungary by his discourses. Those of the "Dubnoer Maggid" are in print, and much
sought after by old-style preachers who cannot rely on their own
resources.

¹¹ אפּיקורוס, as remarked in the preceding chapter, means an
infidel; hence the later Jews have formed the noun אפּיקורסות
to mean apostasy or unbelief.

¹²Jehuda Hallevi, in the Cuzari, pt. 3, § 73, puts the Aggadta in its
true light, of an expression of truths felt by the writers in bold
and too graphic language. The undisguised contradictions, with
none to reconcile opposite views, or to judge between them, were
well known to the Talmudic student; but were not so well known
to our mothers or grandmothers, who on every Sabbath used to
read the week's lesson in "the Deitsch Chumesh," a paraphrase in
jargon, full of the most grotesque specimens of Aggadta. This
work, bearing also the high-sounding Hebrew name צאינה וראינה
(Go ye out and see!) must be mentioned here, because its perusal
has for nearly two hundred years supplied with many thousands of
women in Germany and in Eastern Europe the place of the
preacher.

¹³The word is כביכול. An example of how the Talmud took the
bold narrative of Scripture, is found T. B. Rosh Hashana, 17b,
concerning Ex. 34: 5, etc. Here God is represented as if he was
a leader in prayer in his robes coming down on Mt. Sinai to teach
Moses how to recite the thirteen qualities of mercy: "If the Tora
had not said so, we would not have dared it." The thirteen qualities play a great part in the Atonement and Fast Day Service, and
the leader has to chant them. Or see T. B. Megilla, 21a, on
Deut. 5: 28, where God says to Moses, "and thou stand with me
here," as if it were possible to think that God stands; and T. B.
Baba Bathra, 17a, on God's remark to Satan in the first chapter of
Job: "Thou hast persuaded me, etc."

CHAPTER V

SECRET LORE, OR CABBALA

(Pp. 50-56)

¹ סבה ראשונה, a word found in philosophic as well as in mystic
works.

²The writer heard this thought about the choice of the word ירה
in Job 38: 6, from his father צל.

[1] יְלִיל ראשון. Those who personify wisdom find their authority in Prov. 8: 21, etc.

[2] 'So in the phrase, ליחדא קוב׳ה ושכינתיה. The word שכינה is never thus personified, either in the Mishna or in the old Prayer Book.

[3] 'T. B. Sanhedrin, 38b. The Greek μετάθρονος, "behind the throne," is a plausible explanation. The late Dr. Goldammer, of Cincinnati, tried to derive the word from a Coptic compound, *met-at-ran*, "endlessness;" and there are many other guesses; such as μετατύραννος and Metator.

[4] 'Rashi, following older comments, on Gen. 18: 2, אין מלאך אחד עושה שתי שליחות (one angel never goes on two missions). For namelessness, see Gen. 32: 29; Jud. 13: 6.

[5] 'But only Michael, the special protector of Israel, and Gabriel are named. Many more names appear in the Talmud; none in the Mishna. Michael, Gabriel, and five others are in the later Cabbala, coupled with the seven days of the week and the seven planets.

[6] 'Hagiga, ch. 2, § 1: "They should not discourse on the work of creation to two (at a time); nor on the chariot to even one, unless he is well prepared in wisdom." Maimonides *ad locum* believes that by כיעשה כרכבה proof of the existence of God, his attributes, the nature of the angels, the soul, and future life are meant. Bartenoro, it seems more correctly, says a learning was meant which would enable the adept to "make use of the crown," i. e., work miracles by the mention of divine names (שכות).

[7] 'T. B. Hagiga, 14b. The context shows that mystic lore is meant by the פרדס , not Greek philosophy, as some moderns maintain.

[8] Treatise Megilla, last section.

[9] T. B., 60b, commenting on Ps. 56: 10.

[10] Taken from 1 Chron. 29: 11 ("Thine, O Lord, is the greatness, etc."). They are: 1. חסד (נדולה); 2. גבורה. 3. תפארת; 4. נצח; 5. הוד. 6. יסוד (אהבה); 7. מלכות.

[11] (1) (כתר)חכמה; 2. בינה; 3. דעה (כתר). See Prov. 3: 19, 20. In the later Cabbala, the chain of Sephiroth depends from the אין כוף, or Endless.

[12] The Saxon poem by Cædmon, written in the ninth century, proves this.

[13] Zunz puts the date of the book at about 700 C. E., Laz. Gold-schmidt, in the days of the Maccabees. Saadia inferred from the double pronunciation assigned to the letters כג׳ר כפרת , that the book was written in Galilee; and this consideration induces the

writer to assign the age of R. Akiba to it, Galilee having then become the center of Jewish life.

¹⁵Sepher Jetzira, ch. 1, § 5. The Sephiroth here bear the predicate בלימה, empty space, nothing, from Job 26: 7.

¹⁶(1) נפש (self); (2) רוח (breath, spirit); (3) חיה (the living principle); (4) נשכה (soul); (5) חידה'(the only one).

¹⁸Forty-nine stages of progress (דרגין) upward, but the fiftieth has not been reached; hence the (50) is missing in the alphabet of Psalm 145. The seventy-two names are formed from Ex. 14: 19, 20, 21.

¹⁹The הכלות are repeatedly quoted in Abudraham, where their influence can be traced, but mainly in compositions not now in use.

²⁰Thus, לון is used where the Targum has להון, and the Talmud Babli has להו. But the attempt to write in the dialect of Galilee is not fully carried out; often (e. g., in opening upon Ex. 3: 1) R. Simeon speaks in the Hebrew dialect of the Mishna. Occasionally a word like אשנוגא, plain Spanish for synagogue, tells the tale. Edom and Ishmael are brought forward as great aggregates in commenting on the verse in Deuteronomy, "ye are the fewest among the nations." The Zohar is divided into weekly portions, though Simeon ben Johaï as a Palestinian only knew the three-years cycle. The sages of the Mishna counted either by the Era of Seleucus or by the years of the Emperor; Jadaïm, ch. 4, *sub fine;* Gittin, ch. 8, § 5, where an era from the building and one from the destruction of the Temple are also named as possible, but no Anno Mundi. And see for documentary proof of the fraud committed by R. Moses de Leon, Dr. A. Neubauer's articles in the *Jewish Quarterly Review*, April and July, 1892.

²¹It is יתיק יומין and אבא ואבא. The כטרוניהא in comments on Ex. 14 comes dangerously near the Virgin Mary. The frequent mention of, and great stress laid on faith (כהימנותא) also smack of Christianity. In Comments on Gen. 17, we find "the anointed king (כלכא כש'יהא), who is called by God's name!"

²²Such are the מדרש נעלם and the כהיכנא רי;א (The Secret Research and The Faithful Shepherd), which serve as a supplement to the Zohar, and are published with it; also the הקונ' בראשיה (Expositions of "In the Beginning"), seventy fantastic comments on the first word of the Bible.

²³The prayer בריך שכיה will be given in full in its proper place.

²⁴S. Schechter's sketch of the life and work of R. Israel "Besht," is the first in a volume of essays and reviews by him, issued by the Jewish Publication Society (S. Schechter. *Studies in Judaism*. Philadelphia, 1896).

²⁵The use made by Tholuck and Jewish apostates in Germany to lure men of Cabbalistic tendency over to Christianity has served to expose the poison lurking in the mystic lore.

²⁶Some reference to these innovations will be made hereafter. Isaac Luria gave the *Halacha* a spiritual content. Lev. 11: 33, provides that an earthen vessel, when defiled, must be broken to pieces; these are then clean, and so is a new vessel made of them. The Talmud (T. B. Baba Metzia, 59b) discusses the "oven of Achnai," easily broken into separate tiles; when these are joined again by mortar, there is a clean oven. But there remains the question, is such new oven "capable of uncleanness." R. Eliezer says yes, the others, no. The Talmud tells how R. Eliezer worked miracles to sustain his position; but the others told him coolly that miracles prove nothing, that only the majority can interpret the Law in disputed cases. The story is well known, and the sentiment of the majority highly approved without regard to the question involved. But Luria takes up the question: the earthen vessel is man; he sins and becomes unclean; he is broken into pieces by death, and thus cleansed; the fragments are put together at the resurrection. Is the new man capable of sinning? Luria says no, like the majority which holds that the reconstructed oven is not יקבל טומאה.

²⁷Moed Katan, ch. 3, § 9. T. B. Rosh Hashana, 19a, speaks of the fast of the seventh month (צום גדליה) as "words of Cabbala," because it was established by Jeremiah, and is mentioned by the later Prophets. So also Soferim, ch. 18, § 13. Some old prayers quote verses of the Prophets as "Cabbala."

CHAPTER VI

THE CALENDAR

(Pp. 57-63)

¹Rosh Hashana, chs. 1, 2; esp. ch. 2, § 9. The principle that the day proclaimed by the ruling authority is the true Feast is drawn from Lev. 23: 4: "These are the set times of the Lord, etc., which ye shall proclaim, etc."

²Hilchoth Kiddush Hahodesh, chs. 6, 7, 8, 9. The length of the "mean" month can be learned by a glance at two successive times of Molad in a Jewish almanac. That for Tishri 5658 is September 25, 1897, at 7 h. P.M. 50 m. 8 pts. (i. e., 50 m. 26 ⅔ s). It is easy hence to get that of any other month of earlier or later date, by multiply-

25

ing 29 d. 12 h. 793 pts. by the number of intervening months, and adding the result to or subtracting it from the time named.

³The mean length of the tropical year is now thought to be 365 d. 5 h. 48 m. 46½ s., or of 19 years, 6939 d. 14 h. 26 m. 43½ s. The Persians had a solar cycle of 33 years, including 8 leap years, which is much nearer correctness; but a lunar cycle would have to be much longer to agree better than the Metonic with the true solar year. While the Mishna is full of rules for fixing the new moon, where the question of only one day could be involved, it is silent as to how the Sanhedrin determined upon the necessity of a thirteenth month. It was long an open secret. There is a story (T. B. Sanhedrin, 18a) that a month was once intercalated upon the talk of three cowherds on crops and weather, but it is said there that the sages used this testimony only to confirm their calculation. The rule about the equinox (הקופה) is, however, spoken of among the earlier Rabbis: T. B. Rosh Hashana, 21a. And ib. 25a the mean length of the synodical month is said to have been known to Gamaliel the Elder in the days of the Temple (29½ days ⅔ hours 73 pts.); and it was used to check the testimony of witnesses. The distinction between a "birth," or astronomic new moon, before and one after noontide is noticed ib. 20b.

⁴Rosh Hashana, ch. 1, § 1. There are four kinds of New Year.

⁵Thus New Year 5658 was Monday, September 27, 1897. Before the fixed calendar, while the new moon was proclaimed upon sight, there could be no postponement; hence Purim might be on any day of the week (Megilla, ch. 1, § 1), and the Ninth of Ab happened on a Friday (T. B. Erubin, 41a).

⁶New moon played in Bible times a great part; see I Sam. 20: 24; 2 Kings 4: 23; Isa. 1: 14. The double new moon days are nowhere distinctly mentioned in the Talmud. On the contrary, in the Temple the additional offering for the new moon could not be prepared until the moon had been proclaimed. Rosh Hashana, ch. 1, §4.

⁷The Fasts are enumerated and explained T. B. Rosh Hashana, 18b.

⁸T. B., on Betza, ch. 2, § 1, is full of the distinction between the two days of New Year, which are likened to "one long day," and the "two holidays of exile" in the other Feasts.

⁹See Note 20 to preceding chapter as to eras and modes of dating in earlier use.

¹⁰Dr. H. Barnstein's pamphlet already cited. The writer has seen a Yemen tombstone with the שנת שטרות at the British Museum.

CHAPTER VII

THE SYNAGOGUE AND ITS FUNCTIONARIES

(Pp. 64–71)

[1] The Code of R. Joseph Karo (see Orah Hayim, §§150-155) does not expressly require the placing of the platform in the middle. The custom on certain days of carrying the scrolls around it seems to presuppose such a situation. Maimonides (Hilchoth Tefilla, ch. 9, § 1) speaks of the leader in the services as standing in the middle of the people, all of whom sit. This is according to the Sefardic custom by which the services as well as the lessons are read from the platform.

[2] See the chapters on the Pentateuch Lessons.

[3] See the chapters on Prayer, or Amida. The Sefardim justify their custom of reading the prayers from the reading desk by calling it *Teba*.

[4] Jadaïm, ch. 4, § 5; only books thus written are holy. The Assyrian (אשורי) or square letter is that now in use; the Hebrew (עברי) character, much like the Samaritan, Phœnician, and oldest Greek, is found on Jewish coins and old inscriptions, while the other was as yet used only for sacred writings. The "Assyrian" forms were worked out to the smallest detail; the "tittle of a jot," spoken of in the Gospel of Matthew, is a slight down stroke on the left side of the ל, neglected in printed type, but carefully made in the Scrolls. The opinion of some of the old Sages that the Assyrian letter was as old as Moses, that it was then disused, but was restored by Ezra, is untenable. The "Hebrew" is clearly the oldest form. See the discussion, T. B. Sanhedrin, 21a; T. J., on Megilla, ch. 1, § 5.

[5] See in Megilla, ch. 4, § 3, distinct words for the responsive reading, and for "going down before the Ark." Cmp. Note 1 above, as to Sefardic custom.

[6] The separate placing of the women dates back to the עזרת הנשים (gallery of women) in the Temple Yard; its dimensions are stated, Middoth, ch. 2, § 5.

[7] T. J., on Megilla, ch. 3, § 1. See Bk. IV, ch. I.

[8] They also say prayers in the House of Study. The Talmud deems it a more sacred place than the Synagogue itself. T. B. Berachoth, 3a; Pēa, ch. 1, § 1, and see the decided position taken in Hilchoth Tefilla, ch. 11, § 14.

[9] Megilla, ch. 4, § 3, and T. B. thereon. See also T. B. Berachoth,

21b. The "Treatise of Scribes" (Soferim, ch. 10, § 7) speaks of a custom, which at its date prevailed in Palestine, of holding services with only seven men present.

[10]The analogy of two men and a small boy beginning grace after meal responsively is found, T. B. Berachoth, 48a. Orah Hayim, § 54 and § 4, says the best casuists (פוסקים) are opposed, but R. Moses Isserles thinks it might be done in an emergency. Of course, it is always an emergency. The first discussion of the nine men and one child is found in T. J., on Berachoth, ch. 7, § 2.

[11]Three, or by another opinion, five ordained sages (Sanhedrin, ch. 1, § 3) were needed to ordain by laying on hands. An ordained elder, when solving a religious scruple, took the sin upon himself alone; but only when he interpreted the law contrary to the Halacha. Where he denies or falsifies the plain written law (as where he says there is no Sabbath, or five instead of four paragraphs go into the phylacteries), he is not punishable for the false decision (Horaioth, ch. 1, §§ 3, 4), for every Israelite is supposed to know the plain letter of the written law, and has no business to listen to its denial by any Rabbi or Sanhedrin. Ordination was valid only in the Holy Land. Its substitute, the written certificate, known as Hattarath Horaa, is rather modern.

[12]Maimonides, Hilchoth Tefilla, ch. 8, § 11, insists that the "Messenger of the congregation" should be the foremost in "learning and works," but adds he should have a pleasant voice.

[13]Orah Hayim, § 55, sub. 12; but "sinners" may be counted; even it seems those who openly (בפרהסיא) profane the Sabbath; though the Talmud says of these, that their wine is deemed that of idolatrous drink offering, and their meat the same as pork.

[14]The חזן appears to have been one of the learned class, but of a lower degree than the Scribes, and these were below the Sages; see Sota, ch. 9, app. to last section.

[15]T. B. Megilla, 22a: "One who does it without pay." Orah Hayim, § 53, sub. 22, prefers a paid leader to an amateur.

[16]Soferim, ch. 14, § 14. This usage runs back to Nehemiah 8. The *Gabbai* is still Treasurer or Financial Secretary in most old-fashioned congregations.

BOOK II

THE DEVOTIONS OF THE SYNAGOGUE

CHAPTER I

OUTLINE OF THE LITURGY

(Pp. 75-81)

¹The treatise Berachoth of the Mishna speaks throughout of the devotions as of a daily duty; of public worship as of a privilege to be prized when it can be had (because public prayer is always heard and answered. T. B. on same, 6a). Only as to the "additional," or Musaf prayer, the opinion is expressed by some, that it need be spoken only עיר בחבר, "in town society," i. e., where people meet for public worship. Ibid., ch. 4, § 7.

²The standards, old and new, know no other name than הפלה. The word *Amida* seems to be drawn from a stray remark, T. B. Berachoth, 26b: "Amida (standing) means prayer."

³Berachoth, ch. 1, § 5; see the chapter on the service for the Passover night. As to Rabbi, see T. B. Berachoth, 13b, where later teachers assent to the position that the first verse satisfies the Law.

⁴Berachoth, ch. 4, § 3: "Why does it say, when thou liest down, when thou risest; it means when men generally lie down, or generally rise." Ibid., ch. 4, § 1, gives the limits for the evening reading, and here Rabban Gamaliel remarks, that the Shema may really be read till the morning dawns, and that midnight was only named as a precaution to keep man from sin; § 2 gives the limits for the morning: "When you can distinguish between the blue and white threads, till 9 A. M. ('three hours'); for at that time princes get up." The ancients had sun dials, which would show 9 A.M. at the same figure the year around; but the accepted interpretation of "three hours" is the first quarter of the day, which on a long summer day is earlier, on a winter day, later than 9 A.M.

⁵If one "reads" after 9 A.M., he "loses nothing;" ib., § 2, which T. B. Berachoth, 10b, explains as in text. And at the Synagogue the evening service may be read within 1¼ hours before night-fall. The exception of the Saturday night service is natural; it is unlawful to shorten the Sabbath.

⁶"On the Sabbath it is made up of seven benedictions; on workdays, of nineteen, formerly eighteen.

⁷Jer. T., on Berachoth, ch. 4, § 1, relying on Deut. 11: 13, followed by Maimonides and later codifiers.

⁸Abudraham, in the chapter on work-day morning service, T. B. Megilla, 17b, 18a. A very widely known Midrash, T. B. Berachoth, 6b, ascribes the morning Prayer to Abraham, the afternoon Prayer to Isaac, the night Prayer to Jacob.

⁹See Dan. 6: 10, where Daniel braves the decree of Darius, which threatens death to him who prays. In T. B. Berachoth, 26a and 26b, it is held that one who by accident or forgetfulness has missed one Prayer should recite the next one twice.

¹⁰In T. B., ib., 27b, we read of a violent dispute between R. Gamaliel and R. Joshua, in the second century, over the question: Is the evening Prayer obligatory or optional? The Babylonian teachers of the fourth century are not yet agreed who was in the right. Bartenoro, in commenting on ch. 4, § 1, of the Mishna concludes, that in the dispute those holding it to be optional were right, but that later generations have assumed the evening Prayer as a duty.

¹¹R. Gamaliel and his contemporaries discuss this about the year 100 at Jabneh; see T. B. Rosh Hashana, 34b, 35a, the usage being then fully established.

¹²The name הכוכפין תפלה is used in the treatise Berachoth; in Rosh Hashana, the person who leads in the morning Prayer is simply called "the first," he who leads in Musaf, "the second."

¹³Abraham and Moses always "rose early" to fulfill a divine command; hence the rule. In one passage, T. B. Berachoth, 28b, it is suggested that nothing should be eaten before Musaf, but this view has not prevailed.

¹⁴Taanith, ch. 4, § 1.

¹⁵T. B. Berachoth, 30b.

¹⁶Ib., 4b. The Psalm tells of God's care for his creatures ("Thou openest thy hand and satisfiest the desire of all that live"), and is moreover alphabetic.

¹⁷Ib., same page.

¹⁸Abudraham, pp. 81 and 83 of the Warsaw edition.

¹⁹For the distinction between כינכרות and fasts for rain, see Taanith, ch. 4, § 1. A volume of Selihoth was printed in Jerusalem A. M. 5656 (1895-6) containing among others those for fasts on account of drought, which indicates that in Palestine these fasts must have been kept within living memory.

CHAPTER II

SOURCE AND STYLE

(Pp. 82-88)

[1]Exceptions are found in the prayer on going to bed and a few other passages which are never read aloud.

[2]The "Omnipresent" has been suggested, and will do by way of translation, but it is not the true meaning. Another idea is that הכקום, meaning a consecrated place, was transferred to the Divinity worshipped in that place.

[3]באסם אללה אלרחכן אלרחים, "In the name of God, the merciful, the loving!" T. B. Berachoth, 40a, רחכנא is expressly recognized as a name of God, fulfilling the need of a benediction for such a name.

[4]Joma, ch. 4, § 2; Sota, ch. 7, § 6; T. B., ib., 39a. It is intimated here that after Simeon the Just died, the priests no longer blessed "with the Name" in the country; the High Priest used it ten times on the great Fast. Sanhedrin, ch. 10, § 1, denounces the "thinking" of the Name.

[5]Berachoth, ch. 9, § 4.

[6]T. B. Berachoth, 40b, 46a, 49a; T. B. Pesahim, 104.

[7]Great numbers of these short blessings are found in the Mishna treatise Berachoth, ch. 9, and more in the Talmud upon that chapter.

[8]T. B. Berachoth, 33a.

[9]One will be found in the evening service; one in the earliest part of the morning service.

[10]Generally a petition that the performance of some ceremonial duty may have its full effect.

[11]Several prayers for the Day of Atonement are thus indicated, T. B. Joma, 87b. The composition now known as נשכה, or part of it, is spoken of in Pesahim, ch. 10, § 7, as ברכת השיר (Benediction of the Song), and T. B. Berachoth, 59b, it is denoted by words now in the middle, which then may have been at its beginning.

[12]Will be given hereafter among the benedictions at rising.

CHAPTER III

THE SHEMA IN THE EVENING

(Pp. 89–94)

[1]Berachoth, ch. 1, § 4.

[2]Abudraham protests against these words as out of place at the close of the benediction; they are, however, found in the Seder R. Amram, as printed.

[3]Joma, ch. 3, § 8, and ch. 4, § 1, after hearing the Name. It was inserted after "Hear, O Israel," according to T. B. Pesahim, 56a, in honor of the patriarch Jacob.

[4]We are told, T. B. Berachoth, 14b, that in Talmudic times many in the West (Palestine) said only the first and last verses of this section in the evening; but, for over 1,400 years, all who read the Shema have recited the whole third section in the evening as well as in the morning.

[5]To run the last words, "The Lord your God," together with "True" in the benediction is an old custom, attested by the Talmud (ibid., 14b), and resting on none but devotional grounds. But that the leader should finish the section, and then give out the three words, is a late invention of the Cabbalists, or at least of those believing in the power of numbers. The three sections, with the second line (Blessed be, etc.) added, contain 245 words; three are added to make 248, the number of bones in the human body or of the affirmative commands in the Pentateuch. Hence, for private worship, the three words אל מלך נאמן (God, faithful King) are placed before the first verse to make up the desired number. Abudraham reproves the use of these words on two grounds: first, we must not say anything that interrupts the reading of the Shema; secondly, a name of God cannot be used simply to fill out a number of words.

[6]נפרץ(requires payment), נסים (wonders), חרות(liberty)—all from Hebrew roots.

[7]T. B. Berachoth, 14b, and see notes to next chapter.

[8]T. B. Berachoth, 4b, gives the opening word השכיבנו ، (Let us lie down). The distinction made in the close of the benediction between work-days and Sabbath is mentioned in Seder R. Amram ad locum as not fully established; but the Gaon decides for the special wording on the Sabbath.

CHAPTER IV

THE SHEMA IN THE MORNING

(Pp. 95-104)

'Zunz, in his *Gottesdienstliche Vorträge*, working on suggestions of Rapoport of Prague, is the authority for the proposition that these forty-five words are the nucleus of the benediction.

²Succa, ch. 5, § 4.

³The frequent use of the name Epikuros in the Mishna to designate an infidel proves that the Jewish Sages were well aware of another danger to Judaism besides idol worship. Josephus tries to identify the Sadducees with the Epicurean school.

⁴T. J. on Berachoth, ch. 5, § 4.

⁵A visible effort to keep apart the days of the Messiah and the future world; see the great maxim of Samuel, T. B. Berachoth, 34*b*.

⁶The language of this is drawn in great part from T. B. Hagiga, 13*a*. In the later poetry of Eleazar Kalir, the "Chariot" and the Holy Beasts are much more fully described upon the same authority.

⁷R. Moses Isserles speaks of this piece (Orah Hayim, § 282) as one of the hymns (*Zemiroth*) of Sabbath, which the leader cannot be allowed to omit. It has on late and unreliable authority been ascribed to the Gaon R. Natronaï (ninth century). Abudraham and the Mahzor Vitry give all the insertions for Sabbath as undisputed.

⁸The opening words אהבה רבה are mentioned in T. B. Berachoth, 11*b*, where, however, the majority prefer אהבת עולם, which we now say in the evening; it is indicated by Jer. 31: 3. The Talmud, in speaking of the initial words, probably meant compositions already in vogue beginning with these words. There is hardly any but intrinsic evidence for determining how much of the form now in use (say the German form, as the shorter of the two) is the oldest kernel.

⁹See Note 8 to Ch. III; also for the opening words, Berachoth, ch. 2, § 2; as to the propriety (not necessity) of mentioning the plague of the first-born and the parting of the sea in this benediction, see Shemoth Rabba, ch. 22. "To the living and everlasting King," see T. B. Hagiga, 13*a*. "He has redeemed Israel," is given in T. B. Pesahim, 117*b*, as the proper close of the *Geulla;* especially for a benediction on Passover night.

¹⁰See rebuke for piling up attributes, T. B. Berachoth, 33b.

¹¹See David Kaufmann's account of the London Prayer Book of 1287, in *Jewish Quarterly Review*, vol. 4, p. 20, and compare end of Bk. I, ch. III.

CHAPTER V

RESPONSES—THE KADDISH

(Pp. 105-111)

¹Berachoth, ch. 8, § 8.

²Ib., ch. 9, § 9, and T. J. on same.

³Sifré on Deut. 32: 3.

⁴Megilla, ch. 4, § 3.

⁵This form is given in Berachoth, ch. 7, § 4.

⁶Aboth, ch. 3, § 6, quoting, "God stands in the Congregation, etc., from Ps. 82: 1, and more distinctly, T. B. Berachoth, 6a.

⁷T. B. Berachoth, 3a and 21b; Succa, 39a; Shabbath, 119b. In the last-named passage some Rabbis, noted for their bold homiletics, promise to those who respond, "Amen, be the great name" heartily, that any hard sentence against them will be torn up, though there be a taint of idolatry on them, and through a pun on Isa. 26: 2, that the gates of Paradise will be opened to them: Do not read שׁוֹמְרֵי אֱמוּנִים (who keep faith), but שֶׁאוֹמְרִי אָמֵנִים (they who say Amen). It is still a far way from those who make this response to the parents of him who calls for it. But at least the first two sentences of the Kaddish are very old.

⁸The Seder R. Amram and the Mahzor Vitry contain all the forms of the Kaddish, but as neither as now printed is anything like its original draft, the former containing additions younger by three or four hundred years, the latter, dated in 1208, quoting from the Zohar, published about 1275, but little historical light is thrown on the time when the Mourners' Kaddish (i. e., the aggregate of paragraphs 1, 2, 4, 5) was first used. Moreover, the Mahzor even in its enlarged edition is quite guiltless of the modern effort to multiply opportunities for "saying Kaddish." Thus in its account of the evening service, the leader right after the Amida says the full Kaddish, whereupon "the people go home in peace." Maimonides, in Hilchoth Tefilla, ch. 9, §§ 12-14, goes through the service for weekdays, Sabbaths, etc., stating where a Kaddish comes in, but leaves out all those now allotted to mourners. R. Moses Isserles, in his note on Jore De'a, § 376 (Rules of Mourning), speaks of the habit of mourners to recite a Kaddish, but reproves it, unless they are

little children; otherwise, if they want to honor their dead parents, let them read the service or at least a part of it.

²Mahzor Vitry, p. 74: "The lad, etc.;" p. 112, the legend. This is also printed in the devotional books Menorath Hammaor and Or Zarua, and is credited by these to two older works, Midrash Tanhuma and the Treatise Calla, which do not contain it. N. B.— The writer fully agrees with Dr. K. Kohler (*Jewish Quarterly Review*, VII, p. 606) in the belief, that the Kaddish is thoroughly Jewish and not borrowed; but is not so sure, that its needless repetition by mourners, beyond the קדיש in the old liturgy, is a home-grown institution.

CHAPTER VI

THE CONSTANT PARTS OF THE TEFILLA

(Pp. 112–120)

¹The names of I, II, III and of V, VI, VII, as given in this chapter, together with the intervening IV for Sabbaths and Festivals, are found in Rosh Hashana, ch. 4, § 5.

²So Abudraham, who takes the verb as covering all tenses: he brought us a redeemer from Egypt; he delivers us now, and will send us a redeemer hereafter.

³So Abudraham and other commentators. Israel, he says, is commanded: Be ye holy.

⁴There is a very improbable story, that the two extra responses, which are the beginning and end of the Shema, were introduced during a persecution of the Jews, when they were forbidden to recite the Shema in public.

⁵From Abudraham's comparison of this כתר with the language of the book Hechaloth, there can be no doubt of its Cabbalistic origin and purpose.

⁶Rashi on T. B. Berachoth, 11b, doubts whether the benediction when said in the Temple after the daily sacrifice closed with these words, or: "Who receivest the service of his people Israel with favor." At all events, the conclusion must have included the word Aboda, or its verbal root.

⁷T. B., Rosh Hashana 31a and 31b, gives the ten migrations of the Sanhedrin from that chamber till it rested at Tiberias, where it reached its lowest point, that is, less jurisdiction than ever before; and gives this as a parallel to the receding of the Shechina.

⁸As the servant acknowledging his master should not rely on a

messenger to carry his message, a *Modim* has been drawn up by
many Rabbis, hence called רבנן דרבנן (T. B. Sota, 40, also T. J. on
Berachoth, ch. 1, § 8), which the people read silently, while the
leader proceeds to repeat the benediction: "We acknowledge to
thee, that thou, O Lord, art our God and the God of our fathers,
God of all flesh, our Maker, the Maker in the beginning. Blessings
and thanks to thy great and holy name, for that thou hast kept us
alive and in health; thus keep us further alive and in health, and
gather our exiles to thy holy court-yards, to observe thy ordinances and to do thy will and to serve thee with a full heart. For
all which we thank thee; blessed be the God of Thanks."

⁹כן יהי רצון, not Amen; the latter response is made only when
the priests give the blessing. Qu. Is not this response the origin
of the Masonic "So mote it be?"

¹⁰The West Germans use the longer form on Sabbath afternoons
in the repetition by the leader, not, however, in the silent Prayer.
The Hasidim have it generally for Minha, but not in the night
service.

¹¹T. B. Megilla, 18a, derives the fuller form (literally,"Put Peace")
from the verse, "They shall put my name, etc.," which follows the
priestly blessing; the shorter form is nowhere found in the Talmud.

¹²The High Priest recited V and VI on the Day of Atonement;
Joma, ch. 7, § 1; the second in the priesthood (הממונה) caused
V and VII to be recited every morning; Tamid, ch. 5, § 1; VII was
always preceded by the priestly blessing itself.

¹³T. B. Berachoth, 4b.

¹⁴Mahzor Vitry and Abudraham both give this verse, at which
the worshipper is to "separate his feet" and step back, as the
Talmud intimates a man does after prayer.

CHAPTER VII

MODIFICATIONS OF THE CONSTANT PARTS

(Pp. 121–127)

¹The "Holy King" on these days is deemed indispensable, T. B.
Berachoth, 12b. The insertions in I, II, VI, and VII all ask God
to remember or inscribe. The first mention of "remembrances"
in the "first three and last three" is found in Treatise Soferim, ch.
19, § 8 (say seventh century), where the lawfulness of the insertions is grudgingly granted for the Days of Memorial and Atonement. Maimonides speaks of them as in use in his time. Abudra-

ham, while giving them as in use, still protests against one praying for his needs in these benedictions (ib., 34*b*). This restriction was never respected by the French and German Jews. Mahzor Vitry, p. 366, gives זכרנו, and comments on it.

²See Mahzor Vitry, p. 394.

³According to a response of R. Haï, the last Gaon, Sha'are Teshuba, No. 297, the paragraphs וכבן were written by Rab, the author of many parts of the New Year's Prayer, and there should be no more than three of them. However, in the repetition of Musaf on New Year and of all the Atonement Prayers, the leader adds in the German Minhag another before these three, viz.: "And then be thy name, O Lord our God, hallowed upon Israel thy people, and Jerusalem thy city, and Zion the dwelling of thy glory, and upon the Kingdom of the House of David thy anointed, and upon thy place, and on thy Temple."

⁴Perhaps this should have been treated as one of the late "poetries."

⁵Berachoth, ch. 5, § 2, gives the place in the Prayer; Taanith, ch. 1, § 1, the day to begin and the very words. The solemn words on the first day of rain or dew are later than the Talmud and different in the two rituals.

⁶Betza, 17*a* (a Baraïtha), decides in favor of "Service" as the proper place in which to insert; so does Tosifta to Berachoth, ch. 3, and Shabbath, 24*a*. The words are not given in either place.

⁷See T. J. on Berachoth, ch. 7, § 5 (4), and comp. with same on same, § 6 (5).

⁸In Palestine daily blessings are still in use. T. B. Sota, 39*b*, has the following prayer for the priest after the blessing: "Be it thy will, etc., that this blessing with which thou hast commanded us to bless thy people Israel, be a perfect blessing, free from every stumbling block or iniquity, from now and for evermore." Maimonides inserts it, Hilchoth Tefilla, ch. 15.

CHAPTER VIII

THE WORK-DAY BENEDICTIONS

(Pp. 128–139)

¹Taanith, ch. 2, § 2; Berachoth, ch. 4, § 3. Among the reasons for the number eighteen, the best known are these: The two Psalms known as first and second being really one, the verse, "May the words of my mouth, etc.," asking for the acceptance of prayer,

and the next Psalm, which in its opening line promises the granting of prayer, are thus put after eighteen Psalms, to which the eighteen benedictions correspond. This number is also that of the "Names" in Psalm 29. The "voice of the Lord" occurs in it seven times; hence the seven benedictions on the Sabbath and on Festivals. These are not so much reasons as means of impressing these numbers on the memory, and fixing them as unalterable. In T. B. Megilla, 17*b*, 18*a*, the order of the nineteen benedictions, including that about heretics, is given in full with the reasons for the order in which they follow each other. Astonishment is expressed at the conflict between the tradition, that the eighteen benedictions came from the Men of the Great Synod, and the late authorship of the details, spoken of hereinafter.

²T. B. Berachoth, 29*a*; ib., 33*a*. Two reasons are given for choosing this benediction: first, that to distinguish holy and profane is an act of intelligence; secondly, that the arrival of the work-day should be announced in the first benediction peculiar to that day.

³Berachoth, ch. 5, § 2, and Taanith, ch. 1, §1, which distinguish between mentioning rain and praying for it. Taanith, ch. 1, § 3, makes the third or the seventh of Marheshvan the first day to pray for rain in Palestine. The sixtieth day after the fall equinox is named in T. B. on this section for those in exile, that is, in the main, for Babylonia.

⁴T. B. Berachoth, 28*b*, 29*a*.

⁵This matter is fully discussed in Manasseh ben Israel's letters to the English Commonwealth, and by numberless Jewish apologists and scholars ever since. In the English Prayer Book of 1287, the first word is not, "For the Slanderers," but for the perverts, למשומדים, a later word, while כופרים, denoting those lapsed into paganism, was probably in the first draft, and the thing to be uprooted is the kingdom of haughtiness. Here "the מינים" are to perish in a moment. Angevin England had no censor for Hebrew books. The MSS. of the Mahzor Vitry are to the same effect; but the printed edition leaves blanks for the objectionable words, so that the volume may be allowed to enter Russia.

⁶T. J. on Berachoth, ch. 4, § 3.

⁷T. J. on Berachoth, ch. 2, § 3 (4), in giving an abstract of the work-day benedictions, given in its present form leaves out XII, but as copied in the Mahzor Vitry this abstract has the words, "May the throne of David be established." T. J. on Rosh Hashana, ch. 4, § 7, quotes a Rabbi who speaks of "Rock of David and Builder of Jerusalem" as the close of one benediction; but this

seems from the context to be quoted only as an opinion on such a subject, running counter to the plain usage. Bemidbar Rabba, ch. 18, takes טוב in its numerical value, which is seventeen, as an emblem of the Prayer, counting out XII and IX.

⁸Some of the foremost scholars, like Zunz, have reached the opposite conclusion. Dr. M. Duschak, in a work on the liturgy published in 1866, suggests this solution: Our XII is old as a separate benediction, but when Gamaliel introduced our IX, XI and XII were united, so that the number should remain eighteen, and so the usage remained in Palestine, till the new unit was again broken into its original parts, resulting in nineteen benedictions.

⁹Taanith, ch. 2, § 4.

¹⁰T. B. Berachoth, 29a; T. J. on same, ch. 2, § 3 (4). The Mahzor Vitry has in both forms ישׁפוט, "may judge," instead of ישׁפט, "may be judged," and such is the reading of Alfassi, and this is followed in the text.

CHAPTER IX

THE MIDDLE BENEDICTION ON DAYS OF REST

(Pp. 140–147)

¹T. J. on Berachoth, ch. 4, § 3; T. B. ib., 29a.

²T. B. Shabbath, 119b, recommends him who recites "Then were finished" on Friday evening; for he makes himself, so to say, a partner with God in the work of creation. Yet Tosifta to Berachoth, ch. 3, followed by an evidently genuine passage in the Seder R. Amram, gives for Friday night a form which does not contain it: "From thy love, O Lord, wherewith thou hast loved thy people Israel, and thy compassion, etc., thou hast given us this great and holy seventh day, in love, for greatness, strength, and holiness, etc." This form coincides somewhat with that for the Festivals and with a special prayer of the Day of Atonement. That the Law was given on a Sabbath, see T. B. Shabbath, 86b.

³T. B. Shabbath, 24b, speaks of this abstract, remarking that if the Sabbath is also a Festival, no mention is made of the latter occasion, but it does not give the form; but about this there seems to have never been any dispute.

⁴The opening words, "Thou hast chosen us," are mentioned as such in T. B. Joma, 87b, as well known.

⁵From a discussion at Usha about the middle of the second century, whether the "Sanctity of the Day" should be coupled in the

additional Prayer with the Kingdoms or the Remembrances (see a later chapter), reported in T. B. Rosh Hashana, 32*b*, it seems that the petition for the Kingdom of Heaven had not yet been made a part of the "Sanctity of the Day;" but was probably inserted soon afterward, when the question was finally decided, that it goes with the Kingdoms.

⁶Joma, ch. 7, § 1, and T. B. ib., 70*a;* see Rashi on this passage.

⁷This form was drawn up by Rab and Samuel (see T. B. Berachoth, 33*b*), and met with great approval at the time, being called a very pearl (מרגניתא).

⁸T. B. Betza, 17*a*. Rabbi gives the conclusion, "who hallowest the Sabbath and Israel and the Festive seasons," in full.

CHAPTER X

THE "ADDITIONAL," OR MUSAF

(Pp. 148-154)

¹It is said, T. B. Taanith, 27*a*, that the forgiveness of sins, which was promised to Israel by means of sacrifice, they may obtain now by reading the law of sacrifice; which means the reading from the scroll as a lesson, not the reference to it in a prayer. The leader in Musaf is in Rosh Hashana, ch. 4, § 7, called "the second," who prompts the cornet blowing; the leader in Shaharith, "the first," who gives out Hallel.

²See Abudraham, *ad locum;* he had a truer copy of R. Amram than that now in print, but it agrees with the latter.

³The twenty-two letters are followed by the five having a different shape at the end of words (כנצפך).

⁴T. B. Rosh Hashana, 35*a*, where a later teacher says on the authority of Rab: If one has said, "in thy Law it is written thus," no more is necessary. It is not unlikely that Rab gave that opinion after he had himself drawn up this prayer, along with the special benedictions for the Musaf of New Year to be found in the next chapter. The last verse of the sacrifices of the Day of Memorial begins: "Beside the burnt-offering for the month, etc." This is the only mention of New Moon on the Day of Memorial. It is not to be treated as a New Moon; T. B. Erubin, 40*b*.

⁵Found in Seder R. Amram. There is no trace of it in the Talmud, but the purity of the Hebrew makes the authorship of Rab not unlikely.

⁶The Mishna speaks plainly of a Musaf service on New Moons as

on Middle Days (Megilla, ch. 4, § 2). Perhaps it embraced at first
no more than the closing part, in which a happy month is prayed
for. The part about the sacrificial goat seems to be borrowed from
the form for festivals; its worse Hebrew indicates a later date.
'H. Edelmann, in his annotated Prayer Book (Königsberg,
1845), maintains that the Sabbath and New Moon benediction is the
older and the source of that for the Festivals. The contrary
seems more probable. The Seder R. Amram gives it substantially
as it stands now in the Sefardic Ritual.

CHAPTER XI

THE DAY OF MEMORIAL

(Pp. 155-164)

¹Rosh Hashana, ch. 4, § 5. Among the six extra benedictions in
the Prayer for public fasts were the Remembrances and Shofars;
Taanith, ch. 2, § 3.
²Ibid., § 6; T. B. on same, 32b.
³These pieces are called "the hornblowings of Rab;" T. J. on Rosh
Hashana, ch. 1, § 5; T. J. on Aboda Zara, ch. 1, § 2. In T. B.
Rosh Hashana, 27a, the sentence is quoted, "this day is the beginning of thy works," a memorial of the first day, with the remark
that according to the Mishna the benedictions for the Jubilee were
the same as those for the New Year; showing that a benediction for
the latter, containing this sentence, must have been written after the
Mishna was completed.
⁴But the Mishna already says (Rosh Hashana, ch. 1, § 2): "At
four seasons the world is judged, etc.; on Rosh Hashana all that
come into the world pass before him like lambs." Hence, the
judgment day may have been referred to in the benediction before
it took its permanent shape.
⁵T. J. on Rosh Hashana, near end of ch. 4, quoted in Mahzor
Vitry, p. 352; so also in the Seder R. Amram. R. Gamaliel excuses
those "in the fields" also, that is, those who have no leader to listen
to, from the nine benedictions. But as to those in the Synagogue
his opinions were accepted by his contemporaries. However, the
Orah Hayim, § 58, insists that everybody, even in silent devotion in
the Synagogue, should say nine benedictions, because copies of the
Mahzor are plentiful.
⁶Notwithstanding the many late additions in the printed Seder

26

R. Amram, this is not found; but its identity in both rituals indicates an early origin.

¹Based on an Aggadta, T. B. Rosh Hashana, 27a, that Adam was born on Tishri first. This is found in the Seder R. Amram.

²T. B. Taanith, 25b, R. Akiba said, Our Father, etc., we have no King beside thee; Our Father, etc., show us mercy for thy own sake; and rain came. See Orah Hayim, § 602 (R. M. Isserles), and § 622 (R. Joseph Karo).

CHAPTER XII

THE DAY OF ATONEMENT

(Pp. 165-179)

¹T. B. Joma, 87b. However, there are reasons to suppose that the alphabetic lesser confession is very old. The last word תִיעָנֽוּ is an idiomatic Hebrew formation, which would have hardly ventured on after the language was no longer spoken.

²Maimonides, in his "Order of Prayer for the Year," indicates a single alphabet. In the Mahzor Vitry most letters are doubled, and the alphabetic order is not very strictly kept. The London MS. of 1287 has two lines for each letter, but twelve differ greatly from those now in use.

³Joma, ch. 8, last sec.: "The sin and certain guilt-offerings atone (the faults for which they are prescribed); death and the Day of Atonement with repentance atone." Both Talmuds on this point quote the opinion of R. Judah, the Patriarch, that death and the Day atone, even without repentance, all but apostasy. The phrase, "death atones iniquity," is quite current. See this in the form of prayer, T. B. Berachoth, 60a.

⁴R. Akiba in T. J on Joma, ch. 8, end, expresses the opinion that particular sins ought not to be mentioned, though, of course, they should be thought of and repented.

⁵It is indicated by Samuel (T. B. Joma, 87b) by the initial words, "What are we, what our life, etc." This page of the Talmud indicates in like manner many parts of the present order of confession, and some pieces now forgotten, one drawn up, or at least recommended, by Samuel, beginning, "From the depths of the heart." Here is a confession also by R. Hemnuna, now put at the end of the silent Prayer, but not repeated by the leader:

My God! before I was formed, I was worthless, and now since I am formed, I am no better; I am dust while alive, how much more when dead; behold, I am before thee as a vessel full of shame and reproach. Be it thy will, that I sin no more, and wipe out what I have sinned by thy abundant mercy, and not by sufferings and hard sickness.

[6]T. B. Rosh Hoshana, 17*b*, discusses the atoning effects of reciting the thirteen qualities, and shows from Ex. 34 how God taught Israel to rely on them. The composition, "God, the King," dates back to Talmudic times: "He passes by the first, by the first," is quoted in a Baraitha (T. B. Rosh Hashana, 17*a*).

[7]No trace of these arrangements of Bible verses (O thou, that hearest prayer—Remember us—Remember the covenant) can be found in the Mahzor Vitry, or in older sources. Among the *Selihoth* appended to the Seder R. Amram, there are some collections of Bible verses, but altogether different from those in the text. The divergence between the German and the Polish ritual shows that the collections were finished after the middle of the fourteenth century.

[8]By a custom drawn from one of these verses, men go to a flowing river on New Year's Day, and pray in these verses and the same added words, that God may cast our iniquities into the depth of oblivion. The whole is found in the order of *Selihoth* for the Day of Atonement, appended to the Seder R. Amram.

[9]The writer saw such a service at the great German synagogue of Hamburg as late as August, 1885.

[10]T. B. Taanith, 15*a*.

[11]According to the Seder of R. Amram, his predecessor, the Gaon Natronaï, laid down the rule that "the sprinklings and confessions," as he called the atonement service, should be recited in Musaf only. The sprinklings: "One, one and one, one and two, etc., one and seven," as ordered in Lev. 16, gave him half of the name for the service.

[12]This "permission" is unknown to the Seder R. Amram, to the Mahzor Vitry, and to Abudraham, but is recognized in the Orah Hayim. The ban (or נדוי) was always suspended on the Day of Atonement, but not by announcement in the Synagogue.

[13]Nedarim, ch. 3, § 1; though the opinion of a stricter school is also given, that vows become void only when the former declaration is remembered and silently re-affirmed.

[14]In the Seder R. Amram a formula in Mishnic Hebrew of similar import is given, with the remark that the two colleges denounce the whole ceremony of annulling vows on that day as a כנהג שטוה—a foolish custom.

[15]The release of vows by a self-constituted court of three men

(still well-known among old-style Jews) is treated in Nedarim, ch. 9. Some point must always be alleged: "If I had thought of this, I should not have vowed." Yet Abudraham says, that "from the last past to this year" should be said, in order to avoid the punishment for broken vows.

¹⁶This solemn closing of the fast is unknown to R. Amram, who says: "When Neïla is ended, the leader goes on at once with the evening service."

¹⁷The writer heard of this usage at Bagdad through Mr. Wm. Schur, the author of נצח ישראל, who stopped there on his travels.

¹⁸Taanith, ch. 4, last section.

CHAPTER XIII

PSALMS AND BIBLE VERSES IN THE SERVICE

(Pp. 180–192)

¹ תנכולוהי is Aramaic in all but the root; כ as the suffix for feminine *thee* or *thy* is either Aramaic or very old Hebrew; the forms הכוחה and לכיענו with the old case endings show a late date, when the feeling for the cases was lost, for both are in the wrong case.

²Pesahim, ch. 10, § 4, marks the chapter endings by the last words other than Halleluiah.

³T. B. Arachin, 12, the eighteen days (first of Passover, night and day, counts as one) are enumerated—with double feast days there are twenty-one.

⁴T. B. Berachoth, 14a, distinguishes days on which the individual completes the Hallel from those on which he does not complete it; on the former days he may not interrupt the reading, except on the same terms as that of the Shema; on the other days he may interrupt it anywhere. Maimonides, Hilchoth Megilla, ch. 3, § 7, deems the reading on the latter days a mere custom, and that only for public worship, and disapproves a benediction for "the command." Rashi (see Mahzor Vitry, pt. I, § 226) also deems Hallel on New Moon, etc., a mere custom, and will not say the regular benediction, but rather one like that before the morning hymns (see Ch. XV). It seems that the custom to read Half Hallel and bless before it him who "commanded us to read" was general in the days of Rashi and Maimonides, though they objected. The Seder R. Amram has the benediction.

⁵T. B. Succa, 38b, where the maxim שוכיע כיענה is derived from

2 Kings 22: 16; King Josiah is said to have read the book, though
he only listened to the reading.
⁵In a Baraïtha, T. B. Shabbath, 118b, R. Jose says: Be my share
with those who read Hallel every day. The Talmud explains Hallel
here as the songs of praise in the morning hymns; according to
some commentators, Psalms 146-150, or at least 146 and 148. One
of the Psalms read by the Sefardim before the benediction, i. e., 30,
is found in the same place in the fuller German prayer books.
⁶Orah Hayim, § 131, subs. 4.
⁷The Seder R. Amram speaks of "falling on the face," the usual
name for this part of the service in the later standards. He gives,
under this head, some un-Biblical prayers, also some of the verses
in the text; but makes no mention of a Psalm, either 6 or 25.
⁸Mishna Tamid, last section. On days when "supplications" are
read, the Germans add Psalm 83 to that for the day.
⁹Orah Hayim, § 267, subs. 2, states how early before night-fall
one may receive the Sabbath in the evening Prayer." In the next
subsection the only change for the Sabbath before the Prayer is
noted: namely, in the close of השכיבנו. Not even ושכרו is recognized, though it is mentioned in the Seder R. Amram as now
printed, and was undoubtedly in use, at least locally, when the
Code was prepared.
¹¹These three verses are traced back by Abudraham to the liturgies of R. Amram and of Saadia. He also refers to the Geonim
for the position that these verses (צדקתך) are omitted on days
when Hallel is said.
¹²This custom is unknown to Abudraham.
¹³R. Amram and Abudraham have these two verses even on the
Sabbath and Festivals, for which they are now thought ill-fitted,
as suggestive of sin and repentance and of distress.
¹⁴These Psalms are not thus employed in Russia; the custom is
of very late rise, and is not mentioned in the Orah Hayim at all.
The object of introducing them seems to be to lay the basis for
another Mourners' Kaddish. Some prayer books give additional
Psalms, one each, for Sunday, Monday, Tuesday, Wednesday, and
Thursday nights.

CHAPTER XIV

STUDY AS PART OF THE LITURGY

(Pp. 193-202)

[1]Study and teaching are commanded (outside of the two §§ of the Shema): Ex. 13: 9; Deut. 4: 19; 5: 1, 28, and impliedly Deut. 31: 10.

[2]Zebahim, ch. 5 (which is the place? איזהו מקומן). The Sefardic and fuller German Prayer Books bring in also passages from Ex. 30, as to the basin and as to incense; a Baraïtha in T. B. Kerithuth, 6a, and T. J. on Joma, ch. 4. § 5, on the composition of incense, two other passages as to incense; also a Baraïtha as to the daily order of all sacrificial acts in the Temple.

[3]Beginning of Sifra (oldest commentary on Leviticus). The duty to study trebly each day: text, Mishna, and further discussion, is based on a saying in T. B. Berachoth, 11b. R. Amram enjoins the reading of Zebahim, ch. 5, and the piece from Sifra, and of these alone.

[4]Tosefoth on T. B. Berachoth, 11b, says that the French Jews read these short passages right after the benedictions, following therein the Jerusalem Talmud, but thinks it unnecessary.

[5]The Germans read only the three verses of blessing. The Sefardim in Eastern Europe omit the Talmudic passage. In this they follow Maimonides.

[6]Pēa, ch. 1, § 1. The Western Sefardim have a shorter form of the second sentence, which is by some considered a Baraïtha, omitting, among other things, "devotion in prayer." The Mahzor Vitry says that the Aramaic version of the Thrice-Holy, in "A redeemer will come," is a remnant of daily studies of the Prophets with translation.

[7]T. B. Berachoth, *ubi supra*, gives these benedictions for study before Shema; while אהבה רבה covers all study thereafter. They are ascribed to Babylonians; no Tanna is named.

[8]Tamid, ch. 7, § 4, naming 24, 48, 82, 94, 81, 93, and for Saturday 92: "A Psalm or song for the future to come, a day which is all Sabbath and rest, for eternal life."

[9]T. B. Berachoth. 64a, the verses are: Isa. 54: 13; Ps. 119: 165; 122: 6-9; 29: 11. The Seder R. Amram gives these three pieces for every day in the week.

[10]Shabbath, ch. 2 (במה מדליקין). A section denouncing heav-

cnly punishment on women for certain shortcomings has lately given great offence among English Jews of reform tendencies.

[11] "If the date of ch. 6 could be ascertained, it would very nearly mark the time when the other five chapters came into liturgic use. The Mahzor Vitry recommends the chapters for winter, not for summer reading.

[12] A number of translations in German, French, and English, with critical and explanatory notes, of this treatise, have been published. But the rendering in Leeser's American, or in Singer's English Prayer Book, are sufficient to give a good idea both of style and substance. A chapter of Aboth is familiarly referred to as a Perek (פרק), simply chapter.

[13] Sanhedrin, ch. 10, first part of § 1. This sentence seems to be an interpolation in the Mishna; the section then proceeds to state what sort of men have no share in the world to come.

[14] T. B. Maccoth, 23a.

[15] T. B. Megilla, 31a. The Mahzor Vitry gives this passage as part of the Saturday night service, showing that the "Poles" herein have the old tradition on their side.

CHAPTER XV

THE LESSER AND THE DOUBTFUL BENEDICTIONS

(Pp. 203-211)

[1] While the Orah Hayim already treats this transfer to the Synagogue, or at least a postponement until after washing and dressing, as a matter of course, Maimonides (Hilchoth Tefilla, ch. 7, §§ 3, 4, 5, etc.) still prefers the old way, and insists that any benediction should be omitted for which the occasion has not arisen for the individual on that morning.

[2] T. B. Berachoth, 60b. As to "My God, the soul," see also T. J. on Rosh Hashana, ch. 5, § 1. The substitute, "who revivest the dead," is found in Pesikta de Rab Cahana, ch. 10.

[3] Abudraham, though living at Sevilla early in the fourteenth century, hardly more than a hundred years after the expulsion of the Moors, says: "They recite it—the old benediction—in all Moslem countries because they are in the habit of putting a turban on the head; but in these countries they do not, because they do not put on a turban. They have a wholly different benediction, not named in the Talmud." The Orah Hayim knows only the old benediction.

[4] Tosifta on Berachoth, ch. 6; see also T. B. Menahoth, 43b, a

Baraïtha, ascribing the three formulas to R. Meïr. The former has: "who has not made me a גוי," the latter, "who has made me an Israelite;" a much better reading, which was adopted in the Szold-Jastrow prayer book; for the use of גוי as the designation of a single Gentile is very bad Hebrew. In the Baraïtha there is a dispute as between "bondman" and בור, i. e., thoroughly ignorant man. The latter version is rejected as not in keeping with the rest.

⁵Tanna de Be Eliah, 1st pt., ch. 21.   Seder R. Amram, as now printed, contains it, and the learned editor, Nathan N. Koronel, quotes the Arba Turim, early in the thirteenth century, for the genuineness of this passage. The old sources all omit, "Blessed be the name, etc.," after Hear, O Israel.

⁶Nowhere explicitly named in the Talmud, but implied by the "Benediction of Song" after the morning hymns, as a benediction before performance of duty is more strongly demanded than one thereafter.   Also implied by the criticism on the conclusion, "Honored in many praises," as implying less than all; see T. B. Berachoth, 59b.   The Seder R. Amram, in its present form, gives, "Blessed he who spoke," very much as now found in the Sefardic Prayer Book, as the first piece to be said on entering the Synagogue.

⁷This is clearly the "Benediction of Song" referred to in Pesahim, ch. 10, § 7, and in T. B. Berachoth, 50b, the latter dealing with thanks for rain.   Among the words of praise, we have translated לקלס, to adorn.   It is probably formed from the Greek κάλλος, beauty.   A Greek word indicates Palestinian as opposed to Babylonian origin; also a date later than the destruction of the Temple; but the benediction undoubtedly grew from time to time.   The absurd word הפיענח for revealing, in the Sefardic form, coined out of Joseph's Egyptian name, indicates a later time of authorship than a Greek root would.

⁸There is no trace of this in the Talmud.   Maimonides gives, in his "Order of Prayer for the Year," a few of the verses which precede this benediction, and adds: "Some of the people say this," giving the other verses with the benediction, its "sealing" included. Abudraham thinks it unauthorized.

⁹The command to number days and weeks to reach the Feast of Weeks is found Lev. 23: 15, and Deut. 16: 9.   Before performing any ceremony commanded by the Law, a benediction in this form is spoken.   Tosifta on Berachoth, ch. 6, states and illustrates by many examples that a blessing is due on fulfilling any affirmative precept; see also T. B. Megilla, 21b ("All precepts, etc.").   The particular benediction is not found in the Talmud; but the duty to

count both single days and weeks, and to do it in the evening, is set forth, T. B. Menahoth, 66a. In this connection (65b) the word "Sabbath," in Lev. 23: 15, is determined to be the first of the Passover, so as to bring Pentecost always to the same day of the year, the 6th of Sivan.

CHAPTER XVI

OTHER PROSE COMPOSITIONS

(Pp. 212–221)

[1] T. B. Berachoth, 16b; Cmp. Jost, *Geschichte des Judenthums*, pt. II, p. 152.

[2] See the "Order of Prayer for the Year" of Maimonides. The Seder R. Amram gives it in nearly the same words. It is not traceable to the Talmud, unless it was a part of "Master of all Worlds," which is highly improbable.

[3] Unknown as yet to Maimonides. The Mahzor Vitry has both forms, and wants the leader to recite one and the people to answer with the other. Abudraham's is the oldest Sefardic authority for it.

[4] Abudraham, in giving these petitions for the Sabbath before New Moon, says "Heaven" instead of "Our Father in Heaven," excusing this mode of speech by a passage in Daniel.

[5] Seder R. Amram gives it without question or comment. All the medieval authorities speak of it as "Order of Sanctification" (קרושה).

[6] Thus in the Mahzor Vitry.

[7] Yet the Seder R. Amram does not contain יקום פורקן; nor does Abudraham.

[8] The Mahzor Vitry combines the two pieces into one, adding "this congregation, etc.," to those prayed for in the first part. It answers the objection that it is Aramaic with the remark, that many "poetries" are in that language; as indeed appears from that volume to have been the case then, though it is not so now.

[9] Aboth, ch. 3, § 2.

[10] To indicate the use of this announcement of the New Moon, we have as guides: Maimonides, in his Code, late in the twelfth century, knows nothing of it; Mahzor Vitry (1208) does not discuss it among the usages of the Sabbath, but has it as part of the full text of Sabbath services, without any preliminary prayer; Abudraham (1340) gives it in full, with the preliminary prayer. Neither R. Simha nor Abudraham quotes any older sources.

"Mahzor Vitry, pp. 309 and 392.   It quotes from פסיקתא רבתי
ch. 20, that there is help (הקנה) for the dead, and they should be
helped by prayer and charity.   On p. 173, after קום פורקן, it also
refers to this subject, and indicates a prayer for the dead, especially
for the martyrs, but does not set it out at large.   It was probably
meant to be much like that in the text.

CHAPTER XVII

THE LATE " POETRY "— GENERAL PLAN

(Pp. 222-230)

'The alphabet may be single; such it is in most cases; that is, only
the first word of each line or stanza or the first changing word
follows its order; sometimes it is double or even treble.   Thus,
angels named or denoted by alphabetic order praise in twenty-two
different ways, the verbs of praise being put in alphabetic order.
Generally the alphabet moves directly from Alef to Tav; sometimes it runs backward; sometimes both ways, as in a very old
Seliha for Atonement Day (אל תעשה עמנו כלה); that is, the
odd hemistichs progress Alef. Beth, etc.; the even ones, Tav, Shin,
etc., till the last verse is made up of two hemistichs, Kaf-Lamed.
The play on letters by seeking permutations between letters at the
same distance from the end and from the beginning of the alphabet,
was according to T. B. Shabbath, 104a, a favorite amusement of
the school children of early days.
 'He runs his name in as El'azar ben Rabbi Kalir (sometimes
Kilir), or simply as El'azar.   Abraham Ibn Ezra in Comm. on
Eccl., § 5, criticises his poetry as a maze of riddles, and a mixture
of classic Hebrew with Talmudic words, the former being inflected
in bad grammar.   He may have accused him of bad grammar
through a misunderstanding; but if poems are misunderstood by
such a scholar, they are unfit for devotion.   The pieces in the
Kedusha for the Musaf of New Year, and for the morning and
Musaf services of Atonement, and those placed in the Kingdoms,
Remembrances, and Shofars, are all from Kalir's pen.   Those in the
Kedusha are based on Aggadta that borders on Cabbala; their use
runs counter to what the Mishna says about the "discussion of the
Chariot."
 'Mahzor Vitry, p. 362, § 225.   The Sefardim have pretty much
lived up to the rule.   They have even on Atonement Day no
"poetry" in the first and second benedictions; only a few in the

third, in great part by Jehuda Hallevi, and these lead up naturally to the Thrice-Holy, dealing only with the honor which angels and men pay to God; and there are Seliḥoth in the fourth benediction; that is, prayers for forgiveness where they belong. The long day is filled up to a great extent by poetical and other devotions outside of the Prayer. They have several versions of the Azharoth, or collections of the 613 precepts, in use in different countries.

The *Gallia Judaica, or Dictionnaire Géographique de la France d' après les sources rabbiniques*, compiled by Henry Gross and put into French by Moïse Bloch, and printed at Paris in 1897 under the auspices of the *Société des Etudes juives*, contains literary notices of the Jewish writers in the different towns of France, among them many authors of *Piyutim* in the wider sense of the word. Some of these compositions are found in the modern German Maḥzor, while others have gone out of use; some written at Avignon or Carpentras for a Sefardic public. The most important name in this connection is that of Menaḥem ben Joseph, Hazan of Troyes, the author of the Troyes Ritual (כדר טרוייש), put in shape and published by his disciple, Judah ben Eliezer. The Maḥzor Vitry contains very few of the "poetries" in modern use, and much that is now obsolete; the development of the poetic pieces in the Festival morning service from "Jotzer" to "Silluk" is unknown to its author and to his age.

CHAPTER XVIII

SAMPLES OF POST-BIBLICAL POETRY

(Pp. 231–240)

[1]Many prayer books reprint the thirteen articles of the creed as Maimonides wrote it, each preceded by the words: I believe with full faith. They are: (1) Existence of God; (2) His Oneness; (3) His being incorporeal; (4) His eternity in past time; (5) That he is the creator of all; (6) His revelation by prophets; (7) Moses the greatest of the prophets; (8) The truth of the Tora; (9) Its being unchangeable; (10) God's prescience; (11) The reward of the righteous and punishment of the wicked; (12) The advent of a future Messiah; (13) The resurrection.

[2]It is mentioned by its first two words (ארון יָעוֹלם) in the English ritual of 1287, and must then have been well-known. Some say that Solomon Ibn Gebirol was the author; this is possible. The two additional lines, which the Sefardim insert as 7 and 8, are:

Without estimate or likening, without change or transmutation;
without joining or division, great in strength, and whose is power."
These recall some of Ibn Gebirol's metaphysical language in the
Song of Unity.
    ³T. B. Baba Kamma, 32*b*. R. Jannai cried out: Come, O
Bride!

CHAPTER XIX

CABBALISTIC INTERPOLATIONS

(Pp. 241-244)

¹The Zohar on Exodus recommends this prayer thus: "Says
R. Simeon, when they take out the Book of the Law in public to
read therein, the gates of the heaven of mercy are opened, and
they arouse love above; and a man ought to say thus." Abudraham, writing two generations after the date of the Zohar, as yet
says nothing about the reception of this prayer; nor is it in the
Amsterdam Prayer Book of 1658. It made its way into the
service only slowly after the life-work of Isaac Luria, on behalf of
the Cabbala, had borne full fruit.

²The authorized daily Prayer Book of the United Synagogue of
the British Empire (German Ritual) has met the difficulty in its
edition of 1895 in the following way: It gives "meditations" before
the putting on of the fringed shawl, before laying on phylacteries,
at sitting down in the Succa, and before handling the Lulab, as
drawn up by Cabbalists, but with all the Cabbalistic matter (uniting God and his Presence, and "with fear and love") and all the
grotesque Midrashic matter left out; and it gets rid of the ugly
petition which goes with the priestly blessing, by omitting that
ceremony altogether and leaving it for the Festival Mahzor, of
which there is as yet no official edition.

BOOK III

THE DESK AND THE PULPIT

CHAPTER I

THE WEEKLY PENTATEUCH LESSON

(Pp. 247-253)

¹The present order of lessons is found in every Jewish Almanac, the division of weekly portions, in every Hebrew Bible. The need for *Vaethhannan* on the Sabbath after the 9th of Ab will appear in the chapter on Prophet Lessons; the seven consolations must be read between the Fast and New Year.

²Acts 15: 21; Jos. ag. Apion, 2, 17; T. J. on Megilla, ch. 1, § 1. About the court sessions on Monday and Thursday, see Kethuboth, ch. 1, § 1.

³Of the two passages quoted—T. J. on Shabbath, ch. 16, § 1, and Soferim, ch. 16, § 9—the former only speaks of 175 passages in the Pentateuch which contain precepts; the latter is too late and unauthentic to be a historic authority. When the Treatise of Scribes was written, the division into 175 Sabbath portions was, by its own admission, not used anywhere.

⁴T. B. Megilla, 29*b*.

⁵See Tudela's experience, as given in note 5 to Bk. I, ch. I; also a MS. with Arabic notes on the three-years cycle—Oxford, Neubauer, f. 22—of which more will be said in the chapter on Prophet Lessons.

⁶T. B. Megilla, 31*b*.

⁷Ib. This rule of reading the beginning of the next portion is in a Baraitha, and must have applied to the Palestinian three-years cycle, as well as to the one year. Hence, the opinion there given in favor of reading straight along on Saturday afternoon, Monday, Thursday, and Saturday morning, but overruled, is somewhat strange, as it would require 51 verses, at the least, for every week; too much for a three-years cycle. The Tanna who wanted to have it that way must have favored a cycle of two years.

⁸The absence of a statement to that effect in the book of Nehemiah is the strongest negative proof.

⁹T. B. Megilla, 29*b*, 30*a:* Where the portions כי תשא and אתה תצוה are named as now by their opening words.

¹⁰It appears from a passage in T. J. that the Tora may be finished on a Sabbath and New Moon, which excludes the last day of the Feast; there is also proof that Gen. 5 was read during the Passover; other facts tending this way are collated by Mr. A. Büchler, in his articles in the *Jewish Quarterly Review* for July and October, 1893.

¹¹T. B. Megilla, end of third chapter.

CHAPTER II

LESSONS OUTSIDE OF THE WEEKLY ORDER

(Pp. 254-259)

¹All these lessons, along with those for Purim, Ninth of Ab, Hanucca, and New Moons, are given, T. B. Megilla, 31*a*, *b*, where Baraitha and Gemara are easily separated.

²Ten verses are otherwise the minimum for a lesson (T. B. Megilla, 21*b*); but the battle with Amalek is told in nine verses. This lesson is the only exception to the rule.

³The Talmudic treatise on Fasts (Taanith) treats of the special fasts for drought or other distress, and so still does Abudraham in the fourteenth century. The Mahzor Vitry gives ויחל as the lesson for the afternoon of the Ninth of Ab without quoting authority. The Talmud, l. c. says: Read the account of creation at the מיעמדות, and "blessings and curses" on the Fasts. The present lesson was chosen on account of the atoning virtue of the thirteen qualities.

⁴The Talmud says: "And on your New Moons," which is not the beginning, for it would give only six verses for four men. Some other lessons are also named by a descriptive verse in the middle.

⁵T. B. Megilla, 29*b*.

⁶Megilla, ch. 3, §§ 4 and 5, where the four special Sabbaths are named, and § 6, which speaks also of the conflict between Festivals and the reading on Saturday afternoon, Monday, and Thursday.

⁷T. B. Taanith, 27*b*.

CHAPTER III

HOW THE LESSON IS DISTRIBUTED

(Pp. 260-264)

¹Megilla, ch. 4, §§ 1, 2. At all events the Tora must be read, not recited by heart; T. J. on Megilla, ch. 2, § 1. Only in the Temple,

on the Day of Atonement, the High Priest read the small passage about the day, in Lev. 23, by heart for reasons given.

²Megilla, ch. 4, § 5, as to boys under 13; Baraïtha in T. B. Megilla, 23a: "Even a woman."

³Gittin, ch. 5, § 8: "For the sake of peace they call first a Cohen, then a Levite, then an Israelite," and T. B. on same, 59b. The deduction is drawn from T. B. Kethuboth, 25b, that a Levite is called on after a Cohen; if there is no Cohen, a plain Israelite is called in his place. When there is no Levite, the Cohen first called reads or blesses again the second subsection "in place of a Levite." In modern practice, when more than seven are called, the last may be a Cohen or Levite; see discussion in Mahzor Vitry, p. 95.

⁴A professional reader (קרא) is mentioned, T. B. Taanith, 27b, who directs those called to the desk, especially school children, when to stop. The story about R. Akiba is quoted by the Mahzor Vitry from the "History" of Josippon, the wildest of romancers.

⁵Megilla, ch. 4, §§ 1, 2.

⁶T. B. Berachoth, 11b, gives the first benediction (see Bk. II, Ch. XIV); as to the other, see Soferim, ch. 13, § 8. The form there given differs somewhat from the present.

⁷T. J. on Megilla, ch. 3, last section.

⁸T. B. Megilla, 21b, *sub fine:* "now" each blesses, etc., "for those who come late."

⁹The lawfulness of calling women and small boys is admitted by all the Codes, including the Orah Hayim, though it is said, that to call a woman might be a dishonor to the congregation, as proving the lack of men able to read, as already stated in the Talmud.

¹⁰T. B. Rosh Hashana, 31a, gives the beginning words by initials, which Rashi, after older sources, explains.

¹¹T. B. Megilla, 23a, admitted that the Maftir reads in the Law; dispute whether he is of the seven or not. The latter notion seems to prevail.

¹²Soferim. ch. 17, § 9; T. B. Taanith, 27b, *sub fine.*

CHAPTER IV

THE LESSON FROM THE PROPHETS

(Pp. 265–275)

¹Abudraham, where in the Sabbath morning service he first comes to the Haftara, speaks in general terms of a persecution, during

which reading from the Law was prohibited. He is unreliable herein, as he gives a similar explanation of many usages, for instance, of שכיך and אני ה in the Kedusha of the Additional as a substitute for the reading of the Shema. However, this view, though unsupported by the Talmud, has been commonly received. The statement, 1 Macc. 1: 56, that Antiochus caused the books of the Law to be burned, lays some foundation for it.

²The original scheme was that Isa. 55 and Hos. 14 should be the two Repentances; each ritual set one of them aside for fast day afternoon. The Germans found a good substitute in Ezekiel; the Sefardim read 2 Sam. 18 simply because it is a song, to match the song, Deut. 33.

³Sections XLII and XLIII are then read separately, each with one of the "Punishments."

⁴In every Hebrew Bible the margin of the eight books marks where a Haftara for any portion or day, by either ritual, begins and ends.

⁵Megilla, ch. 4, § 10; but R. Jehuda (ben Il'aï) allows it; his opinion prevailed. The sixteenth chapter of Ezekiel is forbidden in the same place, as being too rude a denunciation of our "mother" Zion.

⁶T. B. Megilla, 31a and b, sets out all Haftaroth for Feasts, Fast of Ninth of Ab, and special Sabbaths. That for fast day afternoon seems to have been evolved later.

⁷Tosefoth on T. B. Megilla, 31b, explains the change in practice from the text by saying: "We go by the Pesikta."

⁸T. B. Megilla, 31b, names "Your New Moons, etc.," which is Isa. 1: 14, to be read when the New Moon of Ab is a Sabbath; also intimates that איכה, ib., verse 21, would fit the chapter for a lesson on the Ninth of Ab.

⁹T. B. Megilla, 23b.

¹⁰Tr. Soferim, ch. 14, § 2.

¹¹Megilla, ch. 4, § 4, allows skipping, but always forward, and though not from book to book, yet from one of the Twelve to another.

¹²All information about this MS. (Neubauer. f. 22) is drawn from Ad. Büchler's article in the *Jewish Quarterly Review*, October, 1893, in which it is copied. The lessons are marked by the first and last verse; those of two verses each have the words פסוקין פסקם (Arabic: two verses only) appended. He quotes other MS. works, in which some Haftaroth in the three-years cycle are mentioned, agreeing with this fragment. T. J. on Megilla, ch. 4, §§ 2, 3, requires three verses at least, though there be an interpreter.

[13]Megilla, ch. 4, § 10, and a Baraïtha under it speak of incidents (such as that of Amnon and Tamar) to be read, but not translated; indicating lessons not now in use.

[14]T. B. Megilla, 25*b*.

CHAPTER V

THE LITURGY OF THE DESK

(Pp. 276–283)

[1]T. B. Berachoth, 54*b*.

[2]T. J. on Rosh Hashana, ch. 4, § 7, has a form for the third benediction after the Haftara, "the God of David," now the "Shield of David." The second in some of the older sources closes, "builder of Jerusalem," which is at bottom the same as the present conclusion.

[3]The following sections in Tr. Soferim are drawn upon for this chapter: ch. 8, §§ 9-14; ch. 14. §§ 8, 9 (Hear, O Israel), and following sections in ch. 14. Maimonides speaks of one benediction before and four after reading, without giving them in full; but says the last closes like the "Sanctity of the Day." It is very probable that the liturgy of the desk was enlarged from time to time. to make up for the loss of the interpreter, perhaps also for that of the preacher. The last benediction after the Haftara, for which there is no Talmudic evidence, is probably as old as the other three. The words, "blessed be Thou," recur seven times in the benedictions before and after; probably meant to represent the seven men called to read the weekly portion.

CHAPTER VI

THE FIVE SMALL BOOKS

(Pp. 284–287)

[1]The following sections of the Treatise Soferim (which is not a part of the Mishna, but later than the Gemara) are drawn on for this chapter: ch. 14. §§ 5, 6, 18· ch. 18, § 4.

[2]Megilla, ch. 2, § 2. The materials needed are the same as for a scroll of the Law.

[3]The Mishna leaves the making of benediction to local custom; this is explained in the T. B. Megilla, 21*b*, to refer to the benediction

after reading, as that before reading falls under the general rule of blessing before the performance of all precepts.

⁴It seems that at one time the public reading of the book began here, with the greatness of Mordecai, not with the greatness of Ahasuerus; at least according to the ruling of some of the Sages; Megilla, ch. 2, § 3.

⁵T. J. on Megilla, ch. 4, § 1; T. B. Megilla, 21*b*. The latter form has prevailed. The double closing is to reconcile two traditions as to the right ending.

⁶T. B. Taanith, 30*a*.

⁷Megilla, ch. 1, § 1. This is of historic interest, as showing the importance of the sessions held on Mondays and Thursdays.

⁸The same rule applies to birthdays. A boy born in Adar of a common year only attains his age in the second Adar, if his thirteenth birthday happens in an intercalary year; Megilla, ch. 1, § 4.

CHAPTER VII

THE INTERPRETER, OR METHURGAMAN

(l'p. 288-292)

¹The great number of Greek words that have penetrated the Mishna and the still greater number in the Jerusalem Talmud and in the Midrash, render this clear. The latter in several passages has plays on Greek words, which shows that these were well understood. At Cæsarea, the services at the Synagogue were sometimes recited in Greek (ἑλληνιστόν); T. J. on Sota, ch. 7, § 1, commenting on the rule, that Hearing of Shema and Prayer may be spoken in any language that is understood. The duty to interpret the Tora, when publicly read, is derived by some from the example of Ezra; T. J. on Megilla, ch. 4, § 1, quoting Neh. 8: 8; though Ezra and Nehemiah must have been quite unwilling to admit ignorance of Hebrew on the part of their hearers and to use a foreign tongue.

²Megilla, ch. 4, § 4. "If the three be three paragraphs, he reads one by one."

³Dr. H. Barnstein, in his pamphlet "Targum of Onkelos to Genesis," already cited, draws from a study of the Yemen MSS. the conclusion that it was written in Palestine in the second century, and inclines to identify Onkelos with Aquila. Rapoport of Prague, about 1826, wrote a work on the Targum, which he called נר אוהב, Friend of the Convert. Zunz, however, believes that the version of Akylas (אקילס) was not Aramaic at all, but Greek, and was much

liked by the Rabbis, because it clung closely to the Hebrew text, while the Septuagint, gotten up by the Jews in Egypt (and which is always followed by the New Testament writers), diverges from it very widely.

⁴T. B. Sota, 49*b*.

⁵Dr. Barnstein's pamphlet, *supra*, p. 22 (quoting from Deren- bourg's *Manuel du Lecteur*).

⁶Orah Hayim, § 145, subs. 3.

⁷Megilla, ch. 2, § 1; T. B. on same (f. 18*a*) remarks, if it be in Greek, one must read from a Greek copy; otherwise it would be a recital by heart, which is unlawful.

⁸The first great objection to *Akdamoth* is its rich Aramaic vocabu- lary, which makes it a sealed book to all who do not study it up beforehand; the other is the introduction of the rather wild fancy about the future fight between Leviathan and Behemoth, and how the former will be served up for breakfast (Ariston) to the right- eous in Paradise.

⁹Megilla, ch. 2, § 9. "Rabban Simeon ben Gamaliel says: They did not allow even sacred books to be written, except in Greek." And see T. B. Megilla, 18*a*.

¹⁰Obadia of Bartenoro, in his commentary on Megilla, ch. 2, § 9.

CHAPTER VIII

PREACHING

(Pp. 293-296)

¹Such ethical rules, given as Halacha, not as in the treatise Aboth as individual opinion, are found, for instance, in Baba Metzia, ch. 4, § 2 (the unwritten higher law); ib., § 7 (duty of restoring wrongful gains); ib., § 10 (tenderness in speech); ib., § 11 (high standard of mercantile honesty). Or take in Eduïoth, ch. 5, § 6, the account of Akabia ben Mahal'el, who spurned the highest office rather than yield his conviction on any point, preferring to be thought a fool all his life to seeming wicked for one moment; and who refused, on his death, to recommend his son to his com- panions, telling him, "thy works may bring thee near to them, thy works may estrange thee." Or Sota, ch. 9, § 5, where the neglect or abandonment of our neighbor, when it leads to his death, is equalled to shedding his blood.

²T. B. Megilla, last sentence, a Baraïtha.

³T. J. on Megilla, ch. 4, §§ 2, 3, which fixes twenty-one verses

for the Haftara, but holds three verses enough, when interpreted, shows that a pretty lengthy paraphrase was expected. The Talmud speaks of great Rabbis acting as interpreters, who would naturally give their own views in the paraphrase. Soferim. ch. 14, § 2, says expressly "when interpreted or preached on." Still the sermons in Talmudic times must have been very short, as we find constant demands for briefness, for fear of "wearying the assemblage" (טרחא דצבורא).

BOOK IV

INCIDENTS AND CEREMONIES

CHAPTER I

POSTURE, SOUND, THOUGHT

(Pp. 299-307)

[1]The Psalm verse (84 : 5): "Happy are they who sit in thy house," and its introduction into the service are some proof. See Bk. I, ch. VII, as to chairs and benches. The German Gentiles called the synagogue "Judenschule," seeing people sitting on benches and reading books. Hilchoth Tefilla, ch. 9, § 1: As a rule, the people sit.

[2]E. g., the "sitting alarm sounds" on New Year; see hereafter. Megilla, ch. 4, § 1: The Book of Esther may be read in sitting posture. On the Ninth of Ab the reader of Lamentations sits on a "low stool or step."

[3]Megilla, ch. 4, § 3: "They raise their hands," means to impart the blessing.

[4]Known as a פתיחה; frequent in the German Ritual of the Solemn Days.

[5]This usage has grown up without the notice of the late or of previous Codes. See Orah Hayim, § 146. The notes, "Magen David," support the text, showing that Neh. 8: 5: "When he opened it, all the people stood up," means only that they were silent.

[6]I Kings 8: 29, 38; also Dan. 6: 11. Mishna Berachoth, ch. 4, §§ 5, 6: If one cannot turn his face, he should turn at least his

heart to the Holy of Holies. T. B. Berachoth, 30a: "Feet as one foot." T. B. Berachoth, 10b: "Tears off his feet" (עיקר את רגליו) ib., 29b.

[7] T. B. Berachoth, 32b. Ib., 27a.

[8] Mishna Berachoth, ch. 1, § 3. On the Day of Atonement, as of old in the Temple, all rise at the response (ברוך שם וגו׳), which follows.

[9] Dan. 6: 11; T. B. Berachoth, 34b. The Mishna does not mention kneeling in prayer at all.

[10] Mishna Joma, ch. 6, § 2: "And when the priests and people who stood in the court heard the plainly spoken Name, as it came from the mouth of the High Priest, they would kneel and bow down and fall on their faces and say: Bléssed is the name of his glorious kingdom forever and ever."

[11] Baraitha in T. B. Berachoth, 34a. See opinions in favor of kneeling and bending, ib., 28b.

[12] נופלים על אפים; the phrase and custom are known to the Talmud, T. B. Megilla, 22b, though only on public fasts; but see Orah Hayim, § 131; also Abudraham's older work, which refers to R. Amram on the question, "whether they fall on their faces" on Purim.

[13] Cuzari, pt. 2, § 80, repels the reason drawn from the lively temper of the Jews, and traces the habit to the former necessity of ten or more men reading from one big book laid before them on the ground. Abudraham puts it on the Psalm verse. Rashi on T. B. Berachoth, 62a, speaks of Bible readers from Palestine, who accompany their chant with the right arm as with a baton.

[14] Ex. 29: 6, 9; Zech. 3: 5. Always so depicted.

[15] T. B. Berachoth, 60b: "He spreads the kerchief on his head, and blesses him who crowns Israel with beauty." This is to be done and said before the fringed shawl or phylacteries are put on. T. J. on Berachoth, ch. 2, § 3, says of R. Johanan ben Zaccai, that by reason of his corpulence he wore no turban in summer, and was otherwise almost naked. The Treatise Soferim puts a person with uncovered head on a footing with one half-clad (פוחח), whose knees and shoulders are bare. As to covered head and fear of Heaven, see T. B. Shabbath, 156b.

[16] This is shown by the unbroken testimony of all antique statues. T. J. on Berachoth, ch. 1. § 3, tells us how the Roman Emperors required everybody to bare his head as a mark of awe, when an imperial rescript (πρόςταγμα) was read, which to the Asiatics seemed a hardship.

[17] 1 Cor. 11: 4, 7: Men must pray and preach with uncovered

heads, while other verses in the same chapter bid women to pray
with covered heads, for reasons not very flattering to the fair sex.

[18]Historic proof of this position can perhaps not be had; but we
know that many forms of salutation among Christians and Mohammedans are marks of religious recognition; see art. SALUTATION in
Encyclopædia Britannica.

[19]Orah Hayim, § 2 (head to be covered when fringed garment is
worn); § 8 (none to walk four cubits distance bare-headed); § 91
(hat or cap at prayers); § 151, subs. 6, § 282, subs. 3 (even children,
who may otherwise be uncovered, must cover the head when reading the Law). Maimonides, writing in Moslem countries, enjoins
only learned men, as a matter of decency, always to keep their
heads covered. In Hilchoth Tefilla, ch. 4, § 1, he does not reckon
the uncovered head among the positive hindrances to prayer. A MS.
lately discovered at Cambridge (see *Jewish Quarterly Review*, October, 1892, p. 23) of a work by R. Asher ben Shaül, a French Rabbi
of the thirteenth century, of "Lorid," probably in France, states that
the benediction, "who crowns Israel, etc." was not customary in
the writer's country as in Spain, because many Israelites there
went with uncovered heads. And there is other evidence to show
that for a long time the Jews of France were careless about covering the head, even at prayers. But Abudraham says the same as to
Christian Spain, in 1340, to the extent that they do not say the
blessing, and do not spread the kerchief; not, however, stating that
his contemporaries in Seville say their prayers bare-headed. (See
Bk. II, ch. XIV.)

[20]Joma, ch. 8, § 1. Taking off the shoes on the Ninth of Ab has
a further reason; it is a badge of mourning.

[21]Megilla, ch. 4, § 8, where the same suspicion attaches to insist-
ence on white garments. Such are, however, worn in our days on
the Day of Atonement: a long, white, lace-trimmed robe, with
linen cap to suit.

[22]Such reading in thought (הרהור) was practiced by the learned
only when defiled, till cleansed by bath or douche; Berachoth,
ch. 3, § 4.

[23]Ib., ch. 2, § 3, and T. B. Berachoth, 15a and b, where Ps. 68:
14, is wildly distorted to favor those who read the Shema distinctly.

[24]T. B. ib., 31a, where 1 Sam. 1: 13, is analyzed. But the Orah
Hayim, § 101, subs. 2, says, he who prays should whisper loud
enough for his own ears.

[25]Orah Hayim, § 101, subs. 2, as a ש׳ אוכרים ; an annotator warns
against raising the voice too much even then.

[26]The response in the Kaddish, "Amen, be his great name, etc.,"

is the most sacred: T. B. Berachoth, 3*a*, 21*b*. For the response, "Give thanks," see T. B. on Succa, ch. 3, § 9.

²⁷The air of כל נדרי is too well known to be here reproduced. As two examples we give here the short quatrain אלי ציון in the dirge for the Ninth of Ab and the tune with which the benedictions before and after the Shema on the Memorial and Atonement days are closed in the evening service.

E - li tzi-ou v' o - re - ho k' mo i - sho b' tzi - re - ho v'

chi-b'su-lo ha-gu-ras sak al...... ba - al n'u - re - ho.

²⁸Known as התינורות. "Pleasant singing" on Sabbath and Festivals is recommended in the German-Polish annotations of the Orah Hayim, to be applied to the זמירות, "musical parts," i. e., Psalms, Red Sea Song, and the poetic insertions in יוצר אור; see רמ״א to § 281. The Sefardic text in § 51, 4, 5, reckons a pleasant voice among the qualifications of the leader, adding that, if a man cannot be found with all the qualifications, the most learned and virtuous in the community be chosen; but R. Moses Isserles, knowing the weakness of his Polish countrymen for fine singing, holds that, between an old ignorant man with a fine voice and a boy of thirteen, without voice, who understands what he says, the latter should be preferred.

²⁹Orah Hayim, § 53, warns the leader against dwelling long on words only in order to show his good voice. The gloss, "Magen

Abraham," on § 529 (Rules of Rosh Hashana), warns him against keeping up the services beyond noon by fine singing. In the very modern work, חיי אדם, §§ 29, 30, the Cantor who sings to show his voice is called disgraced, and a Biblical rebuke is attached to one who spends time on chanting. Girls were, of course, excluded from the old-fashioned Meshorerim, and are even now in orthodox congregations not admitted into the choirs singing modern music; the soprano and contralto parts being sung by the boys of still unbroken voices. This is not done because woman is unworthy to take part in public service; for it has been held that even women and children may be called to the desk to read the Law, if there are not seven men present able to do so (Orah Hayim, § 282), but because קול באשה ערוה, a woman's voice arouses passion (T. B. Berachoth, 24a). The writer thinks that giving to a large choir of Jewish girls an opportunity to become acquainted at least with the responsive parts of the service would outweigh this objection; indeed, it has hardly any force, unless there are solo parts, and these, except for the leader or Cantor, are wholly foreign to the spirit of Jewish services. Many of the strictly orthodox object to any trained choir, because it prevents the worshippers from joining in the responses. They may, of course, join in low tones; but they hate to have their voices drowned by hired singers, often Gentiles, who have no heart in the words uttered. It is to be regretted that Jewish choral music took its rise in Catholic Vienna, rather than in Protestant North Germany, where it might have followed the Lutheran usage of simple airs, set in only two parts, in which the whole congregation is trained to join from their earliest schooldays up. Yet with all its intricacies, the music of Sulzer and of his northern successors, such as Weintraub and Lewandowski, arouses a religious feeling in the hearers just as the Lutheran "Gesangbuch" does. The so-called "musical services" in many American Synagogues, made up of operatic pieces, Catholic masses, and other nondescript matter, cannot be criticised at all from a religious standpoint, as it is usually arranged by some Gentile organist without any view to religious effect. From the standpoint of art it is bad enough; for according to Wagner's great rule, all the elements of art performance should go hand in hand; and a Jewish Temple is hardly the proper background for Lohengrin or for Rossini's Stabat Mater.

²⁰Mishna Berachoth, ch. 2, § 1, as explained in the Talmud, demands *attention* to what is read, not intention to fulfill the command. Ibid., § 4: Workmen on a tree or wall may stay there and read the *Shema;* "which they may not do with the Prayer." Maimo-

nides, in the Jad Hahazaka, rules on Reading the Shema, requires
stoppage of work and attention for all of the first paragraph.

[21]Ib., ch. 4, § 4; ch. 5, § 1; Aboth, ch. 2, § 18. In the Talmud on
the first-named passage there is an opinion that the rule is violated,
if the worshipper does not add requests of his own to the customary
form of words; but this view has never taken root.

[22]Berachoth, ch. 4, § 1. Morning Prayer till noon; Musaf all
day; Minha till dark; evening Prayer all night.

[23]A Baraitha in T. B. Berachoth, 34b.

[24]Mishna Sota, ch. 8, § 1. This has already been treated in the
first book of this work.

[25]T. B. Berachoth, 31b, in a passage already quoted; based on
Hannah's answer to Eli. *Query:* Was the strong language of the
Rabbis based on what they heard of heathen orgies, or about the
Agape?

[26]Mishna, ib., ch. 3, § 5. The Talmud on this section discusses
the matter more fully than modern taste would permit.

[27]Ib., ch. 9, § 4; T. B., ib., 13b.

[28]Berachoth, ch. 2, §1.

[29]Ib., ch. 4, § 1.

[30]Orah Hayim, §§ 66, 102; § 51, subs. 3.

[31]Ibid., § 146, comp. above Note 5. Unfortunately there are many
interludes in the proceedings, when the matter spoken by the
reader or the leader is not such as to command any one's devout
attention, and here free conversation creeps in.

CHAPTER II

THE TROPE
(Pp. 308-311)

[1]The accents can be found with full explanations of their rank
in every good Hebrew grammar, such as that of Gesenius in its
various editions.

[2]The whole is known as Zarka; it begins, Zarka Segol, and ends,
Jethib Pesik Sof Pasuk.

[3]The music below for the trope of Parsha and Haftara in the
German Ritual is taken (with omission of the rarer accents and
combinations) from A. Baer's Baal T'fillah, Gothenburg, 1877, Nos.
105 and 106, in each case the first of three variations, which he gives
in parallel lines. The phrases which cannot well follow each other,
but of which one is a substitute or variation of the other, are
marked in the usual way by double heavy bar-lines.

Parshyoth.
Haphtoroth.
Zar - ko se - gol Mu-
nah Mu - nah re - vi - a Mah-
pach pashto Zo - kef ko - ton Zo - kef go - dol Mer-
cho Tif - ho Mu - nah es - nah - to Po -
zer
T' li-sho k' ta - noh

2
T' li-sho g' do - loh
1
Kadmo v' az - lo
2
Az - lo ge - resh
3
Gershayim
Dar - - go t'vir Ye -
siv P'sik Sof po - suk.
Mer - cho tif' - ho sof po - suk.

Mr. Baer gives, in connection with the trope of the Germans, in Nos. 117-123 certain passages in the Pentateuch, and under Nos. 124-138 certain passages in the Book of Esther, which have traditionally their peculiar tunes (כ׳ענ׳נא).

The following music (Sefardic) for the Haftara and the first verse of Lamentations is also taken from A. Baer's Baal T'fillah (Nos. 938 and 940), and credited by him to an older work by O. Aguilar. The Canto D'Israele, published at Livorno, in its version of the Sefardic trope, differs materially from that below, but agrees with it in its general character.

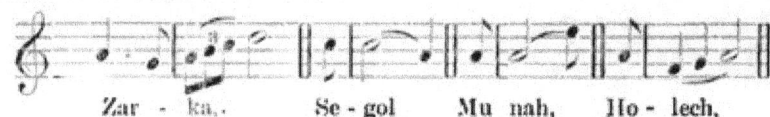

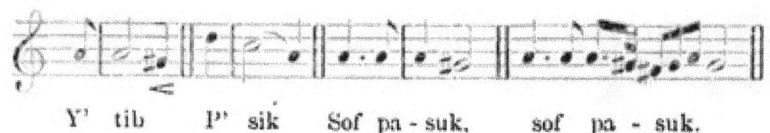

Zar - ka,.   Se - gol   Mu nah,   Ho - lech,

R' bi - a.   Mah - pach,   Pash - ta,   Zakef katon.

Za-kef Ga - dol......   Mercha.   Tif - ha   Mu-nah

Et-nah-ta.   Pa - zer................   T' li-sha k 'ta - na.........

T' li-sha g' do - la.........   Kad - ma.   Veaz - la.   Gersha -

yim......   Ge - resh......   Dar - ga............   Te - bir............

Y' tib   P' sik   Sof pa - suk,   sof pa - suk.

E - cha   ya-sh' ba ba-dad ha-ir rab-ba-ti am ha-y'

ta   k' al-ma - na   rab - ba - ti ba-go-yim   sa -

ra - ti   bam-di - not   ha - y' ta   la - mas.

'Professor Petermann wrote for volume 5 of the *Zeitschrift der deutschen morgenländischen Gesellschaft* an account of the old Church music of the Armenians, showing it to have a notation greatly analogous to that of the trope; that is, not single notes, but larger or shorter phrases. Prof. Paul Haupt (now of Johns Hopkins) has also made researches into the origin of the trope.

²T. B. Megilla, 32a. The author of the saying, R. Johanan, is of the first generation of Western Emoraïm; that is, an immediate disciple of R. Judah, the Patriarch. See also T. J. on Megilla, ch. 4, § 1, where it is claimed that the "giving the sense," spoken of in Neh. 8: 8, was done by reading the Pentateuch with the proper intonation.

CHAPTER III

FRINGES AND PHYLACTERIES

(פ 312-317)

'Berachoth, ch. 3, § 3, as to phylacteries. In case of the fringes, the words of the Law, "ye shall see them," is relied on as showing that they were not required at night. T. B. Menahoth, 43b.

²Menahoth, ch. 4, § 1, says, the lack of the sky-blue, known as הכלת, does not hinder the use of the white threads; then already the sky-blue threads were scarce and dear. T. B. Menahoth, 44a. As explained there, one or two threads of those making the fringe were to be sky-blue. The thread of that color is part of the fringe. Maimonides, in Hilchoth Tzitzith, speaks of the blue threads as if they were then in use, though they were not.

³T. B. Menahoth, 42*a*, as to נֹדִיל.

⁴T. B. Berachoth, 60*b*. Observing Israelites wear a small four-cornered cloth, with a hole cut out for the head, at all times. Before putting this on, the benediction is spoken, in a modified form.

⁵I. M. Jost, *Geschichte des Judenthums*, Vol. II, p. 307, is the writer's authority for the Karaitic custom.

⁶T. B. Berachoth, 47*b*, and elsewhere.

⁷Shabbath, ch. 6, § 1: טוטפות for women's head-bands.

⁸Maimonides, in Hilchoth Tefillin, 4 chapters, gives these and a great many more details. The more modern Codes agree with him almost literally. Among these details is a regular שׁ and a four-headed שׁ, which are worked into the box of the phylactery for the head, to show the direction; the former being on the right, the latter on the left of the wearer, and the strap is put through the loops accordingly.

⁹Hilchoth Tefillin, ch. 4, § 10. In the notes to this is found a discussion between Rabbis of the twelfth and thirteenth centuries, whether phylacteries are to be worn on the Middle Days, as the Unleavened Bread and the Hut should be sign enough. R. Simha, author of the Mahzor Vitry, claims they should be worn on the Middle Days, on the strength of T. J. on Moed Katan, ch. 3, § 4, where leave was given during such days to write phylacteries for one who lost them, though only pressing work should be done on those days. Hence, the German Jews generally lay Tefillin on Middle Days, while the Sefardim and the Hasidim do not. But before Musaf on middle days of the Passover and on New Moons the phylacteries are removed, and on the middle days of the Feast of Huts, before Hallel. As to Sabbath and true Festivals, see Shabbath, ch. 6, § 2, and T. B. Menahoth, 36*b*.

¹⁰T. B. Menahoth, 42*b*, gives the benedictions; the verses were chosen long after.

¹¹Maimonides, in Hilchoth Tefillin, ch. 5, § 4, speaks from this standpoint, when he denounces those who scribble the names of angels and other Cabbalistic nonsense upon the *Mezuza* (parchment strip with the two paragraphs from Deuteronomy for the door-post), thus degrading the highest expression of faith and love into a קְמִיִּ (Amulet).

¹²Megilla, ch. 1, § 8; ch. 4, § 8.

¹³T. B. Berachoth, 14*b*.

¹⁴Cmp. ib., 23*a*, and following pages.

¹⁵T. B. Menahoth, 34-36.

¹⁶The Codes of Alfassi, of Maimonides, the Turim (Toledo, thir-

teenth century), and the Shulhan Aruch, all speak of the Tefillin as a live custom.

¹⁷According to T. B. Menahoth, 34*b*, 35*a*, the order is not material, so long as the two paragraphs that ought to be on the outside are on the outside, and the other two in the middle.

¹⁸T. B. Menahoth, 43*b*, and see the pretty story about the man whom a glance at his fringes saved from sin, and led thus to the conversion and reformation of a fair sinner, ib., 44*a*.

CHAPTER IV

CEREMONIES ON YEARLY OCCASIONS

(Pp. 318-326)

¹Megilla, ch. 4. § 7; T. B. Berachoth, 32*b*; T. B. Menahoth, 109*a*. Baraïtha, in T. B. Kerithoth, 28*b*, excludes the drunken man on the ground of Lev. 10: 8. Lack of piety or learning does not disqualify (Hilchoth Tefilla, ch. 15, § 6), for God blesses (Num. 6: 27), not the priest.

²T. B. Sota, 39, seems not to demand a special washing for the occasion, but it is so construed by Rashi. Maimonides, in the chapter cited, does not demand such washing, nor removal of shoes. The removal of "sandals" is among the institutions of Rabban Johanan ben Zaccaï; T. B. Sota, 40*a*; but, as is there explained, it was not intended as a token of respect, but only because the loosening of the straps might lead to disturbance. The washing by Levites is an invention of the Zohar on Num. 6: 22-27. See Orah Hayim, § 128, for these and other rules observed; and see T. B. Berachoth, 55*b*, for prayer after a troubling dream. A prayer by and for the priests that their blessing may be pure and effective (T. B. Sota, 40) has been given in Bk. II, ch. vi.

³This usage, unknown to the Talmud, seems a survival of the fasts for rain.

⁴Rosh Hashana, ch. 4, §§ 5, 6, 7, 9. R. Gamaliel says: The messenger of the congregation—by blowing the horn—relieves the others of their duty. Hence, to hear the Shofar is enough; so T. B. on same, 32*a*, and the benediction, "to hear the sound, etc.," is correct.

⁵Seder R. Amram speaks of the "sitting sounds," and distinguishes by initials ט and ר and רט, between the two single alarms and the compound alarm, and gives the benedictions in full, not quoting authority for the latter, but stating that R. Abbahu, at

Cæsarea, introduced the three modes of alarm. Abudraham, in the fourteenth century, still quotes the Jer. Talmud for the benediction. As the copies thereof now in use are but a fragment, they may be, and probably are, right in their quotations.

⁶Still unknown to R. Amram, who starts the evening service right after Neïla. Mahzor Vitry: He blows one תקי״עה in memory of the Jubilee.

⁷In Succa, ch. 3, § 4. R. Ishmael gives the numbers of each kind; his rule prevails now against R. Akiba's dissent; § 8, the bunch tied with its own kind; § 9, when to shake it during Hallel; §12, it was taken in the Temple seven days, in the country only on the first; at Jabne Johanan ben Zaccaï made the rule to take it seven days everywhere, in remembrance of the Temple. For mode of shaking, see T. B. Succa, 37b.

⁸Succa, ch. 4, § 5, tells of the circuits round the altar, one each on six days of the Feast, seven on the seventh day; willow bunches were carried in these; § 6, the children ate their citrons; § 9, the water poured from a golden basin amidst cornet sounds; ch. 5, § 1, speaks of the חליל. or concerted music of the middle days of the Feast, known as the music of the Water Fetching House: "who has not seen this pleasure, never has seen pleasure." Ch. 5, § 4, the leading pious men dance, carrying torches, and sing; the Levites play on harps, trumpets, and cymbals; the people glory in their faithfulness to God; for they look westward to the Holy of Holies, while their idolatrous fathers looked eastward to the rising sun. Some slight compensation for the lack of ceremony is made by reading the Sabbath hymns in the morning (Psalms 19, 34, 90, 91, 135, 136, 33, 92, 93) and reciting the Kedusha in the Additional in its fuller form. The concerted music was omitted in the Temple when this day fell on a Sabbath. Succa, ch. 5, § 1. A Yemen MS., lately published, speaks of an old custom of moving the Ark for the day into the middle of the Synagogue, better to represent the circuits round the altar.

⁹Abudraham knows nothing of all this merriment; he has only five men called to read the portion just as on other festivals, but remarks, that the one who finishes the Tora and he who begins it again give banquets to their kinsmen and friends. The Mahzor Vitry already calls those who finish and recommence bridegrooms, and allots to them the honor of rolling each his scroll and carrying it in his arm; but the fun of unlimited calls and repeated reading of the same few verses is still unknown, and so is the procession with the scrolls and flags. The frolic with the scroll in the evening is avowedly a triumph of popular tastes over Rabbinic scruples.

BOOK V

THE JEWISH HOME

CHAPTER I

MINIAN AT THE HOUSE

(Pp. 325-333)

¹No authority for the anniversaries can be found in any of the great standards; the Shulhan Aruch, as far as I can find, does not mention it at all. Other modern writers have not been more successful than myself in finding authorities. However, prayer books with "rules" (דינים) like that of יעב"ץ, the Rabbi of Lissa, not only mention the Jahrzeit, but recommend fasting on such days. The eleven months are put by R. Moses Isserles in a note on Jore De'a, § 621, on the ground that a son should not suppose that his parent was wicked, so that his soul would be in trouble for twelve months.

²T. J. on Moed Katan, ch. 3, § 5; on the basis of the kindred at whose burial a Cohen may defile himself (Lev. ch. 21). The wife is implied there by the exclusion of a married sister; and so is the husband, at least for the purpose of mourning.

³Berachoth, ch. 3, § 1 (before burial, the time known as אנינות). As to mourners proper (after burial), T. B. Moed Katan, 21a.

⁴Moed Katan, ch. 3, § 5. The seven days are by the Talmud on this section derived from Amos 8: 10: "I will turn your feasts into mourning," the feasts being seven days, and adds: There are three days for weeping. And by the letter of the Tora there is only one day of strict mourning, as shown by Aaron's words, Lev. 10: 19: "Should I eat sin-offering to-day?" and so Amos says, in 8: 10, further: "And its end like a bitter day." See T. B. Moed Katan, 16-19.

⁵Moed Katan, ch. 3, § 6; so held T. B. on same, 19a, in accordance with R. Gamaliel's opinion.

⁶T. B. Kethuboth, 8a. Form just as in modern service books. Although the כתובה, or written contract, which is read by the minister after the betrothal and before the seven benedictions is

28

not an act of worship, its opening sentences may be inserted here as a curiosity: "At (such a place) on (such a day) said A son of B to the maiden C daughter of D: Be thou my wife, and I will serve and honor, feed, care for, and clothe thee, like Jewish men who serve and honor, feed, care for, and clothe their wives faithfully, etc."

CHAPTER II

WHAT CHILDREN LEARN FIRST

(Pp. 334-338)

[1]Aboth, ch. 5, § 24. Bartenoro comments hereon, that the letters have been taught before.

[2]T. B. Succa, 42a, a Baraïtha with Talmudic additions.

[3]Berachoth, ch. 6, §§ 1, 2, 3; T. B. on same, 35a.

[4]Berachoth, ch. 9, § 2. "At the sight of זִקִּין, i. e., comets and shooting stars, at earthquakes, lightnings and thunder, one says. "Blessed, of whose power the world is full." T. B. on same, suggests "Creator of the work of the beginning" along with the above; this is now deemed the blessing for the lightning, the former for the thunder.

[5]T. B. Berachoth, 60b.

[6]T. B. Berachoth, 5a.

[7]Ib., the verse being explained: the first word רגזו, "be troubled," that is, set your good impulse at war against the evil one; speak to your heart, i. e., meditate on the Law, to keep down sinful thoughts; if necessary, think of silence, i. e., of death.

[8]See for these responses and their reasons Bk. II, ch. V.

[9]T. B. Shabbath, 21b. Shammaï taught to begin with eight lights and come down to one; the opposite rule, now in vogue, is Hillel's. Those living on the ground floor used to put their lamps before the front door, those living in an upper story in a window. The date of the feast, Kislev 25th, is here given; also its origin in the Maccabean victory by which the Temple was recovered. Nothing is said about benedictions; but the first one is implied by calling the lighting a precept (מצוה), which makes the rule in Tosifta on Berachoth, ch. 6, apply.

CHAPTER III

THE MEAL

(Pp. 339-347)

[1]Berachoth, ch. 7, §§ 1, 2, 3. The following section (4) holds it improper for three, four, or five, or for ten to divide into groups when saying grace, as they would lose the privilege of the address and response, or of God's name therein. The Talmud on this chapter is full of historic illustrations of the manner and form of the address, as far back as the time of King Jannæus. The notion of pronouncing a holier and fuller name of God in the address when 100 or 1,000 men said grace together was dropped through the opposition of R. Akiba, ch. 7, § 3. The custom that the master of the house always "breaks the bread," i.e., says the short grace before the meal, while a guest blesses after the meal, is mentioned T. B. Berachoth, 46a.

[2]Berachoth, ch. 6, § 8, speaks of three benedictions, taking it for granted, that these are spoken after a meal of bread; but discusses whether three are, or an abstract of three is, recited after figs, raisins, etc. As to mentioning the exodus, the covenant of our flesh, and the gift of the Law in the second benediction, along with "the precious, good, and wide land," and the Kingdom of David in the third, see T. B. Berachoth, 48b, and 49a, and reasons there given. The authorship of the first three benedictions is ascribed to Moses, Joshua, and David; which simply means that they had been in use too long to remember their origin.

[3]T. B. Berachoth, 48b, 49a. The refinement about omitting "King" in the insertion for New Moon and Festivals is suggested by the saying, T. B. Berachoth, 48b: One Kingdom does not touch the other as much as a hair's breadth.

[4]T. B. Berachoth, 48b (also Taanith, 31a, and Baba Bathra, 121a). "On the day that the slain of Bethar were given burial, etc.;" הטוב והמטיב being the benediction over good news. The threefold mention of God as King is part of the original draft, to make up for the lack of God's Kingship in the preceding benediction. The petitions beginning "The Merciful" are not mentioned in the Talmud. Maimonides has three such petitions in the short form of grace which he puts in his "Order of Prayer" for common use. The official London Prayer Book has for choice, after the usual form, one even shorter than that of Maimonides, the first benediction, however, unabridged, the second with thanks for all

the things required as above in the Talmud, and "bread in plenty," the third seeking mercy for "thy people, the Kingdom of the House of David" and "the glory of thy temple," according to the traditional requirements. The Seder R. Amram, at the end of the original book, has a special grace for the House of Mourning. The address: "Let us bless the Comforter of Mourners from, etc." (1) and (2) rather short, but with no reference to mourning. (3) "Comfort, O Lord our God, those that mourn, the mourners for Zion and the mourners in this sad case; comfort them after their grief, gladden them after their sorrow, as it is said: Like a man whom his mother comforteth, thus I shall comfort you, and in Zion ye shall be comforted. Blessed, etc., the comforter of mourners and builder of Jerusalem. Amen." In (4) is inserted: "The God of truth, the truthful Judge (the words of the common benediction on hearing bad news; see Berachoth, ch. 9, § 2), the righteous Judge." The London Prayer Book is the only one now in general use which contains for mourners special forms; they are substantially like those of R. Amram. "Workmen omit the fourth benediction;" T. B. Berachoth, 46a.

⁵T. J. on Berachoth, ch. 7, § 5 (4), and see about short grace for workmen, ib., 16a. That the benediction before, hence also grace after bread, include all other food, is stated in T. B. Berachoth, 41b.

⁶Aboth, ch. 3, § 3.

⁷Berachoth, ch. 6, § 6; T. B. Berachoth, 51a, gives all the rules for the "cup of blessing."

⁸T. B. Kethuboth, 7b and 8a; see here the modified address at weddings. The seven benedictions are repeated only when there is a new face.

⁹T. B. Berachoth, 40b.

¹ºBerachoth, ch. 6, § 8; T. B. thereon (44a) gives the form. The Palestinians closed this grace after the five fruits: "For the land and its fruits;" the Babylonians could not join them, and said: "For the land and the fruits," as is the common custom now.

CHAPTER IV

SANCTIFICATION AND SEPARATION

(Pp. 348–355)

¹Shabbath, ch. 2, is taken up mainly with the Sabbath light; see Bk. II, ch. XV, about the reading of this chapter on Friday evening.

¹Hillel and Shammaï were already disputing which benediction to say first; Berachoth, ch. 8, § 1, and as to Passover night, Pesahim, ch. 10, § 2. The order of the thanks for Sabbath and for Festival was settled by Rabbi Judah the Saint, as in the middle benediction of the prayer; T. J. on Rosh Hashana, ch. 4, § 7. That the Sabbath has already been consecrated before Kiddush is made over the cup, see T. B. Berachoth, 52*b* (on ch. 8, § 1).

²There was an opinion that the "season" should be thanked for only on the longer feasts (Passover and Huts); but the view prevailed that it must be done on all yearly sacred days, including Pentecost, New Year, and Atonement; and if it is not done over the cup, anywhere, even on the street. T. B. Erubin, 40*b*. Cmp., this benediction on Day of Atonement, Bk. II, ch. XII. The three verses from Gen. 2 are recommended T. B. Shabbath, 119*b*. See Bk. II, ch. IX, note 2.

³Known by the initials of the five things blessed יקנה״ז (i. e., wine, sanctification, lamp, separation, season); the fourth benediction is analogous to that in the Prayer; see Bk. II, ch. IX. Its full text is not found in the Talmud; but see T. B. Pesahim, 102*b*-105*a*, where the form of the simple and of the compound Habdala is discussed; the number of pairs distinguished varying from 3 to 7. The order of the five benedictions was not settled till the days of Abbaye and Raba, of the fifth generation of Emoraïm. The idea of separating between Holy and Holy is derived from the vail in the Temple, which divided between the Holy and the Holy of Holies.

⁴T. B. Berachoth, 33*a*. Light and spices are named in the Mishna, ch. 8, § 5, by Hillel, in this order: Light, meal, spices, separation. It seems that separation in the Prayer was not yet in use, and the Habdala was intertwined with grace after the Sabbath afternoon meal.

⁵T. B. Sanhedrin, 41*a*, enjoins the duty, and the benediction is given, 42*a*. The late treatise Soferim, ch. 19, § 9, adds a number of verses and phrases, more like incantations than prayers. The Baraïtha commending the duty, ascribed to the "school of R. Ishmael," is also recited as part of the ceremony; also Psalms 121 ("I lift my eyes, etc.") and 67. Soferim, ch. 20, § 1, names Saturday night as the proper time.

⁶Tosifta on Berachoth, ch. 6.

CHAPTER V

THE PASSOVER NIGHT

(Pp. 356-367)

[1]Pesahim, ch. 10 (almost all of it), views not prevailing left out. T. J. on § 2 derives the four cups from the four verbs in the promise of delivering, Ex. 6: 6, 7; so does Midrash Rabba on Gen., ch. 88. Other explanations are given in both places; the above alone is popularly known.

[2]T. J. on Pesahim, ch. 10, § 4.

[3]Rashi drew up this programme; see Mahzor Vitry, *ad locum*. Older sources call for the usual benediction at the first hand-washing.

[4]R. Amram has it without comment, but says, "move the table before the master," not lift the dish; and quotes from T. B. Pesahim how this is done to arouse the child's curiosity. "If his child is smart, he will ask; if not, his wife should ask him; if she does not, he should ask himself."

[5]T. J. on Pesahim, ch. 10, § 4. Here is also the explanation of the two pieces of roast meat, both on the Passover dish, one to represent the "lamb," the other the Hagiga, or Feast offering.

[6]T. B. Pesahim, 116a, gives a dispute which of these passages meets the requirement to begin with reproach and end with praise. Probably both were already in use.

[7]T. B. Pesahim, 115a. "In memory of the Temple like Hillel."

[8]The Piyut for the second night (ואמרתם זבח פסח) is part of those for the morning service of that day, in the repetition of the Prayer. Neither this nor any of the other poetic pieces has an acrostic betraying the author's name.

[9]So Zunz in his *Gottesdienstliche Vorträge*.

[10]Abudraham indicates this insertion by its first words, only to reject it. The writer found it in a publication of a Yemen Haggada, by Dr. Wm. H. Greenburg, London, 1896. This Haggada is accompanied by legendary comment; which is probably used by fathers in Yemen at the table, in order to render the story more interesting to their households.

INDEXES

SERVICES FOR THE SABBATH

I. FRIDAY EVENING

II. SATURDAY MORNING

(Including the "Additional")

INDEX TO THE REFERENCES TO THE SCRIPTURES

(Italics for the page numbers indicate passages quoted in the book, but not necessarily from the liturgy; Roman type indicates those occurring in the liturgy.)

29

INDEX TO REFERENCES TO THE MISHNA

INDEX TO REFERENCES TO THE JERUSALEM TALMUD

INDEX TO REFERENCES TO THE BABYLONIAN TALMUD

Black Death, the, and *Abinu Malkenu*, 164.
Blessing, Priestly. *See* Priestly Blessing, the.
Blue dye-stuff, on the fringes, 312.
Bodleian Library, the, manuscript in, on *Haftaroth*, 274-5.
Boëthos, disciple of Antigonus of Socho, founder of the Sadducees, 23.
Bohemia, Ashkenazim in, 13.
Booths, the Feast of (Huts; *Succoth;* Tabernacles; the Feast), a Midrash concerning, 46; date of, 61; modification of the *Amida* of, 144; *Hallel* on, 180-1; Psalms on, 183; "poetries" for, 223, 227, 323-5; lessons on, 255, 256, 258; number of scrolls used on, 256-7; *Haftaroth* for, 272-3; Ecclesiastes read on, 284; the *Lulab* on, 322-3; *Kiddush* on, 355.
See also Feasts, the three; Festivals, the.
Booths, the Feast of, the seventh day of (*Hoshana Rabba*), cannot occur on a Sabbath, 60; Deuteronomy and the Psalter read on, 192; the lesson on, 254; the *Haftara* for, 272; ceremonies connected with, 323-5; the willow bunch on, 324; Cabbalistic meaning of, 324.
Booths, the Feast of, the eighth day of (*Shemini Atzereth*), date of, 61; prayer for rain on, 123-4; modifications of the *Amida* of, 144; prayers for the dead on, 219; lesson on, 255, 258; the *Haftara* for, 272; interrupts mourning, 331.
Booths, the Feast of, the ninth day of. *See* "Joy of the Law."
Boys under thirteen, and the reading of the Law, 260, 263; on the "Joy of the Law," 326.
Bread, *Kiddush* over, 350.
"Breaking on the *Shema*." *See under Shema*, the.
"Bridegroom of Genesis," 283.
"Bridegroom of the Tora," 283.
Buddhism, and Cabbalistic notions, 53.
Bul, name of the eighth month, 58.

Cabbala, the, and the *Hasidim*, 18, 56; resembles Midrash, 50, 56; philosophy of, 50-1; the Mishna on, 51-2; on the names of God, 52; on the archetype of man, 52; as expounded in the "Book of Formation," 52-3; works of, 53-5; not supported by the teachers of Arabic Spain, 54; in the Bahir, 54; in the Zohar, 54-6; name of, a usurpation, 56; esoteric, 56; in the Prayer Book, 241-4.
Cabbalistic traces in the Prayer Book, 120, 183, 241-4, 277-8, 279, 336-7, 349, 355; objectionable, 242-3.
Cabbalists, the, use "Be it thy will," 87; and *Hoshana Rabba*, 323-4.
Cæsar, Jews in Rome under, 32.
Cagliari, supposed birthplace of Eleazar Kalir, 39.
Cairo, various congregations in, 16; Maimonides in, 40.
Calendar, the Athenian (Metonic), adopted by the Jews, 33, 57; as modified by the Jews, 59, 60.
Calendar, the Jewish, elements of, 57; the month in, 57; dependence of, upon the Passover, 58-9; modified by the Sabbatic year, 59.
Calendar, the Julian, compared with the Metonic, 59.
Calla, assemblies. *See* Babylonia, the schools of.
Candles, benediction over, on Hanucca, 337-8; the lighting of, on Sabbath, 348; in the *Habdala*, 351.
Canticles, the Book of, sacredness of, disputed, 22, 45; text of the Passover "poetries," 227, 286; read on Passover, 284, 286.
Cantor, Christian title corresponding to *Hazan*, 69-70.
Capital crimes, treated of in the Mishna, 30.
Capital punishment, mitigated, 23; the Mishna treats of, 30.
Cappadocia, Jews in, 31-2.
Cavvanoth, 306.

Evening service (*Ma'arib*), the, time of, 76; the *Amida* in, 77; order of, 80; abstract of the *Amida* read in, 80, 142-3; length of, 81; the *Shema* of, 89-94; the Priestly Blessing in, 118-19; modifications of the *Amida* in, 141; Bible verses in, 189-92.

Excommunication, effect of, upon the standing in the Congregation, 69.

Exile, the, the Chief of, powers and character of, 34.

Exodus, the, mention of, in public worship, 76, 91, 103.

Exodus, the Book of, divisions of, 248; *Haftaroth* corresponding to the divisions of, 267-8.

Ezekiel, the Book of, arranged by the Great Synod, 21; the celestials in, 51.

Ezra, reads the Law, 20, 64, 249, 251; founder of the Great Synod, 21; institutes the reading of the Law on Monday and Thursday, 251.

Ezra, the Book of, the language of, 37.

Fasts, the, the services of, modified by persecutions, 43; in the Scriptures, 62; public, for drouth, 81; the *Amida* of, 138; lesson for, 256; not on Sabbath, 256.

See also, Ab, the Ninth of; Gedaliah, the Fast of; Tammuz, the Seventeenth of; Tebeth, the Tenth of.

"Fathers" (*Aboth*). *See Amida* the, the first Benediction of.

Fayum, birthplace of Saadia, 39.

Feast, the. *See* Booths, the Feast of.

Feasts, the three, *Hallel* on, 24, 79; fixed by the Usha Sanhedrin, 29; observance of, discussed in the East, 35; observance of, treated of in the *Shulhan Aruch*, 42; Midrash and Aggadta in the services of, 46; doubling of, 61; the Priestly Blessing on, 69, 126; the services of, on the same plan as those of work-days, 75; four *Amidas* on, 79; length of the services on, 81; the *Shema* benedictions on, 93-4; modifications of the *Amida* of, 115-16, 143-4, 150; the evening service of, 191; "poetries" for, 224-5; interrupt mourning, 331; modifications of *Kiddush* on, 350.

See also Booths; Passover; Pentecost; Festivals, the.

Feasts, the three, the night following, time of service in, 76; the first Middle Benediction of the *Amida* in, 128.

Festivals, the, the Middle Benediction of the *Amida* on, 143-7; modifications of the *Musaf Amida* on, 150-1; Psalms for, 183, 184; the penitential Psalm omitted on, 185; study in the service of, 195; *Nish'math* on, 208; "poetries" for, 223, 225-6, 227-8; benedictions over the *Haftara* on, 277; no sermon on the eve of, 294; the phylacteries not used on, 314; modifications in the grace after meals for, 342, 343, 345; *Kiddush* for, 350-1; modifications of *Habdala* for, 352.

See also Feasts, the three; Atonement, the Day of; Booths; New Year; Passover; Pentecost.

Festivals, Half, the *Amida* of, 112.

Fez, birthplace of Isaac Alfassi, 39.

First Effect, interposed between God and the world, 50.

"Forgivenesses." *See Selihoth*.

"Formation, the Book of," a Cabbalistic work, 52-3; commentaries on, 53.

France, the Jews of, literary work of, 41; use the Targum Jonathan, 290-1.

Frank, Jacob, encouraged by the Cabbala, 56.

Friday, the Day of Atonement cannot occur on, 60; New Year cannot occur on, 60; Psalm for, 188.

Micah, the Messianic prophecies of, revived, 26.

Middle Days, the, the *Aboda* of, 124-5, 144; modifications of the *Musaf Amida* of, 151; Half *Hallel* on, 181; the penitential Psalm omitted on, 185; omission from the services of, 213; lessons for, 255-6, 258; modifications in the grace after meals for, 342.

Midrash, meaning of, 44-5; Palestinian in origin, 45; not embodied in the early prayers, 45; not authoritative, 45; examples of, in the services, 46; examples of, concerning God, 47-8; groundwork of the sermon, 48; in the New Testament, 49; dangers of, 49; resembles Cabbala, 50; on the Psalms, referred to, 100; on the *Amida*, 137; specimens of, in the *Seder*, 361. *See also* Aggadta.

Midrash Rabba, a homiletic work, 294.

Minha. See Afternoon service, the.

Minhag, Portuguese and German, 15-16. *See* Prayer Book.

Minian, requisite number of persons for a public service, 69, 106; during *Shib'a* at home, 330; on *Jahrzeit*, 331.

Minim, Jewish sectaries, 32, 134; none at Nehardea, 37; in the *Amida*, 133. 134; not applicable to the Christians of today, 134.

Miracles, attempt to explain, in *Aboth*, 199-200.

Mishna, the, on the variability of custom, 15; date of the compilation of, 19; on worship, 22; teachers of, 22; on the High Priest, 23; compilers of, 29-30; divisions of, 30; contents of, 30; free from superstition, 30-1; high morality of, 31; the language of, 31; Syrian Jews mentioned in, 31; on the *Minim*, 32; discussions on, at Tiberias, 33-4; parts of, not discussed in the East, 35; quotations from, in the Talmud, 37; addition to, 38; commentary on, by Maimonides, 40; on mystic science, 51-2; use of the word Cabbala in, 56; Eras used in, 62; on the *Amida*, 78; passages from, in the morning service, 79; on the liturgy of the Watches, 81; on the benedictions, 86, 87; on the *Shema*, 89; on the *Shema* benedictions, 103; on responses to benedictions, 105; the *Kaddish* not mentioned in, 108; sections of, in the services, 108; on the prayer for rain, 124, 128; on the number of benedictions in the *Amida*, 128; on the "abstract of the Eighteen," 138; on the "Sanctity of the Day," 140, 146; on the "Kingdom" verses, 156; on *Col Nidre*, 176; on *Hallel*, 180; passages from, in the liturgy, 193, 194, 195, 196, 202; on prayer for the government, 217; on the lessons from the Law, 258; on the number called to the reading of the Law, 260, 261; on lessons from the Prophets, 265; on the Book of Esther, 287, 291; on the Methurgaman, 288; on the fitting up of the Synagogue, 299; on posture at the Prayer, 300; on the frame of mind during worship, 305; studied in a singsong, 311; on phylacteries, 316; on *Shofar* blowing, 320; on the period of mourning, 331; a passage from, read on *Jahrzeit*, 332; on the education of children, 334; on grace after meals, 341, 345; on the *Seder*, 356-7, 360, 362. *See also* Sages, the.

Misnagdim, opponents of the *Hasidim*, 294.

Mohammed, borrows an appellation of God, 83.

Molad, beginning of the month, 58. *See* Months, the Jewish; New moon.

Monday (and Thursday), reading of the Law on, 64, 251, 264; prayers peculiar to, 186-7, 213-14,

in the grace after meals for, 342, 343, 345.

New Testament, the, transliteration of Hebrew names in, 13; on the dispersion of the Jews, 32; examples of Midrashic style in, 49; on the reading of the Law, 249.

New Year (Day of Memorial), the, ceases to be proclaimed, 33; a Midrash concerning, 45-6; Biblical designation of, 59; occurrence of, 60; date of, 61; two days of, 61; the "Additional" *Amida* of, 112; modifications of the *Amida* on, 121-3, 140, 144, 145-6, 155; modifications of the *Musaf Amida* on, 150-1, 155-64; the day of judgment, 158, 160; *Abinu Malkenu* on, 162-4; Psalm on, 183; the evening service of, 191; the Psalter read on, 192; a Mishnic treatise read on, 202; "poetries" on, 225, 226, 227; Cabbalistic petitions in the service of, 243; lessons on the second Sabbath before, 251; lesson on, 254, 258; the *Haftaroth* for, 272; benediction over the *Haftara* on, 277; kneeling during the service of, 301; devotion on, 303; the *Shofar* blowing on, 319-22; ends the *Shib'a*, 331; modifications of *Kiddush* on, 350, 351.

See also "Kingdoms;" "Remembrances;" "Shofaroth."

Nice, Council of, fixes the date of Easter, 59.

Night prayer for children, 335-7.

Nisan, name of the first month, 58; beginning of the year in, 59; length of, 59; the new moon of, 60; the Passover in, 60, 257; number of scrolls on the New Moon of, 258.

Nish'math, introduction to a "Benediction of Song," 208; at the *Seder*, 364.

Noah, a section of the Pentateuch, 248.

Numbers, the Book of, passages from, in the Prayer Book, 82;

divisions of, 248; *Haftaroth* corresponding to the divisions of, 269-70.

Ofan, a "poetry," 225.

Ofannim. See Wheels.

Old Testament, Greek. *See* Septuagint, the.

Om Ani Homa, metrical version of, 236.

Omer days, the (between Passover and Pentecost), in the Cabbala, 53; the Ethics read on the Sabbaths of, 196; the benediction for, 211.

"One Kid!" 365-6.

Onkelos. *See* Targum Onkelos.

Orah Hayim, a section of the *Shulhan Aruch*, 42; quoted, 387, 388, 393, 401, 402, 403, 405, 407, 415, 419, 420, 421, 422, 423, 424, 425.

Ordination, the, of Rabbis, 68.

Ormuzd, protest against, in the benedictions, 96.

"Our Father, our King." *See Abinu Malkenu*.

Paietan, Jewish liturgical poet, 222.

Palestine, under foreign domination, 21; the three-years cycle of the reading of the Law in, 250-1.

Para, one of the four distinguished Sabbaths, 257-8; the *Haftara* of, 271.

Parasha, a section of the Mosaic Law, 247.

Paris, Portuguese Synagogue in, 16.

Parnas, business head of the Synagogue, 71; paid official under, 71.

Parsley, at the *Seder*, 358, 359.

Parthia, the kings of, the Era of, used by the Jews, 62.

Passover, the Feast of the (*Pesakh*), half-yearly meetings of the schools in the month before, 37; sheaf of barley offered during, 58; and the arrangement of the calendar, 59; beginning of the year in the

31

Siddur, the German prayer book, 223; the *Col Bo* edition of, 223.
Sidra, a section of the Mosaic Law, 247.
Silluk, an accent, 308.
Silluk, "poetry," 226; on the Day of Atonement, 229; on the New Year, 237-8.
Simeon, brother of Judas Maccabeus, referred to, 22.
Simeon, Rabbi, sayings of, 198.
Simeon, the cotton dealer, on the *Amida*, 133, 137.
Simeon the Just, date of the death of, 21; last member of the Great Synod, 21, 197; saying ascribed to, 22.
Simeon bar Cochba, the rebellion of, 29; supported by Jews of Cyrenaica, 32.
Simeon ben Gamaliel, Patriarch at Usha, 29; on the Day of Atonement, 178; in *Aboth*, 197.
Simeon ben Johaï, pretended author of the Zohar, 54, 55.
Simeon ben Shetah, Pharisee leader, 25; and grace after meals, 340.
Simha of Vitry, publishes a Mahzor, 41.
Simlaï, teacher at Tiberias, 33.
Sivan, name of the third month, 58; length of, 59; Pentecost in, 61.
Slanderers (*Malshinim*), in the *Amida*, 132-3.
Soferim. See Scribes, Treatise of.
Sof Pasuk, an accent, 308.
Solemn Days. *See* Atonement, the Day of; New Year.
Solomon, prayer of, at the dedication of the Temple, 66.
Solomon the Levite (Alkabets) poet, 188, 233, 244.
Solomon ben Isaac (Rashi), Pentateuch commentary by, 40, 41; disciples of, 41, 42; an authority in Spain, 42; on the *Shema*, 90; on the phylacteries, 317; quoted, 383, 395, 404, 438.
Solomon Ibn Gebirol, poet, 39, 229, 234; "Song of Unity" by, 229, 234.
"Song of Glory," verse on the

phylacteries in, 48; supposed author of, 229.
Song of Songs. *See* Canticles.
"Song of Unity," by Solomon Ibn Gebirol, 229.
"Song of Zion," by Samuel Sulzer, 12.
Songs of Zion, by Mrs. Henry Lucas, quoted, 231-2, 233, 235-6.
Soul, the, in the Cabbala, 53; five names of, 229.
Spain, the Jews of, Sefardim, 12. *See* Sefardim, the.
Spanish Age, the, of Jewish literature, 39-41.
Spanish names used in the services, 281.
Spanish ritual, Jews of the. *See* Sefardim.
Spice-box, at the *Habdala*, 351.
Study, importance of, 193; provisions for, in the liturgy, 193-202; of the Law, benedictions over, 194-5.
Sulzer, Samuel, and Synagogue music, 12.
Sun, the, worshipped by the Israelites, 97.
Sunday, the Day of Atonement cannot occur on, 60; New Year cannot occur on, 60.
Superstition, discountenanced by the Tannaïm, 30-1; in the Babylonian Talmud, 36.
Sura (Mahasia), Abba Areka, head of the school at, 34; the discussions at, form the Babylonian Talmud, 35; regains importance, 38-9; seat of a central authority, 45, 216, 251. *See also* Babylonia, the schools of.
Susa, Purim in, 287.
Synagogue, the, beginning of, 64-5; name and place of the platform in, 64; meaning of the word, 65; mention of, in the Gospels, 65; the Ark of, 65-6; the scrolls of, 66; the desk of, 66; place of men and women in, 66-7; uses of the ante-room in, 67; furnished with benches and chairs, 67; business officials of, 71; how fitted up, 299.

Zemiroth, morning hymns, 224.
See Morning service, the.
Zerubbabel, leader of the first re-
turn, 19; the first of the Chiefs
of the Exile, 34.
Zion, in the Prayer Book, 83.
"Zion," elegy by Jehuda Hallevi,
229.
Ziv, name of the second month, 58.
Zohar, the, the leading text-book

of the Cabbala, 54; author and
pretended author of, 54-5; contents and language of, 55; doc-
trines of, 55; spread of, 55-6;
a prayer from, in the liturgy,
241-2, 243, 278.
Zulath, a "poetry," 225.
Zunz, restores the *Pesikta*, 273;
quoted, 372, 383, 393, 399, 418,
438.